413083

Generation Zombie

D1556435

# Generation Zombie

## Essays on the Living Dead in Modern Culture

*edited by* Stephanie Boluk
and Wylie Lenz

McFarland & Company, Inc., Publishers
*Jefferson, North Carolina, and London*

398.
21
GEN

Library of Congress Cataloguing-in-Publication Data

Generation zombie : essays on the living dead in
modern culture / edited by Stephanie Boluk and Wylie Lenz.
p.    cm.
Includes bibliographical references and index.

ISBN 978-0-7864-6140-0
softcover : 50# alkaline paper

1. Zombies    I. Boluk, Stephanie, 1979–
II. Lenz, Wylie, 1972–
GR581.G46    2011      398.21—dc22      2011017045

British Library cataloguing data are available

Cover images © 2011 Ivan Bliznetsov (Shutterstock)

Manufactured in the United States of America

*McFarland & Company, Inc., Publishers
Box 611, Jefferson, North Carolina 28640
www.mcfarlandpub.com*

In memory of Nicole LaRose
scholar, teacher, colleague, dear friend

# Table of Contents

# Introduction: Generation Z, the Age of Apocalypse

STEPHANIE BOLUK AND WYLIE LENZ

On October 1, 2009, local media in Gainesville, Florida, revealed the existence of a document titled "ZOMBIE ATTACK: Disaster Preparedness Simulation Exercise #5 (DR5)," which outlined a zombie-attack preparedness plan.[1] Rather than appearing in an obviously satirical venue or on a fan message board, this six-page report was posted on the University of Florida's Academic Technology's Support Services website, linked under the heading "Disaster Recovery Exercises," and appended to discussions of four other, presumably more realistic, emergency scenarios. Observing that "it is clear that international media have begun paying increasing attention to the possibility of an outbreak of zombie behavior spectrum disorder" and composed entirely in appropriate administrative jargon, the document includes descriptions of "zombieism," advice on handling an outbreak, and a reference to "documentaries" that deal with the threat of an epidemic (e.g., *Night of the Living Dead* [1968], as well as its sequels and imitators).[2] The report promises to make use of information gleaned from other (real) disaster preparedness models, such as "Campus Closure Exercise (DR4)." When the media revealed the plan to the wider Gainesville public, it and the other disaster recovery exercises were "removed [from the site] at the instruction of UF Administration."[3] The coverage of both the posting and removal of the zombie plan lasted several days and was fairly consistent in content and form, tending to play up the entire incident as a prank, fodder for a "wacky news" segment.

A closer review of the document reveals a sustained and explicit critique of managerial practices (management-speak in particular). Consider the following excerpt:

> Part 2 of the exercise will be a discussion of how the overall impact of a zombie outbreak will affect use of and support for the course management system and will address such issues as:
>
> a. In general, zombified users will be inarticulate and unable to clearly describe technology problems and use cases;
> b. Some support staff may be infected and unable to effectively and efficiently carry out their support responsibilities.
> c. The rapid breakdown of civil society and declining numbers of uninfected users may have adverse budget impacts resulting in a reduction in staffing levels;

1

    d. The spread of ZBSD to institutional administration may complicate policy making;

    e. Conversely, the spread of ZBSD to institutional administration may simplify and streamline policy making resulting in dramatic improvements in administrative responsiveness and service delivery;

    f. Additional security measures will need to be implemented at service delivery points (i.e., the Hub and SSRB).[4]

Transposing this alternate-reality scenario onto the physical geographic and institutional spaces at the University of Florida, the first few items of this list enact a familiar comedic gesture: apply normal social and occupational conventions to a completely abnormal situation. (The notion that anyone would be concerned with the functioning of the university's technology support team during an actual zombie outbreak is, of course, absurd.) But as the list progresses, its targets shift from the general to the particular; in fact, it postulates quite clearly in items (d) and (e) that it may be advantageous in some respects to have the "institutional administration" succumb to a zombie infection. Also included with the document is an "Infected Co-worker Dispatch Form," in which the author gives voice to the usually unspoken desire to be rid of (i.e., to kill) that annoying, unthinking colleague. Perhaps creating and posting the document is not far removed from posting a clipping from *Dilbert* on one's office door in a cathartic attempt to satirize the workplace environment of incompetent managers and co-workers. The scenario of a zombie outbreak allows for a workplace revenge fantasy that gives expression to much darker and more violent desires.

    On October 2, 2009, CNN.com ran an article by Doug Gross titled "Why We Love Those Rotting, Hungry, Putrid Zombies."[5] The journalist interviews several authors and scholars, from producers of popular culture such as Max Brooks, author of *The Zombie Survival Guide* (2003) and *World War Z* (2006), to academics like Peter Dendle and Andrea Wood (coincidentally, a graduate of the University of Florida). Gross concludes, "According to experts—and, yes, there are zombie experts—it's because for all their limitations, the brain-rotted, animated corpses are so darned versatile—helping reflect whatever our greatest fears happen to be at the time."[6] Both this report and the University of Florida "zombie preparedness plan" appeared in the news just prior to the release of *Zombieland* (2009), perhaps the most mainstream zombie film ever produced. Featuring a substantial production budget as well as recognizable and respected actors, it earned almost $100 million total, bringing in $25 million during its opening weekend alone.[7]

    The figure of the zombie not only fronts a million-dollar industry, but the last few years have also seen a rise in zombie-related pranks and culture jamming, such as "zombie walks"[8] and the hacking of traffic warning signs to announce a zombie invasion in cities across the United States including Gainesville, FL, Austin, TX, and Portland, OR.[9] As Brian Greenspan observes, Alternate Reality Games (ARGs) such as *ZombieTruth* and *Lost Zombies* use social media to parody actual governmental and public health organizations, in order to demonstrate how their biopolitical forms of power and control operate within networked culture.[10] The bleeding of zombies into the everyday is further seen in a footnote from the University of Florida document, "ZOMBIE ATTACK." It offers a link to news coverage of a (real) 2009 Twitter exchange between the Boston Police and a member of the public regarding how information would be disseminated in the event of an actual zombie attack:

BOSTON_POLICE: INJURED OFFICER: Officer from District 4 transported to Beth Israel Hospital, human bite to arm, suspect in custody. (8:28 P.M. May 19th.)
WILLCADY: @ Boston_Police if that was a zombie bite, would you tell us? (9:29 A.M. May 20th.)
BOSTON_POLICE: @ Willcady Yes, absolutely. (11:29 A.M. May 20th.)

Tracing the circulation of this post takes the curious reader on a labyrinthine journey through a string of retweets and websites reproducing the exchange.[11] Clearly, this conversation would likely not have traveled so far so quickly had it not first taken place via Twitter. The zombie, a figure of contagion, spreads unchecked through social media; Twitter is, in this regard, the ideal medial staging of the contagion. Yet, this deep structural connection between the form and the content, between the spread of information and fictional/biological forms of plague is not restricted to the twenty-first century. Daniel Defoe's *A Journal of the Plague Year* (1722), a text which itself maintains a similarly porous boundary between fact and fiction, reflects a similar relationship between plague and rhetoric. On the very first page, Defoe writes of how, before the emergence of newspapers, "things did not spread instantly over the whole Nation, as they do now."[12] The development of the newspaper created a paradigm shift that accelerated the dissemination (and confusion) of information via this emergent medial form. Twenty-first century social media may circulate on a level of instantaneity that Defoe could have never imagined, but rumor and plague are conflated in both contexts.[13] Whether eighteenth-century newspaper or contemporary social media, in each of these instances, the rhetoric surrounding infection circulates according to a model of textual contagion.[14]

Zombies have inherited this model characteristic of both plague and plague writing. Its patterns of repetition and recirculation are seen not only in the zombie's bodily infectiousness, but in the recurring return of the living dead, the return of the return as seen in the serial repetition of the zombie in the many interconnected sequels, series and spinoffs (a phenomenon for which Jennifer Cooke has coined the term "episodemic").[15] The complex and interpenetrated genealogy of zombie films, television, comics, games, and literature follows a logic of contagion and compulsive repetition. Since Freud, repetition and the death drive have been conceptually linked, and this logic is reflected in the narratives as well as the systems of production and reproduction of zombie media.[16] A zombie narrative generally depicts a serial process of infection, by means of which humanity is systematically transformed into zombies. The living are compelled towards this condition of permanent inertia, a perpetual motion of (animated) inanimate matter, mirroring Freud's notion of the death drive as the desire for life to return to its original inert and inanimate state ("the aim of all life is death"); the zombie is the contemporary epitome of the repeating dead.[17] The structures of repetition governing the production of zombie media itself and the sheer excess of material available demonstrate that this death drive economy, this process of *becoming-zombie*, functions as an affirmative and generative force. Zombie films beget more zombie films. Zombie video games rarely stop with one sequel, not to mention the mods, fanfiction, and remakes for other consoles and programming languages that comprise a *lively* participatory fan culture based around *death*.

## Genealogy of the Dead

The zombie threat did not always rely on anxiety generated by viral outbreak, however. Responding to the specific technological and cultural anxieties of each historical era, the evolution of the modern figure of the zombie can be roughly divided into three generations: the Haitian voodoo zombie, George Romero's living dead, and the pathologized, infected humans who behave *as if they were living dead,* as seen in the films *28 Days Later* (2002), its sequel *28 Weeks Later* (2007), and the videogame series such as *Left 4 Dead* and *Resident Evil.*

Unlike the vampire or werewolf, the zombie does not have a long literary tradition preceding its emergence in film. Its origins lie in Haitian voodoo practices, made known through English-language reports of zombies in Haiti, most notably William Seabrook's *The Magic Island* (1929), discussed at length by Gyllian Phillips and Chris Vials in this collection. The voodoo zombie is under the control of a witch doctor who performs the resurrection, standing in for a colonial master. In this respect, the Haitian zombie is deeply embedded within the historical imaginaries of slavery and colonialism. Seabrook famously describes the zombie thus:

> Obediently, like an animal, he slowly stood erect — and what I saw then, coupled with what I heard previously, or despite it, came as a rather sickening shock. The eyes were the worst. It was not my imagination. They were in truth like the eyes of a dead man, not blind, but staring unfocused, unseeing. The whole face, for that matter, was bad enough. It was vacant, as if there were nothing behind it. It seemed not only expressionless, but also incapable of expression.[18]

The figure of the zombie as a literally undead human, recently resurrected from its grave, originates in African myth and folklore that migrated to Haiti. It was not until the 1980s that Wade Davis attempted to find a scientific explanation for the process of zombification and proposed that zombies were not undead, but living persons placed in a state of chemically-induced suggestibility, akin to hypnosis.[19] As Jamie Russell has suggested, "Perhaps if the riddle of the living dead had been solved sooner, the zombie would have never taken root in the imagination of the Western world."[20]

The figure entered popular culture most dramatically in 1932 with the release of the film *White Zombie* (directed by Victor Halperin), which was based on the stage play *Zombie* that had premiered early that year. One of its most chilling scenes, reminiscent of Fritz Lang's *Metropolis* (1927), depicts the labor of zombified workers in a sugar mill. Whether hypnotized by the villainous master and magician (played by Bela Lugosi) or the machinery itself, the Haitian workers are so alienated from their surroundings that they continue to mill even as one of their cohorts falls into the grinder. The Haitian zombie was not only an expression of anxieties resulting from the brutal U.S. occupation of Haiti (1915–1934), but for American audiences, the enslavement of the zombies at the hand of a witchdoctor depicted a kind of mechanical servitude that resonated with the "modern times" of 20th century industrialism and its abject instrumentalization and alienation of labor. In her chapter, Gyllian Phillips undertakes a close reading of *White Zombie,* focusing specifically on the representation of creolization. Her chapter re-evaluates the white/black binary that informs most previous scholarship of the film. Chris Vials examines the American appropriation of the Haitian zombie more broadly in early twentieth century radio and film, attending to the specific historical and medial conditions that structure these productions.

## Law of the Dead: Zombies™

An early attempt to contain the spread of the figure of the zombie through legal measures occurred in 1936 when the Amusement Securities Corporation, the finance company that owned *White Zombie,* sued to block another Halperin film from being released with the word "zombie" in the title.[21] The plaintiffs claimed the word was their intellectual property (despite the fact that they themselves were appropriating the term from a longstanding cultural heritage). The American Securities Corporation was the first group to attempt to colonize this term and set legal limits on its signifying properties. Jennifer Fay notes that in "claiming to have invented the zombie (or having helped to finance the film that invented it), and thus to have legal ownership of the concept, this company performs a re-enslavement of this Haitian figure within the logic of intellectual property."[22] Unable to be contained, the Americanized version of the Haitian zombie — a creature more robotic than undead — would continue in film relatively unchanged until 1968 with George Romero's reinvention of the figure. Prior to Romero, *Zombies of Mora Tau* (1957) was the first film to treat the zombie in epidemiological terms. This innovation also surfaces in related forms in science fiction fare of the decade — most potently in *Invasion of the Body Snatchers* (1956) — but it was not effectively made part of zombie lore until George Romero severed the figure from its Caribbean origins in *Night of the Living Dead* (1968). Influenced as much by the Haitian zombie as by pod-people (and Richard Matheson's short vampire novel, *I Am Legend* [1954]), Romero injected a new purpose into the figure by removing the witch doctor, adding the violence of cannibalism, and relocating the menace to an explicitly American cultural land-scape. This figure of the newly infectious zombie is reflected in the countless series, remakes, and sequels, both official and unofficial, which have followed over the past five decades. The blurring of social boundaries that critics frequently point to as part of the political commentary contained within zombie films is further reinforced by the complex, inter-penetrated genealogy of the Romero (and post–Romero) zombie.

Litigation over intellectual property played a further role in the evolution of the zom-bie. First, *Night of the Living Dead* was famously the source of a legal conflict which resulted in the film entering the public domain when the distributor, the Walter Reade Organization, forgot to add a copyright notice after making changes to the title screen. While this error led to a financial blow for Romero, the dissemination of the film through multiple distrib-utors, and its widespread copying and informal distribution, likely contributed to the mas-sive growth in popularity of Romero's innovations in zombie lore. Second, a notable bifurcation in zombie mythology occurred when Romero and John A. Russo, co-writer of *Night of the Living Dead,* disagreed about the future direction of the franchise.[23] Ultimately, Russo would retain the right to use the phrase "Living Dead" in his titles, whereas Romero was left simply with "Dead." Romero's subsequent films — not properly narrative sequels, but rather an informal trajectory of events during a zombie apocalypse — include *Dawn of the Dead* (1978), *Day of the Dead* (1985), *Land of the Dead* (2005), *Diary of the Dead* (2007), and *Survival of the Dead* (2009). Films with the "Living Dead" tag, originally conceived as direct sequels in content (treating the original 1968 film as a docudrama) and functioning as mostly comedic spin-offs, include *Return of the Living Dead,* parts one through five.[24] Perversely, it is this horror-comedy series that most informs the popular conception of the zombie: these monsters have an identifiable origin (toxic waste), fixate exclusively on eating "braaaaains," and are able to articulate this desire. In contrast, the Romero zombies appear without explanation, will eat any part of the body, and remain mute. In Europe, another zombie series was spawned when Italian director Lucio Fulci released *Zombi 2* (1979), a somewhat disingenuous attempt to cash in on the European popularity of Romero's *Dawn of the Dead,* which was released under the title *Zombi* in Italy. (Further Italian sequels fol-lowed.) Finally, there have been Romero-approved remakes of *Night of the Living Dead* (1990), *Dawn of the Dead* (2004), and *Day of the Dead* (2008). The genealogy of the zombie film, from Halperin, to Romero, Russo, Fulci and beyond, can be more accurately repre-sented by a web of self-referential textuality than a typical family tree.

Despite attempts to claim ownership over the zombie, it has eluded containment. In addition to litigation surrounding the two foundational zombie films, *White Zombie* and *Night of the Living Dead,* Marvel Comics held the registered trademark for the word "zombie" in comics from 1975 to 1996. While economic and legal interests have intervened, attempting to quarantine the circulation of the signifier, its very nature seems to have a built-in resist-ance to such efforts. The serial contagiousness of the zombie, its complex "episodemic" structure of branching sequels and spin-offs and ability to aggressively invade other genres, has perhaps given the figure an immunity against the claims of proprietary ownership.

This pattern is further reflected in the recent trend of mashing up zombies with other literary or cinematic genres. There are numerous films based on genre-crossing gimmicks such as zombies + Nazis[25] or zombies + strippers.[26] *Shaun of the Dead* (2004) advertises itself as a zombie romantic comedy (a "zom-rom-com") and Seth Grahame-Smith's mashup of Jane Austen with zombie conventions in *Pride and Prejudice and Zombies* (2009) was a *New York Times* bestseller.[27] The now commonly accepted conventions of zombieism function virally within media, inserting themselves into other genres and contaminating high and low forms with their tropes.

## Evolution of the Dead: Zombie 2.0

The latest mutation of the zombie in popular culture has led to contestations over what, precisely, constitutes a zombie. While lumbering, Romero-style zombies effectively tapped into mid–twentieth-century contagion paranoia, the apocalyptic terror of the living dead was replaced in films such as *28 Days Later* and the *Resident Evil* series with a more explicitly biological model of viral infection. Intriguingly, much like Romero's undead zombies, the biological virus itself occupies a liminal position between living and dead, its status as a form of life contested by scientists.[28] As a force of evolution that still retains undead characteristics, the viral zombie does not replace the older style of zombie as much as find a way to reconfigure it in the light of emerging scientific discourses that tap into deeply felt post–AIDS, SARS, bird flu, and H1N1 anxieties. The zombie has been rationalized and assigned a pathology.

The zombie's undead status and viral nature take on even greater significance in an era of global, networked capitalism. The possibilities for agentive autonomy appear ever more restricted in an era of cloud computing, bots, smart mobs, and avatars that bind our subjectivity to various network protocols of control. To locate the digital zombie literally, in games like *Left 4 Dead,* and metaphorically, through the hordes of zombie computers unleashing Distributed Denial-of-Service attacks, conflates Romero's contagion zombie with the Haitian voodoo zombies. A new witchdoctor resides in these unstable, decentralized networks of power that Brendan Riley, Scott Reed, and Brian Greenspan explore in their analysis of new forms of the digital zombie. From zombie computers to nanobots, previously biological logics of viral life are reimagined as programmable in synthetic structures and distributed via genetic algorithms that give rise to emergent intelligence in the non-living.

This accelerated and pathologized zombie is not only transformed for the age of digital reproduction, but the threat it poses as biohazard also explicitly links the zombie to the millennia-old tradition of plague writing.[29] The once supernatural figure is now a figure of plague. As René Girard has written, there is a "strange uniformity"[30] to plague texts, whether one is considering Thucydides's description of the Plague of Athens or Antonin Artaud's "The Theater and the Plague." Now that the biological mystery of plague has been solved with the identification of its cause (the Gram-negative bacterium *Yersinia pestis*), the zombie appears now to occupy the position of uncontrollable threat that was previously associated with plague. The once apocalyptic and supernatural powers of plague are reconfigured by the zombie. As Sarah Juliet Lauro argues in this collection, the "zombie virus rewrites the plague narrative as a secular rather than spiritual force."

Artaud ascribes agency to plague, suggesting that plague has a deliberate "preference for the very organs of the body, the particular physical sites, where human will, consciousness, and thought are imminent and apt to occur."[31] His description of plague's de-subjectivizing power, the way in which it infects those organs that lie at the very core of an individual's identity, uncannily anticipates the way in which zombie violence is so persistently focused around the brain. As Lauro and Karen Embry have observed elsewhere, those "brain-dead" "brain-eater[s]" can only be killed by destroying the brain.[32] Girard has suggested that plague, in its literary and mythic representations, stands in as a metaphor for reciprocal violence.[33] The modern zombie subjectivizes the movement of plague, spreading infectious violence and thus literalizing Girard's allegory. The zombie essentially distributes and serializes the labor of the fourth horseman of the apocalypse.

A zombie outbreak, much like a plague epidemic, is an event in which the anxieties associated with social connectivity come to the fore — the more boundaries between self and other are broken down in plague time, the more the contagion spreads. Girard's description of plague is equally applicable to zombies: "The plague is universally presented as a process of undifferentiation, a destruction of specificities."[34] In zombie films, the collapse of barriers and attendant social leveling that takes place is embodied through the piercing of skin and the exchange of infectious fluids, which results in the conversion of all hosts of the infection into a homogenous, undifferentiated mass. Jeffrey Weinstock has argued that the concurrent development of hysteria over both AIDS and the computer virus was not coincidental but part of a general "virus culture" that overtook the United States at the end of the last millennium, creating "a landscape obsessed with the fear of contagion, infected with 'infection paranoia.'"[35] He observes that mechanical and biological modes of infection become interchangeable, and that this produces anxieties regarding a post-human condition in which "it is so difficult to figure the computer virus in other than biological terms: in contemporary culture, the body is technologized, the body is a machine." Weinstock's observations concerning the technologized body are in line with Donna Haraway's model of the cyborg.[36]

Zombie scholarship is as much indebted to Haraway's "Cyborg Manifesto" (1985) as it is post-human theories of animality.[37] The cyborg and the animal are dynamically intertwined in the figure of the zombie as it operates in the post-historical landscape of late capitalism.[38] It is this anxiety towards what Haraway describes as the permeability of bodies, towards those proliferating and unstable categories of Otherness disrupting the chain of being in support of human exceptionalism, that is at the very nature of viral plague and zombies. As it stands at the end of history, the zombie is simultaneously a vision of capitalism's fulfillment in the form of a stasis of perpetual desire, as well as a model of proletarian revolution, depicting the emergence of a new classless society. Lauro and Embry extend Haraway's cyborg logic even further in their "Zombie Manifesto."

Lauro and Embry turn to the zombie because, in both its historical and contemporary iterations, it is shot through with the cultural contradictions of capitalism, simultaneously a figure of undead labor and consumption. The zombie literally wears its politics on its sleeve, not only troubling notions of identity and distinctions between subject and object, but these relations are manifested through the most excessively gory scopic regime. Internal and external are indistinguishable on a zombie body composed of exposed internal organs and dangling flesh (a kind of corporeal Moebius strip). At the same time, the zombie (if we use Weinstock's description of virus culture) is simultaneously a figure of pure automation, of programmed memory that infinitely loops. This undead creature is at once horribly animal, horribly machinic, and neither of these.

## Pandemic of the Dead: Plague, Zombies, Apocalypse

Plague, zombies, and apocalypse are deeply entangled with each other. The relationship between the contemporary zombie and apocalyptic imagery and language is made patent through the eschatological implications of a widely-circulated advertising line from the release of *Dawn of the Dead*: "When there is no more room in hell, the dead will walk the earth."[39] As Kim Paffenroth argues in *Gospel of the Living Dead* (2006), "More than any other monster, zombies are fully and literally apocalyptic, as the movies acknowledge.... [T]hey signal the end of the world as we have known it for thousands of years. Also, in the original meaning of 'apocalyptic,' they 'reveal' terrible truths about human nature, existence, and sin."[40] In this collection, Aalya Ahmad links the current and sustained popularity of zombies to this very apocalypticism, arguing that "they signify an un-sated cultural appetite in the Global North for the type of radical transformations that a relatively affluent and politically complacent society cannot achieve."

Again, the historical lineage of plague serves as a model for understanding the relation of zombie narratives to apocalyptic fiction more generally.[41] Fourteenth-century Irish monk John Clyn witnessed every other person around him die of the Black Death in his secluded monastery. Not knowing if any other human beings had survived the visitation of plague, he famously wrote: "Lest the writing should perish with the writer and the work should fail with the workman, I leave behind me parchment for continuing it; if any man should have the good fortune to survive this calamity, or any one of the race of Adam should escape this pestilence, and live to continue what I have begun."[42] Following this concluding passage, a copyist later remarks that it is at this point the author perished.[43] Completely isolated and unsure if there were any other survivors, Clyn literally writes from the perspective of the "The Last Man on Earth."[44] In this respect, he serves as a historical ancestor to both Jean-Baptiste Cousin de Grainville's *The Last Man* (1805), in which the incarnation of Time tells the story of a future sterile earth, and Mary Shelley's novel of the same title (1826), in which a virus wipes out all humanity except for a sole survivor. This fantasy of the Last Man — or the Last Few — in which a band of survivors becomes the last stewards of human civilization, is one of the governing narrative tropes of the post–Romero zombie genre. In their chapters, Nicole LaRose and Terry Harpold each address the role of the Last Few while taking an oblique approach to the zombie by examining one of its limit cases: John Wyndham's *Day of the Triffids* (a story of venomous walking plants that feed on human flesh). Harpold develops a theory of "zombie time" in order to discuss the temporality of the "cozy catastrophe," a sub-genre of apocalyptic fiction derided by many critics. LaRose reads *Day of the Triffids* against *28 Days Later* to demonstrate how both respond to specific moments of crisis in late modern British history.

These literary and cinematic survivalist fantasies move from speculative fiction to a kind of speculative reality. The lessons of countless video games and horror films have, in aggregate, converted long-standing genre conventions into a sort of survival guide: the rules of withstanding a zombie apocalypse have been documented from venues ranging from the BBC's h2g2[45] to the much coarser 4Chan, a seedy imageboard hosting anonymous Internet users who contribute to a thread on the website dedicated to zombie preparedness and survival.[46] Online-based collectives such as the Zombie Research Society blend scholarship in science, the arts, and survival, arguing, "The zombie pandemic is coming. It's not a matter of *if*, but a matter of *when*."[47] These movements are exemplified by Max Brooks' blackly comedic *Zombie Survival Guide* (2003), a handbook that at no point acknowledges its status as fiction.[48] The seriousness with which some participants approach the zombie apocalypse (a fictional enemy that subsumes anxieties surrounding the possible failure of social, economic and technological networks) is as potent as any survivalist literature written for the specter of actual threats such as nuclear war, bioterrorism, or global computer failure (e.g., the Y2K crisis).[49] In fact, as Christopher Zealand's essay on the St. Louis–based Zombie Squad observes, survivalist groups committed to zombie preparedness demonstrate the power of a fictional conceit, which has proven far more effective at generating bipartisan, grassroots activism than disaster, terrorist, and emergency-oriented organizations with explicitly political agendas.

## Ontologies of the Dead

To defend oneself against the zombie, one must understand the zombie; it is necessary, as many critics and historians have attempted, to define an ontology of the zombie that describes its rules and generic characteristics. This has often resulted in humorously didactic definitions—as Simon Pegg emphatically declared in an article published in *The Guardian,* "ZOMBIES DON'T RUN."[50] Indeed, according to a certain logic regarding the generic definition of "zombie," the infected in *28 Days Later* might not qualify as zombies as they are, strictly speaking, not "undead" (even if a virus itself exhibits undead characteristics as discussed above). Yet, given the fact that the film borrows heavily from the idioms of plague memoirs and zombie invasions, and that the humans infected with the "rage" virus can be seen as an attempt to both accelerate the zombie as well as create a frighteningly plausible agent of mayhem, we and others have chosen to persist in reading Danny Boyle's landmark film (and other such digressions from canonical zombie lore) through the lens of the zombie genre. Similarly, many of the chapters in this collection cast a wide net. For example, Andrea Austin's chapter on William Gibson's *Neuromancer* argues that the novel's cyberpunk automatons should be read as zombies. Both Austin's essay and what Brendan Riley terms the *e-zombie* illustrate the way in which multiple orders of zombification mutually contaminate each other. To attempt an unambiguous definition flies in the face of the zombie's fundamental subversive power—its ability to collapse difference. For historical-critical reasons, it is necessary to distinguish the zombie from the ghoul, from the vampire, from the Frankenstein monster (which is, after all, assembled from dead bodies); but what seems to be an essential characteristic of the zombie is its capacity for mutation and adaptation. Just as the zombie resists legal containment, it resists generic and taxonomic containment; it is remarkably capable of adapting to a changing cultural and medial imaginary.

These debates are one of the reasons developing a critical anthology has proven to be a challenge. With each new historical iteration of the zombie, the figure gives expression to the anxieties of that particular cultural moment: issues of labor, race, and slavery for the Haitian zombie; the problem of consumption for Romero (which he addresses differently with each film in the series); the problem of contagious reciprocal violence for *28 Days Later.* The fungibility of the zombie appears to be one of the reasons why it has persisted forcefully and spread widely. It is simultaneously the reason why it is difficult to talk about zombies with critical and historical rigor. It's not so much that the zombie apocalypse encapsulates anxieties about race, or the atom bomb, or recent financial meltdown; it's that the zombie encapsulates anxieties about race *and* the atom bomb *and* the recent financial meltdown, *and....*

This polysemic, opportunistic quality of the zombie has led to appropriations of the figure by varied disciplines and discourses outside of fiction and film. Cognitive philosophy has employed the zombie for thought experiments in support of dualism (the zombie looks and acts just like a human, but lacks conscious experience, thus demonstrating that human subjectivity consists of more than the physical).[51] A mathematical study from the University of Ottawa modeled the trajectory of an outbreak of zombie infection that became a popular cultural meme after its publication.[52] The zombie outbreak scenario has also been used to test various theories of international politics.[53] The metaphor of the zombie has itself been catachrestically extended to the computational and biological sciences with *zombie* hard drives[54] and *zombie* fire ants[55]; increasingly, the term has come to be applied to nearly any agent operating outside of intention and against a normal hierarchy of authority. Jacques Derrida's observation that "metaphoricity is the logic of contamination and the contamination of logic" seems to capture the proliferation and metaphorical transferability of the zombie as it seeps into scholarly and scientific discourses.[56]

Many of the essays in this collection attest to the notion that the zombie's utility as metaphor is virtually without limit, from Karen Randell's exploration of the Vietnam War as a latent presence in *Night of the Living Dead,* to Nicole LaRose's discussion of the zombie in the context of postwar Britain, to Scott Reed's study of the relationship between zombies and player dynamics. We would like to push the zombie's relationship to metaphor even further suggesting that the zombie does not just serve *as* a metaphor for the anxiety *du jour*, but that it *is* metaphor — a kind of walking meta-metaphor, and a self-reflexive metonym for the media through which it circulates. Whether chirographic or print writing, photography, film, video, or networked and programmable media, scholars have deployed rhetoric of the monstrous, the viral, and the undead in order to theorize informational media.[57]

Consider Wendy Chun's observation that "digital media networks are not based on the regular obsoleteness or disposability of information but rather on the resuscitability or the undead of information."[58] In other words, digital information is hard to kill — even when permanent erasure is desired. Data — whether a deleted text message or passing Facebook comment — has a way of being resurrected and recirculated in unforeseen contexts. It is perhaps the accelerated obsolescence and perceived ephemerality of digital culture (Chun describes this condition as an "enduring ephemeral")[59] that makes data's return all the more powerful. As Andrea Austin writes in her essay on cyberpunk, "The zombie is pure, walking memory, memory that refuses to stay dead and buried, refuses to rot away."

This return of memory or the undead of information in digital technology can be attributed, ironically, to those very conditions which contribute to digital media's ephemerality — what Terry Harpold has identified as media culture's attachment to an unrelenting upgrade path. Harpold argues that the failure to process fully the significance of prior predigital and digital technologies is one of the core issues at stake in new media theory and practice and that "we have not yet discharged our responsibility" to those media forms abandoned and buried along the road of technological progress.[60] To intervene on this cycle of undead repetition, Harpold insists that we must pay the digital dead their necessary respects: "Understanding the qualities of a moving field, and not only being swept along by its currents, requires conscientious investigation of its precursors."[61]

The relationship of the zombie to concepts such as Chun's "undead of information" is not unique to the digital field. Writing has been assigned a similarly undead ontology traceable through a long line of philosophers and theorists going back to Plato.[62] Derrida has invoked rhetoric similar to Chun's when he speaks of the "reanimation of knowledge" in his discussions of "dead" writing versus "the living spoken word."[63] Theorists have applied this rhetoric not only to writing, but to film as well. André Bazin famously defines (analog) film as "change mummified."[64] He describes the physical process of capturing motion pictures as an act which "embalms time."[65] As Randy Laist discusses in his essay on *Diary of the Dead,* the undead zombie reflects the specific phenomenological properties of photography and film, as discussed by classic film theorists such as Bazin, Roland Barthes, and Susan Sontag. The indexical trace that light leaves on photosensitive paper transforms the moving picture into a kind of mechanical reanimator of the dead image. The zombie's privileged medium of film is itself zombified. It is also, as Phillip Mahoney suggests in his essay, frequently regarded as having the power to zombify (through the hypnotic qualities of film).

## Scholars of the Dead

Appropriately, then, the essays in this collection represent a wide variety of discourses and apply a diverse range of methodologies in order to examine the significance of the zombie in contemporary culture. Kim Paffenroth opens the discussion of this book by arguing that what is fundamental about the zombie is that it has come to signify an internal threat, the enemy within our borders as opposed to without. Contributors such as Karen Randell, for example, pickup this thread by charting how Vietnam-era films such as *Night of the Living Dead* and *Deathdream* brought the war on to American soil. Meanwhile, Sarah Juliet Lauro examines the zombie through the lens of ecological criticism formulating a theory of the "eco-zombie," a personified environmental avenger that returns power from humanity back to nature. Sean Moreland charts the evolution of the zombie in film, as it has progressively been assigned increasing amounts of sentience (particularly within the Romero saga). From the Scopes Trial to Richard Goldschmidt's "hopeful monsters," Moreland explores the peculiar emergence and convergence of the zombie with important historical debates and developments in evolutionary theory (and their political application to Cold War politics). Phillip Mahoney turns to late nineteenth- and early twentieth-century crowd theory in order to investigate its convergence with the rhetoric of both the mesmerized as well as contagious zombie. Shaka McGlotten and Tyson E. Lewis both use the zombie to approach the problem of "bare life." McGlotten examines Bruce LaBruce's *Otto; or Up with Dead People* and gay men's online hookup culture centered in Austin, Texas, to recuperate a politics of anti-futural zombie sociality. Lewis adopts a similar position from a different perspective, arguing for *ztopia* in an attempt to rehabilitate the zombie as a figure of resistance and political possibility.

Like the zombie itself, the field of zombie studies has also evolved over time, generating a steadily growing critical canon, especially in the last decade. As the zombie genre has proliferated, particularly in film, broad surveys have emerged, such as Jamie Russell's *Book of the Dead: The Complete History of Zombie Cinema* (2005), Glenn Kay's *Zombie Movies: The Ultimate Guide* (2008), and Peter Dendle's *The Zombie Movie Encyclopedia* (2000). These texts rigorously attempt to classify the zombie genre — using the telling expressions such as *ultimate, complete,* and *encyclopedic.* They are fueled by an ambitious desire to establish a totalizing survey of existing zombie films — something which appears to be impossible, given the quantity of zombie films and the uncertainties of popular definitions of the figure. In the same way that litigants have attempted to circumscribe the limits of the zombie through copyright or lawsuit, the titles of these works attempt the difficult task of containing a figure whose nature is beyond containment.

Almost all academic scholarship on the zombie, meanwhile, owes a significant debt to the work of Robin Wood, whose foundational essays on the living dead from the 1970s and '80s mark some of the earliest critical analyses. Wood identifies the way in which the films critique "normality" — the undermining of the heteronormative family and racial, gender, and sexual roles as well as the way in which zombies function as a critique of the lurch towards commodity fetishism and consumer capitalism. He would continue to write on Romero's zombies, publishing an article in 2008 (a year before his death) that frames *Diary of the Dead* against all of Romero's past film. We see Wood's influence in the rise of more focused and tactical approaches to the zombie in the form of Kyle Bishop's *American Zombie Gothic* (2010), Kim Paffenroth's *Gospel of the Living Dead* (2006), and critical anthologies such as Deborah Christie and Sarah Juliet Lauro's *Better Off Dead: The Evolution of the Zombie as Post-Human* (2011), Shawn McIntosh and Marc Leverette's *Zombie Culture: Autopsies of the Living Dead* (2008), as well as the present volume.

Because of the didacticism and political consciousness that is never far from the gory surface of Romero's films (and the economic, political, and racial context from which the Haitian zombie emerged), the zombie has been a privileged object of cultural studies. Compared to the werewolf, mummy, or even the zombie's extremely popular next of kin, the vampire, the zombie appears to have a far more flexible metaphoricity. It is regularly deployed in film as a vehicle for expressing anxieties surrounding class, race, gender, and sexuality. Because the zombie functions as a machine programmed to collapse difference and break down binaries, this operation can be easily mapped onto multiple forms of monstrous others. Marxist readings and psychoanalytic concepts such as Freud's uncanny and Kristeva's abject have been used to develop critical approaches towards theorizing the zombie.[66] Brian Greenspan's essay conducts an institutional critique, turning towards the place of the academy itself and the power structures that govern academic labor through a discussion of the alternate-reality game *Isolation U.* Greenspan's essay makes clear that the zombie has become a nearly too-apt allegory for the university life. He writes that the zombie captures "the desperate situation of the student body in relation to the biopolitical reproduction of human brainpower, or 'immaterial labour,' in the uncanny networks of 'cognitive capitalism.'"

## Death of the Dead

The essays collected here explore the wider ramifications of the zombie in contemporary culture by taking an oblique approach that avoids a zombie essentialism. We are, propose our contributors, witnessing a different kind of Generation Z emerge in the first decade of the twenty-first century. But what does it mean to live in the age of the zombie? Terry Harpold's essay develops a theory of *zombie time,* defined by "the absolute menace of [a] perpetual present, [in which] history (uninfected, serial time) is held apart from posthistory (dead time) by a period (missing time, time-in-crisis)." This condition is, he observes, the "the crux of zombie time: neither living nor dead, but somehow in between both orders, the unmeasured interruption of history's seriality, after which it collapses into the permanent crisis-stasis of posthistory." Contemporary zombie temporality is neither entirely progressive nor entirely suspended, but rather time *deferred.* It resembles in several respects the temporality of much older apocalyptic models, particularly what Frank Kermode in *The Sense of an Ending* characterizes as the myth of "Transition":

> Before the End there is a period which does not properly belong either to the End or to the *saeculum* preceding it. It has its own characteristics. This period of Transition seems not to have been defined until the end of the twelfth century; but the definition then arrived at — by Joachim of Flora — has proved to be remarkably enduring. Its origin is in the three-and-a-half-year reign of the Beast which, in Revelation, precedes the Last Days.[67]

It would seem that the reign of the Beast has been supplanted by that of the zombie. The zombie narrative always teeters on the edge — it does not portray a truly post-apocalyptic world that has been entirely evacuated of humanity and forward-marching time.

That authors and filmmakers rarely visualize a world in which zombie rule is total is telling. The zombie narrative situates itself in that deferred space between catastrophe and posthistory where the march of time begins to shamble and, as Harpold suggests, "the end begins," but is incapable of reaching its logical conclusion. Even as Fran and Peter fly off to their uncertain future in Romero's *Dawn of the Dead,* the audience implicitly understands that their fate will be the same as the companions they left behind. Yet we are spared that moment of total annihilation, the death of death. To truly go beyond would mean arriving at a point at which there can be no sequel, no return of either the living, the dead, or the living dead. The endless deferral and refusal to cross this threshold serves as the precondition for the serial renewal of apocalyptic desire.

On the one hand, to imagine a world where zombie rule is complete may not require any creative leaps of imagination. To make a point that has been well rehearsed, the world of the zombie and the human are complementary reflections of each other. If Peter and Fran had committed suicide (an alternate ending written for the film), most of the world would not look any different; undead bodies would still circulate in the shopping malls and time would move forward. *Shaun of the Dead*'s extended tracking shots in which Shaun walks through his neighborhood unable to differentiate between human and zombie behavior comically illustrates a sameness of the two orders of after-life that haunts the modern zombie scenario.

On the other hand, to imagine a time and space beyond even that of the zombie entails imagining a form of radical otherness. The zombie remains intractably wedded to the logic as well as temporality of the living human. From this perspective we see the biocentric biases implicit in the posthuman zombie (whose unstable boundaries are still contingent on preexistent living/dead binaries). Rather than hot-blooded horror, the terror of this truly post-apocalyptic temporality would perhaps come closer to what Quentin Meillasoux termed the "glacial world"—the evacuation of human subjectivity as it recedes in the face of a universe that is, demonstrably, indifferent to both human and zombie struggle.[68] Unlike the classic cozy catastrophe that, at least for a while, humanizes humanity, rarefying large undifferentiated populations into a focused group of survivors (and, most importantly, a manageable group of compelling characters), this glacial approach resists narrative framing. How does one narrate a world without humans?[69] Thinking in terms of geological time, Mauel De Landa writes: "Over the millennia, it is the flow of biomass through food webs, as well as the flow of genes through generations, that matters, not the bodies and species that emerge from these flows."[70] The significance of a body and a subject, of a *subjectified* body, whether human or zombie, recedes within such a model of time.

It is difficult to imagine a Hollywood blockbuster or a serialized graphic novel written using this model, in which quantum particles, tectonic plates, DNA, and stardust are the protagonists, as opposed to humans and zombies. While the bubble and boil of human conflict and drama remain essential to the extension of the zombie narrative, glacial entropy tells no story because nothing in it moves. What is a virus with nothing to transform through infection? What is a zombie without a human who has yet to become a zombie?

The zombie again and again returns to this time just before the death of death, where—or when—the end of humanity functions as a vanishing point toward which the zombie shambles but never reaches. Time no longer marches but lurches on from one state of exception to another. These almost-end times stretch out, and those that live in them live, necessarily, after an end but before another end. A new generation of humanity emerges in each of these shambling epochs, and in the *n*th end: Generation Z.

**Acknowledgments.** We would like to thank our contributors for all the hard work, patience, and wisdom they invested in the project. This collection would not exist if it weren't for the counsel of Sid Dobrin, whose invaluable guidance helped us to negotiate the unfamiliar terrain of academic publishing. The idea for this project was born in 2009 through our participation in a symposium on "Rhetorics of Plague" at SUNY-Albany; the symposium's organizers, Helene Scheck and Rick Barney, have continued to offer us their support and enthusiasm. We are most grateful to Jean Boluk, Terry Harpold, Patrick LeMieux, and Steven LeMieux for reading and commenting on drafts; their tireless efforts helped inestimably in bringing the manuscript to publication. To the Department of English and our friends, colleagues, and professors at the University of Florida, we owe a tremendous debt.

## Notes

1. Nathan Crabble, "Thank Goodness! UF Has Plans for Zombie Invasion," *Gainesville.com, The Gainesville Sun*, October 1, 2009, accessed February 17, 2010, http://www.gainesville.com/article/20091002/ARTICLES/910021006. The story was picked up and rapidly disseminated in the national media and blogosphere.

2. "e-Learning Support Services," *Academic Technology*, University of Florida, accessed December 11, 2009. (While the document was originally posted at this site, it has since been removed.)

3. Andrew Wyzan, "Zombie Preparedness Plan Removed from Web Site," *The Independent Florida Alligator*, October 6, 2009, 4.

4. "e-Learning Support Services." (See note 2.)

5. Gross, Doug, "Why We Love Those Rotting, Hungry, Putrid Zombies," *CNN.com*, Cable News Network, October 2, 2009, accessed February 17, 2010, http://articles.cnn.com/2009-10-02/entertainment/zombie. love_1_zombie-movie-encyclopedia-white-zombie-peter-dendle?_s=PM:SHOWBIZ.

6. Ibid.

7. Compare this return to *Shaun of the Dead*, which grossed only $30 million total.

8. Zombie walks consist of a group of people showing up in a public space dressed as zombies. Both Philip Mahoney and Brendan Riley discuss the phenomenon in their contributions to this collection.

9. See Dan McGraw, "Austin road sign warns motorists of zombies," *Dallasnews.com*, *The Dallas Morning News*, January 29, 2009, accessed 7 February 7, 2009, http://www.dallasnews.com/sharedcontent/dws/news/localnews/transportation/stories/013009dnmetzombies.1595f453.html; Kristen Gosling, "Sign warns Illinois drivers about zombies," *KSDK.com*, February 3, 2009, accessed February 7, 2010, http://www.ksdk.com/news/local/story.aspx?storyid=166427&catid=3; Joe Byrnes and Karen Voyles, "Don't fear: Zombies are not near," *Gainesville.com*, *The Gainesville Sun*, December 22, 2009, accessed February 7, 2010, http://www.gainesville.com/article/20091222/ARTICLES/912221017.

10. See Greenspan's chapter in this volume for more on ARGs.

11. Adamg, "Boston Police vow not to cover up zombie attacks," *Universal Hub*, Universalhub.com, May 20, 2009, accessed February 17, 2010, http://www.universalhub.com/node/25349. The link included in the footnote takes the reader to a post by Jack Shepherd on the website BuzzFeed: The Viral Web in Real Time, titled "Boston Police Zombie Defense," http://www.buzzfeed.com/expresident/boston-police-zombie-defense. In turn, Shepherd offers a link to an article that served as his source, "Boston Police Department: We Will Let You Know When the Zombies Come," posted at theconsumerist.com, http://consumerist.com/2009/05/boston-police-department-we-will-let-you-know-when-the-zombies-come.html. Laura Northrup, the author of this article, acknowledges that she "learned about this [exchange] via Twitter, naturally," and links to a Dumb as a Blog post titled "Boston Cops: No Lie on Zombie Attacks," http://blog.trutv.com/dumb_as_a_blog/2009/05/via-twitter-boston-cops-confirm-that-any-future-zombie-attacks-will-not-be-covered-up-.html. Dumb as a Blog thanks Universal Hub for "the find." The user leaving the post titled "Boston Police Vow Not to Cover Up Zombie Attacks" does not credit another source, so perhaps it was "adamg" who first posted on this exchange.

12. Daniel Defoe, *A Journal of the Plague Year* (New York: Norton, 1992), 5.

13. Accompanying the outbreak of actual infection is typically a surge in informational and network anxieties. During the recent H1N1 flu crisis, the ability of emerging social networking sites such as Facebook and Twitter to convey misinformation and rumor became as important an issue for health agencies as the control of the virus amongst physical populations. Bringing the two intertwined concerns together, one media analyst commented that proper scrutiny of a new source before re-linking it on a social networking site was the "online equivalent of washing your hands.... Before you pass [an article] on, wash your hands a little." John D. Sutter, "Swine flu creates controversy on Twitter," *CNN.com*, Cable New Network, April 27, 2009, accessed November 15, 2010, http://articles.cnn.com/2009-04-27/tech/swine.flu.twitter_1_swine-flu-twitter-health-emergencies?_s=PM:TECH.

14. What was discovered during the H1N1 epidemic was that Google was able to accurately predict sites of outbreak using the aggregated data of global flu and flu-related searches. The predictive ability of their search was so successful that http://www.google.org/flutrends/ was established as a way for the public to monitor sites of actual outbreak. The relationship between public discourse and public health, between viral media and viral outbreak, were not regarded as being parallel processes, but now deeply intertwined, if not mutually constitutive. Google Flu Trends asserts that there is an indexical relationship between naming and the progress of the physical virus itself. Oddly enough, these advancements in analytic technology resonate with older beliefs about plague in which plague writing (specifically the material on which it was printed) was regarded as a bearer of the disease. As they circulated, these texts were ascribed the power to not only infect readers with their ideas, but the physical disease itself. For more on this complex inter-relationship between textuality and plague, see Ernest P. Gilman, *Plague Writing in Early Modern England* (Chicago: University of Chicago Press, 2009).

15. Jennifer Cooke, *Legacies of Plague in Literature, Theory and Film* (New York: Palgrave Macmillan, 2009), 22.

16. Cf. Sigmund Freud, *Beyond the Pleasure Principle*, trans. James Strachey (New York: W.W. Norton, 1989). See also Gilles Deleuze's discussion of the relationship between the Freudian death drive, memory, and repetition in the introduction to *Difference and Repetition*, trans. Paul Patton (New York: Columbia University Press, 1994).

17. Freud, 46.

18. William Buehler Seabrook, *The Magic Island* (New York: Harcourt, Brace, 1929), 101.

19. See Wade Davis, *Passage of Darkness: The Ethnobiology of the Haitian Zombie* (Chapel Hill: University of North Carolina Press, 1988).

20. Jamie Russell, *Book of the Dead: The Complete History of Zombie Cinema* (Surrey, UK: FAB Press, 2008), 14. If critics of Wade Davis's research in *The Serpent and the Rainbow* are correct, the riddle hasn't been entirely solved yet. The Tetrodotoxin in the "zombie powder" was not sufficient to produce the long-term effects associated with zombification.

21. See "Suit over 'Zombie' Film," *New York Times*, May 26, 1936, p. 27.

22. Jennifer Fay, "Dead Subjectivity: *White Zombie*, Black Baghdad," *CR: The New Centennial Review* 8, no. 1 (2008): 84.

23. The feud eventually culminated in a lawsuit over the parties' respective use of the phrase "When there is no room in hell ... the dead will walk the earth" in advertising materials. For more on the lawsuit, *Dawn Associates v. Links*, see Jonathan Dowell, "Fragmented Copies, Licensing, and Fair Use in a Digital World," *California Law Review* 86, no.4 (July 1998): 872.

24. *Return of the Living Dead* (1985), *Return of the Living Dead Part II* (1988), *Return of the Living Dead 3* (1993), *Return of the Living Dead: Necropolis* (2005), and *Return of the Living Dead: Rave to the Grave* (2005).

25. Consider the films *King of the Zombies* (1941), *Revenge of the Zombies* (1943), *Creature with the Atom Brain* (1955), *The Frozen Dead* (1966), *Shock Waves* (1977), *Oasis of the Zombies* (1981), *Zombie Lake* (1981), *Hard Rock Zombies* (1985), *Braindead* (1992), and *Dead Snow* (2009). Also, in the fifth installment of one of the most popular video game franchises, *Call of Duty,* there is a mini-game mode in which the player takes shelter in a house to fight off waves of Nazi zombies hordes; befitting the notion of zombie apocalypse, the game is technically unwinnable as it only ends once every player has been killed. There is no immediately self-evident reason why so many texts combine Nazis with zombies, aside from the fact that the Third Reich remains a preferred source of evil in American cinema. As Glenn Kay, who compiled most of this list, remarks: "Why so many zombie films return to this subject remains a mystery." See *Zombie Movies: The Ultimate Guide* (Chicago: Chicago Review Press, 2008), 81.

26. For zombie strippers, see *Zombie Strippers!* (2008), *Zombies! Zombies! Zombies!* (2008), and *Planet Terror* (2007). The voyeuristic pleasures of gratuitous sex and death function as a complementary pair.

27. *Pride and Prejudice and Zombies* is only one example of the recent spate of such literary mashups, which typically combine a work of canonical literature (conveniently in the public domain) with newly written passages featuring various monsters. Other examples of the genre include *Sense and Sensibility and Sea Monsters, Abraham Lincoln: Vampire Hunter, Android Karenina, Jane Slayre,* and *The Undead World of Oz: L. Frank Baum's The Wonderful Wizard of Oz Complete with Zombies and Monsters.*

28. The question of whether or not a virus is a form of "life" has been strongly debated by scientists for the past few decades. According to British virologist Norman Pirie: "Now, however, systems are being discovered and studied which are neither obviously living nor obviously dead, and it is necessary to define these words or else give up using them and coin others" (102). Regardless of whether the virus is defined as either alive or dead, what is accepted is that it has played a fundamental part in the evolution of life. One of the more uncanny aspects of the virus is that it appears to contain, much like the supernatural zombie, the powers of resurrection: "Because viruses occupy a netherworld between life and nonlife, they can pull off some remarkable feats. Consider, for instance, that although viruses ordinarily replicate only in living cells, they also have the capacity to multiply, or 'grow,' in dead cells and even to bring them back to life. Amazingly, some viruses can even spring back to their 'borrowed life' after being destroyed.... Viruses are the only known biological entity with this kind of 'phoenix phenotype'—the capacity to rise from their own ashes" (104). For more information on the debate, see the article from which the quotations are taken, Luis P. Villarreal, "Are Viruses Alive?" *Scientific American* 291, no. 6 (Dec. 2004): 100–105.

29. For a discussion of the close kinship between historical plague and zombies, see Cooke or Stephanie Boluk and Wylie Lenz, "Infection, Media, and Capitalism: From Early Modern Plagues to Postmodern Zombies," *Journal for Early Modern Cultural Studies* 10, no. 2 (Fall/Winter 2010): 127–148.

30. René Girard, "The Plague in Literature and Myth," *Texas Studies in Literature and Language* 15, no. 5 (1974): 833.

31. Antonin Artaud, "The Theater and the Plague," *The Theater and its Double,* trans. Mary C. Richard (New York: Grove, 1958), 21.

32. Sarah Juliet Lauro and Karen Embry, "A Zombie Manifesto: The Nonhuman Condition in the Era of Advanced Capitalism," *boundary 2: An International Journal of Literature and Culture* 35, no. 1 (2008): 105.

33. Girard, 836.

34. Ibid., 833.

35. Jeffery Weinstock, "Virus Culture," *Studies in Popular Culture* 20, no. 1 (October 1997): 83.

36. See Donna Haraway, "A Cyborg Manifesto: Science, Technology, and Socialist-Feminism in the Late Twentieth Century," in *Simians, Cyborgs and Women: The Reinvention of Nature* (New York: Routledge, 1991), 149–181.

37. Giorgio Agamben dedicates a book to a discussion of the relationship between humans and animal, and specifically the status of humanity at the "end of history." Working with the Hegelian notion of a post-

apocalyptic/post-historical world, he discusses the "remainder" (*resto*) that survives the death of humanity, who has become animal again at the end of history. See *The Open: Man and Animal* (Palo Alto: Stanford University Press, 2003). Similarly, Jacques Derrida speaks of man's relationship to the animal in eschatological terms when he writes, "The gaze called animal offers to my sight the abyssal limit of the human: the inhuman or the ahuman, the ends of man.... And in these moments of nakedness, under the gaze of the animal, everything can happen to me, I am like a child ready for the apocalypse...." *Specters of Marx: The State of the Debt, The Work of Mourning & the New International* (New York: Routledge, 2006), 14.

38. Lauro and Embry's "Zombie Manifesto" ironically appropriates Haraway's "Cyborg Manifesto," arguing that the authors "attempt to read the zombie as a more effective imagining of posthumanism than the cyborg because of its indebtedness to narratives of historical power and oppression, and we stress the zombie's relevance as a theoretical model that, like the cyborg, crashes borders. Simultaneously living and dead, subject and object, slave and slave rebellion, the zombie presents a posthuman specter informed by the (negative) dialectic of power relations rather than gender" (91).

39. *Dawn of the Dead*, DVD, directed by George A. Romero (1978; Anchor Bay, 2004).

40. Kim Paffenroth, *Gospel of the Living Dead: George Romero's Visions of Hell on Earth* (Waco: Baylor University Press, 2006), 13.

41. For a detailed discussion of the "cozy catastrophe" and its genealogy, see Terry Harpold's essay in this volume.

42. Michael John Brenan, *An Ecclesiastical History of Ireland, Volume II* (Dublin: John Coyne, 1840), 42.

43. For more information on John Clyn and the plague, see Ole Jørgen Benedictow, *The Black Death, 1346–1353: The Complete History* (Rochester: Boydell Press, 2004), particularly 27, 127, 143–4.

44. Vincent Price starred in a 1964 film of this name based on Richard Matheson's *I Am Legend*. Price, as the titular character, must defend himself against attacking hordes of vampires who, in fact, resemble zombies: they are staggering, clumsy, and desubjectivized. Romero's zombies owe a debt to these figures. Sean Moreland's essay in this volume offers an extensive reading of Matheson's *I Am Legend*.

45. "How to Survive a Zombie Attack," *h2g2*, November 11, 2005, accessed November 20, 2010, http://www.bbc.co.uk/dna/h2g2/A6875715.

46. In his essay "The Zombie as Barometer of Cultural Anxiety," Peter Dendle includes a fascinating discussion of the zombie's role in survivalist forum culture: "Survivalists and gun fetishists have found a protective 'narrative' cover amidst the zombie fan community.... While most of these zombie fans state explicitly that zombies do not really exist at the current time, they admit that zombie outbreaks are a possibility or at least represent a useful model for general emergency preparedness.... It is clear that the zombie holocausts vividly painted in movies and video games have tapped into a deep-seated anxiety about society, government, individual protection, and our increasing disconnectedness from subsistence skills." See Peter Dendle, "The Zombie as Barometer of Cultural Anxiety," in *Monsters and the Monstrous: Myths and Metaphors of Enduring Evil*, ed. Niall Scott (New York: Rodopi, 2007), 53–54.

47. Matt Mogk, "Zombie Research Society," *Zombie Research Society*, 2010, accessed November 14, 2010, http://zombieresearch.org/.

48. Brooks also wrote a fictional history of a worldwide zombie outbreak, in which he ironically acknowledges this tradition of the Last Man on Earth. In *World War Z*, the Last Man on Earth (abbreviated as LaMOE) is a character type, an individual suffering from a form of post-traumatic stress; being a Last Man is no longer only a physical, but also a psychological condition. After their heroic efforts to stay alive, these LaMOEs have now become an impediment to reclaiming the nation once the zombie threat has been eradicated: "There was always one or two in every town, some dude, or chick, who managed to survive. I read somewhere that the United States had the highest number of them in the world, something about our individualistic nature or something. They hadn't seen real people in so long, a lot of the initial shooting was just accidental or reflex. Most of the time we managed to talk them down." Max Brooks, *World War Z: And Oral History of the Zombie Wars* (New York: Crown, 2006), 319.

49. Kavita Philip and Terry Harpold, "'Party Over, Oops, Out of Time': Y2K, Technological 'Risk' and Informational Millenarianism," *NMEDIAC* 1, no. 1 (2002), accessed November 21, 2010, http://www.ibiblio.org/nmediac/winter2002/.

50. Simon Pegg, "The Dead and the Quick," *Guardian.co.uk*, Guardian News and Media Limited, November 4, 2008, accessed February 7, 2010.

51. See David Chalmers, *The Conscious Mind* (New York: Oxford University Press, 1996).

52. Philip Munz, Ioan Hudea, Joe Imad and Robert J. Smith, "When Zombies Attack!: Mathematical Modelling of an Outbreak of Zombie Infection," in *Infectious Disease Modeling Research Progress*, ed. Jean Michel Tchuenche, et al. (Hauppauge, NY: Nova Science Publishers, 2010), 133–150.

53. Cf. Daniel W. Drenzer, *Theories of International Politics and Zombies* (Princeton, NJ: Princeton University Press, 2011).

54. See "Zombie," BusinessDictionary.com.

55. See Robert Burns, "New Phorid Fly Species Turns Red Imported Fire Ants into 'Zombies,'" *AgriLife News*, May 11, 2009, accessed November 28, 2010, http://agnews.tamu.edu/showstory.php?id=1187.

56. Jacques Derrida, "Plato's Pharmacy," *Dissemination*, trans. Barbara Johnson (Chicago: University of Chicago Press, 1981), 149.

57. See Boluk and Lenz, specifically 145–146, for further discussion of the relationship between the circulation of media and ontologies of the living dead.

58. Wendy Hui Kyong Chun, "The Enduring Ephemeral, or the Future Is a Memory," *Critical Inquiry* 35 (Autumn 2008): 171.

59. Ibid., 167.

60. Terry Harpold, *Ex-foliations: Reading Machines and the Upgrade Path* (Minneapolis: University of Minnesota Press, 2008), 2.

61. Ibid.

62. Derrida elaborates on the relationship between writing and death in "Plato's Pharmacy." For further discussion of the way in which writing has been regarded as a dead, mechanical apparatus see Walter J. Ong, *Orality and Literacy: The Technologizing of the Word* (New York: Methuen, 1982), specifically 78–82.

63. Derrida, "Plato's Pharmacy," 79.

64. André Bazin, "The Ontology of the Photographic Image," trans. Hugh Gray, *Film Quarterly* 13, no. 4 (1960): 8.

65. Ibid.

66. As Steven Shaviro has argued, "The life-in-death of the zombie is a nearly perfect allegory for the inner logic of capitalism, whether this be taken in the sense of the exploitation of living labor by dead labor, the deathlike regimentation of factories and other social spaces, or the artificial, externally driven stimulation of consumers" (*The Cinematic Body* [Minneapolis: University of Minnesota Press, 1993], 84). Peter Dendle has also remarked that "zombies embody the ultimate Marxist working-class society" (*The Zombie Movie Encyclopedia* [Jefferson, NC: McFarland, 2000], 11). As much as zombie texts take the culture of late capitalism as their point of reference, it is worth noting that there is a reverse vector of influence, with economic theorists turning to the zombie as a central metaphor; cf. Chris Harman, *Zombie Capitalism: Global Crisis and the Relevance of Marx* (Chicago: Haymarket, 2010). This use of the metaphor is inaugurated by Marx who himself frequently invoked the undead imagery in his writing; see Judith Halberstam, *Skin Shows: Gothic Horror and the Technology of Monsters* (Durham: Duke University Press, 1995), 102. This trope is then famously appropriated by Derrida who argues that Marxism is a species of undead haunting our contemporary ideological landscape; see Derrida, *Specters of Marx*. For psychoanalytic readings, see once again Steven Shaviro for his discussion of the cinematic abject and the "abject vacancy" of the zombie (*The Cinematic Body*, 260, 99). For a discussion of the zombie and the uncanny, see Kyle Bishop's "Raising the Dead: Unearthing the Nonliterary Origins of Zombie Cinema," *Journal of Popular Film and Television* 33, no. 4 (2006): 196–205.

67. Frank Kermode, *The Sense of an Ending* (New York: Oxford University Press, 2000), 12.

68. Quentin Meillassoux, *After Finitude: An Essay on the Necessity of Contingency*, trans. Ray Brassier (London: Continuum, 2010), 115.

69. While the conclusion of H.G. Wells's *The Time Machine* (1895) still has a human narrator, the Time Traveller witnesses the terrifying spectacle of a cooling earth which holds residue of life, but nothing resembling the comfort of humanity. The silence and darkness of this cold world fills the narrator with sickening horror. As a counter-example, Reza Negarastrani's has recently advocated the abolishment of "heliocentric slavery," producing a work of radical ecology that celebrates this perspective of the cooling earth ("Solar Inferno and the Earthbound Abyss," *Our Sun* [Venice: Istituto Svizzero di Roma & Mousse Publishing, 2010]).

70. Manuel De Landa, *A Thousand Years of Nonlinear History* (New York: Zone Books, 1997), 259.

# Zombies as Internal
# Fear or Threat

## KIM PAFFENROTH

### The Current State of Zombies in Popular Culture

Zombies are popular today in literature, film, and video games, in a way that no other monster — with some partial exception for the great popularity of vampires since *Twilight* — has been unable to contest, equal, or exceed for some time. So the question is often posed: What is it about zombies that is especially interesting or appealing at the beginning of the twenty-first century? What symbolic meanings or narrative possibilities do they offer that their fellow monsters do not? Or, since zombies are associated with the horror genre, the question can be specified and focused more: What is it that is uniquely horrifying about zombies? And whatever that quality is, how and why is it deemed especially horrifying at this point in world — and especially United States — history?[1]

These two related questions can be pursued partly by elimination. Zombies are frightening because they are depicted as killing and eating their victims, but so do most threats in the horror genre (sharks, serial killers, viruses). Zombies are monstrous versions of human beings, but so are lots of monsters (vampires, werewolves, mutants). Zombies threaten the complete overthrow of civilization as we know it, and possibly the end of all human life, but so do asteroids, meteors, and plagues. The zombie threat is made worse by the fact that their victims then turn into the creature that attacked them. This too is similar to other monsters (werewolves and vampires) and also similar to the sub-genre of infection/plague films. In the case of zombies, however, this may carry a greater sense of dread and revulsion: vampires and werewolves can be seen as desirable, potent, intelligent, virile creatures whom one might like — in some ways at least — to become; a mindless ghoul condemned to wander aimlessly across an empty, ruined earth seems much less attractive.

It is, I think, in a combination of these, where we see the unique horror of zombies, and from which we might be able to answer the further question of "Why are they so popular right now?" Zombies are the only humanoid threat that will bring about the end of civilization by turning all of us into them. Species-killing viruses and planet-killing asteroids aren't human, and the other human monsters don't generally have world domination in their sights.[2] With that description of zombies—an unstoppable, implacable army of primitive, unreasoning humans, set on destroying civilization and turning all "normal" people into subhumans such as themselves—it is probably no surprise that terrorists, especially Islamists bent on destroying the West and killing as many civilians as possible, have been suggested as the fear for which zombies are the fantastical substitute and symbol.[3]

In this essay I'd like to question how widely applicable that identification might be. It is not my contention that filmmakers and writers do not play with the fear of terrorists or other foreigners or that they do not sometimes even traffic in specific images associated with that fear. As the current "other" most feared by many Americans, it would seem inevitable that the zombie trope would be utilized (in part) to play on that fear, as it has been used to comment on racial "others" in earlier films like *White Zombie* (1932), or to examine sexual "others," as in the more recent film *Otto; or, Up with Dead People* (2008). What I would suggest, is that the films' more frequent target, and the ultimate horror and anxiety they wish to provoke, is much more general and deeper than our fears of Islamist or Marxist violence against the United States. As I sometimes say about the social commentary of zombie films: *Fahrenheit 9/11* looked dated just a couple years after it was made, because its referents are so historically and culturally specific; *Land of the Dead* will stand as an effective satire on the abuse and corruption of power for years to come, because its referents are more subtle and general. Or, looked at another way, our neighbors and family members annoy, harm, and frighten us on a much more regular basis than foreign attackers. Romero quipped that his zombies were simply "the neighbors,"[4] and he thereby echoed the evaluation at the heart of Dostoevsky's *The Brothers Karamazov*: "I could never understand how one can love one's neighbors. It's just one's neighbors, to my mind, that one can't love."[5] Neighbors are the least lovable people in our lives, and zombies just make that unlovability concrete and lethal on the screen. Since the *Dawn of the Dead* remake (2004) and *Land of the Dead* (2005) are two films that have invited the analysis I wish to undermine, I'll focus my comments on those, after a review of the Romero films that led up to them.

## The Romero Background

My hesitation with the "zombies are foreign invaders" interpretation begins with one of the best-known lines from what many (myself included) regard as the greatest zombie movie of all time, the original *Dawn of the Dead* (1978). When asked what the ghouls are, Peter responds, "They're us, that's all." "That's all": to Peter, it seems a quite self-evident and simple identification. There is, in other words, nothing very complicated or mysterious, ultimately, about zombies. Perhaps this is why their origin is never sufficiently or convincingly addressed in any of the Romero films[6]: in a way, they've been here all along. If this were a throwaway line in one film, one could ignore its implications—the way one doesn't really have to ask about the movie's tagline ("When there's no more room in hell, the dead will walk the earth"), "Well, if there's no more room in hell, then what happens when you shoot a zombie in the head? Where's it go then?" But tracing the meaning Romero imbues his zombies with shows two ongoing themes: the identity of zombies and living humans, and the greater threat posed by the living humans. Both of these would mitigate against an identification of the zombies as outside forces or the "other."[7]

In *Night of the Living Dead* (1968), the identity of living and dead is clearest in the fact that several of the characters are shown turning into zombies and attacking their living partners. This fate is suffered by Barbra's brother, Johnny, and all three members of the Cooper family. These zombies are no outsiders, but exist in the heart of the group of living survivors. (Their identity as family members exacerbates this and underscores the terror Romero wishes to invoke: not fear of an unknown "other" but fear of the most intimately known and trusted people in our lives.)[8] Ben is misidentified as a zombie in the bleak and ironic ending, while at the beginning, Barbara misidentifies the first zombie as a living person. In the film that created the modern zombie myth, confusion as to who is a zombie and who isn't is an ever-present problem, and a defining characteristic of zombies (and humans).

What drives the film's plot, however, is the second point mentioned above — Romero's contention throughout his films that living humans are more of a threat to one another than zombies are to them. The danger posed by the zombies seems minimal and easily surmountable, if only the seven living people cooperate with one another, but instead they are constantly fighting each other as well as the living dead, who show no tension or disagreement among themselves.[9] The relations between the living humans are characterized by fear, mistrust, suspicion, and a desire on the part of the males for each of them to be in charge of the group — all of this with disastrous consequences— while the zombies appear to be cooperative and docile toward one another, while remaining efficiently and single-mindedly focused on their human foes. The humans' predicament is made worse by their constantly trusting and acting on the information fed to them by the television, whose reliability is shown throughout the film to be suspect and whose "facts" do not to match up with what the survivors can themselves see right outside the door.[10] Whatever the zombies represent, they are not the most dangerous threat to human life, according to Romero: other, living human beings, and especially those closest to us, are the real threat.

These themes continue in the next film, *Dawn of the Dead* (1978). As in *Night*, characters we follow for part of the movie as living beings eventually turn into zombies; in this film, it is in fact half the cast (two of the four main characters). Romero intensifies the residual humanity of zombies by stating something that was never hinted at in the first film — that zombies retain memories of their previous human existence and act on those memories. This is the explanation given for why the mall is so crowded with zombies— because all those people came there when they were alive and they now remember and return there: "This was an important place in their lives," Steve explains when they arrive at the mall and see it packed with undead "shoppers." The identification of living and undead is also made in this film through the camera angle during kill shots: several times these are shot from the zombie victim's point of view, looking down the gun barrel before it fires.[11] In more gentle (and highly uncharacteristic of zombie films) scenes, two of the human characters (Roger and Fran) are shown exhibiting some sympathy or identification with the zombies: the zombies are fleetingly present to them as suffering humans and not just deadly flesh. In the case of the one character, Fran, such compassion and perception may be why she survives the ordeal, by eschewing further violence and rejecting the material allures of the mall.[12] Perhaps most subtly and pervasively, however, the zombies and humans are equated in this movie by both groups striving and sacrificing themselves to occupy and loot the mall: Romero's most potent contribution to the zombie mythos is to portray both living and undead as inveterate, unstoppable consumers.[13]

Exactly as in *Night*, the human survivors again turn out to be more of a threat to themselves than the zombie hordes are. This is shown in several ways throughout the film. The first sequence, inside an apartment building, shows one policeman shooting live people indiscriminately, all while shouting racial slurs at them. The next scene elaborates on the deadly unreliability of the television, already shown in *Night*: here it is said specifically that information is being broadcast which is known to be false and which will send survivors to rally points that have already been overrun by the undead, thereby sending the survivors to their deaths. The climactic sequence of the film has the mall overrun by the undead, only because the carefully constructed defenses were first breached by a gang of human survivors, intent on looting the mall.

But in the end, it is the monstrous consumerism that is the undoing of both humans and zombies. The zombies are killed by the hundreds in their monomaniacal quest to occupy the mall. And once the four main characters secure the mall, the interesting middle of the film shows Romero's real point: safe from the zombies, with every creature comfort, the survivors are utterly miserable.[14] Consumerism is only enjoyable with the necessary social context to make one's consumption noticed and envied by others—and the hungry, mindless jealousy of the zombies milling around outside the mall is clearly not adequate or welcomed. Just as destructive as their urge to consume is the humans' urge to take and possess—epitomized by the raiders' foolish decision to attack the mall, which results in so many of them being killed and eaten, even though they are shown taking things such as bowling balls and television sets—items with no use in a post-apocalyptic world. The two main characters who die also sacrifice themselves to the pursuit of possessions. Early in the film, Roger is killed because he becomes overcome with lust—both for the objects within the mall, and with bloodlust for killing zombies. And at the end, Steve is killed because he tries to attack the raiders, when Peter had advised him to hide and wait for the outsiders to retreat. Significantly, when Steve begins shooting at the bikers, he justifies it by saying, "It's ours! We took it!" In the end, in Romero's most satiric vision, the mall is occupied only by peaceful, tottering zombies, gazing longingly at all the items they now possess, even though they have no real use for them.

Completing the original trilogy of films, *Day of the Dead* (1985) takes the themes of zombie/human identity and the greater dangers posed by humans to their logical extremes. Romero includes in this film a "smart" zombie, Bub, who shows himself in many ways to be preferable to the more evil humans, Rhodes and Logan. Bub is still desirous of monstrous sustenance, but he several times restrains himself from attacking the living humans. He is capable of speech and of knowing the usage of simple items like a razor. More importantly, he is capable of emotion and attachment, of listening blissfully to Beethoven, or letting out a howl of grief and rage when he sees his murdered trainer. For Logan to say of the zombies, "They are us! The same animal, simply functioning less perfectly," would almost seem to understate the point, as both Rhodes and Logan seem incapable of compassion in the film. The humans in this film are more degenerate than in either of the two previous, while the zombies seem to have evolved into more human and humane characters.

This evolution carries over into the relative danger posed by living and undead. From the beginning of the film, it seems clear that the main, sympathetic characters—Sarah, McDermott, and John—have much more to fear from their fellow survivors than they do from the zombies. The soldiers repeatedly threaten them with death, and in the case of Sarah, rape. The scientists are less aggressive toward the other humans, but their treatment of the zombies reaches levels of sadism unknown in the other films: whereas previously the characters would shoot zombies or bash them in the head, now they are shown torturing them, literally hacking them apart into piles of meat. In one scene, this is even depicted as a specifically cruciform torture, with the zombies chained to crosses along one wall of their dungeon. *Day of the Dead* makes explicit the relative evil of living and undead by laying out the various levels of cruelty of which they are capable. A zombie will kill and eat you as quickly as his teeth and claws allow him — it'll probably be over in a matter of a few very unpleasant seconds; a smart zombie like Bub may even evolve the capacity to refrain from such behavior. But a fellow human can rape and torture you for days, and can bring the full weight of his intellect to bear on figuring out new ways to worsen or prolong your torment. Faced with such a grim vision of senseless human cruelty, Sarah is incredulous, but John wisely and sadly attributes it to human nature.[15]

From the original trilogy of *Night, Dawn,* and *Day,* it would be hard to hypothesize that zombies represent some foreign, external force or fear. The living and undead are repeatedly equated in these films, and where any comparison is made, it is usually to the detriment of the living, who are shown to be more cruel and deadly to their fellow survivors. If recent zombie films depict the zombies as a foreign group — terrorists or disgruntled citizens of the Third World — this would be a marked departure from the earlier depictions. Let us see the extent to which the movies' symbolism bears that out.

## Two Recent Versions of the Zombie Threat

The *Dawn of the Dead* (2004) remake begins with one of the most harrowing sequences in modern action or horror films, in which the protagonist, Ana, and her boyfriend are attacked by their neighbor's zombified child; Ana's boyfriend is badly bitten during the attack and immediately turns into a zombie, resulting in a continued attack on Ana. This follows on Romero's dynamic of having family members and friends attacking their loved ones: their violence is more horrifying, as is the violence that must be used to stop them. This dynamic is continued throughout the film: Frank, the father of one of the survivors, has to be killed when he turns, as does Andy, the gun store owner whom the survivors had befriended and tried to help. One of the most hideous scenes is when Andre tries to save his family from the infection, but his girlfriend Luda and their newborn baby both turn and have to be shot; Andre and another survivor are killed in the resulting shootout as well. Two other group members — Steve and Bart — also turn, but they are consistently portrayed unsympathetically and the audience is unconcerned or even pleased at their extermination. With such a heavy toll of characters turning into zombies, the consistent impression in the film is that zombies are from within the group of survivors: they are an internal threat and not from outside — whether that threat is from failed intimacy or callous self-interest.

As for our survivor group fighting the zombies camped out in the parking lot outside the mall, rather than those who arise in their ranks, one scene stands out as especially memorable and significant. This is where the male survivors stand on the roof of the mall and hold up a dry-erase board with the name of some celebrity written on it. Andy, across the street with a high-powered rifle, then shoots the zombie who resembles the named celebrity. If there is any class warfare alluded to in the film, it seems most blatant in this scene, and the survivors are the ones cast as the envious proletariat, taking out their anger and aggression on the helpless, hapless zombies who accidentally resemble the objects of their frustration and envy.

Finally, exactly as with the earlier films, *Dawn of the Dead* (2004) relies on the living humans' failings and vices to bring about their destruction, not the zombies' violence and hunger. Bart and CJ both threaten Ana with rape early in the film. The survivors are also on the verge of shooting one another at several points, and with the tragedy of Andre and Luda, they actually do end up shooting two living people as well as two zombies. Steve locks several of his fellows outside during the final sequence, thereby letting the zombies into mall when the survivors fight their way back in. Though the zombies this time are not particularly sympathetic, several of the human survivors are as distasteful as characters in earlier films, and the human propensity for short-sighted selfishness and violence is the greatest threat to human survival.

In *Land of the Dead* (2005), we are presented with an army of undead attacking a city of survivors. The dynamics are much like *Day of the Dead:* there is a smart zombie ("Big Daddy") leading the horde, and the city is ruled by Kaufman, a villain in the mold of

Rhodes, obsessed with power and cruelty. As several reviewers noted, the allegiance of the audience has shifted at this point to the zombies, who are clearly the aggrieved parties in this story, and away from the humans, who are portrayed as much worse.[16] At the beginning of the film, the zombies are content to "live" in their significantly-named "Uniontown." The humans, on the other hand, occupy a city built on greed and social stratification, in which hordes of Dickensian-looking children and adults dressed in rags live in a shanty town full of crime, drugs, violence, and prostitution, while a few live in a sparkling, high-rising "gated community."[17] The zombies are merely an extension of the stratification that exists in the city: tower-dwellers (safe, insulated, parasitic), shanty-town dwellers (exploited, uncared-for, expendable), and zombies (safe until the humans prey on them, at which point they are slaughtered by the hundreds). The identification of living and undead is again made in this film, in a rather more nuanced way than in the original *Dawn of the Dead*. While watching zombies go through the motions of "real" life (holding hands, pumping gas, playing musical instruments—and even, a minute later, shielding one another from gunfire and trying to save one another from the humans' cruel predation), the main character and a younger man discuss their undead neighbors:

> ROOKIE: [They're] trying to be us.
> RILEY: They used to be us, learning to be us again.
> ROOKIE: There's a big difference between us and them. They're dead. It's like they're pretending to be alive.
> RILEY: Isn't that what we're doing—pretending to be alive?

In this formulation, "human" or "alive" seems not to be a given, but an imperfectly attained goal or process, toward which both living and undead strive, with varying degrees of success.

Are the zombies here representative of exploited, third-world residents, wreaking vengeance on the evil, lazy, capitalist overlords of the U.S.? That is certainly a reasonable extension of what they represent, but I would caution against making it the primary referent. Coming as they do from a place named for a real suburb of Pittsburgh, with a name that evokes memories of a past time when U.S. workers were unionized and treated with respect and fairness, it would seem the Uniontown zombies come from within the U.S. to end the evils that people like Kaufman (another significant name, meaning "merchant") have perpetrated against their fellow countrymen. Consider also the ending, in which the city is not completely destroyed or occupied by the zombies: the zombies wander off, the city is left to be rebuilt by the shanty-town dwellers, and the hardy, individualistic, military-types who were the nominal heroes of the film are left to go establish an outpost in "Canada" (the hardier, more socialist part of North America). Only Kaufman, his hired mercenaries, and some of the tower dwellers are killed or eaten (though the blood bath is spectacular, to be sure). The solution suggested by Romero in this film would seem to be the one he's always hinted at in his ruminations on America: a wiping clean of all the capitalist, racist, consumerist filth that has accumulated on the U.S., to start over with some post-racial, post-capitalist community founded on equality and more humane values.

With all this considered, it would seem these two recent zombie films stand pretty firmly in the Romero tradition of depicting the undead as a threat we carry around within ourselves—either individually or as a society—and not some foreign "other." In this sense they continue the role I see Romero enacting in his earlier work, a mission and message quite close to that of the Hebrew prophets, pronouncing their judgment against the individual and corporate sins that beset and typify the age in which they live. Though the Hebrew prophets and Romero both use imagery of outside, violent forces wreaking destruction on their respective nations, they both conceive the illness and cure as finally internal:

Assyrians and zombies are not the real problem or threat — wickedness, selfishness, greed, and lack of compassion are. And the real cure is not killing some outside enemy — it is personal and communal repentance, in the sense of turning away from the bad habits to which we have become so accustomed and addicted.

## Conclusion

None of this should be taken as though there is some "right" or canonical version of zombies, from which current or future depictions cannot or should not deviate. This is the myopia of fandom one often sees: to cling dogmatically to one aspect of the phenomenon one adulates so fanatically (fast versus slow zombies, *Star Trek* versus *Star Trek: The Next Generation,* scary versus romantic vampires, etc.) and then insist that all other variations or versions of that art form are heretical, deficient, perverted, and worthless — or, at least, inferior. Instead, I'd like to suggest and encourage the opposite extreme: no one version of zombies exhausts all the narrative or symbolic uses or implications of the monster.

There surely are and will continue to be some films and books in which the zombies are stand-ins for the foreign, often stateless enemies of the United States, and the unfolding story will be satisfying because it shows such undead versions of terrorists being slaughtered in various gory and imaginative ways; perhaps other versions with similar symbolism may play with more social satire and show the deficiencies of the United States that gave rise to such a menace, or show how the defeat of the United States by the zombies is due to these shortcomings (whether those ills are the ones feared and decried by right or left will offer further variations). What my review of past and current zombie films is meant to suggest, is that the monster cannot be taken uncritically as merely and automatically an acting out of a xenophobic and/or racist fantasy (or an obvious and direct reversal of such a fantasy). Part of this easy identification of the zombie, I think, comes from a widespread and typical urge to belittle or limit the monster (and those who enjoy reading or watching zombie tales). The monster's very simplicity and lack of personality or individuality leads many to conclude that their stories are straightforward and easy to describe, comprehend, or analyze. But the zombie's minimal approach to monstrosity — it is, simply, an animated, human corpse with way below average human intelligence, coordination, and speed — may leave it open to our projecting a great number of interpretations on to it. With a monster that is so fully and banally human, one interpretation that will surely always be open and likely, is that the zombies are us — not the mysterious or reviled "other," however that is constructed — but us, in all our hungry, grasping, mindless simplicity. We will always be our worst enemies, and the ones we can never fully eliminate.

## Notes

1. I am using "horrifying" to cover an overall effect that would include but not be limited to fright or fear, since many of the films and especially the video games are not meant to be frightening: they're thrilling, but in a grotesque, revolting way. The zombies in them don't scare us, but we very much want to see them shot in the face, so that we will feel relief and satisfaction. We also wish for the zombie attacks to be as harrowing and bloody as possible, not to frighten us, but to exhilarate us, the way a roller coaster does, and also to prepare us for the satisfaction we'll feel when we shoot the attacking zombie three times in the head. Though I focus here on a narrower line of interpretation, most of my analysis can be found stated in more broad terms in my book *Gospel of the Living Dead: George Romero's Visions of Hell on Earth* (Waco: Baylor University Press, 2006).

2. The bad vampires in *Blade* (first comic book appearance in 1973; films in 1998, 2002, and 2004) may have this in mind, but the hero vampire seems to have things well under control.

3. In relation to *Dawn of the Dead* (2004), see M. Degiglio-Bellemare, "Review of Land of the Dead," *Journal of Religion and Film* 9, no. 2 (2005), accessed July 19, 2010, http://www.unomaha.edu/jrf/Vol9No2/Reviews/

LandDead.htm. Related to *Land,* see John Lutz, "Zombies of the World, Unite: Class Struggle and Alienation in *Land of the Dead,*" in *The Philosophy of Horror,* ed. T. Fahy (Lexington: University Press of Kentucky, 2010), 121–136, who opts for a more Marxist analysis, with the zombies standing in for any foreign and domestic proletariats crushed by United States capitalism, but still brings foreign invasion and destruction of the United States into his analysis at many points: "In *Land of the Dead,* this principle is applied on a grand scale. The besieged house is transformed into an entire city allegorically representing America and its relationship to the underdeveloped, exploited nations on the periphery of empire.... This relationship signifies America's exploitative relationship to the underdeveloped nations of the world" (122, 124–25). Cf. J. Russell, *Book of the Dead: The Complete History of Zombie Cinema* (Surrey, UK: FAB Press, 2005), 192: "It [the zombie movie] seems unlikely to be ousted anytime soon. As the West wages its war on Terror and makes imperial incursions into the Middle East, the zombie's role as a veiled commentary on relations between colonial occupier and native subjects and its more contemporary role as a symbol of the mass destruction of the First World may yet have a place in many, many nightmares."

4. Quoted in many places, e.g., G. A. Waller, *The Living and the Undead: From Stoker's "Dracula" to Romero's "Dawn of the Dead"* (Urbana: University of Illinois Press, 1986), 277.

5. F. Dostoevsky, *The Brothers Karamazov,* trans. C. Garnett (New York: Penguin, 1958), 230.

6. In *Night of the Living Dead* there is the vague (and highly suspect, since it comes from the television) surmise that the plague comes from radiation from a returning space vehicle. In *Dawn* not even this thin of an explanation is attempted and the "experts" who appear on television offer nothing except advice on how to dispose of the bodies.

7. A partial exception would be if the living humans represented an evil regime that bolstered its power by claiming it was fighting against the evil "outsiders," represented by the zombies (e.g., if the film mimicked what some saw in the Bush administration and its War on Terror). This comes closest to the dynamic I see in *Land of the Dead,* but without the zombies ever being fully "outside" and without them ever being as big a threat as terrorists.

8. The monstrousness and lethality of the family is often noted as part of the film's increased terror and how it departs from earlier horror films: see D. Pirie, *The Vampire Cinema* (New York: Crescent Books, 1977), 143–45; Waller, *Living and the Undead,* 292; R. H. W. Dillard, "Night of the Living Dead: It's Not Like Just a Wind That's Passing Through," in *American Horrors: Essays on the Modern American Horror Film,* ed. G. A. Waller (Urbana: University of Illinois Press, 1987), 14–29, esp. 28 (originally appeared as R. H. W. Dillard, *Horror Films* [New York: Monarch, 1976], 55–81).

9. Cf. Waller, *Living and the Undead,* 285–86: "What Night of the Living Dead finally suggests, however, is that these human beings are indeed a threat to Ben's survival.... As soon as other people besides Barbara appear, Ben's simple struggle to survive becomes complicated by questions and conflicts about territory, authority, and responsibility — questions that quite obviously do not worry the living dead"; T. Williams, *The Cinema of George A. Romero: Knight of the Living Dead* (London: Wallflower Press, 2003), 22: "The human survivors never unite to defeat the zombies. They are constantly at each other's throats and attempt to devour each other in an ironically metaphorical version of the outside assault by their living dead opponents. Indeed, the dead appear more united than the living in terms of their concentrated focus on a specific aim."

10. On the fatal unreliability of the television in the film, see V. Sobchack, *Screening Space: The American Science Fiction Film,* 2d ed. (New York: Ungar, 1987), 189–90; P. Hutchings, *The Horror Film* (New York: Pearson Longman, 2004), 188–89.

11. Cf. Waller, *Living and the Undead,* 307, 312–13.

12. On Fran's character, see Paffenroth, *Gospel of the Living Dead,* 59–60, 68–69. See also Williams, *Cinema of George A. Romero,* 92, 97; R. Wood, "Apocalypse Now: Notes on the Living Dead," in *American Nightmare: Essays on the Horror Film,* ed. R. Wood and R. Lippe (Toronto: Festival of Festivals, 1979), 91–98, esp. 96–97; A. Loudermilk, "Eating Dawn in the Dark: Zombie Desire and Commodified Identity in George A. Romero's *Dawn of the Dead,*" *Journal of Consumer Culture* 3, no. 1 (2003): 83–108, esp. 92; Shaviro, "Contagious Allegories," 88.

13. Cf. S. Beard, "No Particular Place to Go," *Sight and Sound* 3, no. 4 (1993): 30–31; S. Shaviro, "Contagious Allegories: George Romero," in *The Cinematic Body* (Minneapolis: University of Minnesota Press, 1998), 83–105; D. J. Skal, *The Monster Show: A Cultural History of Horror,* rev. ed. (New York: Faber & Faber, 2001), 376; Loudermilk, "Eating Dawn in the Dark." Zombie walks or marches, one of the increasingly popular manifestations of the zombie culture, play on this dynamic by almost always being staged in malls. See http://www.zombiewalk.com/ to find one near you.

14. Cf. Russell, *Book of the Dead,* 94: "Pointedly lampooning the faux utopian logic behind the consumerist boom of the 1970s, the middle section of *Dawn of the Dead* places its four protagonists inside the zombie-free, empty enclosure of the mall, gives them all they could ask for (cash, food, sports facilities, gadgets and unlimited leisure time) and then quietly watches as they descend into abject misery and self-loathing. Apparently, the zombies aren't the only ones who've lost their souls."

15. Or at least, human society. That would seem the implication of John's idea to leave the archives of the human race behind and start afresh on some island. The way he summarizes all the accumulated knowledge

they are sitting on in the bunker — every tax return and movie, along with records of every war and disaster that's ever occurred — it seems a tale of violence and oppression, but one they can flee by simply ignoring it and never returning to study or remember this cursed history.

16. Cf. M. Dargis, "Not Just Roaming, Zombies Rise Up: Review of Land of the Dead," *The New York Times,* June 24, 2005, accessed July 23, 2010, http://movies.nytimes.com/movie/314246/George-A-Romero-s-Land-of-the-Dead/overview: "In 'George A. Romero's Land of the Dead,' an excellent freakout of a movie, the living no longer have the advantage or our full sympathies"; Russell, *Book of the Dead,* 190: "It's the first film in the series to explicitly ask us to sympathize with the zombies themselves and it extends Romero's living dead mythology in a way which none of his imitators have ever managed to do."

17. Cf. Degiglio-Bellemare, "Land of the Dead," 7: "Romero's new film offers a very important statement on the reality of 'lockdown America,' with its gated communities, its stark class divisions, and its racial demarcations."

# *White Zombie* and the Creole:
# William Seabrook's *The Magic Island*
# and American Imperialism in Haiti

## GYLLIAN PHILLIPS

In 1929, when Haitians' displeasure with the American occupying forces was at its height,[1] William Seabrook published his travelogue on Haitian "voodoo," *The Magic Island*.[2] Cited by most scholars of early horror film as the principle source for Victor Halperin's 1932 film *White Zombie*,[3] Seabrook's book nevertheless offers quite a different representation of Haiti and its folk traditions than the first zombie movie. Recently, the scholarly discussion has turned to the significance of Seabrook's book as an originary text and especially to the ideological implications of the Haitian context of the film. The figure of the early film zombie has been identified as a child of colonial history, representing "slavery's uncanny return."[4] In Haitian folk culture, the zombie is also regarded as a figure of fear representing the return of colonial slave culture.[5] Even the migration of the term, "zombie," into English-language vernacular has its roots in colonial history.[6] In this chapter, I want to enter into the emerging conversation about Seabrook as the source for *White Zombie* by engaging with a figure largely unacknowledged in the discussion of the early film zombie: the creole. Creole cultures represent the inevitable mixing that results from colonialism. To white imperialist America the very existence of the creole is a source of ideological horror because it undermines the white/black binary that keeps the power structures of white supremacy in place. In Seabrook's book, creole culture and the zombie are represented as an ambivalent mix, and this ambivalence is reflected in the book's combination of sensational exploitation and rational explanation of Haitian postcolonial culture. In *The Magic Island*, the zombie is mixed, in part, because it is conscripted to labor in American industry. *White Zombie* attempts, with only partial success, to simplify Seabrook's ambivalence by identifying the creole as the principle villain, in the character of Murder Legendre. Legendre threatens to infect whites with the contagion of native magic and pharmacology by transforming them into zombies. In different ways, both texts attempt to recuperate the American presence in Haiti. However, by reducing the complexities of Seabrook's cultural analysis, *White Zombie* ironically reveals American anxiety, raised by the Haitian occupation, over race relations and over the threat of an American inheritance of French colonial history. By focusing on the concept of the creole traced back to Seabrook, I hope to add my own ambivalent note to *White Zombie* scholarship that has itself replicated the black/white binary. That is, film scholars seem to assume that Murder Legendre is either "white" or "black," not considering that his character might be racially ambiguous. Indeed, it is this very ambiguity which helps to generate the fear embodied by the zombie master.

The central anxiety in Halperin's film, *White Zombie,* is revealed by its title: zombies are one thing, but a white zombie is a sign of horror. Like "white trash" or "white slavery," the term "white zombie" implies the violation of a racial norm. That is, white audiences of zombie pop culture in the 1930s might reasonably expect black zombies to be the norm, thanks to Seabrook's *The Magic Island.* Trash, slaves, and zombies are "normally" black, but when the zombie state crosses the racial boundary to affect a white person, horror results. The source of the horror is the fear, for whites, of a loss of sovereign physical and mental autonomy and/or a fear of "unnatural" servitude.[7] For the Haitian citizen, the fear of the zombie metaphorically represents the fear of returning to colonial, slave status, or objecthood.[8] The threat to white folks, however, as Kyle Bishop points out, is that they might be forced to change places with the "naturally" abject black through zombification. For Bishop, part of this fear is bound up in the miscegenation implied by the black-white binary. The violation of the racial norms in the film then includes both the unnatural displacement of white autonomy, supremacy, and control and the threat of sexual subjugation, or miscegenation. In the film, the zombification of the white woman, Madeline, is a threat to white supremacy in the social and economic power structure, and it also represents a threat to racial purity.[9]

Victor Halperin's 1932 film is not about the American occupation of Haiti, at least not overtly. Although it is set in Haiti, and the characters have 1930s clothing and hairstyles, the exact time is unspecified. The only tenuous connection to American imperialist interests is that the hero Neil Parker (played by John Harron) works in a bank in Port-au-Prince. The film opens with Neil and Madeline Short (Madge Bellamy) in a horse-drawn carriage on their way to the home of plantation owner Charles Beaumont (Robert Frazer). Beaumont is sometimes described by film scholars as an American plantation owner and sometimes as French.[10] Beaumont has generously offered to host the young couple's wedding in his home, but he has ulterior motives: he hopes to win Madeline from Neil. On their way, they encounter a native Haitian funeral in the middle of the road, and then the zombie-master and principal villain, Murder Legendre (played by Bela Lugosi, fresh from *Dracula*). We see his sinister zombie crew in the distance. Once at Beaumont's opulent plantation home, they meet the missionary Dr. Bruner (Joseph Cawthorn) who will marry them. From the outset, Dr. Bruner is the couple's father figure and protector. The wedding goes awry when Beaumont uses a potion, given to him by Legendre, to turn Madeline into a zombie. She appears to die, is buried, and then disinterred by Legendre and Beaumont in order to become the latter's love slave. Neil and Dr. Bruner go in search of the culprits, and the film ends at Legendre's gothic castle[11] where the zombies, their master, and finally Beaumont (who has been himself semi-zombified by Legendre) topple into the ocean. This leaves Neil, Madeline, and Dr. Bruner as a kind of proto-society at the end. While there are (black) zombies in Halperin's film, the titular zombie is not conscripted to field or factory labor. Instead, Madeline is zombified to become, implicitly at least, a sex slave. The black zombies are supposed to be frightening robotic monsters, a la Romero, but Madeline is not a monster; rather, she is zombie as victim.

Until quite recently, the villain of *White Zombie* was identified as a stock character from the tradition of the European Gothic and not with any specific relation to his particular location in Haiti. In Sevastakis, for example, he is a "necromancer" in the tradition of *Dracula* and *The Mummy*.[12] Rhodes complicates Legendre's origins, describing him as a "zombie master" and tracing his similarities to Faust and Svengali, among others.[13] Now that the implications of the colonial setting for the film have begun to be explored, the racial identification of Legendre has become more specific. In particular, two scholars' opposing designations of Legendre result in quite different arguments about the film's representation of racial power structures. On the one hand, Jennifer Fay identifies Murder Legendre as white, and she argues that this racial categorization represents the larger concerns about labor and capital in depression-era America: "That one American is slaving for another — that white men and women are equally vulnerable to various forms of exploitation without pay — tells us that zombified work in any form is not only a tropical malady."[14] Bishop, on the other hand, identifies Legendre as black, and claims that Madeline's zombie status represents the "greatest fear of the colonizers — that the native will rise up and become the dominating force."[15] My argument here, focusing specifically on the threat of the creole, stems in part from the apparent disagreement between Fay and Bishop on the racial status of Murder Legendre.

The confusion is understandable. In the film, he is repeatedly and contradictorily associated with both sides of Haitian history, European and African. Aligning him with Europe are the casting of Bela Lugosi, obviously typed as decayed (Eastern) European aristocracy, the sets for Legendre's cliff-side home which appears to be a gothic castle-cum-plantation house,[16] and the fact that, unlike other "black" characters played by white actors in the film, he is not wearing black-face make-up. However, a number of narrative gaps also seem to align him with Haitian "natives." Perhaps most obvious is the scene in Dr. Bruner's study when Neil expresses his disgust at Madeline in the hands of "natives."[17] A bit later in the conversation, Neil makes the assumption that Beaumont is behind Madeline's poisoning and disappearance, but Dr. Bruner disagrees, replying, "no, no, this is native work." They resolve to go in search of Madeline, which leads them eventually to Legendre's castle.

Is he "native"? Is he a representative of European or American capital? The very ambiguity suggests a third option. Legendre is that postcolonial horror, the home-grown mixed type feared by the American regime. Not only is Legendre a threat, owning both factory and government agents (in the form of his zombie gang, discussed later in the chapter), but he also presents an even more primal source of horror related to miscegenation: when Madeline, and later Beaumont, ingests the secret zombie powder, they are in a sense infected, or at least contaminated. The boundaries of their bodies are violated and invaded, leaving them without essential agency. Whereas miscegenation is a threat to the social order, through the production of mixed race citizens, the zombie metaphor shows that boundaries of identity associated with the skin are permeable and unfixed. The film poses an almost philosophical problem about the nature of bodily autonomy and racial social structures in American culture. Postcolonial culture produces the creole whose very identity undermines the black-white binary necessary to white supremacist power structures.

In order to explore Legendre's dubious racial status and the nature of the creole threat to (white) subjectivity posed by the zombification process, I want to return to the source for the film's central concept of the zombie, Seabrook's *The Magic Island*. The film is by no means an adaptation of the book, which is essentially a popular nonfiction ethnographic travelogue. The film's main debts to the book are the idea of black zombie laborers, raised from the dead, the rationalist explanation (lesser living through chemistry), and its evidence in the Haitian *Code Pénal*. The latter two are quoted nearly verbatim in the scene between Neil and Dr. Bruner after Madeline's supposed death. Although the romance narrative is a completely new addition to Seabrook's central idea, other comparative situations recur in the film, notably in reference to Legendre's status as mill owner and general figure of power in Haiti. By resurrecting these ghost remnants of Seabrook's text in the film, I show the way that the ambivalence of creole culture is implicitly drawn and then erased in *White Zombie*.

## Creolization, Zombification, and William Seabrook

The word "creole" is a loaded term in postcolonial literary studies. Characters who represent "different kinds of whiteness"[18] are familiar figures from colonial and postcolonial literature: some examples include *Jane Eyre*'s famous Bertha, the lesser known *With Silent Tread* (ca. 1890) by Frieda Cassin, Richard Hughes' *A High Wind in Jamaica* (1928), and Jean Rhys's novels, especially *Voyage in the Dark* (1934) and *Wide Sargasso Sea* (1965). Turning to postcolonial literary scholarship gives a conceptual paradigm for considering the mixed nature of the creole. Like miscegenation, zombification in the film is figured as contamination of a "pure" white subjectivity. In colonial literature, "white creoles in the Caribbean diaspora were viewed with suspicion because they were other, a result of their rather too easy association with blacks, or, to put it more bluntly, because of the possible taint of the tarbrush."[19] In colonial and postcolonial literature, the fear of miscegenation represented by the creole and the threat it poses to the construction of a superior white body are often represented with the idea of contagious disease. With the zombie and the creole, the notion of a sovereign independent body, white and self-owned, is invaded by the colonized other, not only sexually and genetically, but also through the body's tissues and membranes. White bodies are under threat in colonial societies, and this local infection stands in for the loss of white subjectivity, independent power structures, and, ultimately, economic ownership. Another postcolonial literary critic, Adelai Murdoch, points out that the very definition of "creole" undermines the apparent binary stability underpinning colonization: "As a result of this discursive and locational slippage, a creole person can be either white or black, colonizer or colonized, as the term articulates an essential ambiguity that both mediates and ruptures the strategies of containment [driving] the dominant designations of difference."[20] This ambiguity and slippage is also evident in Seabrook's text in which he describes the syncretic combination of European and African cultures in Haiti as an "excellent mixture."[21] He also shows that the occupying Americans were less ready to accept this racial and cultural mix. In Seabrook's portrait of the postcolonial rulers of Haiti, the racial indeterminacy of the creole identified by Murdoch serves to unsettle American assumptions supporting white supremacist rule both at home and in Haiti. In *White Zombie*, then, the figure of the creole is transformed exclusively into a threat to white sovereignty which must be purged.

*The Magic Island* is a typical William Seabrook travelogue and was a best-seller in the United States, being one of the first, and perhaps the only, in-depth and readable explorations of Haitian culture in English before the 1930s.[22] Taking field study to something of an extreme, this popular pseudo-ethnologist began his writing career as a journalist, writing sensationalist features for popular newspapers and periodicals, including *The Ladies Home Journal* and *The New York Times*. He was widely known for representing primitive occultist practices from the point of view of a white rationalist who has been granted special cultural access. As Susan Zeiger has pointed out, he self-consciously adopted a performative racial identity, representing himself as uniquely able to get inside black minds and cultures, whether in the Caribbean or in Africa.[23] In *The Magic Island*, in particular, he seeks to become a voodoo initiate and thereby experience its irrational ecstasies first-hand. The chapter describing zombies, "'...Dead Men Working in the Cane Fields,'" is only a small section of a book that begins by taking the reader into Seabrook's witness of a voodoo ceremony simulating human sacrifice (and heavily redolent with perverse sexuality of which he was also a devotee). *The Magic Island* also devotes quite a bit of space to discussing the current political climate of Haiti, including the state of American-Haitian race relations.

In his Haitian travelogue, as in his other works, Seabrook's narrative authority comes partly from his supposed ability to occupy two racial positions at once, and this rhetorical stance aligns him in the book more with the postcolonial Haitians than with the occupying Americans. Perhaps it is this strategy that gives Seabrook's book an openness to what might be described as a creole identity — an openness clearly resisted in the later film. The systematic comparison of these two texts, one the nominal progenitor of the other, shows Seabrook's delineation of the racial and cultural complexities of the creole as outside an explicitly black-white power structure. In the film, the zombies and especially the zombie master represent the figure of the creole. Because the zombies and Legendre are merely a threat in the film, the creole loses the full ambiguity and complexity associated with it in Seabrook's book.

In *The Magic Island,* Seabrook provides a surprisingly nuanced and self-critical analysis of the cultural disconnect between Haitian ruling class and the American occupiers, mainly because he is a champion of the value of primitivism. In a section of the book, titled "A Blind Man Walking on Eggshells," he describes the social-cultural-racial divide between Americans and Haitians with a biting irony, perhaps intended to be missed by most white readers. He argues that along with the gifts of "excellent roads, sewers, hospitals, sanitation, stabilized currency, economic prosperity, and political peace" comes a much more barbed and pointed American "gift": "The most interesting and pervasive of the American innovations is the belated lesson in race-consciousness which we have now been at pains to teach the Haitian upper classes. These urban Haitians, free, vain, independent, and masters in their own land for a long hundred years or more ... had somehow forgotten that God in His infinite wisdom had intended negroes to remain always an inferior race."[24] Seabrook implicitly recognizes the benefits of postcolonial culture, as it moves a little farther away from the polarizations of white supremacy. He also shows the attempts of Americans to reduce the threat to their own racial sovereignty, mainly by importing a kind of Jim Crowism, posed by the mere existence of a "Black Republic." The removal of the threat entails a re-education of the "natives" in their own land, and an education of whites in the U.S. The education of whites at home entails, as Fay points out, both a rewriting and an erasure of this history of American occupation.[25]

William Seabrook is neither a postcolonial writer nor an advocate of Haitian self-rule, so his discussions of race are necessarily contradictory and ambivalent. Seabrook's encounters with the upper-class Haitians, who were usually described in the literature of the time as "mulatto," reveal both his definite appreciation of creolization and the racist assumptions underlying his primitivism.[26] Attending a formal dance given by a highly placed Haitian family, he describes their beautiful daughter as "some ultimate future type, superior perhaps to anything either race alone could breed."[27] He goes on to evaluate this superior racial blend through a lens of cultural eugenics: "The first French colonial planters and slave owners were pre–Napoleonic aristocrats.... The slaves [were imported] ... from diverse and widely scattered African peoples.... Slightly decadent but authentic aristocratic blood, crossbreeding with strong, rich primitive blood makes an excellent biological mixture."[28] Representing himself as a disinterested journalist, Seabrook moves between the cultural divide separating the super-sophisticated upper-class Haitians and the white supremacist Americans. The Haitians in particular are offended and bewildered by the Americans practice of designating any Haitian citizen as a "nigger" regardless of complexion.[29] The idea of indeterminate racial identity, embodied in the creole, is generally perceived by the Americans in Seabrook's book as a threat to their "natural" rule. In its adaptation of elements of Seabrook's representation of Haiti, *White Zombie* represents Legendre as a creole figure only implicitly. Nevertheless, as an in-between figure, he is explicitly evil. The film has evacuated the presence of the real Haitian postcolonial citizenry described in Seabrook, and replaced them with a gothic creation of Haiti's creole past.

His zombie chapter, "'...Dead Men Working in the Cane Fields,'" is typical of the tension in Seabrook's book between American imperial power and Haitian "primitive" culture. In this chapter, which is the source of the zombie concept in *White Zombie* and from which passages are quoted verbatim in the film, Seabrook has stumbled upon a monster of the Americas: "Werewolves, vampires, and demons were certainly no novelty. But I recalled one creature I had been hearing about in Haiti, which sounded exclusively local — the zombie."[30] Seabrook explains that these are corpses "taken from the grave and endowed by sorcery with a mechanical semblance of life."[31] The narrative arc of the chapter begins as a spooky evening folktale told under a rising full moon with "dark rolling hills" in the distance.[32] As Seabrook moves through the chapter to investigate this apparently supernatural phenomenon, however, he gradually uncovers a more rationalist, pharmaceutical explanation: healthy people are turned into zombies with "substances" which produce "lethargic comas."[33] He ends the chapter in the study of Dr. Antoine Villiers, who represents one of the most "scientifically trained mind[s]" and "sound rationalist[s]" in "all Haiti."[34] The conclusion to the zombie tale comes from article 249 of the current (i.e., 1920s) Haitian *Code Pénal*,[35] which is quoted in *White Zombie* when Dr. Bruner, also in his study, is explaining Madeline's disappearance to a distraught Neil. As has been noted elsewhere, this ending to Seabrook's chapter is ambiguous, but it does appear to set the seal on a material-psychological, as opposed to supernatural, explanation of the zombie.[36] The rationalist-materialist approach is underscored by Seabrook's move in narrative space from an evening tale on a peasant's front stoop to a civilized afternoon in a doctor's study.

The division between the superstitious Haitian peasant and the codifications of law and medicine is undermined, however, in the middle of the chapter with the mix of Haitian labor practices and modern American industry. Seabrook describes the sugar refinery operated by Hasco:

> The word is American-commercial-synthetic, like Nabisco, Delco, Socony. It stands for the Haitian-American Sugar Company — an immense factory plant, dominated by a huge chimney, with clanging machinery, steam whistles, freight cars. It is like a chunk of Hoboken.... It is a modern big business, and it sounds it, looks it, smells it. Such then was the incongruous background for the weird tale Constant Polynice [Seabrook's peasant informant] now told me.[37]

Seabrook's industrial scene is indeed incongruous with Haitian folk-magic and/or exploitative folk medicine. Seabrook reveals that Haitian labor subcontractors used "zombie" labor to harvest cane for Hasco at very low wages. The money never went to the laborers, and so they became effectively plantation slaves. While Hans Schmidt does not address the use of zombies by Hasco, he does point out that it was the one corporation to profit substantially from the occupation using underpaid Haitian labor.[38] As Fay points out, with or without zombies, "U.S. policy resurrected a colonial/slave economy" and the zombie is a metaphor for exploited and conscripted labor.[39] Seabrook does not comment on this exploitative labor practice other than to show the juxtaposition between a supposed civilizing influence of American industry and "native magic." I would argue that the "incongruity" is actually an ironic juxtaposition, however, like the dubious gift of "race consciousness" discussed above. In colonialism, mixtures are inevitable. In postcolonial culture, self-rule is established on the basis of the mix between master and slave, which necessarily breaks the dialectic. Seabrook does not attempt to resolve this open dilemma in that he neither condemns nor unequivocally celebrates the American occupation. *White Zombie,* on the other hand, tries to mitigate the colonial anxiety over mixed cultures by locating evil in the mixture. The way in which the film seals over or deflects this incongruity reveals the ambivalence of the potential "synthesis" between American big business and Haitian witch-doctoring represented in Seabrook's chapter.

## White Zombie *Re-does Seabrook*

*The Magic Island* is certainly a source text for *White Zombie,* but the film should not be considered an adaptation. Seabrook's book is a non-fiction travelogue, whereas the film is essentially a fictional romance narrative, with zombification as an extra thrilling obstacle to true love. There are only black, Haitian zombies in Seabrook, no white zombies. Rhodes and Sevastakis have identified the generic precursors of the film's narrative, but Seabrook supplies only the concept of the zombie and the related dangerous and suppressed threat of the creole. The transformation of these conceptual paradigms into character and narrative also simplifies the racial ideologies behind them. In what follows, I will provide some comparative examples between the book and the film, to show the latter's condensation and displacement of Seabrook's more open-ended assessment of Haitian history and culture. For example, the central factory scene where the zombies intersect with American industry is the primary displacement. A few other key scenes help to build our understanding of Legendre as creole and his threat to the white Americans as one of contamination, however. The grave scene shows Legendre as a parallel to the Haitian president deposed just before the American intervention (see n. 1), justifying the continuing American presence by aligning the Haitian ruler with a figure of postcolonial dread. Neil's and Dr. Bruner's search for Legendre is roughly based on a mountaineering expedition undertaken by Seabrook and some other men. In the *Magic Island* expedition, Seabrook and the mountaineers encounter the ruins of a plantation house which evokes Haiti's troubled colonial history. The traces of this history are resurrected in the film in the figure of Legendre who becomes an echo of the past. In the end of *Magic Island,* Seabrook's narrative of discovery is one of respect for the remaining mysteries of Haiti, but the end of the film carefully excises the threat of contamination posed by both the zombies and their master.

In *White Zombie,* the parallel scene to Seabrook's story of the Hasco factory is also the audience's first real introduction to the principal villain of the film, the zombie master Murder Legendre. Legendre in the film replaces a hybrid American "big business" in Seabrook's chapter as the owner of the sugar refinery. In the film's mill scene, we have no sense whatsoever that American interests are involved in the harvest and refining of sugar cane. Instead, the material processing of this profitable commodity is done by the mysteriously "foreign" mill owner, played by Bela Lugosi, recently famous for his role in *Dracula* (1931). Why is an American corporation displaced as the owner of the scene of production and replaced with Murder Legendre? This evacuation of American ownership releases the U.S. from complicity with both neo-slavery and associations with primitive pseudo-magical control of "slave" labor. On a larger ideological scale, I argue, the fear of European-style colonialism found in the spectre of creolization, the threat of mixing and contagion, is relieved by this shift of ownership. Further, Legendre as a character is represented, albeit ambiguously, as a figure of creolization, and serves as an implicit foil to American imperialism, which is exclusively white, rational, and therefore better than the inevitably syncretic models from Europe.

The scene in the sugar mill is a direct contrast to the ultra modern factory scene in Seabrook's book. Described by Fay as "low tech," Legendre's factory indeed does not appear to have any "modern" technology apart from electric lights.[40] In fact, the factory has a deliberately gothic/Medieval *mise-en-scène* complete with manual tread-mill, wood and stone building materials, and the persistent groan of wood-on-wood mechanisms. In other words, this is a far cry from the "clanging" and "steam whistles" of Hoboken-like Hasco, as Seabrook describes. We see the interior of the factory in a long shot as Beaumont, in search of some way to secure Madeline's affection, is taken down into the lower-level office of the owner, Legendre. The camera identifies us with Beaumont's dawning horror as a zombie-worker falls into the giant blades of the machinery to be ground up with the cane. No one appears to react to this except Beaumont. The first thing we see of Legendre is his hand, then a low angle shot of his torso and face, emphasizing his sinister power. The two men's conversation begins framed by a window. We look in from outside, and the view is partly obscured by the frame and other objects. In a sense we, like Beaumont, are initially alienated (outside) but gradually seduced by the mill-owner/zombie master. The next shot is inside the room where Legendre is framed by the objects on his desk. On one side is a quill pen, representing arguably a French-colonial era sign of communication, civilization, and naturally suspect sophistication. On the other side is the head of a stuffed leopard with mouth wide open, associating Legendre with a predatory animal. When he leans in to tell Beaumont the secret way of making Madeline his love slave, this sensual gesture reminds us of a lover leaning in for a kiss or, inevitably, Dracula leaning in for a bite. Overall, the effect is to suggest that material production in Haiti is associated with the dark merger of a gothic-style European feudalism and the appropriation of primitive and pagan domination of others' bodies.

Murder Legendre is not just an image of bad "old-school" European colonialism, as opposed to shiny and modern American imperialism. He is a more mixed bag than that, embodying the danger of syncretism and synthesis. Like his zombie creations, Legendre is a figure for the creole. In the ideology of the film, he serves as a central, though implicit, justification for American imperialism. He is an unknowable figure in many ways, and ultimately associated with the mixed colonial heritage of the Haitian "black republic." To begin with, he is nameless in the film. Although identified as "Murder Legendre" in the script,[41] in the actual film he is referred to as "that person" (by Beaumont early on) and later as a dangerous figure, a man "whose name is [M]urder"—meaning, his proper name? Or the implications of his name? The film is unclear. The effect of his putative name obviously combines the threat of death (Murder) with the effects of legend (Legendre), and the taint of French creole.[42] The effect of his actual nameless status is to make him into an open signifier, ready to accrue whatever meaning is plastered on to him. Maybe this, along with other narrative ambiguities, has given rise also to an ambiguous racial status in the film, as evidenced by the examples of Fay and Bishop cited above.

Another condensation of Seabrook's book with the film's narrative produces an implicit relationship between corrupt Haitian politics and Legendre. Murder Legendre is associated in the film with the central positions of postcolonial control in Haiti, rendering these positions of power suspect. Along with being a captain of industry, albeit Medieval not modern, and a witchdoctor, Legendre is also associated with a central political figure from recent Haitian history, the deposed president Guillaume Sam. Sam's sensational fall from power is echoed in Legendre's graveside conversation with Beaumont in which Legendre reveals the identities of his zombie crew. He identifies each by his former life's work: a government minister, the high executioner, a witchdoctor, and the head of the gendarmerie. When asked what would happen if these men were to regain their souls, Legendre replies, "they'd tear me to pieces." This is not just a thrilling suggestion to whet the appetite of the horror film viewer. In fact, it is an allusion to recent Haitian history, indeed to the events which led to the American "intervention." The parallel is obvious here as Seabrook relates Sam's fate. The latest self-declared president in a series of coups, Guillaume Sam, imprisoned and massacred a large number of politically powerful Haitians, and was then himself deposed by an angry mob of Port-au-Prince citizens: "The mob of course simply tore him into pieces."[43] To reinforce this suspect political connection with Haiti's deposed postcolonial government, the film identifies each of the Haitian zombies under Legendre's control as a prominent member of the ruling class.

In a sense, Legendre and his crew serve as the postcolonial rulers of pre-occupation Haiti. The scene of mob violence as a response to unstable and corrupt leadership, with no sign of democracy in sight, is implicitly represented as the end result of postcolonial self-rule. When a culture mixes the entitlement of European feudalism with the atavistic savagery of African tribalism, the argument seems to go, an inevitable culture of cruelty and corruption is the result. The point here is that the film seems to align Legendre with Guillaume Sam, or at least a figure like him: he is a corrupt leader who has the whole governmental apparatus under his sway and not far from the government is the witchdoctor, or the spectre of primitive native magic. What is the result of this amassing of power using illicit means? Inevitable instability. In fact, the image here suggests the inverse of the creole infection of white identity and the autonomous body. The threat *of* the creole is contamination; the threat *to* the creole is disintegration.

The past colonial history implied by the graveside conversation is further complicated by Legendre's connections with Haiti's earlier colonial history. In another borrowing from Seabrook's text, Legendre implicitly becomes a corrupt plantation owner. Again, this scene implies a mixed and demonized creole identity for Legendre. Neil and Dr. Bruner ride their horses through what appears to be an old orchard, and Dr. Bruner stops to talk to an elderly man (a white actor in black face). Perhaps he's also a "voodoo" initiate, since he offers warnings and *ouangas* to passers-by. Dr. Bruner asks for directions, and the old man warns him off Legendre, describing or naming him (ambiguity discussed above) as "Murder" and describing the "mountain" as the "land of the living dead." The missionary asks the old man to accompany them, but he refuses. In *The Magic Island*, this scene has two origins. One passage from the book describes the geographical "homeland" of the zombies in the "Dean Men Working" chapter as "Morne-du-Diable, a roadless mountain district near the Dominican border"[44] and presumably the inspiration for Legendre's "mountain" castle-plantation as "land of the living dead." In the other passage, which also serves as the ending for *Magic Island*, Seabrook and some companions undertake a journey to the top of Haiti's tallest mountain, Morne La Selle, where they discover the ruined foundations of a colonial plantation estate. Seabrook imagines the horrific slave masters of the colonial past and their suspect sexual proclivities.[45] In the film, however, the ambivalence of colonial history is resurrected in the present since, in a sense, the film rebuilds this mountain-top plantation. Although an accident of independent filming on a budget, the use of the Dracula set (see n. 11) carries semantic weight. The gothic castle-cum-plantation suggests European colonialism, even feudalism. This throw-back to Medieval Europe is wedded with the gothic-exotic landscape of Haiti to produce a physical manifestation of colonial history and the postcolonial horror it has produced.

The climax of *White Zombie* takes place in Legendre's cliff-side gothic castle where the creole contagion is ritually cleansed. Once Dr. Bruner and Neil reach the castle, they are confronted with Legendre and his zombies. Neil tries to shoot the zombies to no avail, but in the end they simply walk off the edge of the cliff onto the rock below. Murder Legendre is himself murdered by the half-zombified Beaumont who partially redeems himself by pushing the zombie master over the edge and then toppling over after him. There is one shot of Legendre's lifeless body being washed over the rocks by the waves. If the zombies and Legendre represent, as I argue, the contagious threat of the creole, they have been literally thrown from their island and "ethnically cleansed" by the ocean waves. The demise of the zombies and their master leaves one zombie behind, Madeline. She awakens from her drug-induced stupor as if from a dream, freed, in the logic of the film, by Legendre's death. At the end we are left with a "pure" society: virginal white woman, American banker hero, and Christian-rationalist missionary.

Madeline in the film is virtually character-free, and so serves in a mostly symbolic function as innocent White Womanhood. The couple's reunion restores white supremacist optimism in a racially pure society as Madeline is freed from the threat of miscegenation, control by Legendre, and the effects of the invasive drug. Neil is not an athletic hero, but is instead a middle-class managerial ideal — the bank clerk or agent. This characterization serves to seal another American anxiety over the relation between imperialism and economic prosperity. While Legendre displaces American industry from its dubious role in the Haitian sugar economy, Neil replaces the entire society of material production, consisting of Beaumont as plantation owner and Legendre as mill owner, with the clean virtual economy of banking. This completes the separation of Haitian labor and American ownership begun in the factory scene discussed above. Americans, thus, are not bothered with the spectre of slave (or near slave) labor conditions in cane fields or processing factories, which uncomfortably calls to mind the race-labor politics of 1930s U.S. culture. In the film's end, Americans come to Haiti and wipe away the taint of the old, post-, and neo-colonial plantation economy with a new rational business model found in offices, not fields or factories. American imperialism, the film implies, has brought modern economic civilization to Haiti.

In the new social unit at the film's end, Christianity is aligned with rationalism in the figure of Dr. Bruner, against the pagan irrationalism of voodoo.[46] He serves as a good twin to Legendre's evil one. Where Legendre seduces and victimizes decadent Beaumont, Dr. Bruner educates and soothes distraught Neil. Even the cinematography and editing in each of these scenes is parallel: in the mill we begin outside the window and are drawn in whereas in Dr. Bruner's study we begin behind Neil's back and are drawn into Dr. Bruner's explanations.[47] Where Legendre is flanked by the pen and the leopard, Dr. Bruner is surrounded by books, the symbols of rational study and accumulation of knowledge. Whereas Legendre is a "witch-doctor" who has appropriated the native powers of dark magic, Dr. Bruner jokingly refers to his status among the natives as "magic" for his role as a priest. In the film, then, the good "rational" magic of Christianity wins out over the bad pagan magic (and pharmaceutical knowledge) of voodoo. The implication of this perfectly clean social unit at the end of the film is that an American-style imperialism is a positive counter-model to old-school European colonialism. The latter, it is implied, leads to a dangerous, unstable mixing. The film's reification of racial divisions—i.e., white versus black rather than the "yellow" creole mix of the Haitian elite — also supports U.S. occupation policy and ideology.

At the risk of undermining my own argument, however, I am bound to remark on some of the problems with this tight ideological seal at the end. Of course, one of the conventions of the horror genre is to refuse unequivocal resolution. Especially as the century moves on, horror films generally do not comfort or completely reassert the dominant social order. In the case of *White Zombie*, the unsettling elements which may undermine the pro-American and anti-creole message at the end are probably simply the result of hasty film-making on a cheap budget and the transition from silent to talkie. The film's own incongruities generate instability in its final social message. The integrity of white womanhood is rescued at the end, but what exactly is it worth? This question is raised, I think, by the characterization of Madeline, in the script and by the actor Madge Belamy. Madeline is almost as robotic before as after her zombification, constrained as she is to be a type rather than even a semi-realized character. In the opening scene when threatened by Legendre in the carriage, her response is delayed and undramatic. In what I call the "cheesecake" scene when we see Madeline in only her underclothes, dressing for the wedding, she is largely static and expressionless. Even when Beaumont is begging her to reject Neil and marry him instead, she seems only mildly nonplussed, saying, "You've been so kind. Please don't spoil everything now." No doubt unintentionally on the part of the filmmakers, Belamy's performance generates the haunting impression that as a bride, Madeline is merely an object in the marriage market and in the gaze of the camera, in much the same way she becomes an object in the more dangerous marketplace of desire.

Neil also fails to achieve the ideal of heroic masculinity that one might expect from the tradition of the adventure film.[48] He does nothing to check Beaumont's obvious designs on Madeline, and when she "dies," he looks helplessly around, saying, "Can't you do something?"[49] The lack of muscular heroism is at odds with the ideological framework at the end, suggesting that Haiti is altogether too much for white folks, and that contamination is inevitable. Even the very land makes Neil sick, though his body has not been invaded by Legendre's power. Finally, Dr. Bruner is also suspect by virtue of the fact that he serves as a kind of double to Legendre.[50] He is, it would seem from his accent, of German ancestry, and this in itself brands him as suspect, given the original aims of the U.S. occupation.[51] In the very last scene of the film, intended to be comic, Dr. Bruner interrupts the married couple's reunion as they are about to kiss—with a tap on the shoulder and request for a match that hints at a disconnect in the social unit rather than a resolution.

The world's first zombie movie remains an intriguing, if sometimes clunky, document to American cultural preoccupations. It has been open to a great variety of readings and approaches, the most recent of which have been mainly concentrated on its representation of race and power. However, these readings have tended to reassert the very racial binary that their postcolonial-based critiques are designed to challenge. By drawing attention to the intertextual relationship between *The Magic Island* and *White Zombie*, I hope to expand the postcolonial frame of reference by positing, in the figure of the creole, the beginning of the end of race. The fact that this figure is essentialized and demonized in the film only points to its centrality as a source of cultural anxiety.

## Notes

1. Haiti has often been identified as the "Black Republic" because of its status as the first postcolonial nation formed out of a successful slave rebellion. Achieving independence from French colonial rule in 1803 and ruled by the descendents of plantation slaves, Haiti is the first officially postcolonial Caribbean nation. With the American "intervention" in 1915, which lasted until 1934, Haitians lost sovereignty for the first time in over 100 years. When I refer in the chapter to Haiti as a postcolonial nation, I mean to indicate the state which pre-dated the American occupation and which implicitly formed a threat to that imperial impulse. A full discussion of this episode of American-Haitian history can be found in Hans Schmidt's seminal 1971 book, *The United States Occupation of Haiti, 1915–1934* (New Brunswick, NJ: Rutgers University Press, 1995). In 1929, anti–American riots and strikes were tearing apart the country and threatening the American regime, which soon thereafter began to plan its withdrawal.

2. William Seabrook, *The Magic Island* (New York: Harcourt, Brace, 1929).

3. *White Zombie*, DVD, directed by Victor Halperin (RKO Studios, 1932; Madacy Entertainment, 2002). The most thorough genealogy of the film is to be found in Gary Rhodes, *White Zombie: Anatomy of a Horror Film* (Jefferson, NC: McFarland, 2001). As Rhodes writes, "It was Seabrook who confronted zombies for the first time in an overt way in an English-language text" (30). Rhodes goes on to trace the specific connections between Seabrook's book and the film. This connection is based principally on the concept of the zombie, Dr. Bruner's explanation of the zombie, and a long quotation in the script from Seabrook's quotation of the Haitian penal Code (30–34). Other film scholars, such as Michael Sevastakis, *Songs of Love and Death:*

*The Classical American Horror Film of the 1930s* (Westport, CT: Greenwood Press, 1993) and Peter Dendle, *The Zombie Movie Encyclopedia* (Jefferson, NC: McFarland, 2001), have also noted Seabrook as a source.

4. Jennifer Fay, "Dead Subjectivity: *White Zombie, Black Baghdad*," *CR: The New Centennial Review* 8, no. 1 (2008): 88.

5. Joan Dayan, *Haiti, History and the Gods* (Berkeley: University of California Press, 1995), 37.

6. Rhodes provides a helpful etymology of the term, beginning with a citation from the French colonial writer Moreau de Saint-Méry, who identified it as a "'Creole word that means spirit'" (75). In his recent book on zombie films, Kyle Bishop, *American Zombie Gothic* (Jefferson, NC: McFarland, 2010), hereafter referred to as *AZG*, 47, has noted the anthropological etymologies which reach farther afield, tracing the term back to the "Angolian Kimbundu term *nzúmbe*" along with the Congo and West Africa. However, Seabrook's book is credited as the first to introduce "zombie" (with that spelling) to identify animated corpses.

7. Kyle Bishop, "The Sub-Subaltern Monster: Imperialist Hegemony and the Cinematic Voodoo Zombie," *The Journal of American Culture* 31, no. 2 (2008): 143.

8. Dayan, 37.

9. The connection between the zombification and the sexual threat is manifested in the film's narrative when Dr. Bruner tries to explain to Neil what has happened. Neil's immediate reaction upon hearing that Madeline is missing from her grave and possibly alive is to cry, "you don't think she's alive!? And in the hands of natives! Oh no, better dead than that!" The fear of miscegenation here is a familiar one in twentieth-century American adventure film before the 1960s and reflects an ever-present cultural anxiety about racial purity and the security of white supremacist power structures (as seen, for example, in *Birth of a Nation*, directed by D.W. Griffith [Epoch, 1915], or *The Searchers*, directed by John Ford [Warner, 1956]). See also, Bishop, *AZG*, 80.

10. For example, Rhodes and Fay. Although I won't discuss it in this chapter, this confusion is almost as interesting as the one over Legendre, which forms the bulk of my discussion. If Beaumont is American, then he forms a kind of ideological link between neo-colonial plantation economy of Haiti and American banking, and this connection needs to be expunged along with the more straightforward threat of Legendre. If he is French, he represents a throwback to Haiti's colonial past, and is therefore an image of the decadent aristocracy which forms the historical roots of Haitian culture (refer to the discussion of Seabrook on decadent French aristocracy later in this chapter). In fact, Beaumont could be seen as a conflation of French and English colonial history, the European legacies of which the film seems to excise and which contributes to the indistinct time and space of the setting.

11. As Rhodes notes, Legendre's castle is actually the set from Browning's *Dracula* which the Halperin brothers rented from United Artists. Though the set is an accident of low-budget filmmaking expediency, it nevertheless carries semantic weight in the implications of the film, seen in my discussion on page 18.

12. Sevastakis, 41.

13. Rhodes, 34–38.

14. Fay, 96.

15. Bishop, *AZG*, 80.

16. Cf. n. 11.

17. Cf. n. 9.

18. Evelyn O'Callaghan, "'The Unhomely Moment': Frieda Cassin's Nineteenth-Century Antiguan Novel and the Construction of the White Creole," *Small Axe* 29, 13, no. 2 (June 2008): 98.

19. Ibid., 102.

20. Adlai Murdoch, "Rhys's Pieces: Unhomeliness as Arbiter of Caribbean Creolization," *Callaloo* 26, no. 1 (Winter 2003): 254.

21. Seabrook, 141.

22. Rhodes, 72–78. Several sources are identified, most unsympathetic to Haitian culture and people, which address "voodoo" if not zombies. A number of news reports tended to sensationalize Haitian native savagery, most notably "Why the Black Cannibals of Haiti Mutilated our Soldiers" in *New York American*, Feb. 13, 1921. Others such as *Haiti: Her History and Her Detractors* (1907) by J.N. Léger painted a somewhat more complex portrait of the syncretic cultural blending of Africa and Europe in Haitian culture.

23. Susan Zeiger, "*Magic Islands, Jungle Ways*: William Seabrook, Popular Primitivism, and the Imperial Imagination," Invitation, American Literature and Cultures Workshop, Univ. of Chicago, May 2010.

24. Seabrook, 127.

25. Fay, 99.

26. As many scholars of so-called primitivism have noted, whether white assessments of African or African American/Caribbean arts and cultures are positive or negative, they are always based in the racist assumption that anyone of African descent is necessarily closer to some past, originary state of humankind. Examples of this postcolonial modernist scholarship proliferate and include, to name only a few, the following books: Petrine Archer-Shaw, *Negrophilia: Avant-garde Paris and Black Culture of the 1920s* (London: Thames and Hudson, 2000), Patricia Chu, "Modernist (Pre)Occupations: Haiti, Primitivism and Anticolonial Nationalism" (171–186) and Simon Gikandi, "Africa and the Epiphany of Modernism," (31–50) both in *Geomodernisms: Race, Modernism and Modernity*, ed. Laura Doyle and Laura Winkiel (Bloomington: Indiana University Press,

2005), Susan Gubar, *Racechanges: White Skin, Black Face in American Culture* (New York and Oxford: Oxford University Press, 1997), and Marianne Torgovnick, *Gone Primitive: Savage Intellects, Modern Lives* (Chicago: University of Chicago Press, 1990).

27. Seabrook, 140–41. Just as a point of contrast, I include here a statement more typical of American administrators in Haiti: "'The Negroes of mixed type [mulattoes], who constitute the majority of educated people and politicians, have the general characteristics of such people the world over — vain, loving praise, excitable, changeable, beyond belief illogical, and double-faced. Many of them are highly educated and polished, but their sincerity must always be doubted'" (Brigade Commander Cole, in 1917; quoted in Schmidt, 146).

28. Seabrook, 141.

29. Seabrook describes his own racial misidentification (and resulting potential social gaffe) of a Mrs. John T. Myers, wife of the brigade commander of the United States, as a light skinned Haitian. Another wife of an American commander refused to go to any Haitian social events, saying, "A coon was a coon" (Seabrook, 155).

30. Seabrook, 93.

31. Ibid.

32. Ibid., 92.

33. Ibid., 103.

34. Ibid.

35. Ibid. "'Article 249. Also shall be qualified as attempted murder the employment which may be made against any person of substances which, without causing actual death, produce a lethargic coma more or less prolonged. If, after the administering of such substances, the person has been buried, the act shall be considered murder, no matter what result follows.'" In an endnote on page 335, Seabrook gives the original French. He has translated "*produisent un effet léthargique plus ou moins prolongé*" as "produce a lethargic coma more or less prolonged" which may add to the ambivalence and confusion at the end of his chapter (a more accurate translation would be "produce a lethargic effect more or less prolonged"; my translation). It is hard to see how a person in a coma can be made to work.

36. Fay, 92. Also see Zeiger for a discussion of Seabrook's reliance on rationalist rhetoric.

37. Seabrook, 95.

38. Schmidt, 171.

39. Fay, 92–3.

40. Ibid., 86–7.

41. Rhodes, 37.

42. Rhodes points out that Marie Laveau, the famous "voodoo queen" of Louisiana, had a daughter named Madame Legendre (38).

43. Seabrook, 281. In 1938, four years after the Americans left Haiti, Zora Neale Hurston would repeat this story in *Tell My Horse* (New York: Harper and Row, 1990). For both Seabrook and Hurston, the tale of Guillaume Sam is a direct justification for the American invasion since "at the precise moment when these events were occurring, the American battleship *Washington* was steaming into the harbour" (Seabrook, 282) and the smoke from the ship was a "black plume with a white hope" (Hurston, 72).

44. Seabrook, 95.

45. The wise and frightened old man warning off white explorers comes in this scene from Seabrook. During their ascent, Seabrook and his companions come across an avenue of "gigantic chestnut trees, planted in double rows" (249) which are clearly the remains of a colonial plantation. Seabrook fantasizes about arriving 150 years earlier when "a marquis might have welcomed us [and] slaves would have attended to our horses" (249). They meet an old man, who Seabrook describes as "Old Authority," who tells them not to go any further: "It was forbidden, he told us, but not by his or any other human authority; on Morne La Selle, as everybody knew, were *loup-garous* and demons" (256). Near the top of the mountain, they discover the foundation-outline of another plantation house. Again, Seabrook speculates on the past glory and horror of those gothic colonial days: "Here once, in a spot as isolated then as it is now, had dwelt slave-owning luxury.... [W]hether the owner, like Count Kenscoff on the lower ridge, had been a monster who amused himself by having his yellow mistress torn by bloodhounds, or a kindly marquis whose slaves had helped him down to Jacmel when the bloody revolution came ... no one will ever know" (268). In this scene, Seabrook emphasizes rather than troubles the ideology that also drives the film. This encounter with a colonial past is a gruesome and thrilling reminder of the dangers of creole mixtures — the "yellow" mistress torn to pieces for sport.

46. Bishop, *AZG*, 80 and Rhodes, 35.

47. Rhodes, 20.

48. Ibid.

49. After her "death," he goes on a drunken binge in a seedy cafe which is represented in an almost surreal way with the other cafe patrons seen only as shadows projected on the wall. As he tries to find an answer to his bride's missing corpse, and then eventually to mount a rescue effort, he is led by Dr. Bruner who commands the entire operation. Upon their approach to the castle, Neil succumbs to an unidentified tropical illness which renders him nearly helpless. His place in that final perfect social unit is secured by others, not by his own

efforts. Perhaps, this paralysis helps to establish one of the abiding features of horror films—the dream-like inability to act against a threat—which gives them their affective power.

50. Rhodes, 36.

51. As Schmidt points out, the invasion of Haiti was part of a U.S. policy of expansion in the Americas and a desire to protect American interests in the region. Along with Cuba and Panama, Haiti and Dominica were among the regions that the U.S. felt were vulnerable to German control (56). As World War I got underway, the impulse to seize these regions, especially to protect the vital shipping access of the Panama canal, was strong.

# The Origin of the Zombie in American Radio and Film: B-Horror, U.S. Empire, and the Politics of Disavowal

## CHRIS VIALS

Released in 1943, Jacques Tournier's film *I Walked with a Zombie* conveys a message about the Caribbean that is ubiquitous among B-horror narratives of the 1930s and 1940s, and that continues to inform representations of Haiti within the Western cultural imaginary. Set on a white-owned sugar plantation on the fictional island of Saint Sebastian, it tells the story of a Canadian nurse named Betsy Connell. The young nurse is brought to the island to take care of the planter's wife, Jessica Holland, who has gotten mixed up in voodoo rituals and, as a consequence, is now a zombie. What is striking about the film is that despite its use of voodoo and zombies to tell a story about the Caribbean, there is a curious acknowledgment of exploitation and social injustice in the region. *I Walked with a Zombie* repeatedly reminds viewers of the history of slavery on Saint Sebastian: the mast of a slave ship sits in the courtyard of the Holland plantation and, throughout the picture, the camera returns to a close-up of the mast's figurehead, a wooden carving of the religious martyr Saint Sebastian dying from arrow wounds. As the island bears the name of a slave ship (named, incidentally, after a plague saint), and since an image of its masthead forms the final shot of the film, slavery emerges as central and inseparable part of its exotic setting.

While the film acknowledges this history, it draws no explicit moral from it, and, paradoxically, it is this interpretive void that is most illuminating. When Betsy first arrives on the island, the planter Paul Holland gestures to the masthead and tries to explain it to her: "The people came from the misery and pain of slavery. For generations, they've found life a burden. That's why they still weep when a child is born and make merry at the burial." He adds, "I've told you ... this is a sad place."

The film's basic social message — "this is a sad place" — should be familiar to anyone who tuned into the coverage of the recent earthquake in Haiti. It is a message about colonial suffering that acknowledges deep, historical wounds but refuses both introspection and responsibility. If a unique discourse of empire emerges from every particular site, then the American discourse surrounding the Caribbean is one with unique roots in B-horror. It

41

works, moreover, to obscure and disavow the true nature of the political relationship between the global North and the global South. Following the tragic 2010 earthquake in Haiti — a disaster that left at least 230,000 dead and over 1,000,000 homeless — the very worst example was represented by the UK's *Daily Mail,* which covered the catastrophe with the headline "Haiti: Rape, Murder and Voodoo on the Island of the Damned" (I will return to this article in my conclusion). Much more typical, however, was the coverage of the New York NBC-affiliate, whose article "The Sad History of Haiti" sympathetically presented the country's past as a tragic, un-ending nightmare only minimally intertwined with the history of the United States.[1]

The figure of the zombie — which has once again become a major phenomenon in global mass culture in the last ten years — played a central role in creating imperial discourses of the Caribbean. For contemporary audiences, the more familiar zombie plot involves a pandemic within the United States (or within the West), and this narrative strand has a separate genealogy that begins with director George Romero's 1968 film *Night of the Living Dead.* Because of the singular influence of Romero — a self-described product of the late 1960s — contemporary zombie films are often vehicles to explore progressive politics (and this has extended into some zombie video games as well).[2] The earliest zombie stories in U.S. popular culture, however, were generally set in Haiti or elsewhere in the region. The walking dead in these older tales were not created through bites from rotting mouths, but by a "master" who used a local herb or voodoo magic to create "slaves" for a particular purpose, most typically for labor. Romero enabled a more progressive bent within the genre by setting the stories in the domestic realm of the viewers and eliminating voodoo as the cause of the outbreak, stripping the genre of its exoticism and disassociating the zombie from Haiti.

But the zombie initially entered global popular culture as direct result the U.S. occupation of Haiti from 1915 to 1934, a fact that has not been adequately explored to date. In the mid–1920s, Marines stationed in Haiti led an author-reporter named William Seabrook on a tour of the country, and his travels there, under Marine escort, inspired him to write the travelogue *The Magic Island* (1929), the first major narrative containing zombies to appear in American popular culture. As historian Mary Renda has noted, his book helped fuel a popular fascination with Haiti, and inspired similar tales of voodoo magic in radio, comic books, and film in the 1930s. Renda argues that such tales allowed ordinary Americans to participate in the project of imperial expansion, and they did so through the logic of exoticism. Much like imperialism itself, which ingests another country without allowing it to become a valid part of the national culture, exoticism injected Haiti into American culture while maintaining its foreignness and presumed inferiority. This, according to Renda, justified the American presence and its paternalistic "tutelage."[3]

But what is perhaps surprising are the ways in which early narratives of zombies in U.S. mass culture in the 1930s and 1940s registered a disease with the misery of colonial labor and imperial exploitation, one which still resonates in popular Western narratives of the third world, zombie or otherwise. Early zombies were often Caribbean plantation workers, black and white, who were employed by a villainous white plantation owner to further his or her nefarious designs. In this essay, I argue that these early tales of zombies in U.S. mass culture — circulating in film, literature, and, most frequently, radio — did not reflect and reinforce a directly imperial logic culminating in an argument for "tutelage," as Renda suggests. Rather, shifting the frame to the theme of labor reveals a deployment of the exotic which ultimately serves a popular isolationism: an isolationism based on a public ambivalence toward colonialism found in the larger public culture of the United States during the 1930s and 1940s. This isolationism ultimately serves empire, however, neither by ignoring injustice, nor through an implicit paternalism, but by disavowing the humanity of its racialized victims and thereby negating the politics of solidarity.

During the 1930s, 1940s, and early 1950s, the zombie appeared in films such as *White Zombie* (1932), *Revolt of the Zombies* (1936), and *I Walked with a Zombie,* as well as in radio programs ranging from *The Shadow, The Clyde Beatty Show, Five Minute Mysteries, Adventures by Morse, Unsolved Mysteries, Strange Adventure,* and *Screen Directors' Assignment.* These productions generally posited the colonial world (usually the Caribbean) as a place of great suffering, either because of a past history of slavery or the exploitative designs of white plantation owners in the present. Such representations were enabled in part by Franklin Roosevelt's Good Neighbor Policy, which placed Haiti in the headlines as U.S. troops pulled out of the country in 1934. This foreign policy change required a new discourse of cooperation that broke with images of voodoo primitivism. But as I will argue, the notion of an oppressed Caribbean workforce was also informed by the relentless vigilance of the African American press, the activism of the 1930s left in the U.S., and the protests of the Haitians themselves. Such agitation not only made Haiti a site of anti-imperial critique, but also put the exploitation of labor more generally at the center of American public debate.

But while these early horror narratives often registered a discomfort with colonial labor, they also used the figure of the zombie to debase the humanity of the colonial subject, offering audiences no basis of identification with his or her plight. Though progressive, even anti-imperial discourses of the 1930s and '40s, were inscribed into the mid-century zombie narrative, the genre ultimately helped to neutralize the quite vocal, activist impulse toward cross-cultural solidarity that marked those decades. While these mid-century horror tales depart from more recent, multicultural readings of the global South in that they generally render its cultures in terms of absolute difference and inferiority, what remains constant is the politics of disavowal. In this regard, the early zombie genre illustrates how popular isolationism paradoxically serves as a basis for empire. Isolationism is premised on the basic idea that the nation will function best if it stays out of world affairs as much as possible — an idea which seems to preclude imperial expansion. But an isolationism that does not acknowledge the living, structural reality of U.S. imperialism — nor question the racial discourses it necessarily creates — quickly degenerates into apathy for its victims. Such is the logic of disavowal.

My examination of the early days of the zombie genre in U.S. mass culture is perhaps the first to consider the medium of radio. The increasing accessibility of commercial radio broadcasts from mid-century have made new archives available to scholars of popular culture, and these archives reveal the frequency with which the zombie tale was used to circulate the narratives about Haiti and the global south to U.S. audiences, particularly in the 1940s. In urban areas in the 1930s, less than 1 in 10 households were without a radio; by 1940, 83 percent of all U.S. households, rural and urban, owned one.[4] Indeed, Americans had much more frequent, daily contact with radio in the 1930s than with any other form of mass culture, with the possible exception of newspapers. As an aural medium, the radio broadcasts were also well-positioned to do the cultural work of disavowal. Using voices and dialect, they dramatically enacted the stark, hierarchical separation between whiteness and blackness that had relied primarily on visual codes in the film genre.

Before discussing the zombie narratives of the 1930s and 1940s, one must briefly contextualize the historical event that led to the creature's dissemination in American culture: the U.S. military occupation of Haiti from 1915 to 1934. Acting on behalf of American business interests, the Marines occupied the island nation and forever altered its political structure. They dissolved the Haitian legislature and installed a puppet government at gunpoint. They suppressed freedom of speech in order to force a new constitution on the country that allowed for more foreign investment, and it is now estimated that around 10,000 Haitians were killed as they rose in revolt. But the long-term consequences were far more dire. Since the founding of their country in 1804, Haitian peasants had generally been able to hold their own against the designs of their leadership; they were able to maintain a viable system of small farms against the wishes of the Haitian elite, who sought to build an economy based around large-scale plantation agriculture. The administrative reforms and infrastructure projects of the U.S. occupation, however, effectively centralized the police and military apparatus of the country, finally allowing the elites, foreign and domestic, to force their economic models and political power on the common people.[5]

Indeed, the people of Haiti have never stopped dealing with this re-composition of their social class structure. Since then, U.S. business and political leaders have continuously sought to expand the inequalities born of the occupation. During the Cold War, the U.S. government ensured the political survival of dictators Francois ("Papa Doc") Duvalier and Jean-Claude ("Baby Doc") Duvalier by providing their regimes with military and economic assistance in exchange for the easy access of U.S. manufacturers to the country's terrorized labor force.[6] And in the 1990s, the United States worked with Haitian elites to curtail the popular, reformist President Jean-Bertrand Aristide, an effort which culminated in a Washington-backed coup d'etat against this democratically elected leader in 2004. Haiti has been in a state of near-anarchy ever since.

The U.S. occupation consistently placed Haiti in American newspaper headlines in the interwar decades of the 1920s and 1930s. It made the island nation a point of interest for American writers and readers alike, and a number of authors, including Eugene O'Neill, John Vandercook, Zora Neale Hurston, and Langston Hughes, created images of Haiti that fired the imaginations of U.S. audiences. Arguably, no single work rivaled the impact of William Seabrook's travelogue *The Magic Island*, published in 1929. This book formed the template for most American stories of zombies and voodoo that followed over the next two decades. Seabrook's personal tale of adventure developed a wide readership in the years after its release in 1929, and even achieved best-seller status in the year of its publication.[7]

*The Magic Island* is not exclusively focused on the living dead per se, but on the general milieu of exotic beliefs and superstitions attributed to Haiti, in which voodoo and zombies figure prominently. Though the story is actually based on the reports of the Marine Faustin Wirkis, Seabrook, as narrator, leads the reader through the primitive world of Haitian "superstition" as if he witnessed it all first-hand. Most elaborate is his description of a voodoo ceremony that he purports to have observed. His breakdown of the ritual, which includes detailed descriptions of drums, wild-dancing, animal sacrifice, and white-robed processions — all in the night air of a jungle enclosure illuminated by both moon and torchlight — would furnish the basis for an aesthetic of horror tapped by a generation of set designers and script writers. He even included visual sketches of ceremonial altars that illustrated the exact placement of crosses, candles, and snakes upon their surface.

But apart from the *mise-en-scène* of the voodoo ritual, *The Magic Island* bequeathed two main narrative elements that were later fused together within the film and radio zombie narratives of the 1930 and 1940s. The first is the idea that female innocence — and femininity itself — is consumed by voodoo ritual, a ritual that creates sexless "automatons." Seabrook describes the ritual as quite sexually charged, with men and women giving themselves over to "ecstasy" at its apex and even going off into the jungle to couple.[8] But this lustful excess requires a human cost. In his account, it necessitates the "sacrifice" of a young black girl named Catherine, whose soul is transferred into the body of a goat during the ceremony; the animal is then slaughtered in her stead in a ritual act of substitution. During the ritual itself, the girl and the goat are effectively zombified; the author describes them as "docile and entranced ... like automatons."[9] Similarly, Seabrook later recounts his meeting with a "country girl" named Classinia, whom he depicts on first encounter as a "smooth-skinned negress ... mild and childlike," "soft-voiced," and "amiable."[10] But when pressed into the service of Haitian necromancy, she rapidly undergoes a horrid transformation. As he discovers her later, "she was no longer a woman, but Papa Nebo, the male-female hermaphroditic oracle of the dead."[11] Seabrook notes with horror that "in the corner of her mouth, as if stuck into the mouth of a wooden dummy, was an unlighted cigar."[12]

Seabrook was ambivalent about the U.S. occupation itself, and actually saw his work as promoting an appreciation of Haitian culture. As has been noted by critics, *The Magic Island* comes out of the same 1920s impulse as Carl Van Vechten's *Nigger Heaven* (1926) and Eugene O'Neill's *Emperor Jones* (1920).[13] As such, it is an exercise in "negrophilia" that exalts the primitive innocence of blacks as a valid antidote to a sexually-repressed, over-civilized, white culture. As Seabrook writes of the voodoo ritual, "their thing ... is rationally defensible. Of what use is any life without its emotional moments or hours of ecstasy?"[14] But as can be seen in the examples above, a heavy strain of Puritanism nonetheless dogs Seabrook's travelogue. As the cases of Catherine and Classinia reveal, there must be a terrible price to pay in a world where so much sexual passion is unleashed. These girls, in effect, bear that cost by becoming "un-sexed" to fuel the sexual energies of the collective.

Although at first glance unrelated, the ritually de-sexed female has its counterpart within Seabrook's narrative in the generally male, zombie plantation worker. Chapter Two of *The Magic Island*, entitled "...Dead Men Working in the Canefields," can be said to have introduced the zombie to the English-speaking world.[15] In this highly influential rendering of a now global monster, the zombie is "a soulless human corpse, still dead, but taken from the grave and endowed by sorcery with a mechanical semblance of life." It is generally created by a "master" for the purposes of labor, becoming "a servant or slave, occasionally for the commission of some crime, more often simply as a drudge around the habitation of a farm, setting it dull heavy tasks, and beating it like a dumb beast if it slackens."[16] While the zombie is a symbol of exploited labor, it is by no means a vehicle to critique colonialism in Seabrook's usage.

In particular, Seabrook's native informant Constant Polynice tells him the story of a "black headman" named Ti Joseph, who created a score of zombies to work on plantations owned by the Haitian-American Sugar Company (Hasco), a U.S. firm. Unbeknownst to the company, which provided "low wages" but "steady work," Joseph registered his zombies to work for Hasco, then kept their wages for himself. His scheme is blown when his tender-hearted wife takes pity on the creatures and feeds them salted pistachio nuts. Zombies, who "as every one knows ... must never be permitted to taste salt or meat," become self-aware upon eating the nuts; upon realizing they are dead, they return once again to their graves, depriving Joseph of their labor. When the author later claims to see some "walking dead men" first-hand (who are employed by a cruel, native overseer on a small farm), he labels them "automatons," the same word he used for Classinia and Catherine. Just as Joseph's zombie workers, described by Polynice as "vacant-eyed like cattle," these creatures go about their menial labor "plodding like brutes."[17] The motif of de-sexing continues in this instance as well, though here more firmly in the form of animalization.

As in subsequent mid-century tales, the figure of the zombie reveals a still active association between the Caribbean and the history of slavery within the white imagination. But in *The Magic Island*, the practice of slavery and the cruelty of colonial labor are displaced onto the Haitian themselves, who cruelly contract the bodies of their deceased neighbors to well-intentioned American companies. Seabrook's zombies aren't just located anywhere in the Caribbean, however, but in Haiti — the site of the first, successful, slave revolt

(Michael Denning even called the Haitian revolution "the first, global, anticolonial revolt").[18] In this context, his book reveals a psychological need to contain the subversive potential of this memory by representing Haiti as the site of the world's last and only docile slaves. In effect, the figure of the zombie functions symbolically to put Haitians back in chains, not as the singing, carefree objects of the paternalist imagination, but as emasculated objects of pity. In sum, the mysterious culture of Haiti becomes, in *Magic Island,* a place of exploitative labor practices—purged of white culpability—with an erotic energy that threatens to destroy the very basis of sexuality for all those who enter it. It is perhaps in this vein that Seabrook writes that being on the island produced "a terror of something blacker and more implacable than [its inhabitants]—a terror of the dark, all-encompassing womb."[19]

In the films and radio broadcasts involving zombies over the next two decades, this basic dynamic remained in place, but with a number of important elaborations. And in tracing the elaboration of the narrative, I am grounding what follows in the films *White Zombie, Revolt of the Zombies,* and *I Walked with a Zombie;* and on radio episodes featuring the walking dead in the programs *The Shadow* (1940), *Adventures by Morse* (1944), *Strange Adventure* (1945), *Five Minute Mysteries, Unsolved Mysteries* (1949), *Screen Directors' Assignment* (1949), and *The Clyde Beatty Show* (1950–51). The two plot lines from *The Magic Island* outlined above—the first involving a ritual sacrifice of femininity, the second involving the employment of zombies on plantations—merge together in the narrative structures of the 1930s and 1940s. In story after story, nefarious designs hatched within the space of a plantation (usually by a plantation owner) somehow ensnare a visiting white couple, threatening their marriage by de-sexing either the man or the woman through zombification.[20] In *The Magic Island,* the open-air voodoo ritual and the creation of zombie laborers were separate affairs, each with its distinct setting, and each distinctly gendered. In subsequent tales of the walking dead, these two motifs became hopelessly entangled.

With the passage of time, the settings of zombie stories widened beyond the borders of Haiti. Though generally remaining on sugar plantations, a number of productions shifted the scene to elsewhere in the Caribbean, particularly Cuba, while others set the action on fictionalized though explicitly West Indian islands. A few of these tales went beyond the West Indies altogether to Asian settings such as Cambodia (e.g., the film *Revolt of the Zombies)* and South American locales like Chile (e.g., the radio serial *Adventures by Morse).*[21] In addition, a host of zombie-themed restaurants and bars popped up in the 1930s and 1940s featuring iconography drawn from the South Pacific. Renda explains, "As white discourses began to merge diverse racial 'others' into a single fluid and generic, exotic object, they tended to emphasize less the specific horrors that had been attributed to Haiti since the early days of the occupation."[22] Be that as it may, the zombie rarely strayed too far from "home," as it were, generally remaining in the Caribbean. The writers' choice to shift the location to an island adjacent to Haiti more properly reveals the American tendency to conflate whole regions. In addition, both the setting and the plot structure of the zombie genre remained remarkably consistent through the Depression, the Second World War, and the early years of the Cold War, despite striking shifts in U.S. foreign policy vis-à-vis Haiti and the Caribbean over those years. More than anything else, this reveals the ways in which pop cultural forms, particularly B-genres, do not rigidly and mechanically correspond with shifts in official policy. As we will see, they sometimes even contradict each other.

In zombie stories after Seabrook, an important shift occurs with respect to the motif of femininity. The loss of either womanhood or female innocence—experienced by the native girls Classinia and Catherine in *The Magic Island*—is visited upon white women in later film and radio stories. As such, the physical and spiritual suffering of Haitian women is displaced onto white, female bodies. In the radio programs "The Zombie" (from the series *Five Minute Mysteries*) and "Isle of the Living Dead" (from *The Shadow*), white female corruption manifests itself in the guise of the plantation owners, who are villainous white women. More commonly, however, the loss of (white) female innocence takes the form of zombification. In *White Zombie*, for example, a young couple named Madeleine and Neil visit the Haitian plantation of Monsieur Beaumont; Beaumont falls in love with Madeleine, and hires a man to turn her into a zombie so as to lure her away from Neil. The title of the film reveals how the idea of a "white zombie" was a novelty in 1932 (but would soon become a familiar trope within the genre). In a later radio program "The Mysteries of the Zombie" aired on *Unsolved Mysteries,* a jealous black servant woman named Clarissima (a slight twist on Seabrook's Classinia) romantically desires the white plantation owner who employs her. When he rejects her advances, she gets her revenge and soothes her jealousy by turning his fiancée Helen into a zombie. The narrator later discovers the result of Clarissima's vendetta. One day in the cane fields, a native tells him that all manner of people labor as zombies. He indignantly replies, "But no white woman!" The un-named native proves him wrong by showing him what the narrator recognizes as the once-delicate Helen, now working amongst the sugar cane as a common, zombified, field worker. Unable to bear the sight of a white woman so fallen in status, he gently puts her out of her misery by feeding her salt.

At the most general level, the Caribbean plantation is a space that breaks up white marriage bonds. But a more specific operation is at work. Transferred to the film and radio narratives, Seabrook's narrative of de-feminization is transferred to white female bodies which are de-sexed through zombification. In the stories mentioned above, the writers make no direct link between the de-sexing of the women and the sexual energies of the racialized masses, as does Seabrook. The connection is implicit, however. In tale after tale, an environment rich with the jungle drums and un-bridled passions of the Other threaten to turn the white woman, the pinnacle of Western civilization, into a de-feminized automaton. The sexual excesses of the island are incompatible with her delicate frame, which is rendered sterile through zombification. As a zombie, she cannot reproduce either her race or her nation.

The discursive function of female de-sexualization is closely linked to the second, main theme in the zombie narratives of the 1930s and 1940s: the theme of exploited labor. Another important shift within the genre, post-Seabrook, is the re-figuring of the zombie "master," the arch-villain of the story, as a white plantation owner. In *The Magic Island,* the cruelty of colonial labor was displaced onto the Haitians themselves, but later stories send a rather different message about labor and capital. When Bela Legosi's villainous white character in *White Zombie* creates walking dead men to work in his sugar mill, he explains to an observer, "They work faithfully. They're not worried about long hours."[23] This 1932 film initiated a plot convention that soon would become a staple of the genre: the multi-racial, zombified, plantation workforce. A series of shots of the sugar mill operation in *White Zombie* reveal undead, mill workers—both black and white—carrying baskets on their heads, slowly turning a gigantic wheel, and trudging about their various tasks.

The character of the white Caribbean planter in these film and radio stories typically creates zombies out of whomever he or she requires for the purposes of labor, be they native workers or white visitors who become ensnared in their web. In a *Strange Adventure* episode entitled "Zombie," to take another example, a white man very narrowly escapes the clutches of a French plantation owner who sought to add him to the ranks of his predominantly black workforce as a zombie. Likewise, toward the end of "Isle of the Living Dead," aired on the program *The Shadow,* a particularly diabolical planter named Mrs. Nesbith reveals that some of her undead hands are "natives," while others are "white men I've hired in their place." But no matter their race, they all receive from her the same degraded treatment. From atop a staircase, she yells to the captive zombies in her basement: "You're no longer men but swine in chains, just as cattle, who labor in the cane fields under my command ... I only keep you alive because I save money using you in the fields instead of native help!"[24]

Clearly, part of the "horror" of these stories is the fear of racial leveling. Blacks and whites are interchangeable in these island labor markets, in which planters can choose to hire natives or to select white men "in their place." But rather than forming a utopia of racial equality, the failure of the authors to afford their black characters any real humanity makes their settings a nightmare world of common degradation. The white man enters the space of the plantation and, at the end of the day, is reduced to the status of blacks. The natives are never raised to the "level" of the whites, nor does the multi-racial workforce rise together. The implicitly isolationist message is that the entire space is to be simply avoided, as its debased system of labor cannot be reformed; rather, its effects are contagious. So pervasive is the leveling that even white women — the bearers of future civilization — cannot produce viable offspring in this space. Their de-sexed bodies cannot reproduce the labor power of the male worker, thus the system is not only beyond reform: metaphorically, it holds no future.

The medium of radio was particularly effective in communicating this leveling. In the 1930s, the new technology of radio took on the national project of creating a shared national culture, and it had distinctly homogenizing effects. At the same time, however, its producers labored to preserve hierarchies of difference that existed prior to its institutionalization. As radio historian Michelle Hilmes has written, radio "established a centralizing structure that could work to control the most immediately threatening aspects of local diversity and maintain local separations."[25] Early radio obsessively accentuated distinctions of race, class, and gender, but it had to do so in a medium without the visual cues upon which earlier genres like blackface minstrelsy depended. It maintained some hierarchies and expanded others by relying on linguistic differences, accentuating stereotypical dialects that it carried over most notably from vaudeville and the minstrel show.[26]

This dynamic arguably extended into the international arena as well. Radio helped to create new categories of inferiority as it brought relatively unknown peoples into American living rooms. What's striking as one listens to these horror radio programs is that it is difficult to distinguish the zombies from ordinary West Indians: even un-zombified Haitians and Cubans speak with slow, drugged, and slavish voices. For example, in the story "The Isle of the Dead," aired on *The Shadow*, the first native introduced to the audience is Mrs. Nesbith's servant "Mungo," whose sluggish, trance-like drawl strikingly contrasts with the eloquent, finishing-school enunciation of his American, English-speaking master. In this context, the aural qualities of the genre were perfectly suited to underscore the horrors of leveling represented by the zombie. In a broadcast culture in which radio actors exaggerated their dialects to make themselves clearly legible as either black or white, the zombie was the only character whose broadcasted voice — generally a guttural moan — was not racially distinct.

As in *The Magic Island*, the zombified colonial laborers of the film and radio stories are still emasculated objects of pity, but the re-figuring of the villain in these subsequent tales represents at least the outlines of a critique of colonialism and a critical awareness of the history of slavery. However problematic the Caribbean plantation is rendered, its system of labor nonetheless appears exploitative and oppressive. To be sure, there are strange echoes of *Uncle Tom's Cabin* and Civil War–era abolitionist discourses in these presentations of plantation life. Most every scriptwriter in the mid–twentieth century would still have been familiar with Harriet Beecher Stowe's famous 1850 novel and its portrait of the South: a world where emasculated slaves are treated like beasts in a plantation culture that erodes the affective bonds necessary to maintain strong morals and healthy families, especially amongst the masters. But the question becomes: why did writers access these abolitionist discourses in the 1930s and 1940s given that they were absent in Seabrook's template?

The answer lies in the official and oppositional politics of the 1930s, which was incorporated (and, in part, negated) in the political unconscious of these B-horror film and radio narratives. Due in part to the ravages of the Great Depression, the 1930s were arguably the moment when the political left had its greatest influence in American culture. Working through organizations like the Congress of Industrial Organizations (CIO), the Communist Party U.S.A, the National Negro Congress, and the American League Against War and Fascism, the left put the exploitation of labor—and the injustices of race—at the center of public debate.[27] It also took up the theme of anti-imperialism as part of its political discourse. Most germane to this analysis, it placed the U.S. exploitation of Cuba and Cuban plantation labor into public debate. As Ben Balthaser has shown, influential artists and writers such as Josephine Herbst, Clifford Odets, Langston Hughes, and the journalist Carelton Beals strove to expose U.S. imperial practices on the island nation. Odets' activities with the American Commission to Investigate Social Conditions in Cuba led to his high-profile arrest in Havana in 1935.[28]

In addition, the demographic shifts resulting from the Great Migration—the exodus of African Americans from the South to the North—had created a sizable, influential block of black voters in Northern cities for the first time. Freed from the constraints of southern-style segregation, this enlarged, urban black population had greatly expanded its cultural and political institutions, from newspapers to civil rights organizations to theater troupes. Politicians at the federal level were forced to begin courting their votes for the first time.[29] By the mid–1930s, African Americans working in this new public sphere, together with their allies on the left, put forth new narratives of Haiti that figured it as a vibrant nation with a rich spirit of independence. While some African American writers such as Claude McKay and Zora Neale Hurston failed to break with the trope of exoticism in rendering its people, Langston Hughes, Arna Bontemps, and CLR James critically called attention to Haiti's class inequalities and its dynamic history of resistance. In addition, the Harlem Unit of the Federal Theater Project produced a number of widely attended plays on the island nation that broke with earlier narratives of the exotic, including Orson Welles' staging of *Macbeth*, set in nineteenth-century Haiti, and the 1938 play *Haiti*, directed by Maurice Clark, which was seen by 72,000 people in New York City alone.[30] Such progressive renderings of Haiti hit the airwaves as well. Most notable was the radio adaptation of *Babouk*, a novel of Haitian revolutionary heroism by communist writer Guy Endore. In 1937, it was broadcast on the *Columbia Radio Workshop*, one of the most popular radio programs at the time.[31]

Finally, new images of Haiti were generated by the Haitians themselves, whose actions helped to transform U.S. policy in the region. In December of 1929, their protests against the U.S. occupation were met with violence by the U.S. Marines, who opened fire on a crowd, killing twelve and wounding twenty-three individuals. Press coverage of the repression provoked an international outcry which ultimately began the process of U.S. withdrawal, completed in 1934.[32] The departure of U.S. occupation forces corresponded with the implementation of Franklin Roosevelt's Good Neighbor Policy, which policymakers advertised as a clean break with gunboat diplomacy. The new agenda was to involve bilateral negotiation, not brute force, in dealings with other nations of the Americas.

The Good Neighbor Policy necessitated a new discourse about Haiti that broke with earlier narratives of exoticism and absolute difference, one that emphasized seeing things "from the native point of view." A wave of scientific studies, inspired by the anthropology of Franz Boas, attempted to reduce the perceived backwardness of Haitian culture in the eyes of the West. Meanwhile, a Euro-American fad for Haitian art in the 1940s broke with the dark exoticism of voodoo drums and zombies in order to emphasize the creativity and dynamism of the Haitian people.[33] On the Haitian end, improved attitudes toward the U.S. were palpable in the writings of Haitian literati and intellectuals. However, this new cordiality took a sharp turn during World War II, when large-scale landowners expropriated peasant lands *en masse* in order to grow a lucrative rubber substitute for the U.S. war effort. In response, a popular, anti–American movement emerged which finally toppled the government of the U.S.–oriented President Élie Lescot by 1946.[34]

These new political forces of the 1930s and 1940s were inscribed into the popular zombie narratives of the period through the motif of the evil white plantation owner, and in the genre's overall figuration of Caribbean plantation labor as a problem. But the use of the zombie in American film and radio ultimately worked to contain and even negate the contemporary progressivist discourses of the Caribbean. Within the American culture industry, the zombie had come to symbolize a world of exploitative labor, but also a mysterious, colonial netherworld that threatened to reduce hapless whites to the same drone-like, sexless state of its natives. There could be no basis for cross-racial identification in such a space — only contamination. The relatively low-profile tiers of the culture industry responsible for B-horror were not in any way bound by the shifting demands of U.S. foreign policy, but only by the immediate need to turn a quick profit via low-budget entertainment. Their representations evolved from broader, long-term, intercultural dynamics. Inadvertently, this industry helped to wean American culture from paternalistic narratives of "tutelage" born of the Haitian occupation, but at the cost of a fundamental disavowal of the entire region.

Disturbingly, the most persistent narrative of the Caribbean in American mass culture before 1945 never transcended the level of B-horror (though Tournier's 1943 film *I Walked with a Zombie*, produced by Val Lewton, momentarily pushed up against the limits of the genre). Moreover, by 1949 it was clear that the zombie tale had been so thoroughly domesticated that it could be parodied on the airwaves as light comedy. That year, CBS featured the story "The Ghost Breakers," aired on the program *Screen Director's Assignment*. It is based on a film from 1940 of the same name which, although it contained comic relief, could not be considered a full-blown farce. By contrast, the 1949 radio play, billed as "A Comedy of Terrors," starred Bob Hope and was set on an island off the coast of Cuba crudely named "Black Island." When the protagonist Larry Lawrence (Bob Hope) arrives on its shores, the result is in no way terrifying. Fresh off the boat, a local woman warns him "The Zombie walks!" to which he blandly replies, "Can we interest you in a subscription to *Weird Stories* magazine?" "The Ghost Breakers" illustrates that, however frightening the zombie may have been in the 1930s, by 1949 the codes of the pre–Romero genre were so internalized by U.S. audiences that this monster and its Caribbean context was neither exotic nor unsettling.

The fact that Haiti entered the dominant, twentieth-century American imagination by way of B-horror has worked against taking the country seriously in the United States. B-horror is not a "serious" genre; it touches on deeply rooted, cultural anxieties, but ultimately turns them into cheap thrills. The Western media coverage of the 2010 earthquake in Haiti underscored the lingering consequences of reading the country through the lens of B-horror. As mentioned in the introduction, *The Daily Mail* in England covered the catastrophe with the headline, "Haiti: Rape, Murder and Voodoo on the Island of the Damned." The newspaper fused the usual narrative of hopeless, third world political violence with a particularly lurid set of images drawn from B-grade horror. In Haiti, we are told by the *Mail*, "Papa Doc" Duvalier ruled the country as Baron Semedi, the voodoo spirit of death, and cut out the hearts of some of his victims while collecting the skulls of others. Meanwhile, on the other side of the Atlantic, U.S. televangelist Pat Robertson revealed an imagination similarly structured by cheap tales of Haiti as a land of supernatural terror. He infamously stated that the earthquake was God's revenge against Haitian slaves, who had signed a pact with the devil to overthrow their masters two centuries ago. Most Western journalists and commentators consciously distanced themselves from such retrograde depictions, but even those who condemned Robertson and his ilk revealed their inability to truly see the long-standing cultural and institutional practices that made such statements possible.

*National Geographic,* for example, consulted popular anthropologist Wade Davis to explain to American readers how voodoo was not some demonic kind of superstition, but rather a set of beliefs with a valid place in the pantheon of world religions. Davis called Pat Robertson's comments "cruel, ignorant, unforgivable, the ravings of a lunatic," and went on to present Haiti as a dynamic, vibrant culture — albeit with a tragic history — whose voodoo-inspired revolution represented a longing for human freedom akin to the colonial revolts of 1776. Davis even acknowledged how the indissociable relationship between Haiti and B-grade horror in the popular imagination is a direct product of U.S. imperialism. He states that

> in the 1920s, the U.S. Marine Corps occupied Haiti. This was during the era of segregation, and most of the U.S. Marine Corps in Haiti were Southerners. Afterward, every one of them seemed to get a book contract, and ... they were all filled with pins and needles and zombies that don't exist. They gave rise to the Hollywood movies ... such as *Night of the Living Dead* and *Zombies on Broadway* and so on.[35]

Despite his tolerant gestures, Davis is complicit in the cultural and political logics that made Robertson and the sensationalism of the *Daily Mail* possible. On closer inspection, one notes that he condemns the cultural productions emerging from the occupation (which he erroneously localizes as Southern), but not the invasion itself. Davis once expressed the belief that the U.S. occupation was a boon for the country, all things considered, and in the 1980s he was even an apologist for the Duvalier regime. His own book *The Serpent and the Rainbow* (1985) re-popularized the image of the Haitian zombie — along with its larger narrative of Haiti as a haunted land of primitive superstition — at the precise moment when Haitians were making enormous sacrifices to destroy the Duvalierist state.[36] In many ways emblematic of the mainstream coverage of the disaster, Davis thus continues the politics of disavowal, albeit with a multicultural inflection, that fails to truly recognize the continuities of the past into the present and is thus complicit in the logics of empire. Like multiculturalism more broadly, his *National Geographic* interview celebrates cultural difference while affirming a core, human sameness, but does so without acknowledging (or questioning) the histories of conflict that continue to create hierarchies and inequalities.

But the old radio shows and films have left a residual culture of imperialism with a stunning tenacity, for the pre–Romero zombie narrative has seen a revival in recent years. The magazine *Men's Journal,* for example, recently led readers through the Haitian countryside on a hunt for zombies in an article entitled "Into the Zombie Underworld."[37] A more egregious sample is *Resident Evil 5,* released by the Osaka-based company Capcom, which became one of the hottest commodities in the booming, video game industry, selling over five million copies worldwide since its release in 2009.[38] The game positions the player as a white American protagonist who mows down hordes of black, zombie-like creatures in Africa, some in urban slums, and others bearing the grass skirts, tribal masks, and spears of 1930s action-adventure films. As a reviewer for *Eurogamer* put it, "It plays so blatantly into the old clichés of the dangerous 'dark continent' and the primitive lust of its inhabitants that you'd swear the game was written in the 1920s."[39] Like its pre–World War II predecessors, the storyline of *Resident Evil 5* contains an awareness of imperial exploitation that sits uneasily within its undeniable, racist frame, thus it fully replicates the earlier genre in this sense as well.[40] If, as Fredric Jameson suggested in his classic study of the postmodern, late capitalism is marked by its ability to pluck from earlier aesthetics, shear them from their original contexts and re-brand them at will in the form of pastiche, then the re-emergence of the early, twentieth-century zombie narrative should come as no surprise.[41]

Capcom's *Resident Evil 5*, Wade Davis' *The Serpent and the Rainbow,* and the media coverage of the recent earthquake in Haiti all illustrate the long reach of the zombie narrative first crafted in the 1930s and 1940s. In order for the colonial and postcolonial suffering wrought by U.S. empire to be truly visible, a new transnational, anti-imperial movement would need to emerge which would create a space for a wholly fresh, popular, narrative genre about the region. Ideally, this genre would neither exoticize nor pity its subjects, nor efface the fundamental relationship of economic dominance, past and present. Perhaps the first step toward breaking the spell of disavowal is to take a long, hard look at B-horror in the full, historical context of its deployment, and finally bury the dead.

## Notes

1. Gabe Pressman, "The Sad History of Haiti," *NBC New York,* January 14, 2010, http://www.nbc newyork.com/news/local-beat/The-Sad-History-of-Haiti-81353577.html; Andrew Malone, "Haiti: Rape, Murder and Voodoo on the Island of the Damned," *Daily Mail Online,* January 14, 2010, http://www.dailymail.co.uk/news/article-1243016/ANDREW-MALONE-Rape-murder-voodoo-island-damned.html.
2. I include here Romero's *The Crazies* (1973), *Dawn of the Dead* (1978) and *Land of the Dead* (2005); Danny Boyle's *28 Days Later* (2002), as well as its sequel *28 Weeks Later* (2007); in the realm of video games, I include *Dead Rising* (2006) and the early games of the *Resident Evil* series, all produced by the Osaka-based CAPCOM. *Dead Rising* actually expands the critique of consumerism implicit in *Dawn of the Dead,* using the zombie as a metaphor for the human and environmental devastation caused by American consumerism around the world. And the root of all evil in *Resident Evil* is a giant pharmaceutical corporation named Umbrella, whose zombie-making "T-virus" was allowed to escape because of its undue influence within local government.
3. Mary Renda, *Taking Haiti: Military Occupation and the Culture of U.S. Imperialism, 1915–1940* (Chapel Hill: University of North Carolina Press, 2001), 6, 21–22.
4. Barbara Dianne Savage, *Broadcasting Freedom: Radio, War, and the Politics of Race, 1938–1948* (Chapel Hill: University of North Carolina Press, 1999), 6.
5. Renda, 29–36, 47–53.
6. Noam Chomsky, "Introduction to Paul Farmer," *The Uses of Haiti* (Monroe, ME: Common Courage Press, 2003), 19–24.
7. Renda, 246.
8. William Seabrook, *The Magic Island* (Hamburg, Germany: The Albatross, 1932), 40.
9. Ibid., 58.
10. Ibid., 74.
11. Ibid., 76.
12. Ibid.
13. Michael J Dash, *Haiti and the United States: National Stereotypes and the Literary Imagination* (New York: St. Martin's Press, 1997), 31–34.
14. Seabrook, 40.
15. This claim needs slight qualification. *The Oxford English Dictionary* records the sporadic appearance of the word "zombie" in the English-language world a number of times in the nineteenth century, beginning in 1819. But none of these sources had the impact of Seabrook's story. Its nineteenth century uses reveal no consistency, which suggests that this figure had yet to take a definite shape in the Anglo-American imagination.
16. Seabrook, 84.
17. Ibid., 85, 86, 91.
18. Michael Denning, *Culture in the Age of Three Worlds* (London: Verso, 2004), 26.
19. Seabrook, 35.
20. It should be noted that female de-sexualization is not universal within the genre. In the film *The White*

*Zombie*, the lead female character is turned into a zombie in order to serve her master as a kind of sex slave. This plotline is the exception to the rule, however.

21. Cambodia and Chile would later become sites where the U.S. was complicit in mass murder. In Cambodia, the U.S. bombings of the country in the early 1970s killed 300,000 and directly led to the rise of Khmer Rouge, while in Chile, the Washington-backed 1973 coup overthrowing Salvador Allende's government brought the brutal regime of Augusto Pinochet to power. In introducing these nations to U.S. audiences, the early zombie stories arguably helped to prepare the ground for their later dehumanization.

22. Renda, 225.

23. *White Zombie*, directed by Victor Halperin (RKO Studios, 1932).

24. "Isle of the Living Dead," *The Shadow*, October 13, 1940.

25. Michele Hilmes, *Radio Voices: American Broadcasting, 1922–1952* (Minneapolis: University of Minnesota Press, 1997), 16.

26. Ibid., 20–21.

27. For the most comprehensive treatment of the influence of the 1930s left on U.S. culture, see Michael Denning, *The Cultural Front: The Laboring of American Culture in the Twentieth Century* (London: Verso, 1997).

28. Benjamin Balthaser, *I See Foundations Shaking: Transnational Modernism from Great Depression to the Cold War* (PhD diss., University of California, San Diego, 2010), 128–77.

29. Savage, 8.

30. Dash, 53–54; Renda, 283–287.

31. Chris Vials, *Realism for the Masses: Aesthetics, Popular Front Pluralism, and U.S. Culture, 1935–1947* (Jackson: University Press of Mississippi, 2009), 198.

32. Renda, 34.

33. Dash, 74–80.

34. Ibid., 86–91.

35. Ker Than, "Haiti Earthquake and Voodoo: Myths, Ritual, and Robertson," *National Geographic*, January 25, 2010, http://news.nationalgeographic.com/news/2010/01/100125-haiti-earthquake-voodoo-pat-robertson-pact-devil-wade-davis/.

36. Dash, 142–143.

37. Mischa Berlinski, "Into the Zombie Underworld," *Men's Journal*, September 2009, 108–113.

38. Those familiar with movie series would be tempted to write off a sequel with "5" in the title as hopeless garbage viewed for only the most undiscriminating fans. This same consumer logic doesn't work with video games, however, a market where each addition to the series is often more widely anticipated than the last. Indeed, *Resident Evil 5* was the best-selling game of the series.

39. Dan Whitehead, Review of *Resident Evil 5, Eurogamer*, February 5, 2009, http://www.eurogamer.net/articles/resident-evil-5-hands-on-chapter1to3?page=2.

40. Midway through the game, the player learns that the African zombies were created by a diabolical, Western pharmaceutical company called Tricell, which turned an indigenous people (called the Ndipaya) into walking dead in order to more easily expropriate their land. The urban slum sequences thus implicitly hold Western companies responsible for not only the region's primitivism, but its failed, postcolonial modernity as well.

41. Cf. Chapter One of Fredric Jameson, *Postmodernism, or the Cultural Logic of Late Capitalism* (Durham: Duke University Press, 1994), 1–54.

# The Eco-Zombie: Environmental Critique in Zombie Fiction

## Sarah Juliet Lauro

> *Before we reached Ground Zero, we had our theories. God released his*
> *wrath. Scientists released a bug. Something passed by the earth.*
> — David Bain, "Under an Invisible Shadow[1]

What one sees in the above quotation is an apt reduction of the major causes of resurrection to three main fields: divine, man-made, and natural. Whether the product of evolutionary forces or man's mistakes, the zombie has always been a natural rather than a supernatural monster.[2] The year after the release of James Whale's *Frankenstein* (1931), which translated Mary Shelley's iconic and archetypal man-made monster for the filmgoer, the Haitian zombie — heretofore the exclusive province of anthropological studies of the Caribbean — was imported to Hollywood. Victor Halperin's *White Zombie* (1932) introduced audiences to a kind of strange living-dead somewhat vaguely defined as being made by a witchdoctor's potion, and seemingly controlled by the use of hypnosis. What these two cinematic monsters shared from the outset was that their creation was distinctly presented as being a work of man rather than of God.

One can trace the way in which these two kinds of mythologies, the mad scientist's living corpse and the Haitian zombie, became tangled, merged, and exchanged traits to produce a new and exclusively Western zombie. As it developed over the course of the twentieth century, indebted to both its mad scientist father and its Black Magic mother, the modern zombie took shape as a critique of science, or at least, an expression of anxiety surrounding the powers that scientific knowledge bestowed upon humanity. Working through a bizarre kind of Oedipal drama, one sees the American zombie come to stand with its Haitian mother — as a monstrous figure tied explicitly to the things of the Earth — turn against its scientific father for his infractions against nature. In examining the progression of the zombie as it develops throughout the second half of the twentieth century in film and in comic books, in pulp-fiction, and in video games, one locates a narrative that, finding its voice over a span of forty years of story-telling, articulates the true culprit not as science, but as Capital, and the avenger is cast not as a supernatural, but an Earthly power.

Whereas predecessor undead such as the European revenant returned to Earth to carry out moral justice, and diverse supernatural creatures were often characterized as emissaries of God's wrath, divine vengeance was never a part of the zombie's makeup. Rather than associating the zombie with holy retribution, the only force appealed to is the natural order; the modern zombie is not conjured, but constituted, and it is more related to evolutionary forces than to forces of evil.[3] However, as a figure of return, the zombie is always revising and reworking its own tropes, as well as the themes evident in other genres of living dead. The tropological zombie returns not once, but many times, to its exploration of the categories of the "human," the "body," the "border," and continually restages its own incarnation of the interzone that makes murky a distinction between the living and the dead, the natural and the unnatural.

The disjuncture between the big tent of "Nature" and the non-natural human, who is made to stand outside of it (designated as "non-natural" because of his proven propensity to try to control, manipulate, and reshape nature), is perhaps best seen in the example of the viral zombie.[4] The connection between recent zombie fiction and literary plagues was recently theorized in a monograph titled *Legacies of Plague in Literature, Theory, and Film*, by Jennifer Cooke.[5] Without re-treading Cooke's ground here, I just want to gesture to an important congruity that will lead us to better understand one of the ways that the eco-zombie likewise enacts a return to old forms.

Plague was historically construed as a kind of sacrifice that the Gods forcefully demanded. In *Plague and Pestilence in Literature and Art*, Raymond Crawfurd asserted that "the Old Testament plague is regarded ... as a direct consequence of God's anger," one that requires a heavy penance paid.[6] Pre-Christian civilization too, associated plague with moral and social crimes, as is demonstrated most notably in Sophocles' *Oedipus Rex*.[7] The association between sin and sickness endures in our era. As Susan Sontag writes in *AIDS and its Metaphors*, "The shame is linked to an imputation of guilt."[8] It surely comes as no surprise that this theme is still evinced in the plague narratives of our own time, even when they take on the shape of a zombie epidemic. What is more nuanced is the way that the zombie virus rewrites the plague narrative as a secular rather than spiritual force. Similarly, the eco-zombie is a new phenomenon, but it has its roots in earlier literary traditions, notably the Gothic characterization of the natural world as darkly powerful.

The subgenre that I am terming the "eco-zombie" exists within the broader category of late 20th century revisions of the zombie myth. The eco-zombie channels contemporary characterizations of a planet angered by humanity's long-term damage—resulting, for example, in drastic climate change ("Extreme Weather," as CNN dubs it)—into a natural progression that comes to look like retaliation for humanity's abuse of its environment. As such, the purely secular eco-zombie seems to infuse into the evolving mythos an element from ancient myths of spiritual undead, positioning the environment in the role of an angered god, and the zombie as a gruesome reckoning. Fittingly, then, the eco-zombie appears to "resurrect" a narrative construct that defined the undead of previous civilizations.

## Accidental Zombies

> *It all starts with some a-hole scientist, doing shit he shouldn't be doing....*
> —Mathew Inman, "How Everything Goes
> to Hell during a Zombie Apocalypse"[9]

In the epigraph that introduces this article, the narrator suggests that a passing meteor may have caused the dead to rise. One finds some instances in which natural phenomena are at the root of zombie outbreaks in contemporary pulp fiction. As the characterization, "Scientists released a bug," suggests, there are also many narratives in which a zombie-making virus has been either engineered or mishandled by humans.

Ever since George Romero's *Night of the Living Dead* (1968) made his cinematic "ghoul" a contagious figure capable of passing on his living-dead state through his bite, the zombie has become increasingly associated with viruses.[10] A certain vagueness of detail often makes it difficult to tell whether one should consider a zombie virus a work of "Nature" or the fault of man. In the most recent iterations of zombie mythology that are constituted in video-games and online social networking applications, comic books and graphic novels, short stories, novels, films, and even art and other types of performances, one finds both "natural" zombie viruses (that is, those which remain untampered with by man), and "engineered" viruses, genetically modified by scientists.

What emerges is a dichotomy in which no matter what the cause of their ghastly reanimation — be it an intentional man-made project seen to fruition only to go horribly awry, an unforeseeable consequence of scientific achievement, or an entirely untouched work of nature — all zombies can ultimately be attributed to a larger driving force: one that is distinctly "natural" only in so far as it can be distinguished from the *super*natural, man's mishandling of nature. The man-made zombie is obviously natural rather than supernatural, but it is also opposed to the Natural zombie that arises, like a meteor passing the earth or a naturally occurring virus, from circumstances unrelated to human behavior.

This section's epigraph, however, redirects our gaze in its characterization of "a-hole scientists" being to blame for the epidemic. One of the most prevalent trends in contemporary zombie fiction is a zombie that is the inadvertent consequence of scientific misconduct or technological innovation. This trend began with George Romero's *Night of the Living Dead* (1968), which is often lauded as bringing the cannibal element to the cinematic zombie. However, what seems more iconoclastic is the film's shifting of the zombie's origin from willful human creation, to unintended fallout from scientific advancement: the cause of the outbreak in Romero's landmark film is most concretely identified as radiation from a human-made space probe orbiting around Venus.[11]

Many of the cinematic living dead resurrected during the aftermath of World War II and the Cold War wove a distrust of military technology into the fabric of a uniquely American mythology. In the 1950s, for example, one sees films that link the creation of living dead to atomic power, as in the *Creature with the Atom Brain* (1953), wherein a scientist uses atomic power to raise the dead to do his bidding, or *Plan Nine from Outer Space* (1958), in which aliens reanimate corpses to mount an attack on humanity. As their leader, Eros, explains, humanity is developing weaponry at a rate that exceeds its maturity. Fearing that humans are on the verge of developing a weapon that could wipe out not only their own planet, but those of other intergalactic species, the aliens tell humans that they are too "stupid" to be in possession of such technology. Though this Ed Wood B-movie is a much-maligned film, it makes explicit the fear which most of the zombie films of this period covertly communicate: human technology has dangerously exceeded its natural domain.

*Night of the Living Dead* forged a zombie that combined deep-seated concerns about contemporary scientific innovation with the living-dead figure, which had historically emblematized the boundary of what constituted the human. Before and after Romero, one sees aliens raising the dead, and one finds mad scientists driven to conquer the limitations of mortality, but Romero's film marks the starting point of an important tropological return, as the zombie begins to revise the supernatural revenant's long-standing associations with divine retribution, to create an undead that is the *accidental* result of human innovation, which delivers to humanity its comeuppance for tampering with nature.

Though this is only made explicit in a very few zombie films, there is always a tacit implication that the zombie arises "naturally" (in contradistinction to "supernaturally") from a confluence of elements, formerly strange to each other, which man has put in contact. Yet, at bottom, the zombie is a most *un*natural creature: it defies the basic principle that divides the living from the dead, animate from inanimate, subject from object. And, in further distinction from the natural order, the most common zombie is a man-made living-dead, an accidental zombie that is an unforeseen result of a scientific project, which serves as a reminder of mankind's dangerous interventions in nature. This contemporary zombie both highlights the epistemological difficulty which the living-dead already poses, and, as its gruesome reflection, illuminates the disturbing fact that in its opposition to nature, humanity now stands with one foot outside of the Natural order.

Still, since in most of the reanimations that we will examine in this article, the outbreak of the living dead is an *unintended* consequence of human malfeasance, there is the intimation that another force is at work: if not the divine hand of God, and not man's willful creation, then we might ascribe this zombie to something like coincidence, or the undirected workings of the universe, or the machinery of physics: all of which fall under the broader category of the natural.

What is tacitly at work here is a partial animation, if not an anthropomorphization, of what, for lack of a better term, I call "Nature." As we see the zombie increasingly associated either with natural phenomena, or with humanity's "unnatural" mistreatment of natural resources, or his foul-intentioned tampering with the elements of biological structure, the trajectory of the myth begins to resemble an asymptote, bending towards a familiar, but unreachable limit: by bringing forth the zombie, nature comes to occupy the place that would have formerly been held by a deity in tales of supernatural revenants, as the force which raises the dead to enact retribution for human sins. Indeed, Nature is imbued with an almost sinister power in this gray area that I call the Eco-Zombie.

## "Natural" Zombies

> He never even acknowledged the weapon. The void in his eyes never changed to recognition of the danger. He walked straight at me, and his face remained blank right up to the end.
> I squeezed the trigger and he fell. The only witness to one of the worst moments of my life was the rustling murmur of the wind through the trees.
> — Joe McKinney, *Dead City*[12]

The natural phenomenon in the zombie mythos consists of everything from the material storm to the immanent will of the planet, and, within the category of matter, from the very big to the very small. The "eco-zombie," as I define it, is a subset of the category of the Natural zombie which draws particular attention to the current state of the planet or makes overt reference to environmental themes, or which depicts the zombie phenomenon as the Earth's retaliation. We might include in this category films in which plants and animals become zombies or carriers of a naturally evolving virus, and unleash an attack on the human population.[13] It is also a long-standing trope of the zombie genre to depict the natural world's indifference to the plight of humanity as it battles extinction under the zombie threat, and this might be considered an element of the eco-zombie's narrative.[14] Obliquely, these narratives convey that the destruction of humanity is in the long-term interest of the planet.

The novel from which this section's epigraph is taken, Joe McKinney's 2006 *Dead City*, depicts a viral zombie outbreak that is directly linked to a series of five hurricanes that batter Houston, Texas, over a period of three weeks. The devastation is cataclysmic, and the wreckage of the city provides a fertile breeding ground for a new virus, which causes living people to become violent and insensible to pain, to decay rapidly, and to crave the flesh of the uninfected. Like the cinematic zombie, it is emphasized, the infected transmit the condition to others through their bite.[15] In a matter of hours, the virus begins to spread throughout most of Texas, reaching San Antonio, where the action of the novel takes place, following Eddie, a cop, in his journey to survive the attack, and reunite with his wife and baby.

A medical doctor clarifies the pertinent details of the outbreak:

> We saw the first cases last night. They came in from Houston on one of the flights bound for the shelters. We had no idea at the time what we were dealing with. It was only in the early hours of this morning that we realized we were dealing with something completely new. Unofficially, we began calling it the necrosis filovirus ... [it] is closely related to the family of viral hemorrhagic fevers that include Ebola, Marburg, and the Crimean-Congo viruses.... The thing about the necrosis filovirus that makes it different from other hemorrhagic fevers is the incubation time ... [it] seems to amplify within the host in just a few hours. After that, well, you've seen the infected walking the streets. They experience depersonalization to such a degree that they essentially become a zombie. The illusion is all the more complete when you see the clouded pupils, the smell, the rotting skin, and the almost complete lack of sensitivity to pain.[16]

Explicitly, this zombie belongs to the category of what I call the new viral zombies, a narrative that emphasizes the condition as specifically biological, and doesn't need the zombie to be a resurrected corpse. The hyperrealism of McKinney's novel makes allusion to George Romero's monsters as a counterpoint.[17] It also insists on medical science as offering a plausible explanation, which puts it in a league with many of the new viral zombies, such as those in *28 Days Later* and its sequel *28 Weeks Later*.[18] One thing that separates McKinney's viral zombie from others is the implication of another cause, or another force, at work.

Written the year after Hurricane Katrina devastated New Orleans, and set just a mere 300 miles away, the allusion here is obvious. Just as the catastrophe which we designate under the shorthand "Hurricane Katrina" was in part a natural disaster, but also the result of human error and greed (notably, city developers who neglected the levees that were constructed to protect the Ninth Ward from flooding), the zombie menace in *Dead City* is not simply the direct result of the hurricanes; rather, the wreckage left in the wake of the storms provides ideal conditions for the virus to evolve. Nonetheless, both this novel and the real world narratives that emerged to describe Hurricane Katrina involve characterizations of nature as having turned against humanity.

Though doubts about a direct connection between Katrina and climate change have been proffered in online journals such as *New Scientist* and *World Science*, strongly worded pieces in more popularly read venues suggested otherwise.[19] The August 30, 2005, issue of *The Boston Globe* ran an article titled "Katrina's Real Name," by Ross Gelbsan. He writes,

> The hurricane that struck Louisiana yesterday was nicknamed Katrina by the National Weather Service. Its real name is global warming.... Although Katrina began as a relatively small hurricane that glanced off south Florida, it was supercharged with extraordinary intensity by the relatively blistering sea surface temperatures in the Gulf of Mexico.[20]

Regardless of the veracity of these claims, Gelbsan espouses the popular rhetoric. A journalist in *Time* magazine notes the prevalence of this discourse: "To hear a lot of people tell it, we have only ourselves — and our global-warming ways — to blame."[21]

In McKinney's novel, the connection between the zombie outbreak and climate change is made much more legible by making Houston the unlikely recipient of five hurricanes in only three weeks. Though global warming is not overtly named, McKinney's characterizations of weather and of the natural world are imbued with a sinister agency. For example, in the scene from which this section's epigraph is taken, when Eddie confronts and kills his first zombie, descriptions of nature are anything but natural: "A sharp, gusty wind blew through the tops of the top branches, tossing them back and forth. The huge oak creaked and groaned under the sudden urgency of the wind. It was strange and beautiful music."[22] Eddie comes upon a zombie in a thicket of branches:

> The space seemed to form a quiet sanctuary, a cave with walls of leaves…. But I saw immediately that it was no sanctuary. A man was already there, on his knees, eating large pieces of viscera from a gaping hole in a dead woman's abdomen. A long, lumpy rope of intestine dangled from his fingers.[23]

Coming across this "abomination" in the clearing sends Eddie reeling: "I let the branches fall from my hand and I stumbled backwards into the yard, still staring at the oak tree that no longer seemed beautiful, but mangled and unnatural."[24] Pulling himself together, Eddie shoots the zombie, with the sound of the menacing wind ringing in his ears.

The novel peppers in mentions of the unusual weather throughout, and, at the end, when the outbreak has been contained, all is right with the natural world as well: "The sky was a vaulted ceiling of absolute blue. There were no clouds…. The Earth was bathed in a blue … startlingly cold and rich and immaculately clean."[25] What the reader is undoubtedly left with is the sense that the zombies were part of the storm, and that what the characters experienced was more than just the fickle temperament of Mother Nature, but, as was said of Hurricane Katrina, that it was an *unnatural* natural disaster.

The eco in "eco-zombie" does not merely stand for "eco-criticism": rarely do zombie narratives overtly further an environmentalist stance by arguing for more protections for the planet. It also stands for "eco-phobia," an increasingly pervasive attitude fearful of Nature's power, to which Ecocriticism is just beginning to turn serious attention. As I define it, the eco-zombie does not denigrate or vilify Mother Nature, it merely returns to her an animating power that distinctly identifies Nature as without the province of man's control.

The 2006 film *Severed* might be thought of as the most overtly ecological zombie film made to date, though an environmentalist strain has long been a part of the genre's makeup. *Return of the Living Dead* (1985) makes an oblique reference to acid rain at the film's end, when the ash of cremated zombies merges with the cloud cover and pours down the contagion in the form of a rainstorm. The trend of incorporating environmental concerns into zombie films stretches back at least to the 1970s. In some of the earlier films, what is made apparent is the subgenre's connection to deep-seated fears about the treatment of the environment by specific industries.

A French film titled *Les Raisins de la Mort* (1978), directed by Jean Rollin, makes explicit an increasing concern over the safety of pesticides. Environmental concern had been on the rise ever since the 1962 publication of Rachel Carson's foundational ecological text *Silent Spring* raised questions about the agricultural industry's use of DDT. Dichlorodiphenyltrichloroethane (DDT) was banned in the United States in 1972 and in most developing countries throughout the next two decades. The plot of *Les Raisins de la Mort*, or *The Grapes of Death*, concerns a region in the French countryside that is plagued by a rash of strange occurrences. The villagers appear changed: they grow somewhat vacant-eyed though they can still speak, and they become violent and homicidal; they develop growths or pustules, and appear to be rotting. Those affected are not zombies in the classic sense of the word: much like the zombies in *Dead City*, they just become irrationally violent and appear to decay rapidly.[26]

The revelation that comes to the characters near the end of the film, that the wine is causing the event, is known to the audience from the beginning. The opening shot is of pesticide sprayers moving through the wines. They wear cloths over their mouths, and as the opening credits roll, the music fades so that all we hear is the labored breathing of the workmen. One man in particular, Kowalski (who is immediately legible as an immigrant — perhaps there is a commentary embedded here about the abuse of foreign laborers in France), returns from the spraying looking unwell. When he boards a train that is seemingly occupied only by two college-age girls, the film's first zombie encounters our protagonist, Elizabeth, a young Parisian who has come to the countryside to meet up with her fiancé. This strange man begins to develop growths and pustules on his face before their eyes, and his erratic behavior frightens them. He attacks Elizabeth's fellow traveler, but she manages to escape on foot. This opening sequence, along with shots of grapes rotting upon the vine and decanters full of wine in the homes of the volatile townspeople, informs the audience early on that the cause of the epidemic is the pesticide, which the villagers are being exposed to through their consumption of the local vintage.

A film like *Raisins de la Mort* uses the living dead to critique the agriculture industry's methods of dispatching pests in the most expedient manner, with little regard for human safety. This was not the only film to invoke pesticide as the zombie-making agent: *The Living Dead at Manchester Morgue* (1975) depicts a zombie made by a sonic radiation wave emitted to kill crop pests; *Toxic Zombies* (1980) depicts an experimental chemical that is sprayed on marijuana crops, creating zombified hippies. There is therefore a precedent not only of films that express concern for the environment, but even more specifically, among those which critique the agriculture industry, an expression of concern about the chemicals that are created by man to influence to growth of plants.[27]

The film *Severed* (2006) offers the most readily visible example of an eco-zombie; the plot concerns a group of loggers in a remote area, and a gaggle of protesters who camp out in the woods, chain themselves to trees, and otherwise try to interrupt deforestation. When Rita, the leader of the environmentalists, "spikes" a tree, a disruptive tactic that causes harm to the loggers who cut into them, sap enters a worker's bloodstream through his open wound, and he morphs quickly into a contagious cannibal.[28] The protestors, loggers, and company-employed scientists are forced to band together and struggle to survive.

The audience comes to find out that the zombies are the result of a genetically-engineered hormone (developed by the scientists) that is injected into the fungi at the base of trees to speed up growth. Early on we see a board meeting wherein a member explains to the CEO that this test area must be protected from media attention, as the new development is boosting profits immensely; they can now get "old growth trees in a third of the time." Shortly after the outbreak, the CEO's rebellious son, Tyler, is sent to find out "why production has stopped."

What makes *Severed* so significant, besides the somewhat heavy-handed ecological critique ventriloquized primarily through Rita, is the clarity of the film's message that capitalist industry, and not science, is the real culprit. Carter, the only scientist to survive the first five minutes of the film, repeatedly insists that he, like the loggers, is just doing his job for the company; there is also a brief moment when he allies himself and the hormone he has helped to develop, menacingly called GX1134, with the cause of the protesters: "I am the only one who is trying to make a difference, I am the only one who can end clear-cut logging!" Presumably then, the scientist also wants to avoid cutting down natural, old-growth trees, but, paradoxically, by creating unnaturally grown ones.

The audience is led to feel pity for the workers who have clearly been oppressed and manipulated by the corporation, the protestors and their dedication to the cause, the CEO's son who heroically sacrifices himself in a vain attempt to save the worthless and cowardly scientist, and even the company's CEO himself, who is morally redeemed when he hisses at a board member: "Don't you talk to me about stock values when my son might be in danger." The true villain of the film, then, appears to be the amorphous beast Capital, which only has an on-screen incarnation in the personage of the board member who institutes the policy of "containment," knowingly sacrificing human lives in the name of protecting the company's long-term investment in the science they have developed.[29]

In *Severed,* and other zombie narratives like it, we find a living dead that specifically incarnates anxieties regarding the abuses of the planet by capitalist industry. This is not a Luddite position railing against civilization and modern progress, but more specifically, the eco-zombie identifies capitalist industry as a sinister engine which drives man to assert his dominion over other creatures, push science into dangerous zones, and defy the moral order by abandoning the good of his fellow man in the pursuit of greater personal gains. The question that these narratives raise for me is whether all zombie stories aren't, in this sense, eco-zombie narratives? For, they are all concerned to some degree with humanity's mistreatment of nature, a broad category which includes at times, mankind itself. More simply put, the eco-zombie replicates the very crux of its predecessor myth: the modern zombie has always articulated a concern with the way humanity warps the natural order. In its original incarnation in Haitian folklore, the zombie was first and foremost a symbol of the peculiar practice of making objects (slaves) of subjects (humans). In its inception, the zombie was a reflection of the abuses of power man was capable of under the profit-driven sway of pre-capitalist mercantilism. The difference, if there is one, to be discerned in the eco-zombie's narrative, is that the force of power that creates the zombies is ultimately undecidable as Natural or as Human.

In 1980, Carolyn Merchant wrote of *The Death of Nature,* arguing that the Scientific Revolution had shifted the model of the earth as an organism to the model of a machine. This demythologizing of nature, she argues, lead to its death:

> The March 1979 accident at the Three-Mile Island nuclear reactor near Harrisburg, Pennsylvania, epitomized the problems of the "death of nature" that have become apparent since the Scientific Revolution.... The long-range economic interests and public image of the power company and the reactor's designer were set above the immediate safety of the people and the health of the earth.[30]

According to Merchant, after Nature was "killed"— symbolically de-animated by being compared to artificial rather than organic components— it was easier to ignore, to subsume to man's interests in development.

More recently, in discussing the epistemological difficulties posed by the concepts of "Nature" and "Ecology," Tim Morton writes, "Nature wavers in between the divine and the material. Far from being something 'natural' itself, nature hovers over things like a ghost."[31] Morton is characterizing the way Nature has been described from Romanticism onwards. Although his assertion that nature is "ghostly" has more to do with Nature's undecidability as either concrete or abstract, tangible or metaphysical, the choice of words resonates with Merchant's insistence upon the death of Nature. The troubling slippage of what constitutes "Nature" is manifested in the eco-zombie genre in the undecidability of whether Nature is meant to be read as a secular stand-in for the deity come to reckon the sins of industry, or whether all the rage of the storm clouds is but humanity's own doing, a representation of our own tampering run amok. At the latter end of this spectrum, the blame for the zombie's creation falls squarely on human shoulders, as in *Severed, Raisins de la Mort* and others. At the former, one finds a narrative like Joe McKinney's novel *Dead City* that enacts a symbolic re-animation of Nature by virtue of its eco-phobia, which seems like an indicator of a larger trend in literature and culture.[32]

## *Unnatural Zombie*

*Nature is Brutal. Respect It.*
— World Wildlife Federation Commercial[33]

The eco-zombie is an undead that results from some gross mistreatment of nature — usually by a corporation, or by someone seeking to make a profit, who thinks little of protecting the natural environment or the inhabitants of it, as when, for example, inappropriately disposed toxic waste results in the creation of zombies; but it can also be more vague, as in *Dead City,* where we encounter a zombie that results from the effects of Global Warming. The representation of Nature within the eco-zombie narrative can also function somewhat like the representation of the natural world in Gothic texts such as Coleridge's "Rime of the Ancient Mariner" or Mary Shelley's *Frankenstein,* wherein Nature is imbued with an almost sinister power. As one can see from this section's epigraph, eco-phobia, or an insistence upon the raw power of nature, is very clearly a larger trend at work in culture today; indeed, it is even espoused by those who, like the authors of the advertisement from which the above quotation is drawn, would protect the environment. Putting the eco-zombie in dialogue with Gothic and Romantic representations of Nature clarifies a central tension that exists within the camp of eco-criticism.

In an article titled "Deep into That Darkness Peering: An Essay on Gothic Nature," Tom Hillard explains the need for eco-criticism to revisit the eco-phobia espoused in Gothic literature.[34] Drawing on Simon Estok's lamentation of the neglect of eco-phobia within eco-criticism, Hillard reminds the reader that the Gothic characterization of the natural world as dark and powerful was replaced by Romantic aestheticization.[35] Keeping in mind Carolyn Merchant's argument about the death of Nature under Enlightenment rationalism, then, one might read the eco-phobic impulse of the Gothic as itself kind of Frankensteinian revivification of Nature. In brief, the overview which Hillard sketches depicts the prevalent worldview as having transitioned fairly swiftly from medieval associations of the natural and the monstrous to the Enlightened ideal; in response, Romanticism took the form of an idealization of nature; the Gothic, then, is that which wants to dwell in a preternatural insecurity about nature's power. Existing on the same trajectory as the Gothic, the eco-zombie returns to the pre–Enlightenment conception of nature as something that was not within man's power, not dead but living, not passive but dominant.

The eco-zombie is not within the grasp of man's power, and its creation seems to point simultaneously to man's incapacity, his lack of control over nature, as it does to his ability to inadvertently destroy the world. What we end up with is the sense that the zombie is not truly controlled by man, but by some amorphous power or order, somewhere between the domains of Nature and Man; part coincidence, part chaos, not quite natural, certainly not supernatural, but possibly a return of the preternatural.[36]

The complex critique of science's relationship to nature that emerges as a central part of the zombie narrative is made more legible when viewed alongside Max Horkheimer and Theodor Adorno's critique of Enlightenment philosophy vis à vis its relationship to technology. In the introduction to *Dialectic of Enlightenment,* Horkheimer and Adorno write that Enlightenment's program was the disenchantment of the world. It wanted to dispel myths, to overthrow fantasy with knowledge."[37] Specifically, this "knowledge" is one that will "establish man as the master of nature," and the system of Enlightenment rationality is one that seeks to replace myths of nature's power by subsuming them to the all-encompassing mythologization of the subject.[38] What we see in the eco-zombie is the opposite of this: it seems to re-animate nature, giving over to it a kind of mythic agency.

Where Enlightenment philosophy differs from its predecessor model, Horkheimer and

Adorno claim, is in its assertion of scientific truth, "the scientific calculation of events annuls the account of them which thought had once given in myth. Myth sought to report, to name, to tell of origins—but therefore also to narrate, record, explain."[39] In applying scientific models to nature, by contrast, man raises himself up as the only God, and "Nature, stripped of qualities, becomes the chaotic stuff of mere classification, and the all-powerful self becomes a mere having, an abstract identity."[40] They describe this model of swapping the "animism" and "enchantment" of myth, which imbued the natural world with supernatural powers, for the sublimation of nature as man's province as reifying, ossifying, petrifying.[41] Quantified, calculated, constructed, the world becomes, as Carolyn Merchant wrote, a dead object.

For Horkheimer and Adorno, the Enlightenment goal was the "subjugation of the world" to the human command by means of logic, reason, and classification systems. The Enlightenment thus signifies for these philosophers a deadening of the world, the erection of a taxidermy museum where once there was a menagerie. What I want to end with here, is the suggestion that what looks like the return of a mythic fear of nature, as it takes shape in the guise of the eco-zombie, or other narratives in popular literature and film, is accompanied by a nearly mythic fear of man himself.

Horkheimer and Adorno write that

> the noonday panic fear in which nature suddenly appeared to humans as an all-encompassing power has found its counterpart in the panic which is ready to break out at any moment today: human beings expect the world, which is without issue, to be set ablaze by a universal power which they themselves are, and over which they are powerless.[42]

What is visible in the eco-zombie is at once the transition from a fear of nature to a fear of humanity (as science becomes the bogeyman responsible, in some way, for the unleashing of the zombie) and, simultaneously, a return to a mythic enchantment of nature (wherein it is ultimately nature, or the natural order, that brings about the zombie as a result of man's tampering). Like an apparition, it seems impossible to nail down this menacing version of Nature in the eco-zombie as ever being definitively separate from the influence of man's control.

Appropriate to its structure as a figure of return, the eco-zombie is a myth that reanimates Nature post–Enlightenment, and returns to it some of its enchanted animism, its preternatural wonder, much the same as was done by the Gothic genre's reaction to the Romantic aestheticization of nature. In this way, the eco-zombie seems to fit with that structuring trope of the postmodern, the *mise-en-abîme,* as it incarnates a return to the return to pre–Enlightenment marvel. Yet, at the same time, it is doing something new: revealing that the powers of man may be more terrifying than the powers of nature. Just like a zombie, the commentary furnished by the new eco-phobia (and the eco-zombie is firmly within this camp) is familiar, and yet different. Further, what we see in the narrative that incarnates the planet's power by representing global warming and climate change subsumes Nature's actions to man's misdeeds; in a sense, we are prompted to ask, is this really a return to the mythic power of Nature, or is it merely, zombie-like, a false resurrection that ultimately attests to the power of man — if only to his power to destroy?

**Acknowledgments.** I wish to thank Professors Colin Milburn, Timothy Morton, Eric Smoodin, and Mike Ziser for their invaluable input on the dissertation chapter from which this article is taken. I am especially grateful to my colleague Erin Paszko for the many conversations we've shared on ecology, disaster, capitalism, and zombies.

## *Notes*

1. David Bain, "Under an Invisible Shadow," in *The Undead, Vol. 3 Flesh Feast*, ed. D.L. Snell and Travis Adkins (Mena, AR: Permuted Press, 2007).

2. I argue in more detail elsewhere that the zombie is actually primarily man-made, inherently natural rather than supernatural. Even when, as in the Vodouist folklore myths of Haiti, the zombie is believed to be created by a holy man, this is not depicted as a supernatural occurrence, but rather the result of his sacred knowledge of the things of the Earth that have potent properties. I argue that this myth has its parallel in Western narratives such as *Frankenstein*, wherein a lone human creator uses natural phenomena (such as electricity) and scientific knowledge (as of chemistry) to raise the dead.

3. Of course, one finds imitators, living dead that don't belong, genetically, to either group, but which may try to capitalize upon the commercial success of the "zombie" by using this name, though in truth their monster is more akin to other types of undead creatures. There are many films which I personally do not consider zombie films, but which are nonetheless included in books such as Peter Dendle's *Zombie Movie Encyclopedia*, Jamie Russell's *Book of the Dead: A Complete Guide to Zombie Cinema*, or Glenn Kay and Stuart Gordon's *Zombie Movies: The Ultimate Guide*. For me, a definitional element of the zombie is that it is *not* supernatural; yet when one classifies the self-declared "zombie movies" of the century, we find, for example, that there are a substantial number of demonic zombies—films in which the undead are raised by an affront to a religious institution, by someone worshipping the devil, or by Satan himself. What we see in this category are mostly offerings from Spain, Mexico, and Italy, notably more conservative, religious countries. These figures are more indebted to other mythologies of the undead (such as the revenant or the golem) than to the man-made zombie of Haitian origin. There are also a few zombies raised by "curses" (perhaps borrowing from the Mummy's mythology), and some by "magic" crystals and enchanted forests, which might best be cross-referenced as a natural zombie, after all. There are also many "zombies" that are raised by Taoist wizards: the Hong Kong zombie was a major cinematic trend of the '90s, but by and large this undead is related to the Chinese hopping ghost rather than the Haitian zombie.

4. The subgenre of the zombie virus narrative emphasizes evolution as a force of nature. In some cases, a natural virus evolves to create zombies, as in the story "Hell and Back" by Vince Churchill (in *The Undead*, 2004, edited by Snell and Hall), in which an outbreak of a virus is named the "Romero-flu" for its uncanny ability to turn people into vacant, zombie-like creatures; or "Mr. Hanson goes to the Lab" by Michael Cieslak (in *Dead Science*, 2009, edited by A.P. Fuchs), in which a natural virus is combated with the Lazarus project, a team of humans who become so panicked about the new disease that they institute a witch-hunt, and quickly prove themselves to be more cruel than the naturally occurring zombies. In film, one also finds many examples of the viral zombie: from Lucio Fulci's biochemical virus that gets unleashed in *Zombi 3* (1988) to the Thai production *SARSWars: Bangkok Zombie Crisis* (2004), which fantasizes the zombie's evolution from the real-life SARS epidemic, the zombie has been increasingly explained as the victim of a wide-scale viral outbreak.

5. For a discussion of how Romero's film firmly instantiated the zombie as a figure of plague, see Jennifer Cooke's *Legacies of Plague in Literature, Theory, and Film* (New York: Palgrave MacMillan, 2009). Cooke writes that since Romero, "instead of a hypnotised slave, the zombie has been a dangerous, infectious embodiment of the living dead who cannibalistically parasitizes the living: Romero made his zombies plague carriers and able to infect others, to turn them, too, into zombies" (165). A recent essay by Steven Zani and Kevin Meaux titled "Lucio Fulci and the Decaying Definition of Zombie Narratives" also traces the zombie epidemic's place in plague narrative history. In *Better Off Dead: The Evolution of the Zombie as Posthuman in Literature, Film, Art and Culture* (forthcoming Fordham University Press, Spring 2011).

6. Raymond Crawford, *Plague and Pestilence in Literature and Art* (Oxford: Clarendon Press, 1914), 9.

7. In *Oedipus Rex*, the first play in Sophocles' Oedipus cycle, the residents of Thebes are suffering from a plague that is associated with unnatural causes.

8. Susan Sontag, *Illness as Metaphor and AIDS and Its Metaphors* (New York: Picador, 2001), 112.

9. Mathew Inman, "How Everything Goes to Hell during a Zombie Apocalypse," comic featured on *The Oatmeal*, accessed September 7, 2010, http://theoatmeal.com/comics/zombie_how.

10. Romero's living-dead was swiftly associated with the zombie despite the film's use of the term "ghoul." Did cinematic audiences make a connection between the body raised by a witchdoctor and the monster that came to life as an inadvertent consequence of interplanetary conquest? Perhaps the connection was drawn because of the sheer numbers of walking dead in Romero's films. Scientific reanimation tended to produce only a few subjects at most, but zombies appeared in groups in the early Vaudou zombie films. While the mythological "ghoul" is flesh-eating, and thus, was perhaps closer to Romero's cannibalistic monster than the mainly innocuous "zombies" that only rarely (and feebly) attacked onscreen in films like *King of the Zombies*, (1931), or *The Zombies of Mora Tau* (1957), the Arab legend of the ghoul ties it to cemeteries, and thus, imbues it with a supernatural power. Whether Romero knew it or not, then, his living-dead are indeed more akin to zombies than to ghouls.

11. It should be underscored that the film is itself intentionally vague on this point. Critics debate whether this is meant to be taken as the definitive reason the dead begin to walk, or just a theory. My reading of the

film focuses on this detail as enabling a landmark moment in zombie mythology; irrespective of Romero's personal feelings about this particular plot point, the film's implication of the space race in the creation of the living dead was a breakthrough for zombie cinema. (Romero's primary inspiration was Richard Matheson's novel *I Am Legend*, which is about a naturally occurring virus that turns people into zombie-like "vampires.") The iconoclasm of the film is its association of the undead with what was already a longstanding trope in science fiction: scientific achievement and technological advancement could have unpredictable, and sometimes horrible, ramifications. For nearly the first time in cinema history, we confronted a living-dead monster that was not a mad scientist's "abortion" (as in *Frankenstein*), but which took on the traits of "nature run amok," and the zombie was re-branded as a wholly accidental and horrifying creation that was the result of man's interference in the natural world.

12. Joe McKinney, *Dead City* (New York: Pinnacle Books, 2006), 41.

13. Actually, the motif of zombie animals more broadly is another increasing trend in zombie literature. There are stories in which gentle, woodland herbivores become hostile zombie animals—as in John Grover's "Unnatural Selection" or David Dunwoody's "Clockwork" (both in *Zombology, Library of the Living Dead*, edited by Rebecca May, 2009). One cannot help but read these examples as nature requiting man's destruction of their natural habitats, or even revenging man's sin of eating animals.

14. This is sometimes alluded to by depicting nature's reclamation of human dominated spaces, as when grass begins to grow on asphalt, and wildlife returns to the city. I think here of the more definitively zombie remake of *I Am Legend* (2007), in which one sees a deer bounding through downtown New York, leaping over abandoned cars. The zombies pose no threat to nature, but only to humanity, and rid of the majority of the population, nature flourishes, illustrating how little the earth would miss us.

15. The infected are quickly dubbed "zombies," and Eddie encounters many experts along the way who explain to him the field of "zombie studies": one character declares that this "amounts to a bunch a freaks in a chat room, talking about what they think zombies would be like if they actually existed" (192). More in line with my own idea of what constitutes "zombie studies," others tell him where the infected can be mapped on the spectrum of zombie classification from cinematic, to folkloric, to philosophical; provide scientific explanations of the outbreak; and even debate the legal ramifications of an entity who is both living, and yet, in some sense, dead.

16. Ibid., 175–6.

17. Ibid., 101.

18. The recent trend of an un-dead undead was viewed as a new development in zombie lore, and sparked debate about what, in fact, constitutes a zombie. Many film critics have illustrated that the zombie need not be definitively reanimated, if it emphasizes depersonalization to the degree that it nonetheless achieves the same effect, calling into question what delineates the human from the non-human. (See for example Peter Dendle, *The Zombie Movie Encyclopedia*, or Glen Kay and Stuart Gordon, *Zombie Movies: The Ultimate Guide*.)

19. Emma Young, "Climate myths: Hurricane Katrina was caused by global warming," *New Scientist* 17:00, May 16, 2007; "Did Global Warming power Katrina?" *World Science*, September 15, 2005.

20. Ross Gelbsan, "Katrina's real name," *The Boston Globe*, August 30, 2005.

21. Jeffrey Klugar, "Is Global Warming Fueling Katrina?" *Time*, August 15, 2005.

22. McKinney, *Dead City*, 40.

23. Ibid.

24. Ibid., 41.

25. Ibid., 284.

26. Nonetheless, the film acknowledges its indebtedness to the zombie genre with a bit of irony. After fleeing from several attackers, the protagonist takes flight across a barren landscape, composed mostly of rock formations, with just a few scattered trees. (Juxtaposed as it is with the shots of the plentiful vineyards that open the film, this change in setting might be read as an ecological warning.) Suddenly, a woman with long, flowing hair appears in a long white housedress. Her arms are outstretched in front of her, and her irises are colorless. This looks like the archetypal figure of the milky-eyed zombie, and particularly of the somnabulistic zombie of early cinema, such as Val Lewton's own white zombie, Jessica Holland, who, like the figure here, appears pale in her nightshirt in *I Walked with a Zombie* (1943). The joke in Rollin's film is that this embodied allusion turns out to be an uninfected blind woman. Thusly, the film concedes that its creatures resemble, and yet differ from, the classic cinematic zombie.

27. Even the sci-fi spoof *Attack of the Killer Tomatoes* (1978), which, in part, might be responding to some films of this ilk, draws upon an existent skepticism of the food industry's practice of tampering with nature: Of the mutation of the tomatoes into vicious, murderous vegetables, one army man says, "Who would have thought? All we wanted was a bigger, healthier tomato."

28. True to the more recent iterations of the mythos, it hardly seems that these zombies are undead; there is barely time for them to die and reanimate before they "change." Indebtedness to Danny Boyle's *28 Days Later* (2002) is obvious; like Boyle's "infected," these zombies are fast, strong, feral, and red-eyed. Interestingly, what both of these films share is that the blame for the outbreak is subtly shared by protesters: in Boyle's film a virus is released from a primate research facility when animal rights activists free the unwilling subjects of

experimental treatment; in *Severed*, Rita's tree spike is actually the immediate cause that introduces the hormone into the human population. Perhaps, then, we are meant to read the radicals as playing the role of human facilitator to Nature's planned revenge.

29. Although one character, Ramon, a severely traumatized logger from a renegade encampment in the woods, proselytizes that this plague is God's vengeance, the viewer is not lead to agree with him. Ramon is shot by another logger in the middle of his sermon, and as he falls from his perch high up in a tree, his body briefly contorts, mid-air, into the shape of a cross. Despite the theatrics, the audience is not lead to think of Ramon's opinion as a revelation; rather, throughout his screen-time he is represented as pitiable, a mad-man, but not particularly profound or wise. True to the contemporary zombie genre, there are no other clues that the phenomenon has any supernatural properties; the idea that the lone scientist ought not attempt to flout God's will by raising the dead has been replaced by the secular notion that when one tampers with the natural order, things can easily "go to hell."

30. Carolyn Merchant, *The Death of Nature* (San Francisco: Harper & Row, 1980), 294.

31. Timothy Morton, *Ecology Without Nature* (Cambridge: Harvard University Press, 2007), 14.

32. This turn of the eco-zombie narrative, whereby eco-phobia becomes a critique of modern industrial capitalism and its abuses of the environment, is revelatory of parallel trends in other types of "eco" narratives, such as disaster films like *The Day After Tomorrow* (2004). The 2010 Cultural Studies Association conference (held at UC Berkeley, March 18–20) devoted a panel to "Capitalism and the (Post)Apocalypse in Film and Fiction." Papers by Erin Paszko, "An Awry Approach to Terrorism through Roland Emmerich's *The Day After Tomorrow*," and Laura Hudson, "Natural Terror: The Eco_disaster Film after 9/11," addressed the genre of the eco-disaster narrative.

33. This is the caption at the end of the controversial WWF Brazil 9/11 ad, which replays the crashing of airliners into the twin towers—after the first two, about several dozen follow suit—in order to make a point about how much more catastrophic the tsunami of the following year was in terms of loss of human life. In her conference paper previously mentioned, Erin Paszko argued that Nature is cast as a terrorist in this advertisement. My interest centers on the ad's juxtaposition of the word "Brutal," and its association with animalism, with a visual representation that crosses references to Nature, to the terrorist, and to God: as if an angry Zeus were hurling airplanes, like thunderbolts, at lower Manhattan. For a discussion of this ad and the fallout, see adfreak.com article "DDB, WWF reeling from fallout over 9/11 ad," accessed September 1, 2009.

34. Tom Hillard, "Deep Into That Darkness Peering: An essay on Gothic Nature," *Interdisciplinary Study of Literature and the Environment (ISLE)* 16, no. 4 (2009): 685–695.

35. In "Theorizing in a Space of Ambivalent Openness: Ecocriticism and Ecophobia," Simon Estok argues that ecophobia should not be dismissed by ecocriticsm, but it is clear that he is locating it as the opposition: "An ecocriticism that takes ecophobia as its core (as feminism takes misogyny and sexism as core issues) will undoubtedly find itself moving toward methodology, will find itself in positions of confluent theorizing, will find itself productively continuing the discussion of environmental issues..." (*ISLE* 16, no. 2 [2009]: 203–225). I would submit that this position (whereby ecophobia is likened to misogyny and sexism) gives it too little credit. Ecophobia should not merely be designated as the camp that fears nature and therefore undermines an environmentalist agenda; it can also espouse a sublime respect for the planet which advocates for the protection of the natural world's complex ecosystems and the maintenance of their equilibrium.

36. In my use of the term "preternatural," I am drawing on the language of Lorraine Daston and Katharine Park's *Wonders and the Order of Nature* (New York: Zone Books, 1998) and their description of the preternatural as "the workings of Nature where she seems to be peculiar in her manner" (231). The category of the "preternatural" as explained by Daston and Park concerns natural phenomena that were interpreted as marvelous—which could not yet be explained by scientific knowledge—but which were not thought of as miraculous or as supernatural. It thus signifies the recognition of the limits of human knowledge.

37. Max Horkheimer and Theodor Adorno, *Dialectic of Enlightenment* (Stanford: Stanford University Press, 2002), 3.

38. Ibid.

39. Ibid., 5.

40. Ibid., 6.

41. For example, "the scientific object is petrified, whereas the rigid ritual of former times appears supple in its substitution of one thing for another" (Horkheimer and Adorno, 7).

42. Ibid., 22.

# Lost Bodies/Lost Souls: *Night of the Living Dead* and *Deathdream* as Vietnam Narrative[1]

## KAREN RANDELL

"The dead of night changed the lives of many ... and ended the lives of some."

This tagline for the 1974 Canadian zombie film *Deathdream* (dir. Bob Clark) could summarize the experiences of many fighting soldiers during the Vietnam War. It doesn't, however: it summarizes the zombie madness brought to a small town by the returning (undead) Vietnam veteran, Andy (Richard Backus), summoned back home by his mother's anguished pleas. Made in 1972, while the war still raged and the anti-war movement gained momentum, this low-budget zombie horror film engages with many issues pertinent to the war era: PTSD, or Vietnam Syndrome,[2] the deaths of over 58,000 American soldiers and the subsequent national mourning, the loss of 2,300 men declared Missing in Action (MIA) or Prisoners of War (POW), and the anxiety that this absence precipitated. The film's tagline thus exploits the tropes of the horror genre but echoes the real anxieties present in an American society disenchanted with the Vietnam War. This chapter will focus on two zombie films made during the Vietnam era —*Night of the Living Dead* (dir. George Romero, 1968) and *Deathdream*— and discuss the ways in which the fantastic specter of the zombie articulates issues of loss and mourning for the American war dead and missing in a way that was not being addressed by the war films of the period.[3]

With the two exceptions of *Lost Command* (dir. Mark Robson, 1966) and *The Green Berets* (dir. Ray Kellogg and John Wayne, 1968), there was no war film set in Vietnam while the war was ongoing. Notions of heroism and the structure of the classical American war genre as buddy movie, so popular during and after World War II,[4] did not translate during the Vietnam War as it was not well-supported by either the public or politicians. It is not surprising that Hollywood, always reliant on a viable economic outcome, did not put into production any other war films. The release of *The Deer Hunter* (dir. Michael Chimino) in 1978 and *Apocalypse Now* (dir. Francis Ford Coppola) a year later mark the beginning of the direct engagement with the experiences of war in a Vietnamese setting. Even then, I would argue, we are often in a metaphorical combat zone. It is not until *Platoon* in 1986,

67

when Oliver Stone makes what becomes the quintessentially iconic Vietnam War combat film, that the traumas of the battlefield are explicitly depicted. As with the First World War, it seems that a period of time was required after Vietnam before these experiences could be "safely" negotiated in the home space of American mainstream cinema.[5] The further away from the war the films are, in terms of temporality, the closer they approach the physical space of the war zone. In this case, the necessity of a temporal gap between the event and a culture's ability to represent this trauma indicated the degree to which the anxieties collectively experienced as a result of the Vietnam War were not sufficiently assimilated until the 1980s.

Where, then, do we see the anxieties of war played out during the conflict itself? Most certainly every night on American TV news reports and in violent returning veteran films such as *Born Losers* (dir. Tom Lauglin, 1967) and *Angels from Hell* (dir. Bruce Kessler, 1968) and in the Vietnam western, such as *Little Big Man* (dir. Arthur Penn, 1970) or *Soldier Blue* (dir. Ralph Nelson, 1970). It also very convincingly finds itself displaced into the horror films of the era. In the following analysis of *Night of the Living Dead* and *Deathdream* I draw on debates in trauma theory to argue how the Vietnam War manifests within these films.[6] The visceral excess displayed within the return of the undead presents, to use Thomas Elsaesser's phrase, a "referred referentiality" within the films of the missing and dead American soldier,[7] a referentiality that signifies the original traumatic event of the Vietnam War. Although the war itself is conspicuously absent, the film obliquely evokes the severe maiming and unclaimed deaths of the soldiers. *Night of the Living Dead* becomes, then, a point of reference for the continuing non-presence in American society of the bodies, living or dead, of the MIA and POW soldiers in Vietnam. Similarly, *Deathdream* becomes an horrific wish-fulfillment narrative in which the trauma of those bereft by the death of the Vietnam soldier, in this case the mother, creates a neurotic return of her dead son that can only be resolved once she can accept his death and display the appropriate societal graveside mourning. These films displace the bodies of the lost and dead into fantasy (horror) narratives that enable the anxieties around this visible absence within the American home front to be visited within the safe space of the film's generic boundaries.

George Romero's *Night of the Living Dead* has been read alternatively as a critique of capitalism[8] and as an apocalyptic narrative concerning Cold War anxieties around nuclear contamination[9]; Richard Dyer reads the film in terms of race[10]; Gregory Waller suggests that *Night of the Living Dead* offers "a thorough-going critique of American institutions and values"[11]; Sumiko Higashi writes that the film is "part of the cultural production registering both repression and resistance during the sixties."[12] While I do not disagree with these readings I would like to offer a parallel reading that suggests that there is a traumatic "trace" within the text: a "recovered referentiality" concerning dead and missing American soldiers (MIA) who fought in Vietnam. *Deathdream*, on the other hand, with the exception of Robin Wood's essay,[13] has received very little critical attention, but, as I will argue in the second half of this chapter, it has much to offer in terms of its engagement with the mourning of the American dead of the Vietnam War.

First, however, we turn to *Night of the Living Dead*. The oxymoron "living dead" not only incorporates anxieties around death, dying and burial, but it also speaks to the absence of men who were either classified as missing in action or prisoners of war. Not only is the MIA soldier absent from living in "the world," a loaded expression used by the majority of serving men in Vietnam to describe the United States, but their liminal status as neither fully alive nor fully dead locates them within the realm of the undead. These particular men are doubly absent: they are not in America and they may or may not be alive in Vietnam either. They persist only in the imagination and memory of their families. Thus, the zombie acts, as Robin Wood has argued, as the "return of the repressed," the corporalization of the corpse that refuses to make itself visible to the American public in the midst of a heavily mediated conflict.

By 1968, and during the film's production, these men were, however, very much "alive" in the American public consciousness. In 1967, the National League of Families of American Prisoners and Missing in Southeast Asia was established by wives and mothers of the missing soldiers. This group continually campaigned for information about their men and worked actively with the Department of Defense. The campaign included interviews with newspapers and television and the public posting of lists containing the names and photographs of those missing to keep their plight a political issue that remained in the public consciousness. Newspaper reports such as this one from the *New York Times* in November 1968, "A United Appeal on Vietnam," demonstrate the way in which this issue was considered at the time to be a bipartisan matter in which everyone along right/left political spectrum was in agreement:

> The United States appeal to members of the United Nations to put pressure on North Vietnamese to lift its secrecy on American Prisoners of War represents one aspect of Vietnam policy on which virtually all Americans are united.... Hanoi persists in flouting civilized practice and procedures by continuing to ignore the humanitarian obligations it assumed when it signed the Geneva conventions on war prisoners in 1957.[14]

The high profile that the missing soldiers had in American society at the end of the 1960s, because of such campaign action, is what is relevant to my argument regarding the cultural resonance of Romero's undead. By 1968 the number of POWs had risen to 400 (from two in 1964); 106 of these men were captured in that year. The number of men listed as MIA also rose dramatically during this period so that by 1973 when 591 prisoners of war came home in Operation Homecoming there were still 2,500 American soldiers listed as MIA or POW.[15]

*Night of the Living Dead* is saturated with anxieties present in American society concerning the absent bodies of men. At the end of Romero's film, the bodies of the undead are piled up and burned and a televised news report features a doctor who states: "The bereaved will have to forgo the dubious consolation that a funeral service can give." In the same way many soldiers' body could not be returned to their families, the film similarly denies the cathartic moment of ritualistic burial. As R. H. W. Dillard points out, in the film "all traditional methods of handling the fact of death fail."[16] There is a tension here between the visceral experience provided the audience of the sight of zombie death and the absence of those mourning the deaths of their living dead. At the conclusion of *Night of the Living Dead*, no rites of burial or memorial are present in the burning of the zombie bodies, whereas the beginning of film privileges the memorial of the dead by opening in a graveyard as two young adults visit the grave of their father. This comparison is key to highlighting the changes that are brought about by the presence of the zombies in the rationalized space of the graveyard; a space normally dedicated to controlling and containing the dead.

At the end of the film the models by which society marks death cannot be formalized. The undead are not ritually buried but burned in an *un*ceremonial pyre. This lack of resolution for the dead body is also apparent for the families of those men MIA or whose bodies literally disappear during combat in Vietnam: burial or cremation, funeral services, graves, and memorials are not possible without sight of a body. The men listed MIA cannot be listed as dead until acknowledgment of the sight of their death or body.[17] *Night of the Living Dead* offers a reading of the presence and absence of dead/undead bodies in America, during a critical moment of political unrest and increased war activity. It presents us with an alternative "returning veteran" film. As Robin Wood argues, "what is repressed must always strive to return."[18] To engage in such a reading, however, one must ask, of course, what is being repressed? The return of the repressed in *Night of the Living Dead* is literally the returning zombie-veteran, this doubled form of *revenant* tapping into what Freud in "Thoughts on War and Death" regards as the most primitive fears that persist in modern society. Freud argues that primitive fears still exist within our modern society that "the dead man becomes the enemy of his survivor and seeks to carry him off to share his new life with him."[19] In *Night of the Living Dead,* this fear is displayed explicitly in the image of the undead that come back to claim the living, whose only motivation is a desire for nourishment and the inclusion of the living in the confines of their borderline existence. In this way, the traumas of the Vietnam War contaminate the home front existence of those waiting for the return of their soldier to the family, a notion that is continued in the later discussion of *Deathdream* in this chapter.

*Night of the Living Dead* opens with what is indicated as an annual trip to a cemetery for a brother (Johnny) and sister (Barbra) to their father's grave: it is a ritual of remembrance. From the beginning of the film there is a link made between nation and death. Romero's name appears superimposed upon the image of the American flag. With the country at war in 1968, the image of the national flag flapping against the background of gravestones was extremely controversial. There is a simultaneous subversion here of American patriotic values—by placing his name across the flag the title suggests that Romero is the true patriot and that we should consider the film in some way a critique of its time, something I will return to at the end of this section. The film's opening on what is for Barbra (Judith O'Dea) a sacred act places the notions of sacrifice and mourning central to the film. At their father's grave Barbra admonishes her brother for his, as it happens, prophetic rehearsal of the classic horror movie trope "They're coming to get you, Barbra!" Thunder rolls to herald the appearance of the first of the undead. Typical of the other characters that will appear in abundance soon, this male character is performed with a stiff gait (reminiscent of Boris Karloff's monster in *Frankenstein* [James Whale, 1931]) and echoes Johnny's earlier tease. Barbra is pursued and caught by the zombie, but she struggles free and runs, first to her car and then to a seemingly abandoned farm house. Her brother, however, is caught by the zombie. The camera movement here positions the audience with Barbra as she runs, moving with her, and, at times, canted. The immediacy with which the camera records the action is placed within the aesthetic of the newsreel rather than classical filmmaking: although the narrative is clearly fantasy, the aesthetic hints at realism, a notion that I will return to later.

Once at the house Barbra is cared for by Ben (Duane Jones) who has already started to make the house safe. Despite having also witnessed the undead at their work, he remains active and alert. Barbra, on the other hand, cannot come to terms with what she has witnessed. She does not, at first, speak; she moves slowly, as if in a trance and pulls absently at her clothes; she seems hot. She continues to do this as she starts to tell Ben of the man that attacked her in the graveyard and of the death of her brother. Her voice is small, childlike, and it falters. As Barbra starts to describe the attack in greater detail, words fail her and she starts to scream hysterically. She leaps up and attacks Ben, screaming over and over again, "We've got to get Johnny! We've got to get Johnny!" She needs his body back, it seems, even though she knows him to be dead. She is inconsolable. Ben slaps her face and she faints. Placing Barbra on the sofa he calmly returns to his plan of action and gets the radio working. This scene is pertinent to the discussion of trauma and its visibility in popular film because it highlights two key issues: firstly, the notion of witness and the trauma of survival, and secondly, the placing of this trauma onto the female character. Gregory Waller suggests that the character of Barbra is a symbol of all trauma survivors: "Barbra can offer Ben no assistance ... [she is] traumatized after she is forced to see the dead and the living dead."[20]

Here we start to see in *Night of the Living Dead* an engagement with the notion of traumatic witness and post-traumatic stress: a notion that is not recognized in explicit terms in the returning veteran films of this period and which is still absent from the American Psychiatric Association's Diagnostic Statistical Manual of Mental Illness. The trauma of witness and of survival is shown here as being one in which Barbra's catatonic state exemplifies, as Waller's discussion suggests, that of the shell-shocked. Writing on the First World War, Trudi Tate states that war trauma was not an uncommon occurrence in civilians and in particular that women were often "subject to trauma."[21] She cites a study by Edwin Ash in 1919 which found that civilians often "exhibited symptoms like those of 'shell-shock of the battlefield'—'loss of voice, paralysis, ... sleeplessness, terrifying dreams' and so forth."[22] Thus, in a moment when civilians were being daily subject to news reports from Vietnam, Barbra's confrontation with the terror of the living dead exemplifies the trauma exhibited by civilians indirect and second-hand engagements with the battlefield. As Tate argues, when civilians "actually did imagine some of the horrible sights of the Great War, they became susceptible to war neuroses."[23] Barbra does not have to imagine though, she witnesses firsthand as the war is relocated onto American soil.

*Night of the Living Dead* is a low-budget horror movie and as such its aesthetics are not concerned with realism. The use of the media (radio and television news coverage) within the diegesis, however, to alert the people to the danger that lurks within their American nation, places a "realistic" edge on the otherwise excessive and visceral *mise-en-scène*.[24] Sumiko Higashi argues that it is the film's evocation of television news that exposes its propinquity with the Vietnam War. She suggests that the "shocking imagery associated with media reports of the Vietnam War ... seems especially apt for a horror film such as *Night of the Living Dead* in which the role of television is pivotal."[25] What Higashi is identifying here is the intertextual link between fictional representation and televised news reports, a link which would have been affectively experienced by the film's contemporary audience. *Night of the Living Dead* has a dual function for the televised news reports, using them to impart information to the audience about the nature of the zombies and as a narrative device to propel the characters to take a particular course of action to protect themselves. The reports within the film mimic the language of Vietnam War reports seen on nightly TV broadcasts in American homes.

For instance, the news reporter refers to a "search and destroy operation." The sense of verisimilitude becomes all the more apparent when we take into account that the field reporter in *Night of the Living Dead* is not an actor at all, but a local Pittsburgh broadcaster named Bill Cardille who, Romero confessed in a 1969 article in *Interview,* was asked to write his own copy on account of budget restrictions.[26] Cardille self-consciously incorporates the Vietnam jargon that he uses in his everyday job on local news into his news report for the film concerning the capture of the zombies. Although the war appears to be absent from the film in terms of plot, the language used to describe the National Guard's attempt to halt the cannibalistic reign of terror introduces it as a narrative device to explain the destruction of the zombies; the language used is shorthand for an audience already familiar with the need for "search and destroy" missions. Given that my reading of the film suggests that the zombies are symptoms of the anxiety of the loss of American life (rather than of the North Vietnamese), this destruction of the monster takes on another horrific turn. Those responsible for control of American society are indiscriminately destroying enemies which threaten the nation without consideration of the reason for their existence. This is exemplified by the shooting of Ben at the end of the film, a classic moment of friendly fire which reveals

America's indifference to both internal and external forms of racial otherness as the film not only speaks to the context of America's overseas war, but the visual evocation of a lynch mob through the all-white gang of hunters and their vicious dogs who surround the farm house also exposes the dark undercurrent of internal Civil Rights–era racial tensions.

Combined with hand-held cameras and grainy film stock, used by Romero for their low cost, the end of the film takes on a new aesthetic, suggestive of contemporaneous television news and documentary. After the *Night of the Living Dead*'s 1968 release, *Variety*'s disparaging review tellingly compares it to "20 year old army stock."[27] In the same year, the *New York Times* noted its "grainy" appearance and "wobbly" camera, but did not make the connection with newsreel. What is apparent at the end of the film is the move to a television news coverage style as the now-dead bodies are piled up for burning. The series of grainy stills of dead bodies are overlaid as the end credits roll to produce a photographic roll call of the dead, a documented image of absence. Thus, order is restored and anxieties surrounding the dead bodies are given a forum for expression when filtered through the lens of horror. These fears, however, are contained within the familiar aesthetic of documentary realism.

Director George A. Romero does not claim to have consciously produced any of the sub-textual readings that academics have attributed to his work. Over the years he has argued that "he was not aware of the politics of the film" and that critics read too much into "the creations they are studying."[28] In an interview in 1995, however, he concedes that the film is open to interpretation:

> It came out of the anger of the times. No-one was gleeful at the way the world was going, so these political themes were addressed in the film. The zombies could be the dead in Vietnam; the consequences of our mistakes in the past, *you name it...* [my emphasis].[29]

To "name it," I would argue that the repeated motif of the undead, the zombie — the present body but absent soul — in *Night of the Living Dead* signals a "recovered referentiality" within the text of MIA and POW soldiers whose absence was a continually validated presence within the public sphere in 1968.

In the six-year time period between the production and exhibition of *Night of the Living Dead* and *Deathdream* the engagement with the Vietnam War in the press and on television became increasingly preoccupied with the behavior of the returning veterans and the development of a "Vietnam Syndrome." In an article on June 7, 1971, in the *New York Times,* "'Syndrome' Found in Returned G.I.s," a mental health officer, Capt. Gene C. Wilkinson, states, "In the sense that the syndrome is a collection of symptoms, we definitely have a syndrome."[30] The symptoms that he goes on to describe of nightmares, flashbacks, restlessness, bouts of depression, and rage are familiar to our contemporary understanding of Post-Traumatic Stress Disorder, but this diagnosis was, as yet, still nine years away. The article also describes the mental condition of soldiers upon return to the United States: "There is alienation at being separated from wartime buddies and resentment over the indifferent welcome accorded them by their countrymen. For all these reasons there is a vague longing to return to Vietnam."[31] This sense of alienation is suggested as not only being related to the quiet return of these men without parade or hero status, but also connected to the difficulty of integration back into American society. Normal life seemed fraught with difficulties; in the same article Pfc. Alan Stogdill declares, "I should have stayed over there ... since we got back to [Fort] Benning ... it's been one detail after another."[32] His frustration is anchored in the feeling that life with his buddies in Vietnam was somehow simpler, however traumatic it appears to those at the home front.

The one-year tour of duty, typical of the Vietnam War, meant that there was a constant flow of returning soldiers to America while the war was still underway. This return of men from war one-by-one is unique to the Vietnam period. On Monday, August 21, 1972, an article by Jon Nordheimer in the *New York Times* described the veterans as slipping "back into America with no bands playing and almost without notice"[33] and in 1970 psychiatrist Robert Jay Lifton had described the soldiers as having to "sneak" back into American society.[34] These articles not only frame the returning veteran as victim by noting the lack of parades and their devalued status, but they also inadvertently represent the veteran as something sneaky and sinister, as a figure to be feared. There was a rapid repatriation for these veterans and within twenty-four hours of leaving Vietnam, they were back in American society. Dr. Jonathan Borus of the Walter Reed Army Hospital has argued that the men were "broken in" too rapidly; in Nordheimer's article Borus is quoted as saying: "My God, the Marines even bring them home in jungle fatigues."[35] Borus argues that these men are still "dressed to kill" when they arrive in the United States. These and other articles highlight the rapid succession of veterans brought into America who still "have the dust on their boots" from Vietnam. The notion of contamination that is apparent in *Night of the Living Dead* can be seen here through the fear that the traumas of war will be brought home with the returning soldiers. *Night of the Living Dead* is a prelude to later returning veteran films such as *First Blood* (dir. Ted Kotcheff, 1982) which portray the veteran as fueled by an unconscious desire to bring the war (and its traumas) home to the USA.

This fear is taken up explicitly in *Deathdream* in which a returning veteran, Andy, comes back to haunt his family and hometown as a blood-sucking zombie. After killing his family doctor, amongst other members of his neighborhood, Andy is driven by his mother to the town's cemetery where she helps him to bury himself in a grave he has prepared on his nightly jaunts. Once buried he is able to return to the dead and his mother can mourn at the graveside. She is the key to his release from the "living dead" and thus her trauma of loss needs to be resolved to enable his resolution. *Deathdream* opens in the combat zone (a low-budget imitation of jungle vegetation); bird song and insects can be heard as two soldiers stalk through the woods. Suddenly, grass and dead leaves on the ground are lit up by a barrage, airplanes are heard overhead, and GIs crouch behind a tree trunk. One soldier gets shot in the back and the second screams hysterically, "Darren! Jesus Christ, Darren!" The barrage lights up the wood again, illuminating the standing soldier as he looks down at his buddy; he is frozen to the spot. While the sound of his screaming fades, the camera pulls back, a single gunshot rings out, and the soldier, shot in the chest, falls backwards to the ground. An extreme close-up of his face becomes blurred as the credits begin. We hear a woman's voice calling, "Andy, Andy, Andy ... you can't die, Andy, you can't die, you promised, Andy, you promised...." as a distorted melody in a minor key heard as the camera pulls back and fades to black. The film cuts to the scene of a suburban house.

Although the film's opening exhibits the telltale musical cues of the horror genre, the iconic jungle combat scene anticipates what would become the conventions of the Vietnam War film. The juxtaposition of the woman's haunting voice with the distorted imagery of warfare set up a doubled notion of trauma: the trauma of battle is bound to the trauma of those left behind. The cut to the family house establishes the source of the ghostly voice, as a mother, father, and daughter sit to eat a roast dinner cooked by mother and badly carved by father. Robin Wood suggests that this prevents the film from falling "into the simplistic trap of innocent-boy-corrupted-by-horrors-of-war."[36] As he states, "It was not Vietnam alone that produced Andy's monstrousness," suggesting that the claustrophobic affectations of his mother and the ineffectual role model of his father are illustrative of the dysfunctional nuclear family under patriarchy.[37] As the family eats, the mother, Christine (Lynn Carlin), relates a tale of telling Andy's girlfriend Joanna that Andy has continued to write. This fabrication and the highly charged and excitable way in which the mother tells her story anticipates her reaction and denial of the news that Andy has died, information that arrives by telegram during the meal. She screams, "No! It's a lie! It's a lie!" Later that night, she is out of bed, sitting in Andy's room, rocking in his chair while holding a candlelight vigil for her son. She intones: "You're all right, you're alive, I know, I can feel it, they lied": as she speaks the superimposed lights of a truck appear on screen, and as the truck stops to pick up a hitchhiker in army combats she continues, "you will come back." This denial of death and subsequent calling up of her son's spirit produces the sinister wish-fulfillment narrative that drives the rest of the film's plot-line: as with *Night of the Living Dead,* the trauma of loss produces a neurotic return of the un-dead and it is the female who once again gives voice to these anxieties.

Although it is the desire of a mother for the return of her son that drives the narrative, *Deathdream* also deals explicitly with the returning veteran and the tensions surrounding his return to civilian society. The narrative evocation of Vietnam Syndrome (PTSD) appears in Andy's behavior towards his neighbors and in the circumstances of the deaths of his victims. Andy does not only damage flesh to gorge himself on the blood of his victims, but also uses a hypodermic syringe to extract blood for later consumption. This link with drug abuse and use of narcotics during and after service in Vietnam is pertinent during this period as news agencies were beginning to report on wide-scale drug use among veterans. An article by Dana Adams Schmidt in 1972 highlights the difficulties that returning veterans had securing work if they received, for instance, an SPN 384 narcotics abuse code in their discharge papers.[38] Companies used these codes when selecting job candidates. One company in Schmidt's report admitted: "'The code number is the first thing we look at when we are hiring a veteran.'"[39] This type of discrimination labeled veterans beyond their immediate return and played into the clichéd stereotype of the unstable and unreliable veteran. This image is reinforced by Andy: his post-war habit can only be fed by the blood of his victims and his catatonic "zombie-state" is reminiscent of a cannabis-induced haze; his reticence to speak about his experiences echoes the silence of the post-traumatically stressed veteran.

One key scene exemplifies the social problem of re-integration. On Andy's second day home the young men of his street, five boys aged between approximately six and thirteen years old, come to visit. Andy sits in a garden chair and does not attempt to get up or move. He remains paralyzed, his static pose giving the illusion of a wheelchair-bound veteran. The children crowd around him and talk fast: "See a lot of action over there, Andy?"; "Hey, Andy, how come you ain't in uniform?"; "You know, my dad got a purple heart in Korea"; "Hey, Andy, I'm having karate!" This last comment is followed by the boy attempting to give Andy a karate chop. Andy grabs the child's hand tight and rises from his chair; the boy whimpers as he is forced to the ground. The family dog, a small terrier, appears at Andy's ankles and barks to protect the child. While still holding the boy with his right hand, Andy scoops up the dog with his left, holding him around the throat. The next action is extreme and somewhat farcical but its excess points to the ways in which the returning veteran was feared and demonized. In Nordheimer's article a veteran bemoans the ways in which civilians are fascinated by, but fail to understand the conditions of warfare:

> Why are they afraid of us? Family, friends and strangers? Why do they ask us questions about how many people we killed? I killed a few, but I don't want to talk about it. It was self-preservation. Why can't they understand that and let us alone?

As a clearer understanding of Vietnam Syndrome began to emerge in the 1970s, Andy's catatonic state, broken by bouts of violence, echoes the destructive elements of this condition. The hyperbolic display of these symptoms in *Deathdream* serves as a dark satire of the shell-shocked veteran.

While the children watch as Andy strangles the dog, the camera cuts between an extreme close up of his face. His eyes become bloodshot and are unblinking, his teeth are clenched and the children look on terrified and in tears. Andy only releases the dog when his father appears, shouting at him to stop. He dismisses the children, and looks directly at Andy. Father and son silently stare each other down. The father does not take his eyes from his son's face, but eventually his eyes narrow in a look of recognition. He shakes his head and walks away. What does this exchange of glances mean? Does the father recognize Andy's extreme and violent behavior? Has he witnessed this type of inappropriate violence before? As Jamie Russell points out Andy's "atrocities back on American soil are little different in scope than those he may have committed while acting in the service of his county."[40] After Andy's first bloody murder, of the truck driver who stopped to pick him up, the police question a waitress at the café where he stopped for coffee. She asks: "Why would a soldier want to do that?" The impossibility of an American soldier committing a brutal murder (at least to a fellow American) highlights the naivety of those on the home front and emphasizes the distance between the returning soldiers' experience of war in Vietnam and the American public's expectations of combat.

While writing this article I have pondered on the academic folly of "over reading" the narrative and aesthetic properties of film in the fashion George Romero wittily accuses his scholarly critics. I would argue that reading these films within their cultural context throws into relief issues and anxieties that were critical during the late '60s and early '70s in North American culture given the ubiquity of the Vietnam War in the newspaper and television of that period. Vietnam Syndrome was clearly an issue that affected civilians as well as the veterans of the war. As I sit at my desk I hear on BBC radio that the 300th British soldier has been killed in Afghanistan (June 21, 2010). To date there have been 2,070 coalition military fatalities in Afghanistan since 2001.[41] The media continues to report on the many global conflicts and disasters occurring in the world and this traumatic material continues to return through outlets such as fantasy and horror genres. In his 2010 article, "After Nearly a Decade of War, PTSD Is Afflicting the U.S. Military," Ryan Jaroncyk debates the statistics available on the current levels of trauma and the treatment available to serving military and veterans of the Iraq and Afghanistan wars. He found that "a study by the RAND Corporation revealed that 20 percent of veterans from Iraq and Afghanistan will suffer from PTSD or severe depression; sadly only 50 percent of these veterans will get the treatment that they need."[42] The diagnosis of PTSD may now have an official status in the military and medical world, but its standing for veterans is still one of contention and fiscal difficulties. This issue then of the (in)visibility and (under)representation of the consequences of war is as pertinent today as it was in 1968.[43] Engaging with the popular and the fantastic brings to the fore the ways in which political and social events permeate our culture. The zombie as cultural cipher allows us an intellectual space to interrogate the issues and to defamiliarize the visceral realities of war that can become, tragically, so matter of fact when seen daily at the newspaper stands and shown on the news channels.

## Notes

1. A shorter version of this chapter, "Lost Bodies/Lost Souls: *Night of the Living Dead* as MIA Narrative," appears in the Film and History conference proceedings, *Film and History: The War Film* (2004), CD-ROM.

2. Post-Traumatic Stress Disorder (PTSD) entered the *Diagnostic Statistical Manual of the American Psychiatric Association DSM-III* (Washington, D.C.) in 1980 as a reasoned nosology of symptoms that may be experienced by those who had witnessed a traumatic event outside of the experiences of everyday life.

3. Although referred to as ghouls in *NLD*, I take the notion of the undead to be inclusively zombie.

4. See Jeanette Basinger, *The World War II Combat Film: Anatomy of a Genre* (Middletown, CT: Wesleyan University Press, 2003).

5. See Karen Randell, "Masking the Horror of Trauma: The Hysterical Body of Lon Chaney," *Screen* 44, no. 2 (Summer 2003): 216–221.

6. See Cathy Caruth, *Unclaimed Experience: Trauma, Narrative and History* (London: John Hopkins University Press, 1995).

7. Thomas Elsaesser, "Postmodernism as Mourning Work," *Screen* 42, no. 2 (Summer 2001): 195.

8. R. H. W. Dillard, "*Night of the Living Dead*: It's not just a wind that's passing through," in Gregory A. Waller, ed., *Essays on the Modern American Horror Film* (Chicago: University of Illinois Press, 1987), 16.

9. Jane Caputi, "Films of the Nuclear Age," *Journal of Popular Television and Film* (Autumn 1998): 100–107.

10. Richard Dyer, "White," *Screen* 29, no. 4 (August 1988): 59–63.

11. Gregory A. Waller, ed., *American Horrors: Essays on the Modern American Horror Film* (Urbana: University of Illinois Press, 1987), 4.

12. Sumiko Higashi, "A Horror Film about the Vietnam Era," in *Hanoi to Hollywood: The Vietnam War in American Film*, ed. Linda Dittmar and Gene Michaud (New Brunswick, NJ: Rutgers University Press, 1990), 175–188.

13. Robin Wood, "The Return of the Repressed," *Film Comment* 14 (July-August 1978): 25–32.

14. Grateful thanks to the Newspaper Morgue at the Center for American History, the University of Texas at Austin. All newspaper clippings from the Veterans clipping file.

15. In 1996 there were still 2,143 American men listed as MIA. See Vernon E. Davis, *The Long Road Home: U. S. Prisoner of War Policy and Planning in Southeast Asia* (Washington, D.C.: Historical Office, Office of the Secretary of Defense, 2000), 7.

16. Cf. Waller, 16.

17. This is particular to the Vietnam War. In the First and Second World Wars the men were listed as Missing in Action, presumed dead. The presumption during the Vietnam War was that they were alive (captured).

18. Cf. Wood, "The Return of the Repressed," 25–32.

19. Sigmund Freud, "Thoughts on War and Death" (1915), in James Strachey, ed., *The Standard Edition of The Complete Works of Sigmund Freud, Vol. XIV* (London: Hogarth Press, 1953), 242.

20. Cf. Waller, 283.

21. Trudi Tate, *Modernism, History and the First World War* (Manchester, UK: Manchester University Press, 1998), 13.

22. Edwin Ash, *The Problem of Nervous Breakdown* (London: Mills and Boon, 1919), quoted in Tate, 13.

23. Cf. Tate, 11.

24. The original was produced in black and white and later prints (post 1973) were colored. My analysis here concerns the original version.

25. Cf. Higashi, 184.

26. *Interview* 1, no. 4 (1969), 23.

27. "*Night of the Living Dead*" review, *Variety*, October 16, 1968, 6.

28. John Russo, *The Complete* Night of the Living Dead *Handbook* (Pittsburg: Imagine, 1985), 37.

29. Paul Wells, *The Horror Genre from Beelzebub to Blair Witch* (London: Wallflower Press, 2000), 80.

30. Ralph Blumenthal, "'Syndrome' Found in Returned G.I.'s," *New York Times*, June 7, 1971.

31. Ibid.

32. Ibid.

33. Jon Nordheimer, "Postwar Shock Besets Ex-G.I.'s; Postwar Shock is Found to Beset Veterans Returning From the War in Vietnam," *New York Times*, August 21, 1972.

34. Robert J. Lifton, "A Re-Examination," *New York Times*, August 20, 1970.

35. Nordheimer.

36. Robin Wood, "Deathdream," in Jamie Russell ed., *Book of the Dead: The Complete History of Zombie Cinema* (Surrey, UK: FAB Press, 2005), 124.

37. Ibid.

38. Dana Adams Schmidt, "Pentagon Studying Coded Data Filed on Misdeeds of Veterans," *New York Times*, March 12, 1972.

39. Ibid.

40. Jamie Russell, *Book of the Dead: The Complete History of Zombie Cinema* (Surrey, UK: FAB Press, 2005), 73.

41. "Operation Enduring Freedom," *iCasualties*, accessed September 6, 2010, http://icasualties.org/oef/.

42. Ryan Jaroncyk, "After nearly a decade of war, PTSD is afflicting the U.S. military," *RAWA News*, accessed September 6, 2010, http://www.rawa.org/temp/runews/2010/10.

43. For a current take on the returning dead of war as social commentary, see Joe Dante's *Homecoming* (2005) which is part of the *Masters of Horror* TV series: episode 1.6 (IDT Entertainment).

# Shambling Towards Mount Improbable to Be Born: American Evolutionary Anxiety and the Hopeful Monsters of Matheson's *I Am Legend* and Romero's *Dead* Films

### SEAN MORELAND

> *And what rough beast, its hour come round at last, Slouches towards Bethlehem to be born?*
> — W.B. Yeats, "The Second Coming"

> *The extinction of old forms is the almost inevitable consequence of the production of new forms.*
> — Charles Darwin, *The Origin of Species*

> *I had come to the conclusion that there was nothing sacred about myself or about any human being, that we were all machines, doomed to collide and collide and collide....*
> — Kurt Vonnegut, *Breakfast of Champions*

> *They are us! The same animal, simply functioning less perfectly.*
> — Dr. Logan, observing the walking dead in *Day of the Dead*

> *Dead is the new alive!*
> — Dr. Ryan Maydan, during Ottawa's 2008 Zombie-Walk

It is an infection — a disease — that much seems to be clear, and if you catch it, it turns you into a merely material shell, devoid of purpose beyond an inextirpable appetite. It transforms you into, or reveals you as all along having been nothing *but*, "pure, motorized instinct," a "lumbering robot," driven not by some higher plan, but by totalitarian microscopic processes that behaviorally manifest as one basic, indivisible drive: consumption-reproduction.[1]

While the first quoted phrase above is taken from an un-named expert in Romero's

*Dawn of the Dead,* who is attempting to explain the walking dead to his traumatized TV audience, and the second is taken from Richard Dawkins' controversial 1976 bestselling piece of (un?)popular science, *The Selfish Gene,* both could equally apply to either the post–Romero conception of the zombie in popular fiction and film, or to the view of human existence that Darwinian evolution's detractors attribute to the "theory" they so ardently oppose. My argument is based, then, on a self-evident observation: there is a fairly extensive discursive overlap between the zombie *chez* Romero and the conception of the human being presented by certain proponents, and many critics, of Darwinian evolution. Consider, for example, the phrasing of what has become something of a "Creationist Manifesto" in the United States, the 1997 document *The Wedge*:

> Debunking the traditional conceptions of both God and man, thinkers such as Charles Darwin, Karl Marx, and Sigmund Freud portrayed humans not as moral and spiritual beings, but as animals or machines who inhabited a universe ruled by purely impersonal forces and whose behavior and very thoughts were dictated by the unbending forces of biology, chemistry, and environment. This materialistic conception of reality eventually infected virtually every area of our culture, from politics and economics to literature and art.[2]

*The Wedge*'s use of the word "infected" aptly captures the diseasing effects its proponents see in Darwinian evolution's reduction of humans to the status of "animals or machines"; they believe that this theory could lead to the destruction of civilization, the erasure of humanity, and the ultimate collapse of our ability to find meaning in life — in other words, to the creation of a world which closely resembles that depicted by the *Dead* films. In the words of Bruce Chapman, one of the architects of the Wedge strategy, a "world without design is a world without inherent meaning. In such a world, to quote Yeats, 'things fall apart; the center cannot hold.'"[3] As Chapman's invocation of Yeats's apocalyptic lyric emphasizes, Darwinian evolution, and scientific materialism in general, is inextricably linked to both philosophical nihilism and the inevitable loss of our collective humanity for proponents of the Wedge strategy. The Wedge strategy, however, is merely one of the more recent salvos in a conflict with a venerable historical pedigree, one which has been particularly prominent in twentieth-century American history.[4] As I hope to show, this is a conflict in which the zombie of popular fiction and film has, for half a century now, played a curiously central role. This scenario has had manifold consequences for the popular reception of Darwinian theories of human evolution, and has also informed the evolution of the zombie film. While the evolutionary war in America has been waging intermittently at least since the epochal Scopes trial of 1925, and the zombie has been a recurrent feature of horror cinema since *White Zombie* (1932), it is with Richard Matheson's 1954 novel *I Am Legend,* and Romero's *Dead* films[5] (Matheson's illegitimate, but genealogically undeniable cinematic descendents),[6] that these disparate cultural manifestations become indissolubly wed.

*The Wedge*'s emphasis on the "materialistic conception of reality" as a contagion reinforces the co-extensive space of the zombie and evolutionary theory in the American cultural imagination. This shared space also encompasses the link between the zombies of popular cinema and the p-zombies of analytic philosophy, as the latter represent a collection of formal arguments against a strictly materialist or physicalist conception of what constitutes a human being. Robert Kirk explains that p-zombies "are of course very different from those seen in horror films, which seem to derive from voodoo beliefs. The idea there is that corpses are caused by magic to perform tasks for the controllers. Zombies of that kind don't seem to raise any special philosophical problems: they belong to the same broad class as marionettes."[7] Kirk's differentiation of the p-zombie from the cinematic zombie is important to remember, despite his devaluation of the richness and complexity of the voodoo-driven zombie, and his failure to recognize that most modern cinematic zombies are not really derived from the voodoo variant. Indeed, the zombies of Romero's films and their many cinematic progeny differ notably from the voodoo-produced zombies of Haitian folklore[8] in that their origins are generally ambiguous and they are not controlled by the will of a domineering zombie master; within their diegetic contexts, these zombies serve no master but their own consumptive drives. Nevertheless, the zombies of the *Dead* films, and their numerous cinematic relatives, *have* been "put to work" in a certain sense, in that they have been subject to frequent expropriation for a wide variety of rhetorical and metaphoric functions outside their fictional contexts, giving new meaning to the phrase "zombie labor."

While proponents of the validity of p-zombie arguments are certainly not necessarily creationists (and neither, I suspect, is George Romero!), they do share a common desire to reject a strictly biological-materialist conception of human existence — one which is shared by religious scholar and Romero fan Kim Paffenroth, whose *Gospel of the Living Dead* (2006) situates Romero's films, and other exempla of the zombie apocalypse genre, in the context of visionary and apocalyptic[9] literature. Paffenroth claims that much of the importance of the *Dead* films stems from their ability to represent "theological ideas of human nature and human destiny."[10] Paffenroth's elucidation of the films' social and epistemological critiques is apt, as is his recognition that "Romero uses horror ... as it is used in the tradition of American Gothic literature," in which "shocking violence and depravity are used to disorient and reorient the audience, disturbing them in order to make some unsettling point, usually a sociological, anthropological, or theological one."[11] His argument becomes less persuasive when he claims that, while the *Dead* films are critical of both scientific and religious institutions and perspectives, their "dismantling of both reason and faith is ultimately much more damning to reason than it is to faith,"[12] since they offer, especially in the case of *Day of the Dead*, "a depressing but altogether realistic indictment of science and rationality, showing not only that they cannot provide people with a new morality to replace that previously supplied by religion, but also that science will even devolve humanity altogether by undermining morality and deadening conscience."[13] In presenting my own reading of the films, I would like to address what I see as two major limitations of this argument.

First, Paffenroth's theological scaffolding distorts the films' merits as works of profound scepticism; as Robin Wood observed, their "occasional religious references are always negative."[14] While the characters in each of the films suggest a variety of explanations for the animation of the dead, some of them religious, some of them (quasi-)scientific, and some of them patently absurd, the films consistently refuse to support any of these attempts at explanation, thus emphasizing the inadequacy of human knowledge, be it gleaned by empirical investigation or religious revelation (a point I will return to below). Second, Paffenroth's implicit dovetailing of p-zombies with the zombies of the *Dead* films as a way of buttressing his theological and anti-materialist reading of the films is, at times, forced. Consider his claim that "the monstrous zombies created by our imaginations, whether in a logician's thought experiment or a director's frame, may yet save us from our own misguided and arrogant urge to degrade and dehumanize ourselves into soulless machines."[15] The phrase "soulless machines," in particular, suggests the evolutionary debates, and echoes *The Wedge*'s accusation that scientific materialism reduces us to "animals or machines." The suggestion that Romero's zombies remind us that we are something more than merely soulless machines or animals effectively occludes the important challenge that the *Dead* films offer to Platonic/Christian/Cartesian notions of the human soul, a point to which I will return below.

Before exploring these issues by looking at them in the direct context of the *Dead* films, it is necessary to consider the descent these films have undergone from a vital ancestor. While many commentators on Romero's *Dead* films have given a perfunctory nod to the fact that Matheson's *I Am Legend* was a major influence, none that I know of have articulated with any depth both the important continuities with and departures from Matheson's narrative. As the relationship between these texts is central to the co-extensive evolution of the zombie film and popular anxieties about evolution in America, I would like to consider some of its implications here.

With its evocation of horrors associated with the mutagenic effects of radioactive fallout and Cold-War political anxiety, *I Am Legend* is situated with other sci-fi-horror hybrids of the 1950s, including "creature features" such as *Them!* (1954) and paranoia narratives such as Jack Finney's *Invasion of the Body Snatchers* (1954). Isabel Pinedo has described the typical 1950s creature feature as "an amalgam of science-fiction and horror elements," and similarly, *I Am Legend* is a deliberate hybrid, which "combines science fiction's focus on the logically plausible (especially through technology) with horror's emphasis on fear, loathing and violence."[16] According to Pinedo, both "creature feature" and the "Golden Age" horror classics, including *Dracula* (1931) and *Frankenstein* (1931), share a basic narrative structure:

> The film opens with the violent disruption of the normative order by a monster, which can take the form of a supernatural or alien invader, a mad scientist, or a deviant transformation from within. The narrative revolves around the monster's rampage and people's ineffectual attempts to resist it. In the end, male military or scientific experts successfully employ violence and/or knowledge to defeat the monster and restore the normative order.[17]

The brilliance of Matheson's novel lies in its subversion of these conventions, as it gradually collapses the "creature feature" formulae it initially seems to establish. It does so in part by revealing that the "monster" responsible for the "violent disruption" has been from the opening scenes of the novel not the vampires, but Neville himself. Neville is now an archaic, vestigial deviant[18] from an otherwise dead race, both an "alien invader" and a "mad scientist." He is responsible for the deaths of innumerable members of a new society that he himself could not, until his final hours, have imagined. The "normative order" is restored not by the destruction of the vampires, whom Neville only belatedly realizes are no longer the "minority" they once were, but by the destruction of the male "scientific expert" who threatens their now-normative way of life.

Mid-20th–century evolutionary theory is a major springboard for Matheson's novel, which was published at the tail end of the consolidation of evolutionary thought known as the modern synthesis.[19] The novel interweaves notions of biological evolution with popular American fears about racial integration and political revolution. Echoing the "last man" fiction popular in the nineteenth century,[20] it portrays the sole surviving member of *homo sapiens* as he bears witness to the wholesale metamorphosis of the rest of humanity into *homo vampiris*. As it concerns an event of speciation occurring from a radical macromutation in a single generation, *I Am Legend* also appears to be informed by Richard Goldschmidt's concept of saltation, often called the "Hopeful Monster" theory, which was disseminated by his book *The Material Basis for Evolution* (1940). The theory derived in part from Goldschmidt's attempt to explain the perceived lack of "transitional forms" in the fossil records (something that generations of creationists have stridently, and often speciously, declaimed). Goldschmidt's largely discredited theory, something of an ancestral influence on Stephen Jay Gould's concept of punctuated equilibria,[21] runs counter to the dominant view, then as now, that evolution by natural selection operates by exceedingly gradual changes over a tremendous span of time. Instead, Goldschmidt hypothesized that speciation might occur in the course of a few generations, through the rapid spread of a radical mutation within a population. Matheson's (conscious or otherwise) adoption of this concept allows for the association the novel makes between biological mutation and social revolution; the "hopeful monster" theory is linked by *I Am Legend* to fears about a Communist revolution on American soil.[22]

Through Neville's investigations, the reader discovers that it is the radiation-induced mutation of a bacterial contagion (dubbed *vampiris* by Neville) which creates this nightmarish new world order. Only much later, and after having killed hundreds of the infected "vampires," does Neville realize that the relationship between the bacteria and its hosts has continued to evolve into a more stable, symbiotic state, and it is this belated recognition that renders the novel's conclusion so unforgettably shocking. Not only does Neville finally realize that many of the infected are still very much sentient, rational beings, however transformed by *vampiris,* but he is also forced to face the fact that it is he who is the Dracula-like monster in this new world. As he has been living locked in his suburban castle, an image of the *ancien regime* he represents, the vampires have continued to adapt, to change, and thus, in a sense, to live, whereas he, still clinging to a non-existent world of property and privilege, has not.

Matheson's collapse of the traditional distinction between protagonist and monster, norm and aberration, thus not only involves a substitution of the American middle class (Neville) for the Gothic aristocrat (Dracula), but also a transformation of the evolutionary anxieties that underlie Stoker's novel. While *Dracula* specifically links the vampire with Victorian notions of racial degeneration, *I Am Legend* inverts this relationship by insisting on Neville's atavism. While *Dracula* emphasizes the destruction of the diseased by the healthy and the retrogressive by the progressive, *I Am Legend* effectively uncouples the popular association between biological evolution and social progress, an uncoupling which is duplicated repeatedly within the *Dead* films. This is particularly noteworthy since it challenges a deeply-rooted and deleterious habit of thought that has long plagued evolutionary theory; as Gould observes, "[t]he attempt to validate human superiority by the doctrine of progress identifies the heaviest burden imposed by Western culture upon evolutionary views of all stripes."[23] Both *I Am Legend* and the *Dead* films, then, are revolutionary insofar as their hopeful monsters annihilate this cherished notion (along with Western civilization itself).

Writing of Don Siegel's 1956 adaptation of *Invasion of the Body Snatchers* in his nonfictional *Danse Macabre* (1981), Stephen King observes, "Over the years, *Invasion of the Body Snatchers* has given a lot of people the creeps, and all sorts of high-flown ideas have been imputed to Siegel's film version. It was seen as an anti–McCarthy film until someone pointed out the fact that Don Siegel's political views could hardly be called leftish. Then people began seeing it as a 'Better Dead than Red' picture."[24] The same sort of allegorical political interpretations have been applied to Matheson's novel, and indeed, while Matheson has denied any deliberate political intention, many phrases in the novel seem to suggest affinities between the vampires and the Red Spectre (the new society is "revolutionary," as well as apparently collectivist). In addition, it is hard to miss the suggestions of racial anxiety embodied by the vampires, who Neville repeatedly refers to as "black bastards"). King goes on to link the paranoiac undercurrent that keeps *Invasion*'s "creep factor" alive with his childhood memory of watching *Earth Vs. The Flying Saucers* in a neighborhood cinema one day in 1957, when the theatre manager announced that the Russians had launched Sputnik, the first satellite, into orbit. It was a revelation King describes as productive of "terror — what Hunter Thompson calls 'fear and loathing,'" which "often arises from a pervasive sense of disestablishment; that things are in the unmaking."[25]

The national anxiety generated by the momentary triumph of the Russian space program had a number of consequences in the American cultural imagination aside from helping to launch the career of the twentieth century's most popular horror author. As Foster et al. explain, "The Soviet launching of the Sputnik satellite in 1957 and the space and nuclear arms races eventually resulted in the perception of an educational crisis in the United States and led to a refurbishing of science education in particular. This included the renewed teaching of evolutionary history."[26] Public opposition to the teaching of evolution continued to wane, and finally, in 1968, the Supreme Court decision *Epperson vs. Arkansas* overturned the anti-evolution laws established in the Scopes era on First Amendment grounds.[27]

Thus, 1968 was an auspicious year for the birth of modern cinema's zombies, as the ghouls of *Night of the Living Dead* would come to be called, since they would eventually become one of the most important images informing the "evolutionary wars" in America. By the late 1980s, a second wave of attempts to pass anti-evolutionary laws at the level of state legislature began to occur with the rise of the "intelligent design" movement in response to the 1987 U.S. Supreme Court case, *Edwards vs. Aguillard*. As many of the urgently impassioned outcries against the "atheistic" tendencies of Darwinism testify, the sense of terrified disestablishment that King describes as his childhood response to Sputnik could just as readily describe the emotional response of millions of American Christians to the teaching of evolution. For them, this "theory" is primarily an "unmaking" of the Biblical creationism central to their religious ideology.

But to return for a moment to 1968 and the birth of the modern zombie, I can't help but see an allusion to the national spasm of anxious disestablishment occasioned by Sputnik in John Russo and George A. Romero's last-minute decision to include mention of a returning space probe as a potential explanation for the apocalypse of *Night*. As Tony Williams explains, "Not in the original script is the vague 'explanation' this sequence gives to the zombie phenomenon—high level radiation from the disintegration of a returning Venus probe." Williams goes on to quote *Night*'s co-writer, John Russo, who explains that the "idea was thrown in simply because the filmmakers felt it 'safer' to have some explanation," and Romero, who agrees that "'it has nothing to do with anything,'"[28] and yet the explanation is clearly resonant in light of King's point about the effects of Sputnik on the national psyche.

Nevertheless, Romero's refusal to privilege this, or any other diegetically presented explanation for the living dead, is central to the unique significance of the *Dead* films and the role they have inadvertently played in America's evolutionary wars. Pinedo writes that

> [i]n postmodern horror, causal logic collapses even when the narrative entertains a logical explanation for the chaos. Thus, a newscaster speculates that a Venus probe that carried high-level radiation back to Earth may be responsible for the dead rising from their graves. What locates this "scientific" account in the realm of horror rather than science fiction is the insignificant role rational discourse plays in the film and the film's sustained focus on the mutilation of the body.[29]

Thus, that the "flesh eating ghouls" kill for "no apparent reason" finally trumps the vaporous rumor of a cause located in radiation from a space probe, but this explanation still serves to contextualize the contemporary American anxieties the film addresses, specifically those concerning space exploration a decade after the traumatic blow struck against American national identity by Sputnik and less than a year before the historic moon landing. As Sarah Lauro and Karen Embry explain, the "zombie is not purely an expression of the pressing social concerns of the historical moment in which it appears (be it colonization, slavery, or capitalist servitude), but, rather, it is given structure by these historical events."[30]

*Night*'s specious causal allusion is one of the many devices the *Dead* films use to loosely connect experimental science to the collapse of civilization. It is a connection drawn from

Matheson's novel, and also less ambiguously exploited by derivative apocalyptic films such as *Return of the Living Dead* (1985, experimental toxic gas), *28 Days Later* (2002, genetically altered virus) and, of course, the most recent adaptation of *I Am Legend* (2007, ditto). The provision of only a tenuous, speculative explanation for *Night's* occurrences remains a hallmark of the entire *Dead* franchise, and is central to its importance. The walking dead of Romero's films remain an over-determined yet irreducible black box, and it is precisely such causal aporia that lead Pinedo to claim that these films confront "us with the necessity for an epistemology of uncertainty: we only know that we do not know."[31] While Paffenroth aptly emphasizes the challenge the films present to instrumental rationality, suggesting that they employ a kind of negative theology to point toward a higher, unknowable power by insisting on the inadequacy of human reason, he also largely seems to miss the point of their deliberate indeterminacy when he writes that

> in *Night of the Living Dead*, it was speculated that the horrible rising of the zombies was the result of human science gone awry, through radiation brought back to earth from a space probe, while in *Dawn of the Dead*, this "scientific" explanation was abandoned for a theological one — judgment from an angry God on a sinful humanity. *Day of the Dead* rather brilliantly combines these two explanations: scientific hubris and encroachment on the prerogatives of an inscrutable and jealous God are precisely what brought down the divine judgment on a proud, sinful humanity.[32]

While each of these attributions corresponds with statements made by characters in the films, there is simply no good reason to take the theological explanations any more seriously than *Night's* Venusian space probe. These character-driven speculations serve to situate the films in terms of ever-shifting American cultural anxieties, including those about the ethical limits of scientific experimentation and the consequences of human evolution, but do nothing to dispense with the epistemological uncertainty (I am tempted to say agnosticism) which is the backdrop of the entire series.

Yet this is only one of the evolutionary threads interwoven with the *Dead* films. With *Dawn*, Romero would return to the outline sketched in "Anubis," his "rip-off" of *I Am Legend*, but he would also radically revise the tone and visual style employed in presenting his ever-evolving concept of the living dead. While *Dawn* is equally pessimistic and cynical about the prospects of humanity and Western civilization, it is also a good deal funnier than the first film, and its humor arises at least in part from its willingness to both increasingly humanize and metaphorize its zombies. Romero has stated that "[w]hat happened to me on *Dawn of the Dead*, I think, was that I tried to make sure the double-entendre things, the things that might have social significance or be socially satirical, were couched in obvious jokes. I was afraid of giving a speech, so to speak."[33] This deliberate decision to adopt a more comic register led to a stylistic departure from both the earlier film and Matheson's novel, which itself owes a great deal to the influence of Kurt Vonnegut, one of Romero's favorite writers.[34] In particular, the satiric/speculative fictional fusion that characterizes *Breakfast of Champions* (1973) also seems writ large in *Dawn*, with its vituperative treatment of capitalist greed, racial hatred, and the dependence on petroleum fuels, but also in its final celebration of the possibility of forming new social groups and interpersonal connections (as Fran and Peter's co-operative survival suggests). This register is painfully absent from *Night's* entirely negative symphony, wherein human connection leads invariably to violent death (for an excellent elaboration of this point, see Dillard's classic essay).[35]

Vonnegut's *Breakfast of Champions* is roughly contemporary with the first deployments of p-zombie arguments by Thomas Kirk and Robert Nagel and shortly precedes the publication of E.O. Wilson's controversial *Sociobiology: The New Synthesis* (1975). Like the former, *Breakfast of Champions* explores scepticism regarding the sentience of other beings, announcing itself as stemming from the narrator's suspicion "that human beings are robots, are machines."[36] Its main character, Dwayne Hoover, becomes convinced by a Kilgore Trout tale that he is "surrounded by loving machines, hating machines, greedy machines, unselfish machines, brave machines, cowardly machines, truthful machines, lying machines, funny machines, solemn machines."[37] Like the latter, it is concerned with the recognition of humanity as one among many species of animal, and attempts to grapple with the consequences of this recognition for its frequently traumatized cast of characteristically Vonnegutian characters. Each of these intersections is also central to the emphatic and stylistic shift Romero makes with *Dawn.* In addition, the narrator's numerous descriptions of the novel's characters as clumsy, lumbering machines, rooted in his solipsistic scepticism about their reality, also anticipates Dawkins' controversial *The Selfish Gene,* which argued that a human body is "really a machine blindly programmed by its selfish genes."[38] Dawkins' book did much to feed the fires (or load the firearms) on both sides of the debate surrounding evolution, and it also serves to reinforce the power of Peter's recognition in *Dawn* that the zombies "are us."[39] This sentiment is echoed in *Day* by the hyper-rational materialist, Dr. Logan,[40] who insists that the zombies are "the same animal, functioning less perfectly," which echoes Dawkins' phrasing that "we, like all other animals, are machines created by our genes."[41]

Interestingly enough, Dawkins would begin his next book, *The Extended Phenotype* (1982), by addressing the explosive reactions *The Selfish Gene* elicited, and in doing so, would explicitly invoke the popular image of the zombie in explaining the misunderstanding many readers brought to the earlier book. He writes that "[s]ome people find it offensive to be called a robot. This is usually because they think that a robot has to be a jerky, moronic zombie with no fine control, no intelligence, and no flexibility."[42] Dawkins goes on to clarify his intended meaning by noting that a "robot is any mechanism, of unspecified complexity and intelligence, which is set up in advance to work towards fulfilling a particular task,"[43] and by emphasizing that "[f]rom being synonymous in the popular mind with a moronically undeviating, jerky-limbed zombie, 'robot' will one day become a byword for flexibility and rapid intelligence."[44]

With *Day of the Dead,* Romero similarly begins to challenge his audience's assumptions that the zombie itself must be "moronically undeviating," by introducing the first of his adaptive zombies, the quasi-domesticated and Stephen King-browsing lab-zombie Bub. As Paffenroth has noted, "Romero himself seems particularly interested in undoing the idea of unintelligent zombies, making their increasing intelligence the theme of his last two zombie movies, *Day of the Dead* and *Land of the Dead.*"[45] This dimension is largely absent from the numerous *Dead*-derived film franchises which spread epidemically in the wake of *Dawn*'s success and is one of the things that so clearly distinguishes Romero's treatment of the living dead from other closely related zombie and contagion films.[46] Many viewers have trouble accepting this element of Romero's vision, I suspect, because it deviates so radically both from cherished beliefs about human exceptionalism, and from the generic expectations and folkloric associations evoked by the word "zombie" itself.

As Shawn McIntosh explains, in "Haitian folklore, there are two types of zombies: spirit zombies (*zombi jardin*) and the type that has made its way into popular culture, the body raised from the dead (*zombi corps cadavre*)."[47] McIntosh goes on to characterize these types as a soul without a body, and a body without a soul, respectively. However, I would contend that it is precisely the dualistic Cartesian formula underlying this distinction that the later *Dead* films call into question. In particular, both Bub, the zombie test-subject of *Day,* and Big Daddy, the driven and tool-using revolutionary-zombie of *Land,* exhibit some degree of sentience and volitional behavior. Through these "zombies with souls," Romero's films further destabilize the rhetorical function of the zombie as a cadaverous caveat against materialism. Like Donna Haraway's simians and cyborgs, Romero's zombies interrogate the convenient distinction between human beings and "soul-less" animals and/or machines, dramatically re-presenting the element of Darwinian thought that has always been the most troubling to Platonists, creationists, and essentialists of all stripes. As Linda Williams explains,

> For Plato, while the human body has a necessary connectedness to the coarse materiality of the animal body, the purpose of human life was to break the chains of that connection in order to attain freedom. Over the long duration of the history of Christian ideas, this concept was essentially reconfigured and retained, but it was the Enlightenment project that offered the reconfiguration of this idea in the context of scientific instrumentalism that most closely approximates the way it recurs in our own time.[48]

In short, the *Dead* films do not simply offer an attack on scientific instrumentalism or materialism; their implied critique goes deeper, to the concept of the human soul itself, which is, as the authors of *The Wedge* so stridently insist, "one of the bedrock principles on which Western civilization was built." This metaphysical conceit, underlying both the Cartesian rational cogito and the Christian conception of humanity, is the greatest "idol of the tribe" to be scrutinized by Romero's cynical cinema, and finally devoured by the evolution of the *Dead*.

In light of this, it is not surprising that many viewers have criticized Romero's later films (especially *Land* and *Survival*) for their portrayal of the dead as slowly adapting to their posthumous state. Some feel that this development detracts from the horror of these antagonists. For example, Jeannette Catsoulis, in a review of *Survival* for the *New York Times*, denigrated the film for the lack of tactical scares provided by its characteristically shambling corpses, writing that "maybe we've become too accustomed to the zipping, hectic ghouls that terrorized films like '28 Days Later,' but Mr. Romero's lumbering corpses, arms outstretched in drunken supplication, no longer scare.... Even to the characters, this new batch of undead is more irritant than threat."

One could conclude from this that Romero's conception of the zombie has become obsolete, and that the social-cinematic equivalent of natural selection has ruled in favor of faster, nastier, and less ambiguous zombies, such as those in Boyle's *28 Days Later* (2004) or Snyder's adrenalized remake of *Dawn* (2004).[49] Nevertheless, I would like to emphasize that these re-visions of the zombie, like Catsoulis and other critics who turn to Romero's later *Dead* films expecting primarily startle-horror, are missing something far more interesting, and ultimately more horrifying, in Romero's representation of the walking dead. This is that the *horror* of Romero's films has, from *Night* onwards, resided not in the dead, both horrific and pathetic as they slowly come to terms with their ambulatory decrepitude and carnivorous drives, but with the living humans of the narrative, who, consistent with Neville of Matheson's novel, fail to effectively adapt to their radically transformed environment. Romero has been explicit about this interest in interviews. He recently stated that "I don't like these rage zombies or virus zombies. My stories have always been people stories, the zombies are an annoyance. It's all about people, how they address the situation, or fail to address it."[50] Here, then, is the most interesting paradox presented by Romero's filmic treatments of the living dead, and the dead-end living. While their interrogation of the relationship between life and death, human and non-human, make the *Dead* films quintessentially post-humanist,[51] Romero's vision, like that of his literary *confrère* Vonnegut, remains, resolutely, all-too-human.

The horror, the incisive irony, and the affective power of the *Dead* oeuvre have always inhered in the contrast between the pessimism of Romero's vision of humanity, and the combination of mindless appetite and almost childlike innocence that his zombies embody. This is amply reinforced by *Survival of the Dead*,[52] which features, among other zombie-accomplishments, a (comically incompetent) zombie plow-pusher[53] and a (comically adept) zombie equestrian.[54] Romero's emphasis on the adaptive possibilities of the dead in *Day* thus both initiates the trajectory that his subsequent films will continue to take, and brings *I Am Legend*'s presciently posthuman engagement with evolutionary theory full-circle in a way that none of the explicit adaptations of Matheson's novel[55] have done. This suggests that, despite the pessimism that characterizes Romero's films, his zombies have been, from the beginning, *hopeful* monsters, especially by comparison to the (hopeless?) human beings from whom they have emerged in their slow shamble toward the steep slopes of Mount Improbable to be (re)born. And one of the most salient consequences of Romero's continued interrogation of the absolute distinction between "us" (the living) and "them" (the living dead) is the vexing ambiguity it inevitably causes rhetorical appropriations of the zombie. As Robin Wood has asked, "What do the Living Dead represent? Our culture, what we used to think of as our civilization, human life itself in all its confusions and unsatisfactoriness? All of the above? When you try to pin it down, something always gets in the way, refuses to fit, resists the meanings we try to impose."[56] Like Dawkins' re-definition of the robot, Romero's ponderous re-visions of the dead, for whom "life goes on,"[57] gradually de-stabilize the rhetorical function of the zombie as an argument against materialism, evolution, capitalism, or any other fixed ideological reference point. In other words, Romero's zombies potently suggest that *Dead* is the new alive.

## Notes

1. As Lauro and Embry state, "The zombie's reproductive drive ... is either an unconscious urge or a mere side effect of its own hunger, for it is through its bite that the zombie reproduces itself. Therefore, the zombie cannot even really be said to have two separate functions—consumption and reproduction—for the zombie reproduces as it consumes." Sarah Lauro and Karen Embry, "A Zombie Manifesto: The Nonhuman Condition in the Era of Advanced Capitalism," *boundary 2* 35, no. 1 (2008): 99.

2. John Bellamy Foster, Brett Clark and Richard York, *Critique of Intelligent Design: Materialism versus Creationism from Antiquity to the Present* (New York: Monthly Review Press, 2008), 35.

3. Bruce Chapman, Postscript of *Mere Creation*, ed. William A. Dembski (Downer's Grove, IL: InterVarsity Press, 1998), 457–8.

4. For a broad historical summary of these debates, see Foster, Clark and York, *Critique of Intelligent Design*.

5. The series comprises, so far, *Night of the Living Dead* (1968), *Dawn of the Dead* (1978), *Day of the Dead* (1985), *Land of the Dead* (2005), *Diary of the Dead* (2007) and *Survival of the Dead* (2009).

6. Matheson has had little to say about *Night*'s merits as an unofficial adaptation, but he has recounted that he "met George Romero who held up his hands in mock defense and said, 'It didn't make any money!' I ran across his film on TV one night and thought, When did they make my novel into a film again? His series of films put the final stake into the idea of making my novel into a film." John David Scoleri, "Richard Matheson," *I Am Legend Archive*, 2008, accessed July 14, 2010, http://www.iamlegendarchive.com/matheson.html.

In an interview for *Cinefantastique Online*, Romero explains that *Night* and its sequels "grew out of a short story [entitled 'The Night of Anubis'] I had written, which was basically a rip-off of the Richard Matheson novel.... In the book and the [previous] films, the very first scene presents us with the last living human being already alone in a world of vampires. That's Matheson's jumping off point for what is basically a siege story. I used zombies instead of vampires; I always thought that zombies were a sort of blue collar, working class monsters that might show up in anybody's backyard. I also felt that, rather than opening with a *fait accompli*, it might be more interesting to observe the world during its collapse, to watch the disintegration of the old guard as its downfall is brought about. I ripped off the siege and the central idea, which I thought was so powerful—that this particular plague involved the entire planet."

Tony Williams adds that "Romero describes 'Anubis' as an allegory about what happens when an incoming revolutionary society—in this case, the mass return from the grave of the recently dead, whose sole purpose is to feast on the flesh and blood of the living—replaces an existing social order." *Knight of the Living Dead: The Films of George A. Romero* (London: Wallflower Press, 2003), 24.

7. Robert Kirk, *Zombies and Consciousness* (Oxford: Oxford University Press, 2005), 24.

8. This folklore was the basis for the earliest examples of zombie cinema, including *White Zombie* (1932) and its sequel, *Revolt of the Zombies* (1936), as well as *I Walked with a Zombie* (1943). For a discussion of the fundamental differences between these zombie-concepts see McIntosh (Shawn McIntosh, "The Evolution of the Zombie: The Monster that Keeps Coming Back," in *Zombie Culture: Autopsies of the Living Dead*, eds. Shawn McIntosh and Marc Leverette [Lanham, MD: Scarecrow Press, 2008], 1–17) and for a teasing out of some of the theoretical implications of these differences, see Lauro and Embry ("A Zombie Manifesto," *boundary 2* 35, no. 1 [2008]).

9. Paffenroth argues that many of these films can best be understood through "the original meaning of 'apocalyptic,' [since] they 'reveal' terrible truths about human nature, existence, and sin." Kim Paffenroth, *Gospel of the Living Dead: George Romero's Visions of Hell on Earth* (Waco: Baylor University Press, 2006).

While I am sceptical about the vaguely theological dimensions of his argument, I find Paffenroth's insistence on the ethical and epistemological questions Romero's films raise to be quite persuasive. In this respect, his claim for the ethical merits of Romero's films resembles Cynthia A. Freeland's assertion that horror films often "continue the traditions of Sophocles, Dante, Milton, [and] Shakespeare ... by offering fictive or symbolic representations of evil." *The Naked and the Undead: Evil and the Appeal of Horror* (Boulder: Westview Press, 2000), 2.

10. Paffenroth, *Gospel of the Living Dead*, 22.

11. Ibid., 2.

12. Ibid., 41.

13. Ibid., 83.

14. Robin Wood, "The American Nightmare: Horror in the 70s," in *Hollywood from Vietnam to Reagan and Beyond* (New York: Columbia University Press, 2003), 29.

15. Paffenroth, *Gospel of the Living Dead*, 11.

16. Isabel Cristina Pinedo, *Recreational Terror: Women and the Pleasures of Horror Film Viewing* (Albany: SUNY Press, 1997), 15.

17. Ibid.

18. Matheson has stated that "Neville was not a monster to me. He was trying to survive, no more. It was an irony that, in the end, he had become the legend, the feared one. I don't believe that the young woman who provided him with the poison regarded him as a monster, merely as a total anomaly in the new society." John David Scoleri, "Richard Matheson," *I Am Legend Archive*, 2008, accessed July 14, 2010, http://www.iamlegendarchive.com/matheson.html.

At issue here is what constitutes monstrosity. It is instructive to consider two opposing conceptions offered by influential theorists of horror. Noël Carroll claims that "the monsters of horror [must] breach the norms of ontological propriety," that is, they must be recognized as unnatural and even impossible by the human characters who inhabit the fictions in which they are found, and by extension, they must be recognized as unnatural/impossible by the reader. *Philosophy of Horror, or Paradoxes of the Heart* (New York: Routledge, 1990), 16.

By this definition, it is, of course, the vampires of Matheson's novel who are the monsters. In contrast, Robin Wood offers a less restrictive conception of monstrosity, one which can be as readily applied to Neville himself as to the hematophagous horde he faces. Wood argues that the monster is "protean, changing from period to period as society's basic fears" change, but that the monster is always that which is contrasted with, and threatens, the norm ("The American Nightmare," 71). As Neville himself slowly comes to realize, "I'm the abnormal one now. Normalcy was a majority concept" (Ibid., 169). The infected in Matheson's novel have become the status quo, making Neville the bogey that threatens the lifestyle of their now-normative nocturnal society. This re-conception of the monster is also central to the *Dead* films, particularly following the inaugural *Night*, as Romero repeatedly emphasizes the monstrousness of the human survivors, often portrayed as more bizarre and threatening than their zombie counterparts.

19. The term was coined by Julian Huxley in *Evolution: The Modern Synthesis* (1942) to describe the synthesis of various biological paradigms including genetics, cytology and paleontology, which had often relied on radically different terms and seemingly opposed conceptions during the early decades of the twentieth century. The synthesis led to a widespread consensus amongst working biologists regarding the basic principles of evolution. For a critical discussion of the historical importance of the modern synthesis, see the second chapter of Gould. Stephen Jay Gould, *The Structure of Evolutionary Theory* (Cambridge: Harvard University Press, 2002).

20. A small but influential literary genre most famously exemplified by Mary Shelley's *The Last Man* (1826).

21. While Eldredge and Gould first proposed the theory in 1972 (Niles Eldredge and Stephen Jay Gould, "Punctuated Equilibria: An Alternative to Phyletic Gradualism," in *Models of Paleobiology*, ed. T.J.M. Schopf [San Francisco: Freeman, Cooper, 1972], 82–115), Gould continued to revise the theory throughout the remainder of his career; it is recapitulated in *The Structure of Evolutionary Theory*.

22. Foster et al. write that the "unification of Darwinian and Marxian materialist views of historical change in the natural world is exemplified in Niles Eldridge and Stephen Jay Gould's argument that the evolutionary history of organisms is best characterized as 'punctuated equilibrium'—long periods of stasis, punctuated

with (geologically) brief periods of change" (Foster, Clark and York, *Critique of Intelligent Design*, 170–1). Gould's detractors often used his supposed Marxist influences in attempts to discredit the theory; Gould notes, "I did briefly discuss the congeniality of punctuational change and Marxist thought ... only to illustrate that all science, as historians know so well and scientists hate to admit, is socially embedded." *Structure of Evolutionary Theory*, 985.

23. Gould, *Structure of Evolutionary Theory*, 588.

24. Stephen King, *Danse Macabre* (New York: Berkeley Books, 1981), 6.

25. Ibid., 9.

26. Foster, Clark and York, *Critique of Intelligent Design*, 11. Perhaps it would be far-fetched to suggest that there is a didactic undertone in the novel about the importance of both instrumental reason and a good schooling in evolutionary biology, since, had Neville benefitted from this post–Sputnik educational program, he may have been better prepared for the grim situation of Matheson's novel.

27. See Gould, *Structure of Evolutionary Theory*, 981.

28. Tony Williams, *Knight of the Living Dead: The Films of George A. Romero* (London: Wallflower Press, 2003), 27.

29. Pinedo, *Recreational Terror*, 26.

30. Lauro and Embry, "A Zombie Manifesto," 101.

31. Pinedo, *Recreational Terror*, 28.

32. Paffenroth, *Gospel of the Living Dead*, 85.

33. Williams, *Knight*, 87.

34. George Romero states that "it's hard to pinpoint where any of the literary influences come from. It's probably a weird combination of [William] James, comic books, Kerouac, Keaton, and Vonnegut. Let's put Vonnegut in there!" Christine Romero and George Romero, interview by Tony Williams, *Quarterly Review of Films and Video* 18, no. 4 (2001): 399.

35. R.W.H. Dillard, "It's Not Just Like a Wind Passing Through," *Horror Films* (New York: Monarch Press, 1974).

36. Kurt Vonnegut, *Breakfast of Champions* (New York: Random House, 2006), 3.

37. Ibid., 261.

38. Richard Dawkins, *The Selfish Gene* (Oxford: Oxford University Press, 1976), 146.

39. I can't help but wonder if Dawkins was familiar with *I Am Legend*, for the novel sprung to my mind immediately upon reading the following in *The Selfish Gene*: "Vampires are great mythmakers. To devotees of Victorian Gothic they are dark forces that terrorize by night, sapping vital fluids, sacrificing an innocent life merely to gratify a thirst. Combine this with that other Victorian myth, nature red in tooth and claw, and aren't vampires the very incarnation of deepest fears about the world of the selfish gene?" (Dawkins, 233). Indeed they are!

40. Logan is not an entirely sympathetic character, and yet there is something about his enthusiasm for exploring the potential of the zombies, and his insistence (which echoes that of Peter from *Dawn*) on the unstable boundary between the living and the walking dead, that prevents him from being *merely* another stereotype of the mad scientist (although he certainly *is* that, as his nickname in the film suggests). Paffenroth writes that "[t]he figure of Logan, like his namesake Frankenstein ... is in fact able to rationalize everything he does in the name of science, expediency, or survival. It is a depressing but altogether realistic indictment of science and rationality" (*Gospel of the Living Dead*, 83). While I find the claim that this is a "realistic indictment of science and rationality" tendentious and strained, Paffenroth is certainly right in pointing out that the film features an anti-science or anti-rationalist undercurrent, one that has characterized much Gothic fiction since *Frankenstein* (1818) and a great deal of horror film since *The Cabinet of Dr. Caligari* (1922), and that is particularly pronounced in most zombie apocalyptic fictions.

41. Dawkins, *Selfish Gene*, 2.

42. Richard Dawkins, *Extended Phenotype* (Oxford: Oxford University Press, 1982), 281.

43. Ibid., 282.

44. Ibid., 16.

45. Paffenroth, *Gospel of the Living Dead*, 6.

46. It has, however, been explored by a number of parodic "zomcoms," most notably *Fido* (2006) and *Shaun of the Dead* (2004).

47. McIntosh, "The Evolution of the Zombie," 2.

48. Linda Williams, "Modernity and the *Other* Body: The Human Contract with Mute Animality," in *The Future of Flesh: A Cultural Survey of the Body*, ed. Zoe Detsi-Diamanti, Katrina Kitsi-Mitakou, and Effie Yiannopoulou (New York: Palgrave MacMillan, 2009), 235.

49. One notable difference between the first three *Dead* films and *Land*, *Diary* and *Survival* is that the latter three, and *Diary* in particular, involve witty, self-conscious commentary on their generic relatives. *Diary* offers a number of pointedly mocking comments on the quick-moving zombies of its competitors, as well as a hyperbolic deconstruction of the "found footage" device. This narrative staple of Gothic fiction since *The Castle of Otranto* (1764) was popularized in horror film following the sleeper success of *The Blair Witch Project* (1998).

50. Chris Eggertson, "BD Sits Down with Zombie Maestro George A. Romero!" *Bloody-Disgusting.com*, May 14, 2010, accessed August 24, 2010, http://www.bloody-disgusting.com/news/20221.

51. Foucault claimed that "at least since the seventeenth century what is called humanism has always been obliged to lean on certain conceptions of man borrowed from religion, science, or politics. Humanism serves to color and to justify the conceptions of man to which it is, after all, obliged to take recourse" Michel Foucault, "What is Enlightenment?" trans. Catherine Porter, in *A Foucault Reader*, ed. P. Rabinow (New York: Pantheon, 1984), 43–44. Because the *Dead* films call such justificatory conceptions into question, they can certainly be understood as post*humanist*. In light of their continued emphasis on groups of human survivors, whether they are truly post*human* is a more problematic question. For a critically incisive conception of the differences between these terms, see Cary Wolfe's *What is Posthumanism?* (Minneapolis: University of Minnesota Press, 2010).

52. As attested by the title, with its echo of Herbert Spencer's phrase, "Survival of the fittest," and its apt tagline, "Survival is not just for the living."

53. Which serves to allude, perhaps, back to *White Zombie*'s slave-laborers.

54. Which serves to allude, certainly, back to *Survival*'s Western ancestor, *The Big Country*.

55. With the arguable exception of the alternate conclusion of Lawrence's 2007 film.

56. Williams, *Knight*, 90.

57. Robin Wood, "Fresh Meat: *Diary of the Dead* may be the summation of George A. Romero's Zombie Cycle," *Film Comment* 44, no. 1 (January 2008): 28–31.

# Ztopia: Lessons in Post-Vital Politics in George Romero's Zombie Films

## Tyson E. Lewis

Thomas Jefferson once speculated whether or not rights (political recognition) extend to the dead. To John Cartwright, Jefferson wrote, "The Creator has made the earth for the living, not the dead. Rights and powers can only belong to persons, not to things, not to mere matter unendowed with will."[1] More often than not, commentators have emphasized how this quotation demonstrates Jefferson's adamant belief that each generation should be liberated from the chains of the past in order to reconstruct democracy anew. Thus, emphasis is placed on the temporal dimension of the present and its particular social and historical context for breathing new life into democratic practices. Writing to James Madison, Jefferson summarizes: "I set out on this ground which I suppose to be self-evident: *'That the earth belongs in usufruct to the living;'* that the dead have neither powers nor rights over it.... We seem not to have perceived that by the law of nature, one generation is to another as one independent nation to another."[2] Equally important here is not simply Jefferson's praise for political reformism but also the clear connection between democracy and the biology of life. Death becomes the limit of political thought, or, stated differently, politics extends only to the furthest edge of life. The terrain of politics is thus supported by a biological distinction between life (the present) and death (the past). In other words, political rights and the biological life of the body coincide without remainder. In circumscribing the field of politics to the question of life versus death, Jefferson enacts what Foucault would refer to as the founding gesture of "biopolitics"[3] as the governing of living populations.

What happens when the clear division between the living (people endowed with active wills) and the dead (mere things, mere matter) that founds Jefferson's notion of political existence is itself divided? What happens when life and death become indistinct, when the basic opposition is held in suspension? If Jefferson can, with perfect confidence, argue that rights do not extend to the deceased, then such confidence seems to waver in the face of certain paradoxical conditions which lie precariously between life and death. The coma patient is just one example of what Giorgio Agamben refers to as "bare life" or a life that is not simply dead or alive but rather renders these oppositions inoperative. In reference to the surprising case of Karen Quinlan — whose comatose body was kept alive for years using advanced medical technology — Agamben argues that her body "had, in fact, entered a zone of indetermination in which the words 'life' and 'death' had lost their meaning, and which, at least in this sense, is not unlike the space of exception inhabited by bare life."[4] Unlike Jefferson's equation between life and rights, the coma patient introduces a remainder that breaks apart the correlation between the surviving body and political recognition. It is the peculiar location of bare life as both inside and outside of the political community that interests Agamben and which seriously jeopardizes any attempt to locate rights strictly within the domain of the living. Certainly the extension of rights *within* the domain of life is a crucial site of political struggle. We can think here of animal rights activists who are attempting to shift the field of political recognition from anthropocentric *bios* (life of human beings in the public sphere), to natural life *zoe* (life belonging to all creatures), yet for Agamben, such political projects bypass a much more pressing and ambiguous problem: the rights of those who are *neither fully dead nor fully alive.*

It is my contention that the zombie inhabits the space of bare life, and that the zombie film is one attempt to gaze at the disturbing realm of bare life in order to examine its political implications. Rather than define the zombie as the living dead, I prefer the self-negating compound used by Marc Leverette "~~livingdead~~"[5] in order to highlight the dislocating location of the zombie as betwixt and between the dichotomous relations upon which Jefferson's foundational gesture grounds politics. It is in this hazy domain that we are forced to rethink the question of politics and its relation to life and death in order to invent a new post-vital definition of politics. In particular, George Romero's film *Land of the Dead* (2005) offers a radicalized version of a post-vital, post-subjective form of revolutionary agency that emerges from within the paradoxical zone between life and death. By comparing Romero's vision of zombie uprising with two other zombie films — Romero's *Night of the Living Dead* (1968) and the campy mockumentary *Rising Up: The Story of the Zombie Rights Movement* (2009) — I will explore the implications of a new coming community of zombies beyond the politics of bare life (the passive existence of bare life) or of liberal forms of representational politics (as viciously criticized in *Rising Up*).

In this sense, I will argue for a rehabilitation of the zombie as a figure of a coming politics. If some have argued that zombie is a sign of total global destruction at the hand of capitalist expropriation,[6] I suggest that the zombie is a more complex figure embodying forms of resistance as well. In this sense, if capitalism is monstrous then we must stay on the terrain of the monster in order to combat its force. As Michael Hardt and Antonio Negri write, "The new world of monsters is where humanity has to grasp its future."[7] In fact, Negri has written that his goal is to "reclaim the monster"[8] and fight against the underlying logic of vampiric capitalism from within the unformed and unruly flesh of the monstrous. Thus, the political clarion call of Hardt and Negri's book *Multitude* is best summarized in the following: "Today we need new giants and new monsters to put together nature and history, labor and politics, art and invention in order to demonstrate the new power that is being born in the multitude."[9] In other words, we need a new "postmodern bestiary"[10] of monsters in order to understand the dialectical figure of the monster as not simply apocalyptic but also as a revolutionary force of social and political transformation beyond the human and into the post-human, post-vital world. Nowhere is this project more urgent than in relation to the current fascination with the zombie.

## Bare Life and the Insult to Death

After a terrifying night of fending off zombie hordes, *Night of the Living Dead* ends on what at first appears to be a triumphant note of human survival. Redemption from zombie hell seems assured as groups of armed officers and civilians clean the countryside of the shambling zombies. But what truly causes a sigh of relief is not simply that "humans win" the struggle against the ghouls but that the binary between life and death is once again reinstated—a binary that is fundamental to the order of *communitas*. Yet this "happy ending" immediately deconstructs itself in several important ways. The aporia opened by the zombie cannot be closed by their mere eradication. Once opened, the strange zone of indistinction between life and death remains to haunt the victory of human might and ingenuity over and against the zombie hordes.

As Agamben argues, bare life is an insult that cannot be gazed upon without horror. In his book *Remnants of Auschwitz: The Witness and the Archive* (2002), Agamben argues that beyond the coma patient, the quintessential embodiment of bare life is the *Muselmann* who suffered in the Nazi extermination camp as "an indefinite being in whom not only humanity and non-humanity, but also vegetative existence and relation, physiology and ethics, medicine and politics, and life and death continuously pass through each other."[11] These living-dead or "mummy-men" are defined by "a loss of all will and consciousness."[12] They appear to lack that ability to speak or respond to command, and thus represent a state of life stripped to its bare survival. Agamben then makes a rather peculiar observation. In an English film shot in Bergen-Belsen of the thousands of naked Jewish cadavers left by the Nazis, the image of *Musselmanner* appear only once at the very end of the documentary. Agamben argues, "The same cameraman who had until then patiently lingered over naked bodies, over the terrible 'dolls' dismembered and stacked one on top of another, could not bear the sight of these half-living beings; he immediately began once again to show the cadavers."[13] In other words, the sight of *Musselmanner* was "unbearable to human eyes."[14] Bare life, betwixt and between life and death, forms a political limit case as well as the limit case for visualization as such. There is something truly obscene in the existence of the bearer of bare life which we cannot gaze upon, which we refuse to witness. It is this threshold where life cannot be fully separated from death—the human from the inhuman—that remains on the extreme edge of the politics of vision and our collective vision of politics.

The close of *Night of the Living Dead* offers relief from gazing upon the zombie as a bearer of bare life, as the obscene surplus outside the defining dichotomy of life and death. Ironically, the pyre of zombie bodies in the concluding frame seems less horrific than the zombies themselves, and thus Romero appears to pull away from bare life at the very moment of its full insurrection. Yet as much as Romero gives us relief by turning our gaze from the ~~livingdead~~ to the merely dead, this relief is instantly thrown back into a new level of anxiety that revolves around that question of the symbolic status of the dead body itself. Agamben writes, "What defines *Muselmanner* is not so much that their life is no longer life (this kind of degradation holds in a certain sense for all camp inhabitants and is not an entirely new experience) but, rather, that their death is not death. This—that the death of a human being can no longer be called death ... is the particular horror that the *Muselmann* brings to the camp and that the camp brings to the world."[15] Thus the "dignity offended in the camp is not that of life but rather of death."[16] As long as death cannot be referred to as death, then corpses cannot be referred to as corpses but merely as cadavers (nameless, faceless, meaningless bodies). The horror of the Nazi death camps is the "serial-production" of cadavers, i.e., "corpses without death."[17] Echoing the theme of the profanation of death, the trapped characters in *Night of the Living Dead* watch a televised public service announcement featuring Doctor Grimes who advises: "The bereaved will have to forego the dubious comforts that a funeral service will give. They are just dead flesh and dangerous." Zombies as bare life are mere materiality stripped of "death" as a socio-symbolic event that defines *a life* — they are truly profane. When death does not properly die then life cannot properly live — thus the strange exceptionality of the zombie whom we cannot mourn and who does not deserve dignity of a formal burial. Hence the strange numbness of audiences faced with images of mass graves — these bodies have been denied the dignity of death.

In the relentless killing of zombies in *Night of the Living Dead* but also in *Dawn of the Dead* and *Land of the Dead*, Romero depicts the serial production of corpses without death — or as one of the raiders in *Land of the Dead* says, zombie bodies are just "trash," a form of disposable waste. Yet in *Night of the Living Dead* the serial murder of zombies does not completely supply closure or a sense of heroic triumph. The hero of the film, Ben, is in the end mistaken for a zombie, shot, dragged with meat hooks, and callously added to the burning pyre of zombie cadavers. In this final scene, Ben's sudden murder indicates that all of us can become mere "corpses without death," that any of us can be killed without trial of murder, that all of us can be rendered bare life by a sovereign decision. Thus the pyre of cadavers offers a brief reinstatement of a dichotomy between life and death *and* a source of new horror — no one's death is safe. Stated differently, all can be killed with impunity or without punishment thus transforming the corpse into the cadaver and thereby desecrating death as a *human* event. In short, death (the corpse) becomes inseparable from ~~death~~ (the cadaver). If murder becomes indistinct from the "extermination" of zombies (as several characters in Romero's films argue) then a frightening indistinction between human liberation and genocide appears unsolvable. The "happy ending" of *Night of the Living Dead* becomes a potentially ominous sign of an even worse fate at the hands of white, gun-wielding men operating outside the law in a permanent state of emergency. As Kim Paffenroth argues,[18] the scenes of white, male mobs shooting zombies cannot be dissociated from lynch mobs, both of which engaged in ruthless killing above and beyond the law. Thus *Night of the Living Dead* ends not with hope but with the emergence of another truly terrifying nightmare this time at the hands of humans themselves. The ~~death~~ of Ben suggests that the very attempt to cleanse the community of the remnant of bare life that traversed its sacred boundaries results in an equally destructive return of violence against the community itself.

In this final moment when cadaver and corpse become indistinct and death folded back on the life of the community, Romero gives his audience a glimpse at what Agamben refers to as "thanatopolics"[19] or a politics that turns against life — a politics of genocide and mass extinctions found within the very heart of Foucault's notion of biopower. Thanatopolitics is not simply a politics of death, but is rather the politics that insults death by transforming the corpse into the cadaver. In other words, thanatopolitics is the serial-production of corpses without death according to a sovereign decision. And if, as Agamben argues, in current society, thanatopolitics and biopolitics have become increasingly indistinct, then so too have the places or spaces of the serial-production of cadavers expanded. If *Night of the Living Dead* begins in the graveyard — the location which Foucault once referred to as a "heterotopian"[20] space beyond the proper and improper distinctions of the law — then *Dawn of the Dead* (1978) reveals the full topological folding of the space of the graveyard into the everyday space of the shopping mall, blurring distinctions between life and death, between the ~~livingdead~~ zombie and the deadalive consumer. The zombie and the consumer become the two sides of the same coin — two faces of thanatopolitics. The ~~livingdead~~ open an aporia that replicates endlessly, producing a thantaogeography of a life without life (passive consumption) and death without death (the cadaver). Life in other words becomes indistinct from the deathless cadaver and death becomes indistinct from the lifeless shop-a-holic. A Jeffersonian vision of the political life becomes an utterly untenable thesis within this overarching aporia.

## Liberal Representative Politics and the Zombie

In his Derridean reading of zombie films, Marc Leverette cites Queer Nation LGBT activist Karl Knapper who stated, if "'queerness is about acknowledging and celebrating difference, and embracing what sets you apart...' then the zombie 'rejects a minoritizing logic of toleration or simple political interest-representation in favor of a more thorough resistance to regimes of the normal.'"[21] It would seem that this is precisely the problematic which the recent mockumentary *Rising Up: The Story of the Zombie Rights Movement* (2009) confronts head on. The film documents the fictitious rise of the National Allied Zombie Initiative (N.A.Z.I.) from its conception to its final demise. The basic premise of the film is that zombies are an oppressed minority that have been exploited by industry (used as everything from crash-test dummies to cosmetic test subjects) and are politically excluded. Rather than simply dead, the zombie poses a political problem for liberal democracies precisely because it exists in a state between life and death where Jeffersonian politics calls into question its own limits. Because zombies cannot speak for themselves, their cause is picked up and championed by other counter-culture fringe groups such as hippies and beatniks who protest the passing of the "Flurman Act" in the 1950s. This act gave license to kill zombies and regulate their lives thus legitimating killing without impunity—in other words, the act gave legal status to the permanent state of exception that defines the zombie. Likewise the fictional "Mitchum Declaration" argued that human rights did not extend to zombies because zombies could not make a claim to rights. In other words, their speechless groaning were not heard as containing a logos but rather were simply noise of pain/pleasure without attending attributes of thought, reason, or will. The voice of the ~~livingdead~~ was simply that: a voice, an inhuman *phone* that lacks an attending *logos*. As such, what *Rising Up* demonstrates is that *bios* (political life of biography) is not simply predicated on a separation of the living from the dead but also *logos* from *phone*. It is *logos* that provides the minimal criteria for announcing a wrong, for initiating a disagreement within the political sphere. If we cannot witness bare life without attending feelings of guilt or shame as Agamben argues, then we likewise cannot hear the cries of the ~~livingdead~~ as containing a post-vital political logic without throwing into jeopardy the structural binaries which maintain the identity of the community of political versus nonpolitical actors.

In the fictional "dark days" of the Flurman Act and the Mitchum Declaration, there emerged a zombie, Chocolate Chip, who could speak. Discovered during an infamous "zombie march" on Washington, D.C., this articulate zombie quickly became the "Rosa Parks" of the zombie rights movement, galvanizing popular interest around the plight of oppressed zombies. With national sentiments won, the zombie rights movement landed an important victory in "Z vs. Dakota" which was the first act to make it illegal to kill a zombie unless in self defense. Yet momentum for zombie rights suddenly plummeted when it was discovered that Chocolate Chip was in fact not a zombie at all but rather a mis-identified syphilitic patient. The 1970s thus returned to outright zombie opposition with citizens protesting against the few rights zombies won in the past decade.

In this absurd act of historical revisionism, *Rising Up* transforms the question of the zombie into the central political problem of liberal democracy. Rather than violent and dangerous monsters outside of the community, this film argues that zombies are yet another misunderstood and marginalized oppressed group who deserve political protection. In this liberal fantasy of inclusion, tolerance, and multicultural sensitivity to otherness, the zombie remains bare life, incapable of political action without the guidance of "open-minded" progressives who can act as spokespeople. Lobbying on behalf of the zombie, these progressives march for zombie rights and for zombie recognition. What I find most compelling in this film is not simply that it highlights the problem of defining rights in relation to life, but that it also demonstrates the failures of liberal democracy in the face of this problem. The liberal democratic system of rights and recognition seems incapable of responding to the existence of bare life without transforming into a farce. Without minimal recognition of a "human" linguistic supplement to bare life, the multicultural tolerance of liberal democracy reaches an aporia which it cannot cross. Thus tolerance is always locked within the framework of a presupposed logic of the same, what Jacques Rancière refers to as "consensus" politics, in which those who count are always already determined ahead of time. As the erasure of politics, consensus merely regulates the distribution of pre-defined and pre-given social roles. As Rancière argues: "the regime [of consensus] in which the parties are presupposed as already given, their community established and the count of their speech identical to their linguistic performance" presupposes "the disappearance of any gap between a party to a dispute and a part of society."[22] In this sense, consensus politics maintains divisions between who counts and who does not, whose voice is heard as pure noise and whose voice is heard as enunciating a political claim. The zombie links Rancière's critique of consensus with the problematic of biopolitics as a question concerning the division between life and death, and ultimately between death and ~~death~~. Within liberal democracy, tolerance is only tolerance for the same, and the framework of rights only extends to those who can be recognized as sharing certain minimal requirements (i.e., to those who can already be identified as belonging to the community ahead of time). In other words, the law cannot account for that which exists on its furthest periphery: the mute zombie. And because of this internally exiled (dis)location, the zombie itself becomes not simply a peripheral question, but a quintessential question that strikes at the very heart of the law.

## Land of the Dead: A New Topography of Revolution

If the zombies in *Rising Up* have no *logos* and no agency and are thus puppets of either the conservative right/industry (who use them as weapons in the cold war and subjects of product testing) or the liberal left (who use them to champion their own good intentions), then in Romero's *Land of the Dead,* the zombie gains an unprecedented level of agency to fight against the tyranny of oppression beyond the limits of liberal democracy and its internal negotiations. Rather than speak and be heard (*phone* transforming into *logos*), the zombie rebels in *Land of the Dead* usher in a post-vital, post-subjective, post-linguistic swarm politics that directly attacks the obscene foundation of the law itself.

As Natasha Patterson states, "The more I watch *Night* and *Dawn*, the more I find something quite exhilarating and, dare I say, empowering in the abolishment of home and consumer culture."[23] This revolutionary quality of the zombie to bring to a halt economic, political, and familial institutions hinges on the annihilation of the subject through the uncontrollable unleash of the post-vital body. In other words, desubjectification of the zombie creates a non-recognizable location for politics—a politics beyond the problematic of identity and recognition that defines multicultural liberalism. Thus Patterson is correct that her pleasure in watching the zombie revolution is predicated on an attending "self-annihilation" of the construction of "Woman" or even "Feminist."[24] In this sense, from the absolute aporia of zombie ~~livingdeath~~ we are able to locate an emergent politics. Between symbolic death of the subject and biological death of the organism exists a space of exception where ~~livingdeath~~ becomes a rebirth beyond birth — a post-vital birth that shifts the staging of politics beyond the mute survival of bare life or the inclusive politics of liberal democracies and outward toward a new, coming community.

In his discussion of Gille Deleuze's famous essay "Immanence: A Life..." (1995), Agamben highlights the centrality of thinking politics outside of consciousness and subjectivity — a politics of desubjectification. For Deleuze the two figures of this "postconscious" and "postsubjective" field of transcendentalism are the young child and, importantly for us, the character of Riderhood from Charles Dickens' *Our Mutual Friend* (1864–65). While on his deathbed, Riderhood, as a specific subject (a scoundrel who is loathed), is separated from the "spark of life" that resides in him. The impersonal life that emerges is, according to Agamben's summary, "neither in this world nor in the next, but between the two, in a kind of happy netherworld that it seems to leave only reluctantly."[25] If a "happy" impersonal life exists in surplus of the subject "Riderhood" (in spite of Riderhood as a particular individual character) then could we not argue that the zombie depicts a type of impersonal existence that is not simply to be feared but rather to be examined for its post-vital potentiality to redefine the parameters of political community? It would seem that this is the ultimate teleology of Romero's films.

In this sense, I have to disagree with the character Riley Denbo (Simon Baker) from *Land of the Dead* who says that zombies are "acting more human" or are "learning how to be us again." The zombies that inhabit Union Town in the opening of *Land of the Dead* are not simply remembering how to be human. The images of zombie lovers holding hands, zombie gas station attendants waiting for cars, or zombie musicians creating sounds with instruments are not depictions of zombies "pretending to be alive" as Riley speculates. Rather, they are playing with the suspended law of the human which divides the living from the dead. As Agamben argues, play opens a "new dimension of use"[26] that "is not limited to abolishing the form of separation in order to regain an uncontaminated use that lies either beyond or before it"[27] but is rather a use that activates through deactivation. The deactivation of the law of *communitas* by the zombie opens up a sphere of new use beyond the human community — a use that is no longer human and not yet post-human either. This is an uncanny use of the human for decisively post-human ends. In this sense, what *Land of the Dead* depicts is not the eternal return of the human but rather a potentiality within the ~~livingdead~~ for creative play or, the emergence of a post-vital resubjectification. Thus Riley's projections are not to be read as objective observations of the emergent zombie culture but rather as a form of wish fulfillment in which biological humans might die but human culture remains immortal and inevitable.

The ultimate moment of overturning hierarchies of living and dead is not simply a profanation of human culture/symbolic systems, but also of capitalist production. It is on this ultimate horizon that we can now locate Romero's own call for a "New World Order ... ruled by the living dead."[28] Even if the character Riley initially fights both the zombies and the capitalists, in the end, it is the zombie army that brings down the reign of capitalist law and exploitation. Rather than kill the zombie liberation army headed by the zombie character "Big Daddy," Riley pulls back, arguing, "No, they are just looking for a place to go ... just like us," thus initiating a radically different relationship between the living and the ~~livingdead~~ beyond thanatopolitics. In this sense, Riley's hopeful "world without fences" is a post-identity, post-vital, multi-racial motley crew — a multitude of the uncounted and excluded who lack a clear political *logos*. In surplus of any identifiable social location as this or that, and lacking any specific or articulate political platform, this coming community overcomes the dystopia of human subjectivity which, for Romero, is contaminated by a disease far worse than the pathogens which cause zombification: the disease of racism and the capitalist law of expropriation. This opens the space for a new emergent, post-vital politics against the sovereign division between the living and the dead — a great refusal to separate the two and thus ground community in a decision against bare life. Welcome to Ztopia.

In *Land of the Dead* the sovereign is cinematically embodied by the character of Kaufman (Dennis Hopper) who tyrannically rules over the chaos of the zombie world.[29] Existing above the law, Kaufman and the bearers of bare life hold an identical structural location within Romero's thanatogeography: both are the internally excluded supplement to the society of humans at "Fiddler's Green" — the nightmarish suburban/casino/fortification that forms the backdrop for much of the action in *Land of the Dead*. Kaufman as sovereign is granted the executive right to kill without impunity. He is the force of the ~~law~~, or the pure force that emerges when the law is suspended by the decision over and against life and death. Like the white militia at the end of *Night of the Living Dead* or the biker-mob in *Dawn of the Dead*, Kaufman epitomizes the obscene side of a sovereign decision to abandon life to direct and unmitigated violence. As Agamben summarizes, "the sovereign and *homo sacer* [the sacred bearer of bare life from Roman law] present two symmetrical figures that have the same structure and are correlative: the sovereign is the one with respect to whom all men are potentially *hominess sacri,* and *homo sacer* is the one with respect to whom all men act as sovereigns."[30] What is missed in *Rising Up* is this fundamental link between the zombie, the sovereign, and the force of ~~law~~. Zombie politics cannot be located within the law without appearing to be a farce, a comical charade. The relation between sovereign and zombie exists before and subsequently in excess of the social contract and is thus a violent, pre-linguistic, pre-subjective relation of direct force. The proper thanatogeography of zombie politics is in the direct relation to the obscene obverse of the law that founds the law yet exists in surplus of the law: the sovereign decision. In *Land of the Dead* the indistinction between zombie masses and the sovereign is heightened when the human character Cholo DeMora (John Leguizamo), recently transformed into a zombie, battles with Kaufman. The divine violence of the zombie (which breaks the law of *communitas*) and the mythical violence of Kaufman (which is the force of ~~law~~ over bare life) are held in suspension creating a threshold between law and force, nature and exception, to the point where the two become indistinguishable.

This is the messianic space of post-vital politics, the emergence of ztopia. For Agamben, messianic time is a time between the chronological time of *bios* (the recording of great events in the history of the *polis*) and the end of time (the apocalypse). Neither chronological or secular time, it is the time of the now, the time of action. This moment presents time as a remnant, wherein "the division of time is itself divided."[31] The messianic present is a creative time that exceeds chronological time by introducing future eternity as an internal surplus to the everyday and likewise bleeds the chronological as excess into the eternal. In other words, it is a zone of indistinction or undecidability that short-circuits definitive boundaries between the past, present, and the future. Hence, as Agamben states, "the messianic world is not another world, but the secular world itself, with a slight adjustment, a meager difference."[32] The messianic reveals an immanence between this world and the future world, and, in this sense, is not the apocalyptic end of time but rather the time that remains before the end of time.

The messianic time of revolution produces what Agamben refers to as a real "state of exception." In this state of exception, there is an indiscernability of the law in that the law ceases to operate in relation to an inside and an outside. The suspended law neither gives a commandment or a prohibition. Here Agamben's points to St. Paul's treatment of the relation between the Jew and the non–Jew in his Letter to the Romans. In the messianic moment, Paul argues that a third figure is produced that breaks down the division of the Jew and the non–Jew constituted by the law — a division within the division that renders it inoperative. Between the Jew and the non–Jew resides the Jew of the flesh and the Jew of the breath. For Agamben this division of the division means "the partition of the law (Jew/non–Jew), is no longer clear or exhaustive, for there will be some Jews who are not Jews, and some non–Jews who are not non–Jews."[33] The remnant is the non–non–Jew who cannot be fixed either within or outside the law, cannot be defined either as a Jew or a non–Jew. The law that separates is held in potentiality, giving itself back to itself, and thus potentially opening up a space for a radical rethinking of community beyond the logic of the sovereign ban that founds the law.

Applying Agamben's theory of the messianic to *Land of the Dead*, we could argue that this film is not at all a zombie apocalypse but rather a zombie messianic time of action — a revolutionary time of collective politics that challenges the last hierarchical divisions between the living and the dead. Note that the zombies here do not wait for representative elites to lobby for their rights or for the executive order from the sovereign but rather take matters into their own ~~livingdead~~ hands/teeth, bringing forth a radical redistribution of the city, a break with the consensus that divides the living and the dead. This is a space where the laws of racist oppression and capitalist expropriation are deactivated through a rupture with the fundamental sovereign decision that lies outside yet founds the law.

The zombie is an inscription of this dislocating location of a post-vital politics, opening the messianic time before the end of time (the strange and unnerving gap between the end of the *bios,* of the subjective "I," and the cession of biological life). Rather than apocalyptic as Paffenroth argues, Romero's films in the final instance reveal a messianic kernel. *Land of the Dead* is not an image of hell on earth but is rather a messianic beginning of a final revolution between the human and the post-human. The zombie is no longer the harbinger of the end of politics but rather the beginning of a new post-vital politics that exists before the end of time (the total end of the world) and the beginning of a new world (a new form of post-vital existence).

## Conclusion

At the beginning of his book *Homo Sacer: Sovereign Power and Bare Life,* Agamben ambiguously argues that bare life is a kind of "protagonist" whose very existence as the one "who may be killed and yet not sacrificed"[34] offers a new location for thinking politics. Romero's *Land of the Dead* seems to pick up Agamben's challenge to think through the post-vital politics of this uncanny protagonist — a protagonist who is neither human nor inhuman, neither living nor dead. The political demands of this protagonist remain largely empty without articulate positions or negotiating platforms. Rather, the emergent coalition between zombies and humans represents what Agamben would refer to as a "whatever singularity." "In this conception [of whatever singularity]," continues Agamben, "such-and-such being is reclaimed from its having this or that property, which identifies it as belonging to this or that set, to this or that class (the reds, the French, the Muslims [and, we might add "the living"]) — and it is reclaimed not for another class nor for the simple generic absence of any belonging, but for its being-*such,* for belonging itself."[35] Whatever existence is an unrepresentable community of singularities (a ztopic zone of desubjectification) that can no longer be clearly delineated according to oppositions such as friend vs. enemy, or living vs. dead. Rather it is a space of open play. In this sense, I disagree with Henry Giroux who has recently argued that the zombie represents nothing more than "a politics in which cadres of the unthinking and living dead promote civic catastrophes and harbor apocalyptic visions, focusing more on death than life."[36] Here Giroux sees the zombie as a representation of transnational-global capitalism as a voracious, unthinking, murderous monster. Certainly transnational-capitalism is a vampire, but if this is the case, then, as Marx said, capitalism produces its own gravediggers. Perhaps we can even go so far as to re-write this famous analogy and suggest that if capitalism is undead, then it produces not so much gravediggers as ~~livingdead~~ who rise from the grave of capitalism itself in the messianic light of a post-vital form of political revolution.

One of the most important images of the messianic moment when whatever divides the division separating bare life from the *bios* of the community is limbo. While originally conceived of as a punishment for unbaptized children, Agamben argues that this image of punishment as privation from God's law "turns into a natural joy"[37] beyond "perdition and salvation."[38] Perhaps "Land of the Zombies" is such a limbo, and perhaps we can read Romero's many zombie films as attempting to realize the latent potentiality of absolute punishment to transform into a type of joy beyond salvation. It is in the final moments when the zombies and the human workers break with the sovereign decision over and against life and death that a new political possibility rises that is not reducible to either the mass killing of bare life or the limited negotiations of liberal democracy but rather a radical eruption of a coming community. This is a politics that lacks an articulate *logos* and can only be heard in the monstrous groans of the zombie Big Daddy who is not so much a ghostly shell of human society as the infantile birth of a new post-vital potentiality.

## Notes

1. Thomas Jefferson, *The Writings of Thomas Jefferson, Memorial Edition*, vol. 16, ed. Andrew A. Lipscomb and Albert Ellery Bergh (Washington, D.C.: The Thomas Jefferson Memorial Association of the United States, 1903–04), 48.

2. Ibid., vol. 15, 392.

3. Michel Foucault, *The History of Sexuality: An Introduction: Volume One* (New York: Vintage Books, 1978).

4. Giorgio Agamben, *Homo Sacer: Sovereign Power and Bare Life* (Stanford: Stanford University Press, 1998), 164.

5. Marc Leverette, "The Funk of Forty Thousand Years; or, How the (Un)Dead Get Their Groove On," in *Zombie Culture: Autopsies of the Living Dead*, ed. Shawn McIntosh and Marc Leverette (Lanham, MD: Scarecrow Press, 2008), 185–212.

6. Henry Giroux, "Zombie Politics," *Mammon or Messiah Meta*, accessed June 19, 2010, http://caimbhri-ainmyrddin.blogspot.com/2010/03/henry-giroux-zombie-politics.html.

7. Michael Hardt and Antonio Negri, *Multitude: War and Democracy in the Age of Empire* (New York: Penguin, 2004), 196.

8. Cesare Casarino and Antonio Negri, *In Praise of the Common: A Conversation on Philosophy and Politics* (Minneapolis: University of Minnesota Press, 2008), 196.

9. Hardt and Negri, *Multitude*, 194.

10. Tyson Lewis and Richard Kahn, *Education Out of Bounds: Reimagining Cultural Studies for a Posthuman Age* (New York: Palgrave, 2010).

11. Giorgio Agamben, *Remnants of Auschwitz: The Witness and the Archive* (London: Zone, 2002), 48.

12. Ibid., 45.

13. Ibid., 51.

14. Ibid.

15. Ibid., 70.

16. Ibid.

17. Ibid., 72.

18. Kim Paffenroth, *Gospel of the Living Dead: George Romero's Visions of Hell on Earth* (Waco: Baylor University Press, 2006), 18, 38.

19. See Giorgio Agamben, *Homo Sacer: Sovereign Power and Bare Life* (Stanford: Stanford University Press, 1998).

20. Michel Foucault, "Of Other Spaces," *Diacritics* 16.1 (1986): 22–27.

21. Marc Leverette, "The Funk of Forty Thousand Years; or, How the (Un)Dead Get Their Grove On," in

*Zombie Culture: Autopsies of the Living Dead,* eds. Shawn McIntosh and Marc Leverette (Lanham, MD: Scarecrow Press, 2008), 188.

22. Jacques Rancière, *Disagreement: Politics and Philosophy* (Minneapolis: University of Minnesota Press, 1999), 102.

23. Natasha Patterson, "Cannibalizing Gender and Genre: A Feminist Re-Vision of George Romero's Zombie Films," in *Zombie Culture: Autopsies of the Living Dead,* eds. Shawn McIntosh and Marc Leverette (Lanham, MD: Scarecrow Press, 2008), 112.

24. Ibid.

25. Giorgio Agamben, *Potentialities: Collected Essays in Philosophy* (Stanford: Stanford University Press, 1999), 229.

26. Giorgio Agamben, *Profanations* (London: Zone Books, 2007), 76.

27. Ibid., 85.

28. Patterson, 109.

29. See also Simchi Cohen, "The Already Dead and the Dying," *JGCinema.org,* accessed June 19, 2010, http://www.jgcinema.com/single.php?sl=zombie-as-homo-sacer-romero.

30. Agamben, *Homo Sacer,* 84.

31. Giorgio Agamben, *The Time That Remains: A Commentary on the Letter to the Romans* (Stanford: Stanford University Press, 2005), 62.

32. Ibid., 69.

33. Ibid., 50.

34. Agamben, *Homo Sacer,* 8.

35. Giorgio Agamben, *The Coming Community* (Minneapolis: University of Minnesota Press, 1993), 1–2.

36. Giroux, "Zombie Politics."

37. Agamben, *Community,* 5.

38. Ibid., 6.

# Soft Murders: Motion Pictures and Living Death in *Diary of the Dead*

## RANDY LAIST

The undisputed godfather of contemporary zombie lore, George A. Romero, has always represented living death as a supremely adaptable metaphor for examining a broad palate of socio-political issues. Romero has manipulated the zombie figure as a vehicle for satire and commentary so successfully that Robin Wood famously described Romero's *Dead* movies as "the most uncompromising critique of contemporary America (and, by extension, Western capitalist society in general) that is possible within the terms and conditions of a 'popular entertainment' medium."[1] Neither alive nor dead, neither entirely ourselves nor entirely Other, neither human nor nonhuman, the zombie is particularly well-suited to emblematize certain social structures which have a similar phenomenological capacity to violate the border between subject and object, including race, capital, and technology. Romero has very deftly manipulated this pliability of the zombie image. *Night of the Living Dead* (1968) introduces the shuffling corpse as an emblem of Nixon's America, *Dawn of the Dead* (1979) turns its zombies into soulless consumers, *Day of the Dead* (1985) reorients the zombie narrative to attack the values and structure of the military, and *Land of the Dead* (2004) explicitly attacks capitalism itself. Being completely empty of any positive qualities, the zombie is a semantic device of an extremely plastic nature.

The fifth movie in the *Dead* series, *Diary of the Dead* (2007), contains some of the most explicit social commentary in all of Romero's movies. Indeed, one critique of the film might be the insistence with which it propounds—through voiceover narration, narrative content, and unsubtle parallels in dialogue and *mise-en-scène*—a reading of the film that equates zombieism with the proliferation of new media. The conceit of the film is that it is entirely composed of footage shot by a group of film students who happen to have a camera with them when the zombie apocalypse breaks out. The filmmaking itself becomes part of the story, and we are provided an opportunity to observe the zombie-movie cameraman become so absorbed by the carnage he films that he himself becomes complicit with the zombie attacks. Camera and gun are repeatedly described as two equivalent technological

101

means of responding to the zombie menace. The voiceover narration spoken by Debra, the omnipresent editor of the film we are watching, tends to provide critiques of the pre-apoc-alyptic environment of new media when the narrative logic suggests that she should be describing the post-apocalyptic situation of the zombie plague. *Diary*'s inescapable insin-uation is that the new media condition and the zombie apocalypse condition partake of the same essential structure, and so it is metaphorically appropriate, if technically unlikely, that the Internet stays up and running after the rest of society has collapsed.

"New media" provides a loose term for the techno-social phenomenon that *Diary* interrogates, but the college kids who compose the band of survivors at the center of the movie are not particularly preoccupied with web surfing, social networking, blogging, pirat-ing music, gaming, or many of the other activities which are included under the broad con-ceptual tent defined by "new media." The Internet is of interest to Romero and his characters in *Diary* principally as a platform for the dissemination and consumption of motion picture footage. The specific aspect of new media that fascinates Romero is the effect it has of turning everyone who owns a telephone into a cameraman with a global audience. The camera (rather than the keyboard) is the totemic object that underwrites Romero's metaphor in *Diary,* making the movie less of a commentary on new media per se and more definitively a parable about a viral contagion of filmmaking that is responsible for the current epidemic of living death. Furthermore, at the same time that *Diary* contends with the social effects of twenty-first century technologies, it is also the most backward-looking and self-conscious of all Romero's movies. It is as if the framework of new media leads Romero into a post-modern hall of mirrors in which cameras film cameras filming cameras, and when Romero holds a mirror up to himself, what he sees is not a self, but a shadowy figure with a box for a head and a lens for an eye, a cybernetic entity that is neither a living person nor an inan-imate object.

*Diary* takes us back to the beginning, and back before the beginning. Breaking away from the sequence of the previous four movies, which had followed a narrative of increasing intelligence and ascendency of the zombie horde, *Diary* "reboots" the franchise by taking place during a first outbreak of zombieism. If it weren't for all the twenty-first century gad-getry, *Diary*'s survivors could be right down the road from the farmhouse in which Ben and his companions took refuge in 1968. Indeed, at one point in *Diary,* the radio plays a clip from a news story broadcast in the original movie. But Romero also takes us back to before the beginning, establishing his characters as young filmmakers making a low-budget horror movie about people returning from the dead. In case we miss the parallel to Romero himself in 1968, the dialogue includes a self-referential sequence in which the filmmakers argue about the gait of zombies. It is official zombie legend that the original differences of opinion between Romero and his collaborator on *Night,* John Russo, resulted in the parallel evolution of two separate zombie worlds; one populated by Romero's signature zombies, which shuffle, and the other populated by a more dynamic style of revenants who have the ability to sprint for short distances.[2] The reference to this debate is more than just an in-joke; it signifies to the audience that *Diary* intends to visit the original scene of the crime, to pull back the curtain on the entire zombie movie paradigm to show us what we are watching when we watch zombie movies. Since *Night of the Living Dead,* we have all grown accustomed to what we can easily identify as the most prominent landmarks of the zombie movie landscape: guns, vehicles, abandoned buildings, and the undead themselves, all of which provide compelling starting points for deconstructing the zombie mythos. But what had previously been invisible yet omnipresent had been the movie camera itself. Throughout the *Dead* series, the zombie plague has been variously attributed to radiation from outer space or a virus, but *Diary* reveals that it is the movie camera that has always been ultimately responsible for bringing the zombies to life, or at least, to what simulacrum of life they manage to achieve. When Romero turns the zombie-movie maker's camera into the mirror, we recognize that the filmic quality of the zombie has always been part of its uncanny appeal.

Film itself, after all, achieves its magical effect through a paradoxical conflation of life and death. If the zombie conflates the existential values of life and death on a semantic level, film enacts the same maneuver in the experience of the filmgoer, who is regularly accustomed to seeing people who are long-since dead sing and dance on a silver screen, or to cheering on as heroic characters murder their enemies on a scale that would qualify as sociopathic atrocity in real life (i.e., if their victims were really human, instead of only appearing to be human). The filmic image, for all of its lifelike power, is trapped in an automated death-trance. The film stock on which *The Wizard of Oz* was originally shot may degrade, Dorothy's skin may appear to decompose, Judy Garland may age and die, and the American cultural context that gave life and meaning to Victor Fleming's movie may fall away into oblivion, but regardless of all of these signs of morbidity, Dorothy will relentlessly continue to skip down that yellow brick road. Romero is not the first cultural critic to discern the zombieism of the photographic image. The trope of living death is a leitmotif throughout much of the writing on film. Marshall McLuhan observes that "The camera tend[s] to turn people into things, and the photograph extends and multiplies the human image to the proportions of mass-produced merchandise."[3] In McLuhan's formulation, photography has the power to de-animate human beings as people and to reanimate them as an anonymous global plague of lifeless pseudo-people. Guy Debord defines the spectacle — a broad set of phenomena among which filmic images hold a privileged place — as "a concrete inversion of life, an autonomous movement of the nonliving."[4] Jean Baudrillard describes the camera lens as "a laser [that] comes to pierce lived reality in order to put it to death."[5] Roland Barthes examines "that rather terrible thing which is there in every photograph: the return of the dead."[6] André Bazin begins his famous essay, "The Ontology of the Photographic Image," by speculating that "at the origin of painting and sculpture lies a mummy complex."[7] In order to express the strange phenomenology of film, each of these writers needs to strain the definitions of life and death, bending them out of their existential separation and into an unnatural interactionism. Arguably the most famous writer on the phenomenology of filmic images, Susan Sontag, liberally employs the metaphor of living death throughout her commentary on photography. "One of the perennial successes of photography," she observes, "has been its strategy of turning living beings into things, things into living beings."[8]

Romero seems to allude deliberately to Sontag in his depictions of the parallelism between the camera and the gun. Sontag's influential book, *On Photography,* observes that "there is an aggression implicit in every use of the camera."[9] In a frequently quoted passage, she insists that "to photograph people is to violate them, by seeing them as they never see themselves, by having knowledge of them they can never have; it turns people into objects that can be symbolically possessed. Just as a camera is a sublimation of the gun, to photograph someone is a sublimated murder — a soft murder, appropriate to a sad, frightened time."[10] The camera is like a gun in that it is a weapon, but it is a very peculiar kind of gun, one that doesn't destroy its victims, but damns them to an inanimate immortality. This difference is what makes murder-by-camera a "soft" murder; incomplete, dishonest, evasive. The camera cannibalizes what it films, but (like a zombie) it does not devour what it feeds on, but *infects* its subject with the fate of existing in a new ontological register defined by the implosion of the values of life and death.

The filmed subject is not the only victim of the zombifying effects of the photographic event. Sontag was just as interested in the dehumanization of the photographer as in that of the photographed subject. Sontag could be describing the plot of *Diary of the Dead* in her description of the attitude of the war photographer: "While real people are out there killing themselves or other real people, the photographer stays behind his or her camera, creating a tiny element of another world: the imageworld that bids to outlast us all."[11] In Sontag's description, the person with the camera is cut off from the class of "real people," caught up in their existential struggles of killing and dying. The camera operator is already a part of that zombie-world that the camera is responsible for bringing into being. One of the media montages that punctuate *Diary* with extra-narrative commentary juxtaposes a news report that "there are now more than 200 million video cameras in people's hands worldwide" with Debra's haunted voiceover perception that "Jason was compelled" to film the grisly events around him, as if he were in the grip of a mechanical will that is only residually human. The world of *Diary* is one in which there are fewer and fewer "real people" as the dehumanized perspective of the camera operator becomes more commonplace and habitual. Finally, in addition to the style of zombieism which afflicts the subject of photography and the operator of the camera, both Sontag and Romero suggest that the consumption of filmic images infects an audience with a disturbingly zombie-like point of view. Sontag suggests that "living with the photographed images of suffering ... does not necessarily strengthen conscience and the ability to be compassionate. It can also corrupt them. Once one has seen such images, one has started down the road of seeing more — and more. Images transfix. Images anesthetize."[12] If the camera operator is separated from the domain of "real people" by a relationship to lived experience that is exclusively scopic, the audience looking, as it were, through the camera operator's eyes, participates in this disembodied conceptual posture at an even greater remove from the originary event than the camera operator. Debra's voiceover comments that "it's strange how looking at things through a lens, a glass, rose-colored or shaded black, you become immune. You're supposed to be affected, but you're not." Transfixed and anesthetized, seduced and desensitized, infected and immunized, the audience of horrific images experiences a perverse admixture of erotic and thanatoid sensations.

As the most self-reflexive of his movies, *Diary of the Dead* is Romero's most personal and most penetrating interrogation into the nature of the zombie metaphor. Romero shows us a world in which zombie, filmmaker, and audience collaborate together in the mutual project of cannibalizing living subjects in order to turn them into the living dead. As a visual representation, the zombie personifies the living death of the filmic image. As a filmmaker, the zombie movie cameraman becomes a participant in the conversion of living subjects into living-dead ghouls. As a viewer, the zombie movie filmgoer experiences both the vicarious zombieism of sympathizing with the events on the screen and the immediate zombieism that creeps up from within as a result of his participation in a videotaped mass-culture defined by moving pictures; inanimate things brought to post-biological life, living subjects brought to an animated variety of quasi-existence. The zombie is the natural mascot for an Internet-facilitated culture of consumer-generated video content in which everyone is always simultaneously subject, filmmaker, and audience. *Diary of the Dead* offers one explanation for the boom in zombies' popularity at the beginning of the twenty-first century, a time during which everyone has becomes intimately involved in every stage of the phenomenon of cinematic zombification and in which Sontag's soft murder is being committed constantly, in every direction, spreading virally in an epidemic of insatiable voyeuristic cannibalism.

Each of these stages of filmic zombieism is on display in a sequence that acts as a kind of prologue and prospectus to the rest of *Diary*. The scene purports to be raw footage from a television news camera that records the first major incident in the zombie outbreak.

Debra's voiceover narration tells us that the cameraman who filmed this footage and who is the first person we see in the movie uploaded the footage onto the Internet out of a desire to "tell the truth" about what happened. But "the truth" that the footage reveals is only incidentally about the historical facts of the incident. The much more prominent "truth" on display is that the camera plays a central role in a spectacle of dehumanization that was well underway before the zombies ever came along to flesh out the metaphor. The cameraman is on a routine assignment to film a typical incident of familial murder-suicide in the slums of Pittsburg. The cameraman waves away an ambulance that threatens to block his shot, demonstrating that he is not particularly interested in assuring the well-being of the victims. The overheard conversations of nearby police echo the cameraman's emotional distance from the scene he is recording. "Who knows his name? Who cares? He's got no ID, no papers." Like a zombie, this immigrant family is nameless and without unique human qualities. The police are only giving voice to the work the cameraman is doing of substituting a speechless image for a human being. When the dead family springs back into life to attack the callous EMTs, law officers, and television reporters who have gathered like vultures to cannibalize their deaths, it represents a stark poetic justice. What had previously been ignored in the telling of the story, the dead people, as well as death itself, returns with a vengeance, disrupting the structure designed to conceal their deaths behind a screen of bureaucracy, documentation, and regimentation, a process in which the camera plays a crucial role. Moreover, the dead people return as the anonymous, dehumanized specters that the onlookers had perceived them to be. The scene as a whole illustrates the symbolic logic according to which zombies are a kind of product of the filmic gaze.

But in this scene, it is not only the anonymous dead immigrants who become zombified. In a motif that the rest of the movie will continue to explore, the cameraman and audience also become seduced into a variety of living death. In his banter with the reporter, the cameraman makes it very clear that they are not here out of any emotional connection to the incident they are documenting, they are just in it "for the paycheck," and if they weren't here at this murder-suicide, they'd be off at some other equivalent scene of carnage. Their interest in the deaths of the nameless immigrants is motivated entirely by the mechanical imperatives of a capitalist economy. We are shocked by the cameraman and reporter's indifference to the human tragedy, but then we are even more shocked when the actual segment begins and the reporter mouths the tragic story with all of the clichéd expressions, both verbal and facial, that we are so used to hearing on the local news all of the time. The reporter herself is a quasi-zombie figure who exists exclusively to inhabit the role of a personified camera, able to turn from one scene to another without any emotional continuity or subjective perspective, devoid of any personal thoughts and feelings. The camera's way of showing concern is only a different disguise through which it expresses its ghoulish curiosity. When the corpses on the gurney begin to flinch and lurch unexpectedly, the reporter's first response is annoyance. "Aren't they supposed to be dead?" Death gets ratings (and YouTube hits), so the cameraman's aesthetics include a ghoulish preference for death over life. The cameraman, and the global media enterprise of which he is the footsoldier, feeds on death. As the zombies run amuck, the cameraman continues to film. Although we do not see the face of the cameraman, we are immersed in his camerawork, through his zooms and pans, which constitute the language of his response. Throughout the scene, we can perceive that his most controlling emotion is the desire to capture as much of the action as he can on film. It is only after the reporter is killed by zombies that the cameraman comes out from behind the camera to express anything like pity or despair. And even after the cameraman escapes from the filmic trance, the camera itself continues to look on coldly with its own inhuman gaze, and so do we, the audience.

Had it not been for the zombie outbreak, this news report would have been only one of an infinite series of similar images of death that compose the humdrum background of the contemporary mediascape. But the audience of this segment gets more than it bargains for. Against the quotidian dehumanization the news media bring to bear on social reality, the zombie shocks us into a violent understanding of what a horrific thing dehumanization is—how brutal, mindless, and contagious—even as it tantalizes our own voyeuristic appetite for horrific scenes of dehumanization, arousing the latent zombieism of the viewer. This footage continues to live on through the Internet; we see it playing in the background computer at two points during the movie. These dead people keep coming back to life every time the footage is played; it is our appetite for gore that sustains the zombie's living death. Debra's voiceover connects this episode to the main narrative by explaining that the movie that we are about to watch is an extended attempt to accomplish the same purpose that the Channel 10 cameraman was trying to do by uploading this footage to the Internet: "So that people, you, could be told the truth." The direct address to the viewer represents a challenge to see through the narrative metaphor of the zombie outbreak into the social critique that Romero wants to expose, even as Debra's narration is edited together with real news clips from Hurricane Katrina, 9/11, and other contemporary disasters that we vaguely recognize from the world of nonfiction. At the same time that the film reappropriates this disaster footage into its fictional narrative, the extradiagetic provenance of these images keeps one foot planted in "the real world," indicating a conflation of the fictional zombie outbreak and our own twenty-first century glut of televised catastrophes.

Debra's introductory voiceover explicitly addresses the movie's theme of the hybridization of real life and artifice. Unlike previous films such as *The Blair Witch Project* (1999) and *Cloverfield* (2008) which also depict horrific occurrences from a subjective-camera perspective, *Diary* includes an account of how and for what purpose the film we are seeing was edited together.[13] We see Jason, Eliot, and Debra assembling the footage on their laptop, and Debra confesses that she manipulated the final cut with more than simply reportage in mind. "I've added music occasionally for effect, hoping to scare you. You see, in addition to trying to tell you the truth, I am hoping to scare you, so that maybe you'll wake up." The implication of Debra's wake-up call is that, for all of our mobility and appearance of life, we are actually a society of shambling sleep-walkers, transfixed by an uncritical relationship to visual representations of reality. The Channel 10 cameraman had attempted to shock us into consciousness by showing us the objective, photographic truth of what his camera witnessed. The emotional strength of this clip is its merciless lack of editing, the impression that it is an unfiltered window into a living reality. Debra's final cut of the movie she makes for us takes a different approach, however, manipulating the raw footage with horror-movie editing and sound cues designed to make us feel rather than merely see. Debra's understanding of how to make the camera tell the truth implies that the filmmaker's task is to manipulate the medium in order to reproduce the phenomenological experience of an event, rather than merely the objective appearance of an event. Although the Channel 10 cameraman and Debra seem to be approaching the project of photography from two opposite perspectives, they both participate in the essential feature of photography: that it operates across the borders of conventional categories of subjectivity and objectivity. Sontag described all photography as representing an interaction between "the supposition that cameras furnish an impersonal, objective image" and "the fact that photographs are evidence not only of what's there but of what an individual sees, not just a record but an evaluation of the world."[14] On the one hand, a photographic image represents a blunt thing in the world, while on the other hand, the same image represents a slice of the photographer's personal experience, saturated with language and life. By explicitly addressing this ambivalent status of photography as both a documentary object and an aesthetic presence of a speaking artist, *Diary* provokes us into recognizing photography itself as a kind of zombie art, one which draws its magical power from a transgression of the boundaries between living subject and inanimate object.

In *Diary of the Dead*, the camera is the most prominent vector of zombieism, committing its "soft murder" on everyone it lays its eye on. When we first meet the film students, they are filming a scene in Jason's movie in which a character played by Tracy is fleeing the shuffling mummy played by Ridley. Everything transpires according to the conventions of horror movies. The mummy shambles but nevertheless gains on the fleeing heroine, the heroine's dress rips off, she trips, but as soon as Jason yells "cut," the heroine pulls off her wig, we see that the mummy's makeup is unglued, and Tracy's feminist deconstruction of standard horror movie tropes quickly informs us that the horror scene we thought we were watching was only a self-conscious parody of a horror scene. The threat posed by the undead creature was only a simulation, and we breathe a sigh of relief. But when we reach the end of *Diary*, we see the same scene unfold again, only this time in "reality." Ridley, still wearing his mummy costume, has in fact become undead. Tracy, still wearing her damsel-in-distress costume, flees from him through a dark wood, getting her dress ripped off and tripping in her non-sensible shoes. Furthermore, both scenes are presided over by Jason, who chases after the "actors" with his camera in order to capture the action. Over the course of the movie, Ridley and Tracy have gone from playing characters in a cheesy horror movie to *being* characters in a cheesy horror movie. Ridley has been literally zombified and Tracy has adopted the living death of becoming a character in a movie rather than a real person. Ridley seems to become the literalization of Bazin's description of film as originating out of a "mummy complex." It is as if the camera has imposed its own logic on Ridley and Tracy, sucking them into its own landscape of clichés and conventions, and presiding over their conversion into specters, devoid of free will and doomed to mechanically enact the same brainless scenario throughout eternity. Debra's voiceover tells us that, although Jason made a horror movie for his senior thesis, he really wanted to film documentaries, but through the magic of the camera to warp the fabric of the real, the horror movie becomes a documentary and vice versa. Ridley's "real" zombie is even able to be called off from his pursuit of Tracy when Jason shouts "cut," suggesting that the cameraman is the final arbiter of reality. A parallel process seems to be at work in the world at large. When the student filmmakers first hear the news reports of zombie attacks, Tony tries to calm everyone down with the commonplace critique of the news that it is mostly "horse shit" that is blown out of proportion to "sell soap." As good as Tony's advice would be under rational circumstances, these characters have already entered into the horror-movie mirror-world where the paranoid myths propagated by the mass-media come true, bursting out of the shadowy realms of the subconscious and taking visual form in high-definition. In the process of paranoid fictions becoming true, the documentary subjects of *Diary of the Dead* become transposed into fictional characters and derealized phantoms.

Jason keeps the camera rolling after his student movie has been abandoned, carrying the same structure of perception over from the horror movie scene into the real world, which correspondingly takes on the dimensions of a horror movie. Initially, Jason's companions resist being abducted into Jason's "shockumentary." They shrink from the camera, as we all do, in the interest of preserving their interiority, their individuality, and their humanity. But the quiet insistence with which Jason badgers them into playing the role his camera is hungry for effectively demonstrates the "soft" aggression that Sontag observed in the photographer's activity. Jason adopts the impersonal logic of the camera in his approach to his material and enthusiastically plays the role of the objective camera eye, interviewing his friends as if they were strangers, a technique which does in fact have the effect of ripping these characters out of their social context, their relationship to Jason and to each other, and whatever subtle uniqueness they may have as human beings and retranscribes them into the impersonal role of documentary subjects. In his interviews with his friends, Jason follows filmic convention by "shooting them in the head," filming them in the head-and-shoulders medium close-up interview gaze. The convention for definitively capturing someone on film, it turns out, is the same as the generically agreed upon convention for definitively eliminating a zombie with a gun. A photograph of someone's elbow or chest does not capture the subject; the photographer and the zombie-killer both have to shoot the head in order to successfully bag their quarry. This parallel between photography and zombie-killing suggests that there has always been a basic symbolic correspondence between the zombie and the subject of photography. In *Diary*, the parallelism between the gun and the camera as tools of depersonalization is made explicit when both instruments are condemned as "too easy to use," when a rogue national guardsman levels the barrel of his rifle with Jason's camera (a shot that resonates with other shots in *Diary* in which a cameraman points his camera into a mirror), and, finally, when Jason himself is being eaten by a zombie. When Jason is tackled to the floor by an undead Ripley, still dressed in the mummy costume Jason assigned to him for the purposes of his movie, Jason clutches for the object just out of reach, not the conventional gun, but his camera. His last words, "shoot me," refer less to his wish to be put to death by a bullet than to his corresponding wish for his death to be captured on film as the climax of the movie of his life. Jason is more interested in living on as a filmic image than he is in living on as a real human being. The gun and the camera work in concert to extinguish Jason as a real human being ("hard murder") and simultaneously to grant him a supra-biological existence as a victim of photography's "soft murder."

The term "The Dead" in *Dawn of the Dead, Day of the Dead,* and *Land of the Dead* clearly refers to the hordes of zombies which appear in each of those movies. The title *Diary of the Dead,* however, attaches the dreaded zombie moniker to the subjects telling the story. The shuffling ghouls are not coming into the narrative from "out there," they are the ones telling the story which, given the narrative arc of increasing sentience throughout the Romero series, becomes the most powerful expression of zombie agency. Alternatively, and perhaps more literally, the title suggests that all those documented in this visual account of the outbreak have perished. In this case, we are privileged to a real zombie sighting, dead people walking around through the fantastic properties of film.[15] A parallel interpretation of the title is that the people telling the story are in some sense already dead *while they are telling the story.* In this case, the state of death is not the literal cessation of biological function, but something more elemental, a more abstract kind of death. Simultaneously, the title of Jason Creed's film (which is the same film as Romero's), *The Death of Death,* can refer simultaneously to the corpses who return to life as well as to the filmic reanimation of our heroes. Death has not only disappeared from the world as a result of the zombie plague, but also, correspondingly, as a result of the proliferation of media images that never die. The Christian metaphysics which John Donne expressed in "Divine Sonnet X" with the famous line, "And death shall be no more; death, thou shalt die"[16] represented the death of death as the release of the human spirit. Romero's existentialist suggestion, on the other hand, is that when death is eliminated from the world as it frequently is in our sanitized mediascape, human beings lose their most significant connection to what is meaningful, what is real, and what is human. Romero's immortal zombies, embodying a grotesque, fleshy style of deathlessness, become the walking symbols of our contemporary disconnection from the humanizing influences of an authentic recognition of our shared mortality —

a recognition that is deliberately obscured by the viral proliferation of "mummified" images that usurp the human presences they purport to preserve.

Jason, who is the chief diarist of *Diary of the Dead,* is the most prominent person in the film who exemplifies the condition of living death. The sense of his ghoulishness is amplified by the fact that we never see his face very clearly because he is always behind the camera or, when he is being filmed by somebody else, his head is always half-hidden by the camera he is holding. It is not until after he dies in the story that we see some footage from earlier of him explaining to the camera that he's "really excited to be given this opportunity" to record the chronicle of horror of which his own death will be the climax. But rather than establishing an ironic contrast between Jason's prior naiveté and his tragic death, this footage reveals the consistency of Jason's vision; he hasn't learned anything, he is the same ghoul at the beginning of the story that he is in his final moments, when he explains, "Who the fuck wants to survive in a world like this? All that's left is to record what's happening for whoever remains when it's all over." His loyalty has consistently been on the side of death against life. Whenever there is a confrontation with the zombies throughout the movie, Jason is clearly aligned more with the zombies than with the humans. He lurks around with his camera while the other humans panic and attempt to defend themselves. Jason is a perfect embodiment of Sontag's dictum that "essentially the camera makes everyone a tourist in other people's reality, and eventually in one's own."[17] At the hospital, the Amish barn, and looters' warehouse, Jason, who is always filming, never participates in the action, as if he were only spectrally present. Indeed, when he's lost in a dark room, he is frightened by his own reflection in a mirror, as if he had mistaken himself for a zombie. Upon finding Jason, Tony admonishes him, "There's a dead man walking around here, let's go" — a line which seems to refer doubly to the literal zombie on the loose and Jason himself, who is so mesmerized by gazing at reality through the camera lens that he has wandered away from other human beings and into the darkness.

Furthermore, as with all zombies, Jason's undead condition is infectious. Debra spends most of the movie criticizing Jason for his zombie-like relationship to reality. She had defiantly refused to continue using the camera, haunted by the eerie sense that it's "too easy to use," that the camera seduces the operator into its own disembodied currents. She stopped practicing camerawork in college because she "didn't want to be like" Jason. She attacks him for "dicking around" with his camera while everyone else is worried about their friends and family. Her voiceover narration continually propounds the theme of the social perils of media-glut and voyeurism. Yet after Jason's death, she resolves to "finish Jason's movie," and the final product we are watching is proof that she has in fact made good on her conversion to Jason's mentality. This transformation in Debra's character is even more shocking for being completely unexplained. It is as magical and as non-psychological as the process whereby one zombie infects another. A similar fate sweeps up Tony, who had spent much of the movie both criticizing Jason's obsessive filming and denying the possibility of the existence of zombies. Ultimately, however, he is compelled to acknowledge the power of these twin varieties of living death. Just as it becomes clear beyond a shadow of a doubt that the dead are returning from the grave, Tony tacitly confesses that he "can't resist" the temptation to slip behind the camera lens and trade real life for the mediated quasi-life of the camera-operator. Both Debra and Tony are infected against their will by Jason's photo-zombieism, so it is appropriate that at the end of the movie, they are both symbolically buried alive in a sterilized chamber lined with video screens where their only access to the real world will be through surveillance cameras. Debra and Tony are reconstituted as the Adam and Eve of the new media image-world. Although they are shown becoming closer to one another throughout the movie, their relationship is curiously asexual. The fact that they are joined in their one-room techno-Eden with Dr. Maxwell seems to ensure that their relationship will remain that way, asexuality being the appropriate condition for both zombies and images. The only child Debra and Tony will have is the film we are watching, which can be uploaded and infinitely reproduced as one more shambling unit of living death to join the horde of comparable media images.

Jason's anonymity as a character in *Diary* is a metaphor for the anonymity of the director of any movie. The very transparency of the director makes him or her an omnipresent figure. The audience of a film does not *see* the director, they *become* the director, adopting the camera's zombie-like lack of existential contact without even realizing that they are doing so. In his DVD commentary on *Diary*, George A. Romero uses the second-person to refer both to the director and the audience when he describes filming a conventional zombie cannibalism scene. "You can go in and while the zombies are feasting, you can feast yourself, and you can stretch it out for five minutes and go in for close-ups and all that." The audience participates in the cannibalism of the camera. The cameraman's descent into zombieism carries us along into the vortex of living death. To watch sadism is to become a sadist. The earliest critics of *Night of the Living Dead* were disturbed by precisely this concern that zombie-movie violence could become an infectious social problem. A 1968 review in *Variety* proclaimed that "until the Supreme Court establishes clear-cut guidelines for the pornography of violence, *Night of the Living Dead* will serve nicely as an outer-limit definition by example. [The film] casts serious aspersions on the integrity and social responsibility of its Pittsburg-based filmmakers ... as well as raising serious doubts about ... the moral health of filmgoers who cheerfully opt for this unrelieved orgy of sadism."[18] The fact that *Night of the Living Dead* is comparatively mild by horror movie standards of the twenty-first century bears out Sontag's observation that "photographic seeing has to be constantly renewed with new shocks, whether of subject matter or technique, so as to produce the impression of violating ordinary vision."[19] Sontag and the *Variety* reviewer seem to agree that violent images "desensitize us" to violence in general, but in Sontag's analytic, the violent content of visual media is only one aspect of and perhaps a metaphor for a more pervasive violence that filmic images do to conventional attitudes about reality and representation. All images are violent, because they murder the living world in order to replace it with a shadow world, even as they possess the enchanting capacity to lull us into preferring the shadow world to what we faintly remember as something known as "lived experience." *Diary of the Dead*, with its moralistic stance on the ethical dangers of the filmic imagination, seems to suggest that all movies are zombie movies.

Of course, Romero's critique of the pernicious effects of various registers of media violence is embedded within a film that revels in splatter effects and which invites its audience to do so as well. Romero seems to acknowledge his lack of trustworthiness as a moral truth-teller by casting himself in a background role as a military officer who presides over a disinformation campaign about the zombie epidemic. Pony-tail tucked out of view, General Romero presents a version of the Channel 10 cameraman's footage that has been re-edited to support the official narrative that there is no zombie epidemic. If this very minor character were played by anyone else, this detail would support the dominant reading of the movie that filmed reality is the opposite of real reality and therefore corrosive to any viable morality, but with Romero in the role of the arch-deceiver, the entire message of *Diary of the Dead* is undermined along with the credibility of the teller. Rather than a contrast between the "fake" military footage and the "real" uncut footage at the beginning, Romero's confession that he is a liar infects the movie as a whole with forgery. When we return to the "raw" footage from the beginning of the movie, it is possible to discern that this long take is actually punctuated by several "hidden cuts," the splatter effects have been CG'ed in post-production, and the sound cues have no relation to any television camera's microphone. What's more, as a long opening shot, the opening sequence of *Diary* semi-deliberately alludes to long opening shots from other films such as *Touch of Evil* (1958), *Rope* (1948), and even the "mock" long opening shot from Robert Altman's *The Player* (1992) (incidentally, another movie about the power of cinematic vision to warp the texture of reality). This apparently "live" footage is actually an elaborately choreographed simulation of reality. Romero provides us with the appearance of life while simultaneously cluing us in to the awareness that the kind of life we are witnessing has already been drained of its vital essence — its living facticity. The filmmaker participates in the zombification of reality itself. Romero amplifies this suggestion by casting writers and filmmakers who have been influential in the contemporary zombie boom including Quentin Tarantino, Wes Craven, Stephen King, Simon Pegg, and Guillermo del Toro as the background media voices whose presence permeates *Diary*. The characters in *Diary* live in a world where the producers of zombie fiction have become the newscasters of a new dispensation in which "real" and "fake" are as unnaturally melded as the conditions of "living" and "dead." But the use of these cameos also serves to turn the movie inside out, to suggest that what we thought of as our "real" world outside the zombie movie is actually undergoing the same hybridization of vital and inanimate values that *Diary* evinces; truth and fiction no longer have distinct ontological status.

It is in the context of this deconstruction of the real/fake binary that we can best understand Dr. Maxwell's strange indictment and exoneration of Jason's camera-facilitated zombieism. "There will always be people like you," he tells Jason, "wanting to document, wanting to record some sort of diary.... Well, this is a diary of cruelty. And in war time, when the enemy can be marked as 'this son of a bitch' or 'that son of a bitch,' then cruelty becomes justified." At first, it seems as if Dr. Maxwell is going to echo Debra's moralistic condemnation of the cameraman's self-distancing from his context, but he complicates this simple moralism by concluding that a world characterized by dehumanization requires a dehumanized chronicler. If Jason/Romero is in fact guilty of photo-zombieistic cannibalism, their guilt is mitigated by the fact that the "reality" that they are documenting is already zombified. Dr. Maxwell and *Diary of the Dead* itself both seem to arrive at the point of view Sontag described using cannibalistic imagery in *Regarding the Pain of Others*: "the vast maw of modernity has chewed up reality and spat the whole mess out as images."[20] Dr. Maxwell's statement is indeed nihilistic, but he has had a lifetime to grow inured to a nihilistic worldview. In a movie that targets the youth market, Dr. Maxwell is a belletristic dinosaur, the very caricature of all of the values that are being and have been replaced by the YouTubification of society — and normally, according to the conventional horror movie formula, would be the first character wiped away by the new plague. But this modernist throwback to whom the teenagers pay minimal attention, in addition to being the only one who is able to fully comprehend the depths of the movie's cynicism, is also the most ruthless survivor. As the millennial netizens, filled with naiveté and self-confidence, are picked off one by one, Dr. Maxwell manages both to be a very effective zombie-killer and also to hold on to his humanity. Although Dr. Maxwell gives his blessing to Jason's compulsion to participate in the zombified mirror-game of contemporary hyperreality, Maxwell himself opts out of the whole system, preferring low-tech weapons such as arrows and swords to the cameras and guns of his young companions, a preference that reflects his passion for old media, particularly the "slow media" of books and theater. His grounding in the values of literacy and history seem to protect him from the zombie-like fascination with digital images that infects, literally or metaphorically, almost all of the movie's young characters.[21] His presence in the movie erects a preserve of humanism that stands apart from the posthuman, hyperreal zombieism that overwhelms the rest of the movie. While it is true that his fate is to be "buried alive" with Debra and Tony at the end of the movie, his tomb is lined with all of his cherished Great Books. Since he had earlier mentioned that he never knew or wanted a home anyway, he finds himself in a book-lover's utopia, locked away forever with an endless supply of classic literature. In a deeply cynical movie that both critiques and enacts the cinematically-facilitated zombification of its characters, its makers, and its audience, Dr. Maxwell's literary humanism represents a possible alternative to the epidemiology of moving pictures and living death.

## Notes

1. Robin Wood, *Hollywood from Vietnam to Reagan ... And Beyond* (New York: Columbia University Press, 2003), 287.

2. The differing locomotion of Romero and Russo zombies is helpfully spelled out — along with several other major differences between the two types of zombies— at *TVTropes.org* under the heading "Zombie Apocalypse."

3. Marshall McLuhan, *Understanding Media: The Extensions of Man* (New York: Signet, 1964), 170.

4. Guy DeBord, *Society of the Spectacle*, trans. Ken Knabb (London: Rebel Press, 2002), 7.

5. Jean Baudrillard, *Simulacra and Simulation*, trans. Sheila Faria Glaser (Ann Arbor: University of Michigan Press, 1994), 28.

6. Roland Barthes, *Camera Lucida*, trans. Richard Howard (New York: Hill & Wang, 1981), 9, 7. André Bazin, "The Ontology of the Photographic Image," trans. Hugh Gray, *Film Quarterly* 13, no. 4 (1960): 4.

8. Susan Sontag, *On Photography* (New York: Picador, 1977), 98.

9. Ibid., 7.

10. Ibid., 14–15.

11. Ibid., 11.

12. Ibid., 20.

13. Although using the camera to present a subjective point of view is at least as old as Robert Montgomery's *Lady in the Lake* (1947), the widespread availability of portable video cameras in the early '80s and of digital cameras in the '90s has led to a flourishing horror sub-genre of "found footage" films, which is still going strong and of which *Diary of the Dead* is a prominent example. Like many Gothic novels which claim to be manuscripts documenting true events, found footage films titillate audiences by creating an aura of plausibility around fantastic situations. The ur-text of all found footage films is the Italian exploitation film *Cannibal Holocaust* (1980), but the genre broke into the mainstream with the runaway success of *The Blair Witch Project* (1999). The formula has provided the basis for a number of other commercially successful films recently, such as *Cloverfield* (2008), *Quarantine* (2008), and *Paranormal Activity* (2009).

14. Sontag, *On Photography*, 88.

15. See also Tyson E. Lewis's article on bare life and Shaka McGlotten's article on dead and live life in this collection.

16. John Donne, *The Complete Poetry and Selected Prose of John Donne*, ed. Charles M. Coffin (New York: Modern Library, 2001), 250.

17. Sontag, *On Photography*, 57.

18. Quoted in Adam Lowenstein, *Shocking Representation: Historical Trauma, National Cinema, and the Modern Horror Film* (New York: Columbia University Press, 2005), 154.

19. Sontag, *On Photography*, 99.

20. Susan Sontag, *Regarding the Pain of Others* (New York: Farrar, Straus, and Giroux, 2003), 109.

21. Correspondingly, in *Land of the Dead*, zombies become mesmerized and rendered complacent by the flickering images of fireworks, a parallel to the flickering images of film.

# Mass Psychology and the Analysis of the Zombie: From Suggestion to Contagion

## Phillip Mahoney

> The mob spirit grows and expands with each fresh human increment. Like a cannibal it feeds on human beings.
>
> — Boris Sidis

> The becoming-real of the Imaginary Party is simply the formation — the contagious formation — of a plane of consistency where friendships and enmities can freely deploy themselves and make themselves legible to each other.
>
> — Tiqqun

### Zombies and Crowds

Today, the association of zombies and crowds occurs on the manifest level of both zombie films and popular discourses of mass psychology. Once George Romero cemented the previously loose association between hordes of zombies and riotous crowds, it became common for zombie films to incorporate images of hypnotized audiences, stampedes, and political protests, often, as in *28 Days Later* (2002)[1] and Zack Snyder's remake of *Dawn of the Dead* (2004),[2] in their opening scenes. In addition, and perhaps as a result of Romero's revolutionary intervention into the zombie film genre, cultural commentators in general often employ zombie rhetoric when they describe the masses as hypnotized automata, easily manipulated by those in power.[3] In other words, today, equating masses and crowds with zombies is itself a practice of the masses and not the exclusive rite of the critical elite.

The very pervasiveness of this rhetorical coupling, however, threatens to naturalize it, veiling its historical contingency behind an apparently intuitive logic. Even worse, the contemporary knee-jerk comparison between zombies and crowds is almost always a pejorative one. Returning to the discourse of early crowd psychology will allow us to uncover a crucial portion of the process by which these two figures, the zombie and the crowd, came to merge within contemporary Western consciousness. It will also help us to construct a

113

vocabulary for exploring the positive aspect of the identification of crowds with zombies, and vice versa.

Though I begin by indicating some of the broader points of convergence between the zombie mythos and crowd psychology, my analysis will ultimately focus on the deployment of two key concepts from early crowd psychology within the zombie film genre: suggestion and contagion. Over the course of zombie film history, I argue, the zombie undergoes a transition from a suggestible creature, to a contagious one. Reading the fictive medium of the zombie film alongside the "scientific" discourse of crowd psychology promises to do more than simply expand our knowledge of zombie film trivia, however, by showing how the zombie film offers us the means to think past some of the classic deadlocks of crowd psychology and theories of collective action. My broad contention is not simply that critics of zombie films would do well to study crowd psychology, but rather that crowd psychologists do themselves a great disservice by ignoring the mythos of the cinematic zombie.

Crucial in this regard is my argument that the displacement of the logic of suggestion by one of contagion entails a concomitant sublation of the figure of the tyrannical leader in favor of a horizontal, collective relation between equal members. Read this way, the typically dystopian vision of the zombie collective becomes available for a utopian recasting. The zombie, I argue, is a particularly powerful figure of the multitude, one that challenges us to imagine collective life, not through the humanistic and psychological terms of sympathy and identification, but through the inhuman terms of what the radical French collective Tiqqun calls "contagious formation."[4]

Crowd psychology did not become a widely-recognized discourse in its own right until the 1895 publication of *The Crowd* by conservative French sociologist, Gustave Le Bon. While other writers had written about the crowd earlier in the century, Le Bon's vitriolic indictment of the crowd was, somewhat ironically, more accessible to a mass readership. Announcing the dawn of a new "era of crowds" in Western civilization,[5] Le Bon's work bemoaned the inevitable replacement of the "divine right of kings" by the "divine right of the masses" and predicted nothing less than the complete destruction of society.[6]

The following year, *The Crowd* was translated into English and made available in America, where it influenced a number of sociologists, such as Franklin Giddings, Boris Sidis, James Mark Baldwin, and Edward Ross,[7] many of whom wrote for popular publications like *The Atlantic Monthly* and *The Popular Science Monthly*. Although *fin-de-siècle* America was a time of worker's strikes, lynch mobs, and urban crowding, the "crowd" became a significant rhetorical figure for these writers primarily because it offered the possibility of understanding broader and more abstract collectives, particularly the national, democratic public.[8] In this sense, "crowd psychology" is something of a misnomer, as the term "crowd" most often stands, not for an aggregate of physically proximate bodies, but for virtually every other conceivable form of human collective: races, classes, publics, nations, and mass audiences.

Because of its generally conservative bent, earlier crowd psychology often takes on an apocalyptic style and tone that anticipates cinematic representations of wide-scale zombie invasions. Most writers agreed with Le Bon that the ascendancy of the crowd represented a terrible threat, if not, as in the case of Le Bon, to aristocratic society, at least to organized democratic society. Combining the discourses of Italian criminology, French psychiatry, and evolutionary biology, crowd psychologists established the crowd, in the words of Boris Sidis, as a veritable "demon of the demos," capable of throwing "the body politic into convulsions of demoniac fury."[9] Of course, later zombie films, particularly *The Last Man on Earth* (1964),[10] would eventually literalize Sidis' figurative notion of a body politic possessed by demons.

It is perhaps this unruly fear of the crowd that inspires the discursive excesses one finds in the works of early crowd psychologists. In his efforts to grasp the chaotic multiplicity of the crowd, it is not enough for Le Bon to compare the crowd to "women, savages, and children"[11]; he has to avail himself of cellular,[12] animal,[13] mechanical,[14] and bacteriological[15] metaphors, as well. Thus, when Le Bon imputes to the crowd a tendency to associate "dissimilar things possessing a merely apparent connection,"[16] he might just as easily be speaking of his own reasoning in reference to it. The very concept of the multitude seems to encourage rhetorical overproduction, as if no single metaphor, allusion or definition can account for it.

In this connection, it is not uncommon for early writers of the crowd to call upon the sublime imagery of nature to help them represent the inchoate figure of the crowd or the masses. Le Bon describes the individual in the crowd as a "grain of sand amid other grains of sand, which the wind stirs up at will."[17] In his 1897 essay for *Popular Science Monthly,* titled "The Mob Mind," Edward Ross draws upon water imagery to illustrate the fickle minds of the American masses, which "drift without helm or anchor" on the "ripples" and "currents of opinion."[18] Meanwhile, for Boris Sidis, "the mob is like an avalanche, the more it rolls, the more menacing and dangerous it grows."[19] The threat of the many pushes against the boundaries of linguistic representation itself, undermining the putatively rational and scientific discourse of crowd psychology and revealing it, instead, to be motivated by a complex mixture of fascination and horror.

These fleeting moments of discursive excess in early crowd psychology become the very substance and focal point of later zombie films, which often depict uncountable hordes flowing in massive and uncontainable tides through urban landscapes. As Christian Thorne writes, "Zombie movies are always going to be about crowds."[20] Filmic zombies are herd creatures, unimpressive singly, but dangerous in large numbers. Thus, it is relatively easy for the uninfected to fend off an individual zombie, but, because of its slow, plodding persistence, a crowd of zombies is typically fatal. The cinematic zombie generally remains lost, furthermore, in the anonymity of the multitude, so that we rarely identify with or even remember any particular one. This is perhaps one of the clearest and most important differences between the zombie and other classic horror monsters. The individual/protagonist zombies of later films like *Deathdream* (1972)[21] and *I, Zombie: The Chronicles of Pain* (1998)[22] are, in this case, merely exceptions that prove the rule. Much more common today are the vast, pulsating hordes, whose sheer numbers frustrate the viewer's attempt to construct a knowable totality by seething beyond the borders of the cinematic frame.

As others have noted, however, the cinematic zombie is both literally and figuratively multiple, signifying numbers *sensu stricto* and a number of politically-charged anxieties.[23] Kyle Bishop sees the recent resurgence of the cinematic zombie as an expression of widespread fears of terrorist attack,[24] while earlier zombie films, he argues, tap into deep-seated cultural anxieties regarding the "dominance of the white patriarchy, the misogynistic treatment of women, the collapse of the nuclear family, and the unchecked violence of the Vietnam War."[25] Adding bio- and nuclear warfare, disease (particularly AIDS), and, of course, mass revolt to the list hardly exhausts the metaphorical breadth of the zombie, which, through a kind of unconscious logic that embraces contradiction, is capable of representing vastly divergent threats.

Such metaphorical overdetermination on the part of both zombies and crowds causes considerable confusion when it comes to defining the object in question. In the discourses surrounding these figures, therefore, one finds a preoccupation with classificatory distinctions that rarely does more than highlight the futility of such an endeavor.[26] Rather than enter into such debates, it is perhaps more useful to determine what the lack of a hard and fast classificatory schema tells us about zombies and crowds. It is possible, in other words, to see this very absence of a single determining feature as the most salient, *positive* aspect of zombies and crowds.[27]

The figurative excesses that one finds in reference to zombies and collectives, in which metaphors and figures of speech are piled haphazardly one atop another, make up only one side of a double, and seemingly contradictory, strategy of representation. Though the first thing writers tend to notice about crowds and zombies is this sublime, overdetermined quality, I would argue that such overdetermination is, in fact, the effect of a logically-prior blankness, or constitutive emptiness. As figures of the multiple, zombies and crowds confront us first with a kind of uncanny featurelessness, which we are then compelled to "fill in" with content.

In the case of the crowd, it is turn-of-the-twentieth-century American social psychologist James Mark Baldwin who gives the most extreme version of this radically denatured quality. In a chapter on the "Theory of Mob Action," in his ambitious *Social and Ethical Interpretations in Mental Development* (1897), Baldwin asks, "Has man collectively no thought, no sense of values, no deliberation, no self-control, no responsibility, no conscience, no will, no motive, no purpose?"[28] The immediately supplied answer, of course, is: "No, he has none."[29] "The suggestible consciousness," he continues, piling negation upon negation, "is the consciousness that has no past, no future, no height, no depth, no development, no reference to anything; it has only in and out."[30] The man of the crowd is, quite simply, a man without qualities, a denatured and denuded *no-body*. Similarly, the classic features of the zombie are typically expressed in a negative register; the zombie is represented as soulless, unconscious, without will, insensitive to pain, and indestructible, so that even the zombie's deadness (itself a rather negative feature) must be cast negatively, as "undead."

The zombie's negatively figured undeadness and the crowd's constitutive indeterminacy allow them to occupy an "empty space" within Western consciousness, where they function, in the words of Slavoj Žižek, as ideal "containers" for a host of divergent, "free-floating, inconsistent fears" and concepts.[31] At the most fundamental level, zombies and crowds can thus be said to represent what Giorgio Agamben, in *The Coming Community* (1993) calls "whatever singularities": limbo life-forms connected, not "by any common property, [or] identity,"[32] but through their very lack of positive features. Rather than attempt to determine their proper attributes, fix their true identities, or fill in their content, I take this negative determination of zombies and crowds seriously, looking to this very negativity as a way of constructing a new understanding of collective life itself.

## From Suggestion...

The indeterminacy of the zombie and the crowd derives from two concepts which receive their most detailed elaboration in the discourse of crowd psychology: suggestion and contagion. After listing the three basic attributes of Le Bon's crowd mind—"a sentiment of invincible power," mental "contagion," and "suggestibility"—Mikkel Borch-Jacobsen points out that "the second and third (the most decisive, in [Le Bon's] argument) are manifestly non-characteristics, or nonspecific characteristics."[33] "Neither substratum nor substructure," Borch-Jacobsen argues, "but rather a soft, malleable, plastic, infinitely receptive material without will or desire or any specific instinct of its own,"[34] Le Bon's crowd cannot even be said to possess a spirit or character at all. The two predominant "characteristics" of the crowd, mental contagion and suggestibility represent little more than the ability of the crowd to absorb, from outside, what would properly be called characteristics.

While distinct in their application, as I will show in a moment, suggestion and contagion are similar in that they are both something like "anti-properties," which connote an innate or constitutive "openness" to external influence. In this sense, the crowd *is* nothing other than its potential to become something else. Such is the dominant note of early theories of the crowd. Thus we find early crowd psychologists grouping suggestibility and contagion under various headings, such as innate gregariousness, organic sympathy, and imitation, all of which emphasize the tendency of crowd members to take on the characteristics and features "suggested" to them by some external stimulus.

Le Bon identifies the root of this suggestibility in the most primitive structures of the brain. In a crowd, Le Bon writes, individual, conscious thought becomes inhibited, allowing the unconscious behavior of the "race" to rise to the surface. According to him, the acts of the crowd "are far more under the influence of the spinal cord than of the brain," making the crowd "closely akin to quite primitive beings."[35] This attempt to locate suggestibility in the "primitive" part of the brain may go some way toward explaining both the prevalent racism of early zombie films and the convention that developed of aiming for the head when attempting to destroy a post–Romero zombie.

Though many of Le Bon's American followers read suggestion and contagion as synonymous, I follow Freud in drawing a careful distinction between the two.[36] According to this reading, suggestion describes the manner in which the leader influences the impressionable crowd, and contagion designates the effects of one crowd-member upon another. Thus, while both phenomena presuppose the basic impressionability and lability of the crowd, they proceed in entirely different directions. Suggestion can be described as a vertical phenomenon, expressing the leader-crowd relation, while contagion represents the horizontal movement through which the leader's original suggestion spreads, like a disease, throughout the body of the crowd. Finally, as the above remarks imply, suggestion and contagion designate a clear temporal sequence: *first,* the leader plants "suggestions" in the crowd, *then* the original suggestion is intensified by the contagious interaction of individual crowd members.

The concept of suggestion grew out of an interest, among nineteenth-century French psychiatrists, in hypnosis. Thus, as early as Le Bon's *The Crowd,* one reads, "an individual immerged for some length of time in a crowd in action soon finds himself ... in a special state, which much resembles the fascination in which the hypnotized individual finds himself in the hands of the hypnotizer."[37] Freud's "Mass Psychology and Analysis of the 'I'" (1921), from which this essay takes its title, provides the most elaborate application of this analogy, clearly mapping the "two party" scenario of hypnotist and hypnotic subject onto the relationship between the leader and the crowd.[38]

With the hypnotic phenomenon of suggestion, the discourse of crowd psychology begins to take on the affective coloring that would make it an ideal source for early zombie films. This is clearest in the reactionary and apocalyptic tone of Sidis' writings on "social suggestibility."[39] Taking up Le Bon's sketchy analogy between the hypnotized subject and the member of the crowd, Sidis describes the "subwaking self" that emerges in collective life:

> The crowd contains within itself all the elements and conditions favorable to a disaggregation of consciousness. What is required is only that an interesting object, or that some sudden violent impressions should strongly fix the attention of the crowd, and plunge it into that state in which the waking personality is shorn of its dignity and power, and the naked subwaking self alone remains face to face with the external environment.[40]

Sidis' crowd member is essentially a hypnotized subject, whose will is overcome by the force of the hypnotist's suggestions. The particular content of the crowd, according to this understanding, remains to be written, as it were, so that the crowd is the mere *effect* of an "outside." Furthermore, the hypnosis-suggestion complex is, by this reading, responsible for the dystopian view of the zombie as a metaphorical figure for the labile and impressionable masses.

*White Zombie* (1932)[41] offers the most memorable example in the zombie film genre of the hypnotist-leader with the character of "Murder Legendre," played by Bela Lugosi. At first, however, the film seems unable to decide whether Legendre's power over others is a result of voodoo or what Le Bon terms the "prestige" of the charismatic leader, a "mysterious force" that accounts for the latter's influence over the crowd.[42] This mysterious force, Le Bon argues, in a rare assumption of the first person, "paralyses our critical faculty, and fills our soul with astonishment and respect."[43] Thus, in *White Zombie*, we see Legendre sculpting and burning voodoo dolls, through which he gains control of Madeline and Beaumont, but we also see him control Beaumont's valet by a mere wave of his hand. Perhaps even more memorable are the protracted close-up shots of Legendre's eyes, which float against a black background and thus suggest that the true source of his power lies in his manipulation of the hypnotist's gaze.

In his impressive study of the film, *White Zombie: Anatomy of a Horror Film*, Gary D. Rhodes shows how the "history of hypnotism and mesmerism ... informed *White Zombie*, particularly in the controlling power of Legendre's eyes."[44] Rhodes does not connect the use of popular notions of hypnotism with the suggestions of the crowd-leader, and there is little reason to suppose Halperin had any such idea in mind in this film. Jennifer Cooke also sees hypnosis as a key element of zombie films in general, but she makes a distinction between early films, like *White Zombie*, that feature the "master-hypnotist" and later films, such as *Night of the Living Dead*, that depict the leaderless "crowd ... susceptible to suggestion and contagion."[45] Indeed, like many of the early zombie films, there are only a few scenes in *White Zombie* in which we are treated to a "crowd" of zombies. (The scene in the sugar mill, in which scores of natives slave away mindlessly at their forced labor, is one of the most chilling in this regard.) The central drama of the film, in fact, focuses on the titular "white zombie," Madeline, who is an exception to the rule precisely for being a white "individual" apart from the crowd of native zombies.

Halperin would not make the association between zombie lore and crowd psychology explicit until his much less successful *Revolt of the Zombies*[46] of 1936. Here, we have the standard zombie love story made famous by *White Zombie*, with the important difference that now the action begins in World War I, with a troop of hypnotized, zombie-like Cambodians who are conquering the battlefield. The film involves the search for the "secret of the zombies" located in the lost city of Angkor. Armand is the main male character of the film, a jilted-lover who has lost his fiancée, Claire, to her new love, Cliff. Of course, Armand learns the secret of the zombies, which, like *White Zombie*, involves a strange blend of Hollywood-style voodoo and hypnosis. Drunk with his new incredible power, Armand begins creating his own zombie army. His soldiers, however, are not traditional zombies; they have not been resurrected from the dead, but are rather living men placed under a hypnotic spell.

Though many of the motifs of *White Zombie* reappear here, they take on a decidedly more political cast, encouraging us to retroactively interpret some of the more ambiguous elements of the earlier, more successful film. Like Freud's "Mass Psychology and Analysis of the 'I,'" which is often touted as a prescient account of the mass psychology of fascism,[47] *Revolt of the Zombies* somewhat counter-intuitively takes the "artificial" crowd of the army as a paradigmatic expression of crowd psychology.[48] Freud focuses on artificial crowds because, according to him, even Le Bon did not go far enough in stressing the influence of the leader in reference to crowd phenomena.[49] As if taking its cue from Freud, *Revolt of the*

*Zombies* recasts the hypnotic gaze of the voodoo priest as a function of the fascist military leader. This is seen most clearly in the return of the image of Legendre's eyes, here superimposed over the troops of catatonic, but indestructible soldiers.

For all appearances, Halperin simply recycled the footage of the eyes used in *White Zombie,* but it is perhaps too hasty to dismiss this repetition as a result of directorial economy. I read this repetition, rather, as a late realization on the part of Halperin of the unexplored political significance of the otherwise apolitical hypnotist's gaze found in *White Zombie.* These political overtones appear from the start of *Revolt,* when Armand tells his friend Cliff about the ancient "priest-kings" who "mentally" controlled and directed their followers, as if they were mere "robots." Ever the sturdy individualist, Cliff responds, "I don't believe you can turn men into automatons ... or, as you call them, zombies." The floating eyes, of course, become the final proof of just how wrong Cliff (who Armand eventually turns into a zombie) is. Toward the film's end, the same footage of the menacing gaze, which primarily directed the actions of individual characters like Madeline and Beaumont in *White Zombie,* is used here to illustrate Armand's command over thousands of unconscious, "subwaking" soldiers.

Though we find many of the clichéd voodoo elements here as well — albeit with a slight "oriental" alteration — this mythology is soon replaced by an explanatory framework that resonates much more with what Wilhelm Reich would call "the mass psychology of fascism."[50] With his first victim, the hapless servant Buna, Armand mixes and burns a mysterious white powder, the fumes of which put Buna into a catatonic trance.[51] But when Armand issues commands, Buna simply remains frozen in his rigid pose. Suddenly, though, the eyes of *White Zombie* reappear, superimposed on a black surface, and when Armand repeats his command to "lower your arms," Buna finally obeys. From this moment on, the eyes become the central source of Armand's strange and unexplained power. Through them he is able to amass a tremendous army and control the actions of important military figures from incredible distances, thus exercising what French sociologist Gabriel Tarde refers to as "remote suggestion."[52] Such "remote suggestion" on the part of the leader betokens the movement that zombie films would make from a concern with localized zombie invasions to global ones. Thus, what in *White Zombie* involved a simple "two party" relationship between hypnotizer and hypnotized, is transposed in the later film onto a broad political field and rewritten as a relationship between the charismatic leader and his horde of followers.

The film closes with an ironic thematic twist that offers the zombie as a paradigm not just of fascist formations, but of revolutionary ones as well. After the soldiers are released from their spell, they turn on Armand. This time, however, the servant, Buna, leads the masses in their "revolt" against the tyrannical leader. We have, of course, been waiting for Armand to get his just deserts and so are led to identify with this new collective. Yet, the film makes another inventive use of recycled footage by narrating the revolt of the newly emancipated soldiers with shots of the earlier, amassing "zombie" troops. Thus, what again looks like the effect of mere convenience or directorial laziness actually functions as an invidious comparison between the soulless, military zombies and the conscious, enlightened rebels. This thematic irony is properly Freudian, for it demonstrates how a similar pathology undergirds both the "artificial" and institutionalized forms of collective behavior and its more spontaneous, revolutionary manifestations.

Though *White Zombie* was the far more successful Halperin production, *Revolt of the Zombies* is notable in that it presages the coming cinematic zombie collective, particularly through its repeated indulgence in a fetishistic spectacularization of uncountable zombie masses. The hypnotized and affectless soldier-zombies of *Revolt,* however, still form what

Freud terms an "organized" or "artificial" crowd,[53] a thematic element that would become common in zombie films of the '50s. *Creature with the Atom Brain* (1955),[54] for instance, discards the voodoo clichés of the '30s to recast the zombie as a "mass man" or "organization man," living within the midst of "normal," suburban America.[55] Zombie films from the '50s are also noteworthy for offering an early zombie-version of what Tarde calls a "spiritual collectivity," a term which reflects how suggestion can operate, not just on a localized agglomeration of physically proximate bodies, but, through the press and mass publications, on a national, or global scale.[56]

In this transitional phase, elements of crowd psychology are spotty, at best. Even a pioneering film such as *The Zombies of Mora Tau* (1957),[57] "the first film in which the zombies clearly exist without a voodoo master or leader controlling them and the first in which the zombie condition is contagious,"[58] does little to advance the crowd psychology motifs present in *Revolt of the Zombies*. Aside from a couple of excellent scenes of a small group of fifteen to eighteen zombies rising from their tombs in an ancient African temple, there is relatively little indication, in this film, that the zombie is an expressly mass phenomenon.

More relevant to a crowd psychological account of the zombie mythos is the advent, during this transition, of zombie experts. From the pre–Romero to the post–Romero films, the zombie evolves from a simple material fact to be controlled and suppressed, to an object of "biopower," a subtler "form of rule"[59] that "combines military might with social, economic, political, psychological, and ideological control."[60] Previously no more than a threat to be destroyed, in the '50s and '60s, the zombie becomes a "subject" of genuine curiosity to doctors, scientists, and government officials. In a similar fashion, crowd psychology proper would seem to begin with the idea that one can no longer simply crush the crowd through military might. "A knowledge of the psychology of crowds," Le Bon writes, "is today the last resource of the statesman who wishes not to govern them — that is becoming a very difficult matter — but at any rate not to be too much governed by them."[61] This new awareness of the need, not simply to suppress, but to understand the zombie-collective is dramatized most memorably in the clash Romero stages in *Day of the Dead* (1985)[62] between the soldiers, who want to exterminate the zombies, and the scientists, who insist on learning more about them. But even as early as 1966 we see a rather prescient example of medical interest in the zombie in John Gilling's *Plague of the Zombies* (1966).[63] Set over and against the military and governmental regimes of biopower, the zombie, during this phase, begins to take on an ambivalent status from the perspective of the human viewer. Threatening individual identity and rationality, on the one hand, but placed in the role of revolutionary struggle against the abuses of the State, on the other, the zombie occupies a tenuous limbo zone in which it becomes available as a *potential* site of emancipatory, collective revolt.

## ... to Contagion

It is only natural that the emergence of the logic of contagion in the zombie film would lead to an increased interest, on the part of regimes of biopower, in understanding the zombie phenomenon. As long as suggestion was the rule, the zombie fit neatly into a predominantly racist and colonialist hierarchy that privileged the rational, white individual over the irrational and impressionable "tribe." Zombie-crowds were threatening only insofar as they were controlled by the wrong individuals, so that the true threat, in these early films, was not the zombie-crowd as such, but rather the evil individual who held it in "his" thrall.

With the appearance of Romero's groundbreaking *Night of the Living Dead* (1968)[64] all of this begins to change. Romero not only makes the figurative association of the zombie and the crowd explicit, he also changes the basic structure of the zombie-horde, by effacing all trace of voodoo lore and installing contagion as a primary aspect of a mass zombie phenomenon.[65] Adhering to a logic of contagion consonant with early crowd psychology, *Night of the Living Dead* also does away with the typical charismatic leader,[66] allowing the zombie horde to emerge as a central object of spectral fascination and a threat in its own right.

It has become commonplace to identify *Night of the Living Dead* as a pivotal turning point in the zombie film mythos; however, in terms of the transition from a logic of suggestion to one of contagion, *Night of the Living Dead* represents not so much a radical break as a crucial change of emphasis. As we have already seen, in early crowd psychology, the suggestion-contagion complex implies a relatively short temporal sequence: first, the leader "suggests" an idea to the crowd, and then the suggested idea spreads from one member to another, growing more and more powerful through a process of mutual reinforcement. Here I am simply stretching this temporal sequence out over the thirty-six years between *White Zombie* and *Night of the Living Dead*. Even with the shift to the latter contagious film, however, we can still discover a formal trace of the leader's suggestive function in the necessity of a first cause, usually a virus or radioactive disaster. In this way, the original cause of the zombie phenomenon is to be found in the structural place previously occupied by the hypnotist-leader. Perhaps even more striking, in this context, is the curious adherence *Night of the Living Dead* demonstrates to the older trope of hypnotic suggestion, through its use of slow, lumbering zombies. It is almost as if Romero's early zombies experience a kind of hypnosis hangover in which they fail to realize that there is no longer a leader controlling them with suggestions.

It is thus unclear, with Romero's breakthrough film, to what extent we have really transitioned from a vertically ordered logic of suggestion to a horizontally ordered logic of contagion. In many zombie films — and *Night of the Living Dead* is no exception here — the first cause often feels perfunctory, as if it were a mere afterthought.[67] From the point of view of a radical collective politics, the challenge for the contemporary zombie film is to find the means to completely excise this transcendent cause, to locate the source of the collective phenomenon of contagion in the body politic itself. In the final moments of this essay, I thus offer an alternative interpretation of the obligatory first cause, one which tries to position it more squarely within a decentralized, non-hierarchical logic of contagion.

In a chapter titled, "The Leaders of Crowds and the Means of Their Persuasion," Le Bon identifies three ways in which the leader's suggestion may be successfully propagated throughout a crowd: affirmation, repetition, and contagion.[68] In truth, with this last term, the leader is not involved in any significant manner, for once he has affirmed a notion and then repeated it over and over again, it leaves his hands and the automatic and deterministic process of contagion takes over. The meaning of affirmation and repetition will be self-evident, and Le Bon himself spends little time explaining them. His discussion of contagion, however, is worth repeating at length, as it quickly slips into a microbial language that resonates strongly with the zombie mythos:

> When an affirmation has been sufficiently repeated and there is unanimity in this repetition ... what is called a current of opinion is formed and the powerful mechanism of contagion intervenes. Ideas, sentiments, emotions, and beliefs possess in crowds a contagious power as intense as that of microbes. This phenomenon is very natural, since it is observed even in animals when they are together in number.... A panic that has seized on a few sheep will soon extend to the whole flock. In the case of men collected in a crowd all emotions are very rapidly contagious, which explains the suddenness of panics.[69]

When we disconnect suggestion from contagion, or the effects of the leader from the effects of the crowd members upon each other, we see that, as is the case with cinematic zombie-crowds, contagion appears to be a rather anti-psychological phenomenon, something that occurs on the basic biological level of animals, or even on the more fundamental bacteriological level of microbes.

The association of crowds with microbes or cells is common in early crowd theories. In his summary of Wilfred Trotter's book on the "herd instinct," for instance, Freud writes that the concept of a herd instinct is, in reality, an "extension of multicellularity ... an expression of the inclination ... of all similar living creatures to unite in ever larger units."[70] In an 1895 article for *The Atlantic Monthly*, Boris Sidis speaks of the cellular organization of the mob, arguing that, like all "low organisms, the mob possesses an enormous power of propagation."[71] "Under favourable conditions," he continues, "mobs multiply, grow, and spread with a truly amazing fury."[72] Even a recent writer such as Aaron Lynch uses language that resonates with the viral and bacteriological bent of zombie films when he compares social "thought contagion" to a "software virus in a computer network or a physical virus in a city."[73] Like these other viruses, he writes, "thought contagions proliferate by effectively 'programming' for their own retransmission."[74]

Though, in the above examples, contagion still figures negatively, as a force to be limited and contained, more recent works, such as James Surowiecki's *The Wisdom of Crowds*[75] and Howard Rheingold's *Smart Mobs*,[76] to name just a few, offer the essentially contagious arena of social networking technology as a possible source for decentralized, collective cooperation. In his essay "Networks, Swarms, Multitudes," Eugene Thacker cautions against a naïve "techno-utopianism," but his notion of the "living network" as a decentralized, dynamic, and intensive site of nodes acting in concert points toward the radical potential of that other "unliving" network, the zombie swarm.[77]

Whereas the logic of suggestion gave us the "subwaking self," epitomized in zombie films by the zombie's dead-eyed stare and lumbering, somnambulistic gait, contagion provides the means for representing rapid propagation of a virus-like infection. Thus, as these two logics disconnect, the zombie loses the appearance of a hypnotized sleepwalker and becomes fast-moving, as in *Zombieland* (2009),[78] and, at times, even intelligent. (In *Burial Ground* [1980],[79] for instance, one of the zombies uses a scythe to lop off a head.) There seems to be a progressive tendency here, as if, as it evolves, the cinematic zombie is becoming more physically and mentally fit.

We find particularly fast-moving and sophisticated zombies in Umberto Lenzi's *Nightmare City* (1980),[80] in which a radioactive disaster sets off a massive invasion of what we might do better to call contagious "beings." True to traditional, post–Romero lore, the radioactive disaster causes the infected to lose red blood cells, which can only be replenished by consuming fresh blood. Naturally, when a zombie bites into the neck of a human in order to feed, the latter becomes infected as well. As Lenzi claims in the interview included with the DVD, he was concerned with showing the very real situation of a spreading virus. *Nightmare City* thus shows zombies at all stages of infection and, in general, adds more and more zombies to the screen as the film progresses. This tendency culminates in one of the final scenes, in which a group of a hundred or so zombies is shown, from the vantage of a helicopter, running through a field. Here, the contagion has spread so far and wide that the camera must reach extreme heights in order to encapsulate an entire zombie-crowd in the frame.

But the resemblances between Lenzi's contagious beings and the typical zombie stop here. As Lenzi points out in the interview, his creatures are not traditional zombies at all; he even hesitates to give them an explicit name, telling us simply to "call them what you want." As with the soldiers of *Revolt of the Zombies*, Lenzi's beings have not been raised from the dead, but are merely infected humans. In a pivotal scene, the two protagonists, Miller and his wife, Anna, even fail to realize that their friends are zombies, precisely because the latter appear so human. In this connection, Dendle has criticized the film for its cheap make-up (which often consists of little more than a few haphazard oil smudges),[81] but such a criticism seems to me beside the point, as it is predicated on the very idea that Lenzi's film appears to be challenging — namely, that zombies and humans are ontologically distinct beings. Lenzi's zombies move like humans, use tools and improvised weapons like humans, and even work together to perform complex tasks, often, as we will see, better than humans. In fact, in their carefully orchestrated attacks against key power establishments, such as the TV station, the city's power supply, the hospital, and the military base itself, Lenzi's creatures more closely resemble political saboteurs or members of a radical leftist organization such as the Weathermen than they do traditional zombies.

As I will argue, Lenzi's "call them what you want" attitude toward these contagious creatures is significant in terms of their value as a model for collective action. Agamben writes that "the coming community" will not be based on shared properties or predicates (in the case of zombies: undead, slow, soulless), but rather on a simple effect of naming, of "being-called."[82] The radical French collective, Tiqqun, develops Agamben's gnomic utterances regarding the future collective in more detail in their *Introduction to Civil War* (2010), a work that will figure largely in the concluding remarks of this essay.[83] Here, I simply want to point out that by telling us to "call them what you want," Lenzi betrays a general lack of interest in classificatory distinctions and thus identifies the zombie, not as a creature with this or that essential property, but as what Tiqqun, following Wittgenstein, calls a "form-of-life."[84]

The idea that Lenzi's zombies are not ontologically distinct beings — that they do not *belong* together simply on the basis of a set of shared properties — becomes most important when we examine their relationship to the human protagonists, on the one hand, and regimes of biopower, on the other. Like other films of the '70s and '80s, particularly those with obvious political overtones, *Nightmare City* places the zombies alongside the human protagonists in the sense that both zombies and humans are engaged in a broader conflict against the media, the military, the government, and the scientific/medical complex. The difficulty, as we will see, is simply that the humans do not realize their proper place in this new distribution of beings.

In an early scene, just after the zombie invasion has begun, the protagonist, a TV reporter named Miller, gets in a heated argument with his boss and General Hutchison, of the Defense Department. General Hutchison and the owner of the station are agreed that the outbreak must be kept secret from the public. In bombastic liberal language, Miller argues that it is his duty as a reporter to "keep the public informed." The general answers him with a rhetorical question: "Are you aware of the uproar that would be followed by such a broadcast?" This response is significant because it draws what, from the perspective of the liberal, Miller, is an invidious comparison between the masses of impressionable viewers and the contagious zombies. If the public finds out about this crisis, the general's reasoning goes, mass panic will spread throughout the body politic and the State will be forced to contain two separate, but structurally analogous, "viral" outbreaks of hysterical humans and infected zombies. Thus, the State now finds itself positioned against two potential enemies.

To understand the true import of this new political spectrum, we must, I think, deal with the cause of the zombie phenomenon. As in *Night of the Living Dead,* the advent of the radioactive virus occurs off-screen, before the proper action of the narrative. The virus, the initial impetus of the outbreak and thus the foundational moment of the film itself, feels like little more than a grudging concession to a cause-and-effect logic that one would rather not have to oblige. The real interest is the zombies and who cares how they got that way. There is something just about this feeling, for the specific content of this viral outbreak (a scientifically engineered drug, a chemical deposit from a meteor, a voodoo curse) is, in a very specific, formalist sense, immaterial. What the radioactive virus stands for, what it effectively creates, is a clear front between "friends" and "enemies." The radioactive virus, meaningless in itself, feels so perfunctory in this and so many other zombie films precisely because it is, in the words of Agamben, "what is most difficult to think: the absolutely non-thing experience of a pure exteriority."[85]

Thus, in *Nightmare City*, the radioactive virus simply makes apparent a front of civil war that was always already there, albeit in a state of latency. In the wake of the virus, Miller, the TV reporter, can no longer deny that he is diametrically opposed to the owner of the TV station for which he works. Furthermore, the previously obscure relationship between the media and the military becomes painfully obvious as both parties collude on ways of befogging the public. The virus thus makes legible what Jacques Rancière calls a new "distribution of the sensible,"[86] by dividing the multitude from the regimes of biopower. This new distribution of the sensible, this pure event of the outside, operates as a "call" that instantiates a vibrating frontier "between the State and the non–State."[87] The great failing on the part of the humans, in this regard, is their ultimate reliance on a logic of predicates that divides beings according to their "condition[s] of belonging (being red, being Italian, being Communist)."[88]

Hence, we see the poetic justice in the slipshod smears of motor oil that mark the minimal formal difference between the *putatively* living and the paradoxically *animated* undead. As a pure event of the outside, the virus is nothing other than a marking, naming, or calling, that divides those who are in power from those who are against. As Ernesto Laclau argues, "the people" does not express an already constituted sociological reality (a particular class, race, or nation), but "actually constitutes what it expresses through the very process of its expression."[89] We are sorely mistaken if, like the human protagonists of *Nightmare City*, we insist on seeing the zombies as a pre-given group to which one can belong on the basis of properties. "Zombie" here is nothing more, nor less, than the name for this new instantiation of "the people," "the multitude"—call them what you want.

According to his interview, Lenzi refused, against the directions of the original script, to allow the human protagonists to simply fly off to safety at the film's end. After the helicopter picks him up, Miller awakens as if from a nightmare and the whole drama begins again with a repetition of the initial zombie invasion. On the one hand, this decision on the part of Lenzi is purely practical: if the humans failed to contain the virus, there would be no place to escape to. On the other hand, Lenzi's improvisation is politically and thematically sound: the drama can only repeat again and again until the humans recognize their ultimate solidarity with the infected "zombies." Miller will be forced to relive this scenario until he makes the correct choice — until, in other words, he realizes that he is on the same side as the zombies against the State.

Freud never doubted the efficacy of human groupings, but he saw clearly that the patently human group was founded on an identification rooted in a more fundamental rivalry, jealousy and envy.[90] Such rivalrous human identification is built upon an a priori, property-based logic of belonging that begins with what one *is*. By contrast, Lenzi's "beings" are nothing other than a response to an empty call from the outside, represented here by the radioactive virus that creates a legible front between Us and Them. This seems to be the only appropriate way to interpret all the failures of human collective action in this film: from the identically-clad, choreographed dancers, who are butchered on live TV, to the doctors and nurses killed in the midst of an operation, to the group of hysterical humans stranded in an elevator. All of these human groupings fail, precisely because they cannot see that the real distinction is not between humans and zombies, but between Us and Them.

Lenzi insists that the radioactive virus is to be seen as a prescient, fictive vision of the AIDS epidemic. Whether or not we buy Lenzi's claim to foresight, the idea that zombies are not ontologically different entities, but merely humans afflicted with a life-altering virus is productive for our understanding of the possibilities of collective human action. We should see them, in other words, as touched, or animated, by a new "form-of-life," what Tiqqun designates as the "elementary human unity."[91] The zombies of *Nightmare City* do not identify with one another, nor do they experience the jealous rivalry that is the necessary source of such identification. Instead, the "zombies" of *Nightmare City* are, in the words of Tiqqun, "more faithful to [their] penchants than to [their] predicates."[92] The fact that this penchant is a penchant for fresh blood does not prevent us from taking a lesson from them about the future of collective action. By embracing their viral "desubjectivization,"[93] by becoming "anonymous,"[94] by becoming "whatever singularities,"[95] Lenzi's creatures demonstrate how the act of holding on to a new form-of-life "spontaneously manifests ... its own community,"[96] transforming the weak relationship of hostility into one of genuine enmity.[97] By holding to this new form-of-life, the zombies construct a vibrating front of "civil war" between friends and enemies, while the humans are stuck in between, remaining merely hostile to the government and the infected subjects it wants to eradicate.

Lenzi's zombies enact for us the "contagious formation" that is the ideal of Tiqqun's anarchistic program for collective organization.[98] Such a contagious formation, in which "friendships and enmities" come alive and "make themselves legible to each other,"[99] can only come about because of the zombie's constitutive indeterminacy, which leaves the latter open to the pure event of an "outside" and thus allows it to break free of the limits of a property-based, human logic of collective "identity."

I want to close this discussion of the zombie as a model for collective organization with a brief consideration of the "zombie walk," a practice that puts this idea into action in a very literal and dramatic manner. According to Simone do Vale's essay "Trash Mob: Zombie Walk and the Positivity of Monsters in Western Popular Culture," the first zombie walk took place in Toronto in 2003, and included only six participants, who dressed up as their favorite zombie-film characters and roamed the streets, primarily for the sake of their own entertainment.[100] Since then, thanks to new social technology, the phenomenon has spread, with zombie walks being hosted across the world.[101]

Though she distinguishes them from "flash mobs," do Vale still sees zombie walks as a celebration of the participants' "power as a mass."[102] Despite the fact that, in recent years, the zombie walk has often served charitable functions, it would seem that it is the very indeterminacy surrounding this phenomenon which allows it to take on a number of political significations. Like a typical flash mob, in other words, the zombie walk may be said to manifest the empty form of the social itself, essentially demonstrating nothing other than the very ability of people to organize en masse.

In the call for zombies found on message boards and websites devoted to zombie walks, the term "zombie" operates as what Ernesto Laclau, in his book on populism, calls an "empty signifier," a term which "can be attached to the most diverse social contents," precisely because it has no particular "content of its own."[103] On the *Toronto Zombie Walk* site, for instance, no specific direction is given regarding costuming or make-up.[104] In a typical zombie walk, "[e]ach zombie," as one writer puts it, must decide "for him or herself what 'type' of zombie [to] play."[105] Here, particular predicates (redneck zombie, prom-queen zombie, escaped-from-the-hospital zombie) are of far less importance than the mere fact of "being-called."[106] In this manner, the zombie walk constructs a front of civil war, which divides the putatively "living" and isolated, individual spectators from the undead collective.

This zombie multitude, finally, is itself peculiarly "animated" by a purely linguistic call to the celebration of the empty form of sociality itself.

The zombie walk is a final, physical proof of the supersession, within the zombie mythos, of a logic of suggestion by a logic of contagion. The very sites and message boards that "call" for zombie crowds are themselves multiple and fleeting. Their organizers remain largely anonymous, preferring to deny their obvious leaderly functions in order to blend into the undifferentiated horde. We need only understand that the particular term that is applied here is of little consequence. What is important is that, for now, "zombie" effectively operates as an "empty signifier," capable of calling into existence an active, global front dividing those who respond to the call — in "whatever" fashion — and those who do not.

## Notes

1. *28 Days Later*, DVD, directed by Danny Boyle (London: DNA Films, 2002).

2. *Dawn of the Dead*, DVD, directed by Zack Snyder (Universal City, CA: Universal Studios, 2004).

3. A simple Google search is enough to demonstrate this point. An article on the website *Kill Your Television* speaks of the creation of "network zombies," while, in a debate with Bill O'Reilly, Glenn Beck infamously refers to his own viewers as zombies. At *CSRwire*, John Rooks diagnoses "zombie consumerism," and, finally, a new conservative book warns against what the author calls "Obama-Zombies." See Ron Kaufman, "The Creation of Network Zombies," *Kill Your Television*, 1997, http://www.turnoffyourtv.com/commentary/network.zombies.html; Foster Kamer, "Bill O'Reilly Calls Glenn Beck Insane, Glenn Beck Calls his Viewers 'Zombies,'" *Gawker*, August 25, 2009, http://gawker.com/5378821/bill-oreilly-calls-glenn-beck-insane-glenn-beck-calls-his-viewers-zombies; John Rooks, "Zombie Consumerism," *CSRwire*, 29 September 2009, http://www.csrwire.com/csrlive/ commentary_detail/1179-Zombie-Consumerism; Jason Mattera, *Obama Zombies: How the Liberal Machine Brainwashed My Generation* (New York: Threshold, 2010).

4. Tiqqun, *Introduction to Civil War*, trans. by Alexander R. Galloway and Jason E. Smith (Los Angeles: Semiotext(e), 2010), 179. The anonymous collective Tiqqun is most likely connected to the authors of *The Coming Insurrection* (2009), a book attributed to the equally obscure Invisible Committee, which gained some attention in the U.S. after being negatively reviewed by Glenn Beck on his show. For more information, see Judith Rosen, "Glenn Beck Helps Turn Anarchist Book into Bestseller," *Publishers Weekly*, February 18, 2010, accessed June 8, 2010, http://www.publishersweekly.com/pw/by-topic/industry-news/publisher-news/article/42133-glenn-beck-helps-turn-anarchist-book-into-bestseller.html; Alberto Toscano, "The Story of the Tarnac 9," *Organic Consumers Association*, January 11, 2009, accessed June 8, 2010, http://www.organicconsumers.org/articles/article_19366.cfm.

5. Gustave Le Bon, *The Crowd: A Study of the Popular Mind* (Mineola, NY: Dover, 2002), x. Originally published in 1895 as *Le psychologie des foules*.

6. Ibid., xi.

7. Ericka G. King, "Reconciling Democracy and the crowd in Turn-of-the-Century American Social-Psychological Thought," *Journal of the History of the Behavioral Sciences* 26 (February 1990): 334.

8. Ibid., 338.

9. Boris Sidis, *The Psychology of Suggestion: A Research into the Nature of Man and Society* (New York: Appleton, 1898), 313.

10. *The Last Man on Earth*, DVD, directed by Ubaldo Ragona (1964; Los Angeles: 2007).

11. Le Bon, *The Crowd*, 10.

12. Ibid., 4, 72.

13. Ibid., 78.

14. Ibid., 8.

15. Ibid., 78.

16. Ibid., 34.

17. Ibid., 8.

18. Edward A. Ross, "The Mob Mind," *Popular Science Monthly* 51 (1897): 397.

19. Boris Sidis, *The Psychology of Suggestion*, 303.

20. Christian Thorne, "The Running of the Dead," *Commonplace Book*, 24 July 2010, http://people.williams.edu/cthorne/articles/the-running-of-the-dead-part-1/.

21. *Deathdream*, DVD, directed by Bob Clark (1972; West Hollywood: 2004).

22. *I, Zombie: The Chronicles of Pain*, DVD, directed by Andrew Parkinson (Miami: 1998).

23. Kyle William Bishop, *American Zombie Gothic: The Rise and Fall (and Rise) of the Walking Dead in Popular Culture* (Jefferson: McFarland, 2010), 95.

24. Ibid., 11.

25. Ibid., 95.

26. Though he admits that the "substantial overlap among the various movie monsters precludes the possibility of an all-encompassing definition of a zombie," Peter Dendle nonetheless decides to "limit [his] coverage to movies in which the creatures are actually revived corpses, or are explicitly referred to as zombies." Peter Dendle, *The Zombie Movie Encyclopedia* (Jefferson, NC: McFarland, 2001), 13. Unfortunately, as Dendle himself points out, this disqualifies many films with creatures that "exhibit most of the familiar traits but are not actually reanimated corpses." Ibid., 13. In the case of literature on the crowd, one finds a similar effort to distinguish between mobs, riots, masses, publics, etc. Canetti follows the classificatory impulse the furthest, distinguishing between "baiting crowds," "flight crowds," "prohibition crowds," "reversal crowds," and "feast crowds." Elias Canetti, *Crowds and Power*, trans. Carol Stewart (New York: Farrar, Straus and Giroux, 1962), 48. Perhaps Mills' arbitrary definition is most telling, however: "[A]s a rule, when I describe a crowd I mean a gathering that cannot fit into a room but can, on the other hand, be contained in a public hall or square." Nicolaus Mills, *The Crowd in American Literature* (Baton Rouge: Louisiana State University Press, 1986), 9.

27. For the idea that indeterminacy can be a positive feature of collective organization, I am indebted to Ernesto Laclau's post-structuralist conception of "populism." Ernesto Laclau, *On Populist Reason* (London: Verso, 2005). See, in particular, Chapter 4, "The 'People' and the Discursive Production of Emptiness."

28. James Mark Baldwin, *Social and Ethical Interpretations in Mental Development*, 5th ed. (1897; rept. New York: Macmillan, 1913), 246.

29. Ibid.

30. Ibid.

31. Slavoj Žižek, *Tarrying with the Negative: Kant, Hegel, and the Critique of Ideology* (Durham: Duke University Press, 1993), 149.

32. Giorgio Agamben, *The Coming Community*, trans. Michael Hardt (Minneapolis: University of Minnesota Press, 1993), iii.

33. Mikkel Borch-Jacobsen, *The Freudian Subject*, trans. by Catherine Porter (Stanford, CA: Stanford University Press, 1988), 139.

34. Ibid.

35. Le Bon, *The Crowd*, 11.

36. "It is not our intention here to contradict Le Bon, we simply wish to stress that the last two reasons for the change affecting the individual in the mass, namely contagion and heightened suggestibility, are clearly not of the same kind.... Possibly the best way to interpret what he says is by relating contagion to the effect that the individual members of the mass have on one another, whereas the manifestations of suggestion in the mass, which are equated with the phenomena of hypnotic influence, point to a different source." Sigmund Freud, "Mass Psychology and Analysis of the 'I,'" *Mass Psychology and Other Writings*, trans. J.A. Underwood (London: Penguin, 2004), 24. Originally published as *Massenpsychologie Und Ich-Analyse* (Zurich: Internationaler Psychoanalytischer Verlag, 1921).

37. Le Bon, *The Crowd*, 7.

38. See, in particular, the chapter titled "Being in Love and Hypnosis," in which Freud writes, "The hypnotic relationship is (if the expression will be permitted) the formation of a mass of two. Hypnosis offers a good comparison with mass formation, being actually identical with the latter. From the behavior of the mass it isolates one element for us, namely the behavior of the mass individual towards the leader." Freud, "Mass Psychology and Analysis of the 'I,'" *Mass Psychology and Other Writings*, 68.

39. Sidis, *The Psychology of Suggestion*, 297.

40. Ibid., 300.

41. *White Zombie*, DVD, directed by Victor Halperin (1932; Marina Del Ray, CA: RCF, 2008).

42. Le Bon, *The Crowd*, 81.

43. Ibid.

44. Gary D. Rhodes, *White Zombie: Anatomy of a Horror Film* (Jefferson, NC: McFarland, 2006), 30.

45. Jennifer Cooke, *Legacies of Plague in Literature, Theory and Film* (New York: Palgrave Macmillan, 2009), 167. It is imperative that I make a further distinction between Cooke's insightful study and my own. Because she views hypnosis as a perennial feature of the zombie film, from *White Zombie* to *Night of the Living Dead*, she ultimately equates what I identify as two distinct phenomena: "suggestion and contagion" (167). Thus, for her, the disappearance of the early figure of the "master-hypnotist" in *Night of the Living Dead* paradoxically signifies *both* the emergence of the crowd proper and the continuation by other means of the phenomenon of hypnosis (167). In other words, taking hypnosis as her organizing principle, Cooke sees the crowd as a feature of the late zombie film alone. By contrast, in taking the crowd as my organizing principle of the zombie film genre, I see hypnosis as a feature relevant only to the early zombie film. I think future study alone can determine the relative productivity of these conflicting distinctions.

46. *Revolt of the Zombies*, DVD, directed by Victor Halperin (1936; Philadelphia: Alpha Video, 2003).

47. André E. Haynal, "Groups and Fanaticism," *On Freud's "Group Psychology and the Analysis of the Ego,"* ed. Ethel Spector Person (Hillsdale, NJ: The Analytic Press, 2001), 112.

48. Freud, "Mass Psychology and Analysis of the 'I,'" 45.

49. Ibid., 27.

50. Wilhelm Reich, *The Mass Psychology of Fascism*, ed. Mary Higgins and Chester M. Raphael (New York: Farrar, 1970).

51. The irony is that Buna already obeys Armand's every command, making the inducement of hypnotic trance rather superfluous.

52. See Mary Esteve, *The Aesthetics and Politics of the Crowd in American Literature* (Cambridge: Cambridge University Press, 2003), 84.

53. Freud, "Mass Psychology and Analysis of the 'I,'" 45.

54. *Creature with the Atom Brain*, DVD, directed by Edward L. Cahn (1955; Culver City, CA: Sony Pictures, 2007).

55. See Dendle, *The Zombie Movie Encyclopedia*, 38.

56. Gabriel Tarde, "The Public and the Crowd," *On Communication and Social Influence*, ed. Terry N. Clark (Chicago: University of Chicago Press, 1969), 277. Originally published in 1901, as a part of *L'Opinion et la foule*.

57. *The Zombies of Mora Tau*, VHS, directed by Edward L. Cahn (1957; Culver City, CA: Sony Pictures, 1986).

58. Dendle, *The Zombie Movie Encyclopedia*, 212.

59. Michael Hardt and Antonio Negri, *Multitude: War and Democracy in the Age of Empire* (New York: Penguin, 2004) 13.

60. Ibid., 53.

61. Le Bon, *The Crowd*, xiv.

62. *Day of the Dead*, DVD, directed by George Romero (1985; Campbell, CA: Anchor Bay, 1998).

63. *The Plague of the Zombies*, DVD, directed by John Gilling (1966; Campbell, CA: Anchor Bay, 1999).

64. *Night of the Living Dead*, DVD, directed by George Romero (1968; Fort Mill, SC: Sterling Entertainment).

65. For a helpful summary of thematic innovations of *Night of the Living Dead*, see Dendle, *The Zombie Movie Encyclopedia*, 6–7.

66. Gregory A. Waller, *The Living and the Undead: From Stoker's* Dracula *to Romero's* Dawn of the Dead (Chicago: University of Illinois Press, 1986). Although he compares *Night of the Living Dead* to earlier representations of the vampire, Waller traces an evolution that is structurally similar to the one I trace here between pre– and post–Romero zombie films. For him, the Freudian "primal horde" found in Stoker's *Dracula* is "ruled by a superior leader" (277), whereas the zombies in *Night of the Living Dead* are "diseased, instinct-driven automatons [that] walk the earth without a leader" (280).

67. About *Night of the Living Dead*, Dendle writes, "The distributors wouldn't release the film until the crew tagged on some sort of explanation for the phenomenon ... hence the references to an explorer satellite sent to Venus bringing back mysterious high-level radiation." Dendle, *The Zombie Movie Encyclopedia*, 121. As Waller points out, "To assert that 'mysterious radiation' in some unexplained way causes the dead to roam the land in search of human flesh is finally little better than no explanation at all." Waller, *The Living and the Undead*, 275.

68. Le Bon, *The Crowd*, 78.

69. Ibid.

70. Freud, "Mass Psychology and Analysis of the 'I,'" 72.

71. Boris Sidis, "A Study of the Mob," *The Atlantic Monthly*, February 1895, 192.

72. Ibid.

73. Aaron Lynch, *Thought Contagion: How Belief Spreads Through Society* (New York: Basic Books, 1996), 2.

74. Ibid.

75. James Surowiecki, *The Wisdom of Crowds* (New York: Anchor, 2004).

76. Howard Rheingold, *Smart Mobs: The Next Social Revolution* (Cambridge: Perseus, 2002).

77. Eugene Thacker, "Networks, Swarms, Multitudes" *CTheory.net*, May 18, 2004, accessed November 28, 2010, http://www.ctheory.net/articles.aspx?id=422.

78. *Zombieland*, DVD, directed by Ruben Fleischer (Culver City, CA: Sony Pictures, 2009).

79. *Burial Ground*, DVD, directed by Andrea Bianchi (1980; New York, NY: Shriek Show, 2002).

80. *Nightmare City*, DVD, directed by Umberto Lenzi (1980; West Hollywood, CA: Blue Underground, 2008).

81. Dendle, *The Zombie Movie Encyclopedia*, 36.

82. Agamben, *The Coming Community*, iii.

83. Tiqqun, *Introduction to Civil War*.

84. Ibid., 16.

85. Agamben, *The Coming Community*, xvi.

86. Jacques Ranciere, *Dissensus: On Politics and Aesthetics*, ed. and trans. Steven Corcoran (London: Continuum, 2010), 36.

87. Agamben, *The Coming Community*, xix.

88. Ibid.

89. Laclau, *On Populist Reason*, 99.

90. Freud, "Mass Psychology and Analysis of the 'I,'" 75.

91. Tiqqum, *Introduction to Civil War*, 16.

92. Ibid., 23.

93. Ibid., 204.

94. Ibid., 206.

95. Ibid., 205.

96. Ibid., 181.

97. Ibid., 31.

98. Tiqqun, *Introduction to Civil War*, 179.

99. Ibid.

100. Simone do Vale, "Trash Mob: Zombie Walk and the Positivity of Monsters in Western Popular Culture," *There Be Dragons Out There: Confronting Fear, Horror, and Terror*, edited by Shona Hill and Shilinka Smith (Oxford: Inter-Disciplinary Press, 2009), 131, accessed August 27, 2010, http://www.inter-disciplinary.net/wp-content/uploads/2009/11/FHT-2-Final.pdf#page=143.

101. Ibid.

102. Ibid., 136.

103. Laclau, *On Populist Reason*, 76.

104. *Toronto Zombie Walk*, http://www.torontozombiewalk.ca/index.html.

105. Dan Linehan, "Zombie Walk: Death Imitates Art," *The Mankato Free Press*, July 6, 2009, accessed August 27, 2010, http://mankatofreepress.com/local/x1048527008/Zombie-walk-Death-imitates-art.

106. Agamben, *The Coming Community*, iii.

# Gray Is the New Black:
# Race, Class, and Zombies

## Aalya Ahmad

*There are in fact no masses; there are only ways of seeing people as masses.*
— Raymond Williams, *Culture and Society*

When we think of zombies, let us not only think of American zombie films. While the ghoulish undead are increasingly familiar to movie audiences as a dominant figure of contemporary monstrosity, much less attention is accorded to written zombie narratives. Indeed, critical study of the horror genre has been firmly rooted in film, with a far more tenuous toehold in literature. Moreover, unlike the vampire or the ghost — two monstrous entities with canonized literary ancestors — the zombie has only become familiar, if not quite respectable, through the history of the cinema. This situation has changed somewhat recently with the enormous popularity of Max Brooks's elaborately episodic *World War Z* (hereafter referred to as *WWZ*)[1] and Seth Grahame-Smith's clever mash-up, *Pride and Prejudice and Zombies.*[2] Zombie narratives have emerged in a variety of genres, from graphic novels to trading cards to games. Yet literary works remain an under-examined area of investigation. While many contemporary short zombie horror stories[3] could and should be discussed, this essay will direct its focus towards *WWZ,* ending with some reflection on the Canadian writer Tony Burgess's grim, starkly beautiful novel, *Pontypool Changes Everything.*[4]

The film-centric focus of critical analysis of horror leaves scholars of horror literature to extract the marrow of useful theories from film criticism, which is what I intend to do here. One reason for such a focus is that, in literary criticism, the study of horror fiction has been eclipsed by the looming shadow of the Gothic. I term the prevalent notion that all horror can and should be traced back to eighteenth-century Gothic literary forebears, the "Gothic consensus." This consensus does not leave much space for contemporary zombie fictions, those bastard children of colonialism, adopted first by George Romero and then, gleefully and gorily, by the "splatter punks." Why do we find zombies so compelling? As Peter (Ken Foree) says in *Dawn of the Dead,*[5] "they're us." For Judith Halberstam's version of the Gothic, however, monstrosity is located in "someone else," a markedly foreign Other that "condenses various racial and sexual threats to nation, capitalism and the bourgeoisie in one body."[6]

Monstrous identities are produced in particular ways; according to Halberstam, they are "imagined communities which are 'conceived in language not in blood'"[7] and which find their way from the exotic locales of eighteenth-century Gothic literature to more familiar and contemporary settings. Halberstam argues that racism "may be drawn from imperialistic or colonialist fantasies of other lands and peoples, but it concentrates its imaginative force upon the other peoples in 'our' lands, the monsters at home."[8] The monstrous figure of the vampire, associated with feudal Europe, was gradually displaced by the rise of the serial killer in industrial, capitalist America. This conjunction of mass culture and mass murder resulting in what Mark Seltzer has termed the "mass in person."[9] In turn, the serial killer seems to have moved over lately to make way for the post-industrial, late capitalist, globalized zombie horde, the impersonal mass, as the leading "monster narrative" of contemporary horror. The contemporary zombie might be seen as an updated vampire, condensing in its rotting body a number of threats to both capitalist and "imperialistic or colonialist" expansion, including challenges to racism and class privilege. In this essay, I will compare *WWZ* and *Pontypool* as examples of these challenges.

The zombies of the Global North have migrated from their origins in the *voudun* practices of enslaved colonial subjects struggling and resisting in Haiti; first refashioned as occult exotica by W.B. Seabrook and others in the early twentieth century in the form of "white zombies"; then shifting shape into Romero's silent, implacable ghouls and the more vocal variety with a comical fetish for brains; finally, metamorphosing into a malleable monster that can assume different forms (running or slowly lurching in pursuit, ghoulishly feeding or rabidly murderous, purposefully seeking or mindlessly wandering). Far from being an enslaved soulless corpse strictly under the control of a *bokor*, the zombie, once unleashed, freely ranges over cities and countries, in massive hordes that overwhelm organized resistance, no matter how expert or militarized.

In spite of its migrations and transformations, the zombie remains redolent of the subaltern, continually challenging experts, institutions, and authorities' attempts to categorize and contain it. In apocalyptic narratives, zombies spectacularly rehearse what both the late Canadian film critic Robin Wood and Carol Clover identify as the collision of hegemonic "White Science" with subjugated, but powerful "Black Magic," to use the terminology of [Canadian ethnobotanist Wade Davis's book on *voudun* culture in Haiti] *The Serpent and the Rainbow*:

> White Science refers to Western rational tradition. Its representatives are nearly always white males, typically doctors, and its tools are surgery, drugs, psychotherapy, and other forms of hegemonic science. Black Magic, on the other hand, refers to Satanism, voodoo, spiritualism, and folk variants of Roman Catholicism. A world of crosses, holy water, séances, candles, prayer, exorcism, strings of garlic, beheaded chickens, and the like, its inhabitants are blacks, Native Americans, mixed-race peoples (especially Cajun and Creole) and third-world peoples in general, children, old people, priests, Transylvanians—but first and foremost women.[10]

The resurgence of such subordinated identities in fiction takes on monstrous forms, as Wood points out,[11] because "what escapes repression has to be dealt with by oppression."[12] Wood's claim that horror's "apocalyptic" phase renders it "the most important of all American genres and perhaps the most progressive, even in its overt nihilism" is founded in large part on the zombie films of George Romero.[13] The increasing "nihilism" of Romero's zombie apocalypse is welcomed, clearing the way, in its vision of utter social breakdown, for the possibility of a "new social order." It must be noted, however, that the zombie narrative masks its revolutionary potential under the guise of cataclysmic breakdown rather than organized struggle. Paul Virilio argues that this fantasy of a "general accident" is peculiar to our times: brooding on the risk of a sudden, catastrophic event that is "the hidden face of technical progress":

> No technical object can be developed without in turn generating "its" specific accident: ship=ship wreck, train=train wreck, plane=plane crash.... [A]cceleration has reached its physical limit, the speed of electromagnetic waves. So there is a risk not of a local accident in a particular location, but rather of a global accident that would affect if not the entire planet, then at least the majority of people concerned by these technologies.[14]

Virilio specifies that the attacks on September 11, 2001 (even though this atrocity was deliberately planned), were precisely such an occurrence of a general accident enabled through these technologies. The cultural aftershocks of 9/11 revived apocalyptic disaster and war film genres, shone a spotlight on imperialist aspirations and disrupted the dominant narrative of the United States as an infallibly virtuous superpower. These subversive ripples strongly recalled cultural work already performed by apocalyptic horror fictions depicting devastating outbreaks and desperate survivors. It is not surprising, therefore, that the decade since 2001 has seen an enormous spate of remakes of horror films and that cultural preoccupation with the zombie apocalypse persists in the context of an ominous sense of ongoing atrocities occurring on a global scale. Virilio notes the cultural tension between the Otherness and the familiarity of zombies:

> Depending on the time and the latitude, the multitude of bodies with no soul, living dead, zombies, possessed, etc., is imposed all throughout history: a slow-motion destruction of the opponent, the adversary, the prisoner, the slave; an economy of military violence likening the human cattle to the ancient stolen herd of the hunter-raiders, and by extension, in modernized and militarized European societies, to the soulless bodies of children, women, men of color and proletarians.[15]

Zombies function therefore as gray go-betweens between subaltern and supremacist, black and white, selves and others, lurching over borders as inexorably as they break through farmhouse walls. Wood observed of the Val Lewton film *I Walked with a Zombie* (1943) that it "proceeds to blur" all of its initial, "apparently clear-cut structural oppositions": "Canada-West Indies, white-black, light darkness, life-death, science-black magic, Christianity-Voodoo, conscious-unconscious."[16] Zombies are now traded back and forth on the auction blocks of intertextual, trans-cultural venues and media, both as the gory allegorists of apocalypse and the ragged gladiators of "splatstick" entertainments. Increasingly trans-generic and trans-cultural, their growing popularity has given rise to "zomedies" and even "zom-rom-coms," zombie romance comedies. The British zomedy *Shaun of the Dead* (2004),[17] the Canadian *Fido* (2006),[18] and the American *Dead and Breakfast* (2004),[19] as well as the more recent *Zombieland* (2009),[20] all indicate that the zombie film is becoming more presentable, more popular, and more obviously intended for mainstream consumption.[21] In *Fido*, for example, all the elements of the apocalyptic Romero narrative are present, including a fortified zone, zombies wandering the perimeters, disaster capitalists, and intimate conflicts raging within surviving families. Scottish comedian Billy Connolly plays a lovable, domesticated zombie, at least as long as his electro-shock collar stays on.

Familiarity with film's zombies may breed contempt, evinced in an increasing propensity to settle the roaming monsters into entertaining "zombielands." The zombie is now bound to the service of stock Hollywood master narratives such as boy-meets-girl, boy-battles-zombies, boy-gets-girl.[22] Yet, many zombie fictions, even such a gentle satire as *Fido*, do retain their postcolonial bite. They are carnivals of the *status quo*, raising the radical possibility of an apocalypse that not only exposes, but also destroys entrenched systems of power feeding on racism, patriarchy, gross inequality and other institutionalized follies. They are so popular, I contend, precisely because they signify an unsated cultural appetite in the Global North for the type of radical transformations that a relatively affluent and politically complacent society cannot achieve. In short, zombie gray is the new black.

Zombie narratives condense comedic "splatter" and radical, apocalyptic "punk" in a sensibility that has been memorably named by Philip Brophy "horrality" or "horror, textuality, morality, hilarity."[23] This term, coined to describe the differences between horror films post–1975 and their "more traditional generic" predecessors, has been particularly applicable to zombie narratives since Romero's films created a *mythos* of the living dead for the Global North. Brophy observes that modern horror "is involved in a violent awareness of itself as a saturated genre" and exhibits the tendency, often in a grimly funny fashion, to "recklessly copy and re-draw [its] generic sketching,"[24] a trait which has also been identified with postmodernist texts. The contemporary zombie narrative is inescapably intertextual, a text that is engaged in a constant exchange with other genre texts every time it is read or watched anew.[25] In *Dead and Breakfast,* for example, the zombies suddenly break into the famous zombie dance sequence from Michael Jackson's *Thriller*[26] music video, released in 1983, while *Fido* is set in a town named Willard, a reference to the town in *Night of the Living Dead.*[27] These "knowing winks" are, as Mark Kermode writes, one of the chief pleasures of horror fandom.[28]

Another good example of such textuality in zombie film can be traced through Peter Jackson's *Braindead/Dead Alive.*[29] The Great White Explorer at the beginning of the film discovers a "Sumatran rat-monkey" that infects people with a zombie virus (the border between Black Magic and White Science is played here for laughs). He is bitten by the rat-monkey and swiftly dispatched by his crew of locals, but the creature is taken to a zoo where it bites and infects the protagonist's overbearing mother who soon begins to deteriorate and whose behavior becomes alarming. She eats his girlfriend's dog (or, as the protagonist points out, "not all of it"). The film's humor is inseparable from its notorious gore, cartoonish in its sheer, over-the-top, sickening excess. Bodies are exploded and reanimated as malignant wreckage, including tops of heads that are sheared off but whose eyes still blink. A vengeful walking, gurgling digestive system, complete with gas-emitting lower intestine, stalks the protagonist, who finally takes a lawnmower to the zombies encircling him, and ends up ridiculously skidding in a "splatstick" pile of blood and guts. Nods to *Braindead/Dead Alive* appear in other zombie films: for example, the reanimated Nazi ghouls of the Norwegian zomedy film *Død Snø*[30] messily slaughter a victim who is wearing a *Braindead* tee shirt. *P&P&Z* also renders homage to *Braindead*'s gross-out by having a "stricken" Charlotte Lucas slowly degenerate into a groaning "dreadful," like the evil mother in Jackson's film, mindlessly consuming the pus that drips from her zombifying body onto her plate.

Written zombie fictions derive their horrality not only from such intertextual weavings, but also from expanding and embroidering upon Romero's vignettes of survival. "Orality" should therefore be added to "horrality," for it is important to preserve horror's connections to the old art of oral storytelling.[31] Linda Badley, following Walter Ong's *Orality and Literacy: The Technologizing of the Word,*[32] points out that "[i]n preliterate culture you knew only what you could recall, and the oral performer functioned as a library or computer whose information could be accessed by a key word or sound formula." Badley sees horror as "postliterate culture in process of becoming ... a language for an age of secondary orality."[33] Badley, however, maintains the Gothic consensus's emphasis on the Gothic novel as the literary antecedent to the "postliterate" horror novel. In so doing, she ignores the enormous quantity of short fictions that have not yet forsaken primary orality, not only through their intertextuality, but also through such diegetic narrative devices as framing tales in settings such as campfires, gentlemen's clubs, and survivors' accounts.

*World War Z*'s framing narrative as an "oral history of the zombie wars" also aligns with horror's storytelling tradition. Like other written zombie horror fiction, *WWZ* follows the Romero mythos (the book is dedicated to the filmmaker), but Brooks extends Romero's social critique to include many references to current preoccupations with the decline of the United States as a global hegemonic superpower. For example, a purged and demoralized CIA fails to acknowledge the zombie threat it is first warned of in the Warmbrunn/Knight Report, which ends up neglected in the bottom of a drawer.[34] At the same time, it is implied, the stop-loss program of the U.S. military and the wars on drugs and terror have fatally weakened the ability of the United States to manage the outbreak: "This generation had had enough, and that's why when the undead began to devour our country, we were almost too weak and vulnerable to stop them."[35]

*WWZ* could be read as a descendant of Chaucer's *Canterbury Tales* with zombie apocalypse substituted for the Black Death: a series of accounts, narrated through interviews, of various survivors' experiences. These are arranged to give a rough chronology of the apocalypse and aftermath, beginning with the doctor who treats "Patient Zero" in China, the "richest and most dynamic superpower."[36] China is also the location where the zombie outbreak begins, in the areas the government has designated to be flooded by the gigantic Three Gorges Dam project, resulting in the forced displacement of thousands of villagers. Fengdu, drowned by the dam, is one of these villages, also known locally as the "City of Ghosts." The outbreak therefore retains the discourse of Black Magic as a "curse" by vengeful spirits,[37] mingled with White Science (medical and government authorities), while simultaneously recalling Western fears of infection in the form of tainted formula, lead paint and other toxins from Chinese manufacturers.

Throughout *WWZ*, the frightful possibility of a zombie apocalypse is measured against grim realities from the past and the present. The first public zombie attacks, for example, are located in South Africa, in the township of Khayelitsha, a site of poverty and violence where people, conditioned by years of apartheid's brutal oppressions, have cultivated "an instinct born in a time when they were slaves in their own country" to flee at the sound of "they're coming." Even though they do not know "they" are zombies, people run because "everyone knew who 'they' were, and if 'they' were ever coming, all you could do was run and pray."[38] A global Great Panic ensues and entire populations flee, creating a fictional affinity with those oppressed by real-life regimes.

Brooks continues Romero's critique of hegemonic agents of repression such as the military. For example, a veteran bitterly recalls the last-ditch stand against the undead in the spectacular scene during the battle of Yonkers, in which doomed American soldiers, encumbered by their high-tech military gear, vainly battle millions of zombies. The global sweep of Brooks's chronicle brings the American nightmare into the realm of a contemporary, globalized *Zeitgeist*, while its commitment to storytelling supplies a diverse range of perspectives and narrations that linear film narration cannot match. Oral history includes "the human factor," characterized by "opinions" and "feelings," that more official accounts of the zombie apocalypse fail to capture.[39] In the framing narrative, we learn that the collected stories of *World War Z* have been dismissed as "too intimate" by the commissioners of the post-apocalyptic UN official report, who want "a collection of cold, hard, data."[40] The framing narrator protests that the human factor is what distinguishes us from the zombies. As we know from Romero's films, the "human factor" in both its positive and negative aspects is also the key to either the downfall or the survival of those facing an apocalypse.

Greed, prejudice, arrogance, and ignorance are also portrayed as deadly infections. These factors serve to escalate the worldwide outbreak and to impede potential solutions, which leads to the zombie plague bursting the boundaries of "official" containment. While these follies can be traced through individual and group acts during Romero's films, *World*

*War Z* shows them occurring on a global scale. Desperate refugees carrying the infection are smuggled through Tibet. They are illegally transported by "snakeheads"[41] (human smugglers) into the "First World ghettos" of the "self-righteous hypocritical North,"[42] where certain outbreaks, particularly those in lower-income areas, are "neglected."[43] The first name for the zombie plague, "African rabies," is a clear reference to the racism-tinged panics that accompanied the growing awareness of HIV/AIDS in the 1980s and the ongoing racism-fuelled indifference towards the scourge in Africa.

In the opening story of "Patient Zero," the puzzled Chinese doctor who discovers the first zombie — a young boy — contacts an influential friend, who, when he grasps what is happening, gives orders to the doctor in a "flat robotic voice, as if he had rehearsed this speech."[44] His response implies that not only were the authorities already aware of the possibility of a zombie outbreak, but that, in fact, they may have been anticipating it. This not only opens the account *in medias res,* but further suggests that these same authorities may somehow be responsible for the outbreak, even though its original cause is concealed from the reader. In less than an hour, the "Goanbu" or Chinese secret police arrive to remove both the zombie and the infected villagers.[45] A "War on Drugs" soldier in Kyrgyzstan encounter zombies, only to have the story covered up by Canadian authorities that attribute his report to "exposure to unknown chemical agents" and "a healthy dose of PTSD," sending the soldier for evaluation. The soldier remarks: "Evaluation ... that's what happens when it's your own side. It's only 'interrogation' when it's the enemy."[46] Social inequalities, as well as racism and totalitarian manipulation, escalate the crisis. For example, the black market in harvested organs from China causes an outbreak in Brazil, where wealthy people go for organ transplants. The implication is that this outbreak is caused by the careless and cannibalistic predations of the rich on the bodies of the poor. The narrator, a former surgeon, drops hints about "executed political prisoners" from whom the organs might have been removed while the "donor" is still alive and indignantly exclaims:

> Who knows how many infected corneas, infected pituitary glands ... Mother of God, who knows how many infected kidneys [China] pumped into the global market. And that's just the organs! You want to talk about the "donated" eggs from political prisoners, the sperm, the blood? ... Few of you Yankees asked where your new kidney or pancreas was coming from, be it a slum kid from the City of God or some unlucky student in a Chinese political prison.[47]

While money flows in from these surgeries, however, underwriting the narrator's "herbal Jacuzzi," he is content to set these questions aside. Another follower of "big-time, prewar, global capitalism" peddles a phony zombie "vaccine" Phalanx, generating huge profits by exploiting people's fear.[48] This amoral businessman sees "the opportunity of a lifetime" in the first reported outbreaks of "African rabies" and finds a "workable pitch": "A cure would make people buy it only if they thought they were infected. But a vaccine! That's preventative! People will keep taking that as long as they're afraid it's out there!"[49] Zombies draw our attention to the hungry gaze that capitalism focuses on people: what Naomi Klein calls "disaster capitalism" or "orchestrated raids on the public sphere in the wake of catastrophic events, combined with the treatment of disasters as exciting market opportunities."[50] A critique of disaster capitalism is found in practically all zombie apocalypse fictions, as survivors learn that some of the complicated, crafty living are worse than the simple, mindless dead, described by Louis Gross as "the proletarian" to the living's bourgeoisie.[51] As one Internet commentator said of the then-upcoming television series based on the comic book series *The Walking Dead,* "Zombie stories treat the ghouls as the environment, and not as the antagonist. The antagonist in a good zombie story is other (living) people."[52] The "Phalanx King" expresses no regret for his exploitation: "I chased my dream and I got my slice."[53]

The bankruptcy of the system that allows such practices to flourish is demonstrated by the complicity of the politicians and corporate-owned media, with devastating consequences.[54] The former White House chief of staff explains that Phalanx was a welcome placebo because it "calmed people down and let us do our job": "What, you would have rather we told people the truth? That it wasn't a new strain of rabies but a mysterious uber-plague that reanimated the dead? Can you imagine the panic that would have happened: the protest, the riots, the billions in damage to private property?" To this official, echoing the businessman, who blames the inevitable panic on the media for finally blowing the whistle, the truth is "political suicide."[55] Phalanx is thus aligned with the popular medications Adderall and Ritalin, prescribed as coping aids for a stupefied, fearful population who cannot keep "track of it all," meaning the global 24-hour news cycle suffusing twenty-first-century awareness with appalling stories, in which those of marauding zombies become just another piece of bad news. As a former suburban housewife plaintively asks, "How do you know which one is really real?"[56] This character, at first reminiscent of the catatonic Barbra in *Night,* after surviving zombie attacks and pulling one zombie's head off to save her child, eventually becomes the mayor of a rebuilt, fortified community where houses on stilts are accessed through retractable walkways and ladders. She gets one of the last words in *WWZ,* which returns to some of its interviewees at the conclusion: "You can blame the politicians, the businessmen, the generals, the 'machine,' but really, if you're looking to blame someone, blame me. I'm the American system, I'm the machine...."[57]

In the post-apocalyptic U.S., class differences are reversed as manufacturing skills become paramount. Formerly privileged white-collar workers are burdens on the new society, as the head of "DeStRes," the agency set up to handle rebuilding efforts, explains:

> You should have seen some of the "careers" listed on our first employment census; everyone was some version of an "executive," a "representative," an "analyst," or a "consultant," all perfectly suited to the prewar world, but all totally inadequate for the present crisis. We needed carpenters, masons, machinists, gunsmiths.[58]

In Romero's films, technical "apocalypse know-how" is also crucial to survival — knowing how to handle weapons or to fly the helicopter in *Dawn of the Dead,* for example — and, as with *Dawn,* the senseless accumulation of consumer goods becomes not only obsolete, but also sinister. In *WWZ,* a diver refers to the unsettling experience of having to navigate the massive amounts of inessential goods that were dumped overboard in harbors by those fleeing during the Great Panic: "Plasma TVs always crunched when you walked over them. I always imagined it was bone."[59] In addition to the uncanniness of these heaps, the corpses of dead luxuries joining the undead underwater, this sentence also evokes the apocalyptic zombie's onscreen origins.[60]

Notably, the much maligned, first-generation immigrants, formerly inhabiting subaltern cultures, become the saviors of post-apocalyptic America. A "mixed group of instructors" is "tasked with infusing these sedentary, overeducated, desk-bound, cubicle mice with the knowledge necessary to make it on their own"[61]:

> These were the people who tended small gardens in their backyards, who repaired their own homes, who kept their appliances running for as long as mechanically possible. It was crucial that these people teach the rest of us to break from our comfortable, disposable consumer lifestyle even though their labor had allowed us to maintain that lifestyle in the first place.[62]

The breakdown of class privilege is "scarier than the living dead" for the formerly "high-powered" elite: one woman with an MFA cannot handle being instructed by her former cleaning lady, whom she insists on addressing by her first name "Magda."[63] "Mrs. Magda Antonova," formerly and familiarly subaltern, is dignified with her surname in the aftermath of the apocalypse. The former White House chief of staff who welcomed the cover-up of Phalanx is interviewed while he is shoveling dung for fuel.[64] In *WWZ*, in effect, another, internal, American Revolution has happened.

The breakdown of the more absurd and reprehensible aspects of "the machine" is an occasion for revolutionary celebration in zombie narratives. A Texan bodyguard recounts the memorably absurd failure of the gated compound containing thinly disguised versions of well-known Hollywood celebrities and their entourages who broadcast a reality show from within their plush haven's walls. These "pampered parasites" are "Romanovs": "that little rich, spoiled, tired-looking whore who was famous for just being a rich, spoiled, tired-looking whore" is clearly an allusion to Paris Hilton and her ilk.[65] The celebrities sit back and watch the "peons" fighting the zombies, but they are themselves invaded and overcome by a frantic horde of people who have bought into the idea that celebrity privilege equals safety. Confronted at last with reality, the celebrities' security forces walk out on them in disgust.[66]

The dramatic reversals and restructurings of society that follow the zombie wars challenge preconceived perceptions of individuals, cultures, and nations. The "prewar paradise" of Iceland, for example, becomes "a cauldron of frozen blood" while Cuba, in an ironic reversal, becomes a refugee haven, accepting boat people from the United States.[67] "The Arsenal of Victory" undergoes subtle changes as Cuban society becomes more open as a result of an influx of refugees in a kind of "infection" of ideas.[68] In the post-apocalyptic world, the Cuban peso is "king."[69] The Russian chaplain who euthanizes infected soldiers as an act of "Final Purification" founds a new type of spirituality.[70] This leads to a "religious fervor" in the new "Holy Russian Empire" which begins to show signs of totalitarian corruption at the close of *WWZ* as priests are organized into "death squads" and hints abound that Cold War–type hostilities might resume.[71]

Other reversals of established systems of order abound: global life expectancy is "a mere shadow" of what it used to be. The post-apocalyptic U.S. implements universal health care.[72] New corporal punishment laws are put in effect, putting people in stocks and whipping them in the town square: "What were you going to do with thieves and looters, put them in prison? Who would that help? Who could afford to divert able-bodied citizens to feed, clothe and guard other able-bodied citizens? ... [S]eeing a senator given fifteen lashes for his involvement in war profiteering did more to curb crime than a cop on every street corner."[73] Some survivors who are abandoned in the isolated zones foment rebellions, which are later brutally put down by a resurgent post-apocalyptic American government, as the Yonkers veteran notes: "That was the first time since crossing the Rockies that I ever saw tanks. Bad feeling: you knew how that was gonna end."[74]

The zombie apocalypse stops the machine, but the machine's effects clearly linger on in the survivors. Some survivors, in their desperation, become "quislings" or zombie sympathizers, while others resort to eating human flesh for food, representing, as Wood reminds us, "the logical end of human relations under capitalism."[75] Survival, it is implied, may entail becoming as impersonal, amoral and bloodthirsty as the living dead themselves. Survivors must defeat not only the zombies, but also representatives of the old order struggling with the new for post-apocalyptic hegemony. In *WWZ*, "greed, fear, stupidity and hate" are eternal issues for those trying to survive and rebuild.[76]

Zombie narratives such as *WWZ* and *Pontypool*, as we will see, can thus be read as a kind of postcolonial dystopia in which "the political disfigurement of the oppressed" causes their transfiguration. Such dystopias reverse the utopian "foundation myths of nations."[77] In contrast, we hear from the de-nationalized and displaced, the walking wounded, racked with survivors' guilt, narrating their stories of the zombie wars. If utopianism is based on "assumptions of human perfectibility,"[78] then zombie dystopias presume that, before the situation improves, people will turn to cannibalism and that things will inevitably fall apart. Zombie horror does not gloss over the traumas of social upheaval. In *Regarding the Pain of Others,* her meditation on the photography of war atrocities, Susan Sontag describes the zombies that arise at the climax of *J'Accuse* (1938), French director Abel Gance's antiwar film:

> "Morts de Verdun, levez-vous!" ("Rise, dead of Verdun!"), cries the deranged veteran who is the protagonist of the film, and he repeats his summons in German and in English: "Your sacrifices were in vain!" And the vast mortuary plain disgorges its multitudes, an army of shambling ghosts in rotted uniforms with mutilated faces, who rise from their graves and set out in all directions, causing mass panic among the populace already mobilized for a new pan-European war. "Fill your eyes with this horror! It is the only thing that can stop you!" the madman cries to the fleeing multitudes of the living, who reward him with a martyr's death, after which he joins his dead comrades: a sea of impassive ghosts overrunning the cowering future combatants and victims of la guerre de domain. War beaten back by apocalypse.[79]

Filling our eyes with zombie horror, it is suggested, allows us to regard the pain of others with a little less complacency. For example, *WWZ* optimistically postulates that Israel, the first nation to enact quarantine in the face of the zombie outbreaks, invites the Palestinians into the quarantine zone, thereby settling the longstanding conflict in the Middle East by uniting against the zombies.[80] The Palestinian narrator recounts his disbelief at hearing what was thought to be a "Zionist lie."[81] The Israelis use sniffer dogs to distinguish the infected from the healthy at their checkpoints. At first, they take away an elderly Palestinian man, confirming the narrator's suspicions, but then they also drag away an American Jewish man who is screaming, "I'm one of you!"[82]: "Everything I thought was true went up in smoke..., supplanted by the face of our real enemy."[83] A civil war in Israel is waged between those opposed to the repatriation of Palestinians, a pullout from the West Bank and Jerusalem, and the razing of settlements: "A lot of Israelis had to watch their houses bulldozed in order to make way for those fortified, self-sufficient residential compounds."[84] War is beaten back by apocalypse as long-established hostilities are overturned. At the Honolulu Conference following the apocalypse, where the American president proposes that the living launch an offensive and return from their "safe zones," the complete reversal of pre-war hegemonies becomes clear as more zombies are to be found frozen in suspended animation in the Global North:

> Many of the colder countries were what you used to call "First World." One of the delegates from a prewar "developing" country suggested, rather hotly, that maybe this was their punishment for raping and pillaging the "victim nations of the south." Maybe, he said, by keeping the "white hegemony" distracted with their own problems, the undead invasion might allow the rest of the world to develop "without imperialist intervention." Maybe the living dead had brought more than just devastation to the world. Maybe in the end, they had brought justice for the future.[85]

The Chilean narrator finds this reaction understandable but ultimately unproductive: "They just wanted revenge for the past.... After all we'd been through, we still couldn't take our heads from out our asses or our hands from around each other's throats."[86] No nation, it is implied, holds the monopoly on oppression. When a South African radio broadcast is set up to combat ignorance, "misinformation," and "the various indigenous solutions people believed would save them from the undead," the radio station operator who is narrating this segment remarks, "Everyone was furious with his own people. Everyone was ashamed."[87] This shame causes a rash of suicides among radio operators who monitored the anguished voices from all over the world.[88] Although the American president's proposal is scorned by the narrator as "typically Norteamericano," it is also presented as redemptive and heroic. This vision prevails as the inheritors of the zombie apocalypse set out in the final pages of *WWZ* to rebuild their world along radically different lines. It will be interesting to see whether or not the soon-to-be-released filmed version of *WWZ* retains its critical consciousness of the American tendency to capitalize on disaster. The Chilean narrator cynically remarks of the American presidential speech: "I guess, if this was a gringo movie, you'd see some idiot get up and start clapping slowly, then the others would join in and then we'd see a tear roll down someone's cheek or some other contrived bullshit like that."[89] Earlier in the book, however, a filmmaker creates narratives of resistance to help fight the suicides and despair that torment the survivors.[90] Although the filmmaker is depicting technological fixes that don't work, his films do raise the morale of the survivors because "Americans worship technology."[91] The filmmaker justifies his "contrived bullshit" by emphasizing the need for stories of courage and hope: "The lies our government told us before the war, the ones that were supposed to keep us happy and blind, those were the ones that burned, because they prevented us from doing what had to be done."[92] This dueling and ambivalent perspective on narrativity and Hollywood sentimentality amplifies the subversive power of orality in the written text. It resists being the "gringo movie," undermining hegemonic patterns of representation and dissolving black-and-white portraits of nationalized and racialized identities.

*WWZ* thus continually sidesteps essentializing narrative moves by self-consciously contrasting itself to simplistic Hollywood heroic narratives. Gray also applies to the ethical choices that people are forced to make during the zombie apocalypse. As Selena (Naomie Harris) tells Jim in *28 Days Later*, survival necessitates being prepared to kill infected loved ones "in a heartbeat." This horrific possibility recurs in *WWZ*, but the book also juxtaposes the narratives of unsympathetic characters such as "the Phalanx King" or the cosmetic surgeon, with more innocent, likeable, or downright heroic characters. For example, Sharon, a mentally disabled girl found "in the ruins of Wichita," provides one of the more moving accounts of the book. While Sharon's understanding is limited, she can mimic the moan of a zombie almost perfectly and describes being barricaded, along with other women and children in her community, inside a church that is being overrun.[93] As we struggle to piece together Sharon's fragmentary words to understand what is happening, it becomes agonizingly evident that women are killing their children to save them from being devoured. A woman who has already lost her own daughter to the zombies, saves her, shooting Sharon's mother before she can kill her daughter.[94] This church may be the same one that an army patrolman, interviewed much later on in the book, discovers: "We once broke into a church in Kansas where it was clear the adults killed all the kids first."[95] In this way, seemingly disparate and fragmented stories are interwoven and cross-referenced throughout *WWZ*.

In a similarly heartbreaking story, another young woman, Jesika Hendricks, recalls the agonizing choice her family makes to consume human flesh to survive. She describes the gradual disintegration of communal ties among a band of survivors fleeing north, changing from a friendly group that cooperates and shares or trades its resources to a dangerous situation in which "people started getting mean":

> There were no more communal fires, no more cookouts or singing. The camp became a mess, nobody picking up their trash anymore.... I wasn't left alone with neighbors anymore, my parents didn't trust anyone. Things got dangerous, you'd see a lot of fights.... The only time anyone ever came together was when one of the dead showed up.[96]

Eventually, Jesika's parents abandon their scruples to hunger and trade her radio for a bowl of "steaming hot stew. It was so good! Mom told me not to eat too fast.... She was crying a little." Later, she understands the "look" that changes her father's face when her parents fall ill and she has to care for them. It is left up to the reader to guess how she does this, presumably by killing others or making some other appalling choice. At the close of the novel, although the interviewer makes reference to "trials" of those who practiced cannibalism, the Yonkers veteran says that it is better not to judge "questionable survival methods." Such awful choices, *Realpolitik* on a national scale, save humanity in the form of the Redeker Plan. Originally a ruthless blueprint for the survival of an apartheid regime, the plan is adopted, first by the South African post-apartheid government "of all colors"[97] and then by other nations. Redeker himself is depicted as being unable to live with this plan and is committed to a psychiatric institution under another name.[98]

The effect of telling from multiple, international perspectives, rather than showing a limited (American) range in a linear Hollywood film, allows the reader to move beyond the borders of the text to imagine the heterogeneous range of situations, conflicts and scenarios evoked, but not covered by the accounts compiled in *World War Z*. For example, some passing allusions to "Flight 575" by a former "snakehead" leads the reader to imagine what might have happened on board. A British survivor recounts the castles and stately homes of Europe being fortified against the besieging zombie hordes, referring to, but never elaborating upon, several spectacular failures such as Versailles and Muiderslot in Holland.[99] Another sequence left to the reader's imagination is the battle of "One Tree Hill" with five hundred Maori "versus half of reanimated Auckland."[100] In this way, *World War Z* is a written work that is also self-consciously about a zombie film that, after we have read it, will be "now playing" in the theatres of our minds. At the same time, the global scale of *WWZ* forces the conventional zombie narrative of a handful of survivors to expand and to overrun both its national and its textual boundaries. It will be interesting to see whether the forthcoming film adaptation with its main character — the frame-narrator who is compiling the oral history — will be able to make such transmediated gestures.

If *WWZ* in its (h)or(r)ality ambitiously imagines a global apocalypse, the apocalypse depicted in *Pontypool Changes Everything*, although equally rooted in social causes, retains the intimacy of a particular locale — rural southern Ontario. Although the book was written in 1998, it was reissued in 2008 following Bruce McDonald's film adaptation, for which Burgess wrote and re-wrote the script. Burgess adapted a portion of the book into a linear story that follows the struggles of only one of the sets of characters depicted in the book. The book, on the other hand, is another Chaucerian web of non-linear, but interconnected tales, again escaping the limitations of narrative film through its mirror maze of reflections of and on the apocalypse.

In his afterword to the new edition of *Pontypool Changes Everything*, Burgess self-consciously distances himself from his earlier self, "insufferably preoccupied with literary malformations."[101] Burgess's zombie virus is itself a literary malformation, a tongue-in-cheek amalgam of influential semiotic theories. Like Baudrillard's simulacra, the virus is endlessly copying itself.[102] In keeping with the conventions of the zombie genre, however, institutionalized experts, including academics, are notably at a loss to explain or control the outbreak. One character avers that "a whole host of disciplines are working together on this one," "teams of doctors, semioticians, linguists and anthropologists worldwide."[103] He also claims, ridiculously, that the "immature virus looks a bit like a sunfish ... it has two long, pointy fangs, which it uses to practice scratching at the paradigms it will eventually invade."[104] In a nod to Julia Kristeva, "the mature virus," we are told, "resembles the figure of abjection," leaving the reader to hopelessly try to imagine a figure of "death infecting life," "what disturbs system, identity, order," "in-between," "ambiguous" and "composite."[105] Another expert adds Chomskyan linguistics to the mix: "It gestates in the deep structures prior to language. Or, at least, simultaneous with language. In the very primal structure that organizes us as differentiated, discontinuous copies of each other."[106] *Pontypool*'s protagonists—Les/Greg/narrator/Grant Mazzy—are also "differentiated, discontinuous copies of each other," just as "H/ellen," a mental patient, is an amalgam of two female characters, Les's wife Helen and Ellen Peterson. H/ellen quotes Walt Whitman's line about "the beautiful uncut hair of graves" from "Song of Myself."[107] Earlier, we read that Ellen's husband, Detective Peterson, mumbles "Bad boy Walt Whitman" as he succumbs to the virus. *Pontypool*, unlike its film adaptation, resembles *WWZ*. It is a song of many selves, chronicling the breakdown of relationships, whether personal or societal.

Whereas Burgess's zombies are frightening, murderous creatures, they are also pitiable and in some ways indistinguishable from what Burgess calls "unsound bodies" or the socially vulnerable—the physically and mentally handicapped, children, and drug addicts. For example, Ellen's empathy for the zombies is created by her experience of having suffered a stroke: she thinks, "*These poor people have all suffered strokes*" [italics in original].[108] The abject zombies and the "unsound bodies" of *Pontypool* are informed by a historical social subtext that keeps *Pontypool* firmly within the same apocalyptic zombie tradition as *WWZ*. In 1998, under the Conservative provincial government of Mike Harris, a "Common Sense Revolution" or the imposition of capitalist neoliberalism in Ontario was in full swing. Social programs were gutted, particularly those for the vulnerable: single mothers, welfare recipients, drug addicts, and the mentally ill, many of whom were forced onto the streets and kept there by the cuts to social housing and income supports, as well as the closure of hospitals and the elimination of thousands of hospital beds.[109] *Pontypool* describes these displaced persons as "high-functioning mercenaries," whose "strange ability ... frightened the proto-Yuppie colony that had just recently moved into the area."[110] The Harris government also slashed funding to education (such as Burgess's graduate program in semiotics) and created a culture in which non-profit-oriented work and study was devalued.

This social and cultural upheaval unmistakably forms the backdrop for the creation of Burgess's zombies. These all-too-human monsters, whose infection deprives them of the ability to communicate with each other, are forced to attempt an escape through the open mouths of their victims. In this Ontario, the zombie's look, "familiar to the followers of zombies," "though inanimate, is fresh with the experience of abjection, of failure."[111] A recurring theme is the inability to express and to communicate. This characterizes all the "unsound bodies" in *Pontypool*: Robin Wood's Othered monsters—zombies, junkies, women, and children. The first deaths of zombies we see are, unlike the splatstick of many zombie films, tinged with empathy:

> The killer's neck is broken and he stands over the nurse with his head dropping to his chest. His mouth is open, a bright red gasket through which the bleating of animals can be heard. The sound he makes isn't human; the message, however, is unmistakable. He's saying: "*This doesn't work, I'm failing.*"[112]

Empathy haunts *Pontypool*'s characters in much the same way that survivor's guilt haunts the characters in *WWZ*. *Pontypool* makes a similar point that empathy creates vulnerability. At the same time, the novel is insistent that the loss of empathy means the essential loss of humanity, even though it is perilous. For example, it is not clear whether or not Detective Peterson is stricken by the zombie virus or by empathy when "he feels the bowling ball holes of the hunter's eyes slipping behind his own sockets."[113] This slippage is also conveyed in the film by the sequence in which Sydney Briar (Lisa Houle) struggles with infection, stuttering over and over again on the word "kill." Only by convincing her that she has actually said "kiss," can she fend off being transformed into a zombie. The non-stricken characters similarly struggle with language and expression, in a way that could not be conveyed by film that demands sound—Ellen, in the aftermath of having to kill her husband, "makes a fist of her long hand to push against her mouth. The crying that she feels is very young, and she cannot trust herself to let it up."[114] Ellen subsequently encounters a strange group of zombies who are "working" (dumping garbage into the pond and picking it up again, possibly duplicating Harris's workfare programs for welfare recipients). Fearful abjects, they are filled with anticipation of violence: "Why, if he's cold, won't he freeze?"; "You don't hate him yet. But if you don't know him will you stab him with a knife?"; and "If you don't want to kill him, does that mean that you want to run him over with a car?"[115] Ellen finds herself consoling the hapless killers, leading the reader into a chapter entitled "Policy" in which the zombies invert her language of compassion: "It's OK": "It's OK to kill biting, y'know." "And I know it's OK to tear fuckin' fuckers' heads off."[116]

In another segment, a junkie on the streets of Vancouver is portrayed as a type of innocent zombie, smiling at onlookers while blood drips down his chin. The narration provides a calm commentary on his frightening state. It is an inner monologue told in retrospect: "Oh dear. Sometimes you can't help but notice how sick you're becoming":

> You know that you have been barking at people lately. In fact, that's why you got thrown out of the Columbia Hotel. "Do you know you've been barking at people in the lobby?" You shrug miserably at this kind of question. *No, I'm afraid I didn't know....* You make a face like Buster Keaton, tilting your jaw. *Yes, the problem is huge, altogether too far gone, I think* [italics in original].[117]

Like the zombies, the nameless junkie cannot communicate these thoughts. He ends up in a psychiatric ward being forced to watch "hateful" films like *Terms of Endearment*, which the patients turn into *"Agonizing Screams of Endearment"* by adjusting the volume.[118]

Les's struggle with mental illness paradoxically protects him from the zombie virus.[119] He struggles with the "delusional worms" surrounding him as he escapes and "rightly thanks his illness for peeling back at least one layer from the hideous stop of the sky."[120] Later, as Les makes his escape, he reflects that he has "isolated a part of himself that he commits to sanity, and from here he has decided that the difference between his relapsed psyche and the outside world is so negligible that to worry about losing touch is not the most urgent game."[121] Les's delusions of "The War in Ontario" and "the Underground"—about finding bodies in the garbage he picks up—echo the heartlessness of Harris's "Common Sense Revolution" which social justice groups such as the Ontario Coalition Against Poverty (OCAP) described as a war on the poor.[122] His hallucinations of cannibalism are nightmarish allegories of late capitalism as a

> Canada's Wonderland made of bodies. Giant bloodslides. Houses of torture where children's kidneys are twisted like sponges in the fat hands of musclemen. There would be buns crammed with the cooked knuckles of teenagers, and a king, sitting on a mountain of kings, eating his own shoulder.[123]

In keeping with the bleak tradition of zombie narratives, Les Reardon does not survive, appearing as one of the many silent, uncommunicative bodies in the aftermath of the zombie apocalypse in Dr. Mendez's autopsy lab. Dr. Mendez's attempt to dignify the deaths of so many invites empathy as his one-sided conversations with corpses become another failure of language. Later, the doctor beseeches his callous teenage helpers not to be "seagulls" and to "cry every so often."[124] Like the monstrous babies to be found elsewhere in the book — Les Reardon's son and the creature that drags him to the bottom of the lake — the silent, tearless teenagers, indifferent to the pile of corpses they are cleaning up, do not inspire hope.

The indiscriminate slaughter detailed in *Pontypool*'s "novel" section becomes grimmer and more documentary than hallucinatory, taking the form of *WWZ*-type vignettes. Not all of the deaths can be ascribed to the zombie plague. In a rapid succession of scenes, "a man with his hands clasped behind his neck kneels in a barn in Pontypool. One of two men standing behind him steps forward and fires a handgun through the back of his head," while a baby in Niagara Falls falls out of its highchair and down a flight of stairs.[125] Elsewhere, a "tiny fish-hook is dropped into the lettuce at a salad bar by a madman and swallowed by a dieting accountant."[126] These awful deaths are mingled not only with the zombie mayhem, but also with satire: "A public poll is taken about the confidence people have in Emergency Task Forces; however, most of the respondents are zombies, and half of the pollsters are killed on front porches."[127]

> In Barrie, a defiant population takes to the streets to embrace their cannibal brothers and sisters. An emotion-choked voice blares from a megaphone, pleading for people to return home. The snapping of compassionate necks can be heard clicking through the town and army personnel descend with guns blazing under tear-streaked faces.[128]

These vignettes escalate into devastation: "The population of Norwood is zero. Guelph, three hundred. Maybe. St. Catharines, eight hundred." We are told that "Hamilton is particularly disastrous. Pockets of homicide flare up with crazy unpredictability, confounding a military strategy that flexes itself, finally, in an anguished genocidal nightmare. Hamilton: population definitely zero."[129] This scene is duplicated at the conclusion of the film adaptation, when the radio station is bombed, reducing zombies and survivors alike to rubble. It is *Night of the Living Dead*'s ending writ large, the sheriff's posse replaced by aerial bombardment. While the film takes *Pontypool*'s communication breakdown out of Ontario and into the federal "two solitudes" with its premise that speaking French protects one from zombification, the "strange new edicts" in the book ban "all forms of communication" apart from "militarese": "Speaking, listening, reading, even sign language are punishable at the brute discretion of Ontario's own licensed assassins.... [T]he only words spoken aloud in Ontario through the winter are militarese, punctuated with a sharply barked 'Sir'!"[130]

The devastating conclusion of the film is a grim reminder of the wars in which Canada is currently engaged, which flourish on nothing so much as breakdowns of understanding, erasures of difference and spectacular failures of empathy. The arrival of such monsters in Canadian cultural productions ought to serve as a warning that no national identity can remain fixed and complacent in the globalized world that is mirrored so darkly in our zombie tales.

## Notes

1. Max Brooks, *World War Z* (New York: Three Rivers Press, 2006).
2. Seth Grahame-Smith and Jane Austen, *Pride and Prejudice and Zombies* (Philadelphia: Quirk Productions, 2009).
3. These include (but are not limited to) Richard Matheson's early zombie tale "Dance of the Dead" (later filmed by Tobe Hooper as a *Masters of Horror* episode in 2005) and the short stories in the Romero-inspired shared-world anthology *Book of the Dead* (Skipp & Spector, 1989), notably Joe Lansdale's "At the Far Side of the Cadillac Desert with Dead Folks" and David J. Schow's unforgettably gory "Jerry's Kids Meet Wormboy." Nina Kiriki Hoffmann's "Zombies for Jesus" joins these memorable satires on the rise of evangelical Christianity. Also noteworthy are S.P. Somtow's historical horror story "Darker Angels" (*Confederacy of the Dead*, 1993), Dennis Etchison's tale of exploited zombie temp workers on "The Late Shift," Neil Gaiman's "Bitter Grounds," Poppy Z. Brite's "Calcutta, Lord of Nerves," and Dale Bailey's short story "Death and Suffrage," which forms the basis for the *Masters of Horror* episode "Homecoming" directed by Joe Dante. The 2008 collection, *The Living Dead*, edited by John Joseph Adams, compiles many of these short stories.
4. Tony Burgess, *Pontypool Changes Everything* (Toronto: ECW Press, 1998).
5. *Dawn of the Dead*, DVD, directed by George Romero (Laurel Group, 1979).
6. Judith Halberstam, *Skin Shows: Gothic Horror and the Technology of Monsters* (Durham: Duke University Press, 1995), 3.
7. Ibid., 14.
8. Ibid., 15.

9. Mark Seltzer, *Serial Killers: Death and Life in America's Wound Culture* (New York: Routledge, 1998), 2.

10. Carol Clover, *Men, Women and Chainsaws: Gender in the Modern Horror Film* (Princeton, NJ: Princeton University Press, 1992), 66.

11. Robin Wood, *Hollywood from Vietnam to Reagan ... and Beyond* (New York: Columbia Univerity Press, 1986, 2003).

12. Ibid., 64.

13. Ibid., 76.

14. Paul Virilio, *Speed and Politics: An Essay on Dromology* (New York: Semiotext(e), 1977, 1986), 92–3.

15. Virilio, *Speed*, 76.

16. Ibid., 77–8.

17. *Shaun of the Dead*, DVD, directed by Edgar Wright (Studio Canal, 2004).

18. *Fido*, DVD, directed by Andrew Currie (Lions Gate Films, 2006).

19. *Dead and Breakfast*, DVD, directed by Matthew Leutwyler (Ambus Entertainment, 2004).

20. *Zombieland*, DVD, directed by Reuben Fleischer (Columbia Pictures, 2009).

21. Not only in the growing popular entertainment of "zombie walks," but also in commercials such as the recent Ford Fiesta ad that presents the compact vehicle as a better zombie survival option than its competitors, the Honda Fit and the Toyota Yaris (whose drivers are pursued and devoured). In these ads, as Stephanie Boluk observes in correspondence, the critiques of consumption circulating around the figure of the zombie have come full circle.

22. Edward Said, *Orientalism* (Toronto: Random House, 1978).

23. Philip Brophy, "Horrality," in *The Horror Reader*, ed. Ken Gelder (London: Routledge, 2000).

24. Ibid., 227–8.

25. The term "intertextuality" has been broadly expanded since Julia Kristeva, interpreting Bakhtin, advanced the concept. Here I take it in its original sense as indicating the connections between texts, discourses and traditions as "a mosaic of quotations" (Kristeva, *Desire in Language*, 66–69).

26. *Thriller*, directed by John Landis, performed by Michael Jackson (1983).

27. *Night of the Living Dead*, DVD, directed by George Romero (Image Ten, 1968).

28. Mark Kermode, "I Was a Teenage Horror Fan: or How I Learned to Stop Worrying and Love Linda Blair," *Ill Effects: The Media/Violence Debate*, ed. Martin Barker and Julian Petley (London: Routledge, 1997), 60.

29. *Braindead/Dead Alive*, DVD, directed by Peter Jackson (WingNut Films, 1992).

30. *Død Snø*, DVD, directed by Tommy Wirkola (Euforia Film, 2009).

31. Clover makes the interesting assertion that intertextuality or "horror's habit of cross-referencing" is a "standard feature of oral cycles." *Men, Women and Chainsaws*, 9.

32. Walter Ong, *Orality and Literacy: The Technologizing of the Word* (New York: Routledge, 1982).

33. Linda Badley, *Film, Horror and the Body Fantastic* (London: Greenwood Press, 1995), 37.

34. Brooks, *World War Z*, 48.

35. Ibid., 53–4.

36. Ibid., 6.

37. Ibid., 10.

38. Ibid., 30.

39. Ibid., 1.

40. Ibid.

41. Ibid., 13.

42. Ibid., 22.

43. Ibid., 61.

44. Ibid., 9.

45. Ibid., 9.

46. Ibid., 21.

47. Ibid., 27–8.

48. Ibid., 54–5.

49. Ibid.

50. Ibid., 6.

51. Louis S. Gross, *Redefining the American Gothic: From* Wieland *to* Day of the Dead (Ann Arbor/London: UMI Research Press, 1989), 86. For another reading linking serial killers, zombies and capitalism, see Annalee Newitz's *Pretend We're Dead: Capitalist Monsters in American Pop Culture* (2006). In the context of the financial crisis at the time of this writing, the discourse of "zombie banks" as a mark of disaster capitalism's opportunism is particularly apt.

52. "ZeroCorpse" commenting on *The Walking Dead* in "Holy Zombies, This Looks Good," http://www.fark.com/cgi/comments.pl?IDLink=5630682.

53. Brooks, *World War Z*, 58.

54. Ibid., 56.

55. Ibid., 60.

56. Ibid., 66.

57. Ibid., 334.

58. Ibid., 138.

59. Ibid., 305.

60. I am indebted for this insight to Stephanie Boluk in our email correspondence.

61. Brooks, World War Z, 139.

62. Ibid., 140.

63. Ibid., 141.

64. Ibid., 59.

65. Ibid., 84.

66. Ibid., 88.

67. Ibid., 230.

68. Ibid., 232.

69. Ibid., 337.

70. Ibid., 297.

71. Ibid., 331.

72. Ibid., 2.

73. Ibid., 149.

74. Ibid., 322.

75. Wood, *Hollywood*, 22.

76. Brooks, *World War Z*, 148.

77. Ronald Niezen, "Postcolonialism and the Utopian Imagination," in *Postcolonial Theory and the Arab-Israel Conflict* (New York: Routledge, 2008), 38.

78. Ibid., 39.

79. Susan Sontag, *Regarding the Pain of Others* (New York: Farrar, Straus and Giroux, 2003).

80. Brooks, *World War Z*, 32.

81. Ibid., 37.

82. Ibid., 41.

83. Ibid., 44.

84. Ibid., 43–4.

85. Ibid., 266.

86. Ibid.

87. Ibid., 197.

88. Ibid., 198.

89. Ibid., 267.

90. Ibid., 160.

91. Ibid., 166.

92. Ibid., 167.

93. Ibid., 73–7.

94. Ibid.

95. Ibid., 325.

96. Ibid., 129.

97. Ibid., 107–8.

98. Ibid., 111.

99. Ibid., 189.

100. Ibid., 332.

101. Burgess, *Pontypool*, 237.

102. Ibid., 147.

103. Ibid., 168.

104. Ibid., 169.

105. Julia Kristeva, *Powers of Horror: An Essay on Abjection* (New York: Columbia University Press, 1982), 4.

106. Burgess, *Pontypool*, 167.

107. Ibid., 125.

108. Ibid., 115.

109. Charlotte Gray, "Will Voters' Response to Health Care Reforms Determine the Fate of Mike Harris?" *Canadian Medical Association Journal* 160 (June 1999): 1623–1624. See also Cheryl Forchuk, Libbey Joplin, Ruth Schofield, Rick Csiernik, Carolyne Gorlick and Katherine Turner, "Housing, income support and mental health: Points of disconnection," *Health Research Policy and Systems* 5, no. 14 (2007), http://health-policy-systems.com/content/5/1/14.

110. Burgess, *Pontypool*, 161.

111. Ibid., 58.

112. Ibid., 30–1.
113. Ibid., 29.
114. Ibid., 67.
115. Ibid., 108–9.
116. Ibid., 112.
117. Ibid., 118–21.
118. Ibid., 129.
119. Ibid., 38.
120. Ibid., 42.
121. Ibid., 62.
122. Sandra Jeppeson, "From 'The War on Poverty' to 'The War on the Poor': Knowledge, Power and Subject Positions in Anti-poverty Discourses," *Canadian Journal of Communication* 34, no. 3 (2009): 487–508, 491.
123. Burgess, *Pontypool*, 64.
124. Ibid., 140.
125. Ibid., 255.
126. Ibid., 256.
127. Ibid.
128. Ibid., 259.
129. Ibid., 261.
130. Ibid., 254.

# Cyberpunk and the Living Dead

## Andrea Austin

### Alchemy

The zombie is a conveniently dual-purposed figure in many popular films and novels, standing either for civilization as a system or process that is deadening to the individual or, in the form of an inchoate, rampaging horde, for anything and everything that threatens to tear down "civilized culture" and/as the established order. In much of pop culture, then, the zombie is distinctly oxymoronic, both the empty product of capital or labor or even more generally, society, and at the same time, a primal and animalistic force poised to wipe out all such organization. Moreover, the zombie perfectly conveys a major trope of post-industrial culture in its simultaneous dependence upon and fear of technology: the transformation of human beings into mindless machines. Edgar Wright's insistence on the resemblance between zoned-out iPod users and a plague of zombies, for example, is instantly recognizable in the prelude for the parodic *Shaun of the Dead* (2004) precisely because the trope has now become cliché. The specter of technological zombification has been repeated in countless films, television shows, and popular novels for several decades. Yet if cyberpunk did not invent the trope, it was cyberpunk that most thoroughly explored it, anatomized it, peeled back the skin from the sleek surface of its too-obvious allegory to reveal the grotesque, inner workings of a more detailed and murderous fascination.

Notorious in the sheer variety of its living dead, from neural imprints, personality constructs, and AIs to meat puppets and flatlined hackers, cyberpunk drew first breath from its proposal of machine insurgence and the material ghost. Nor was the proposal ever mere critique, a mere cautionary tale warning us that technology would steal our souls; it was as often overwhelmed by the electric hum of the dead-alive as infinity-nexus of evolutionary possibility, and easily as in love with the perils of dystopia as with its pleasures.[1] A cerebral intensity marked cyberpunk's living dead, an intensity that went well beyond the robotics and reanimation antics of an earlier generation's mad scientists, and that did so in order to define a popular technology that spread like infection to transform both flesh and mind. For cyberpunk writers, the zombie is a gesture beyond, linking the future-impulse of science fiction, the horrific other-worldly impulse of the gothic, and, most importantly, the crucible

147

impulse of competing possessions. This chapter explores that gesture in William Gibson's iconic novel, *Neuromancer* (1984).

## Ballistics

*Neuromancer* has become one of the most well-known and frequently taught texts of the cyberpunk movement.[2] It is a beautiful and complex novel, recounting through a deliberately disjointed, sometimes retrospective narrative, and in a profoundly poetic and often elliptical style, the story of Case, a young man with a neural jack who specializes in digital break and entry. Case is recruited by the artificial intelligence, Wintermute, to join a select group of talent with one purpose and one purpose only — to break into the mainframe system that houses the AI.

The story is quintessential cyberpunk in its array of cybernetically-enhanced characters, its *in medias res* beginning, its non-conclusion, its edgy, street-scene language, its vivid depiction of a near-future dominated by the corporate interests of pharmaceutical and computing conglomerates, and its layered plot threads with key events in both physical and virtual terrain. Its resistance to dialectic oppositions is likewise typical of the genre, as is its encouragement of cognates for the posthuman. The ontological difference between the cyborg, the clone, the ghost, and the zombie is a shifting house of cards, and all are allied with the evolution of the human into something either more or less, but variously collected together under the rubric of a prefix that gestures beyond the meaning and origins of what it modifies. What interests me most about *Neuromancer,* however, is not its refusal of apparent opposites (like human and zombie) or even its expansive "posthuman" (which includes the zombie) but rather, its violence against more fundamental assumptions of concurrence. If, as Timothy Leary has asserted, "the cyberpunk is a meaning grenade thrown over the language barricade,"[3] then the cyberpunk zombie is an existential shotgun, blowing apart the couplings of "human" and "alive," "survival" and "evolution," "memory" and "past," "sensation" and "corporeality," and most profoundly, "awakening" and "transcendence." Each sundering of these complementary terms brings Case a step closer to an anticipated vanishing point, and by the end of the story, the trope of the technological zombie — which also happens to be Case's beginning — has been ripped inside out.

## Falling into Flesh

When we first meet Case, he is a shell trying hard to live down to his name. He is a fallen man. A once-elite hacker who cheated his boss and was re-paid with a virile neurotoxin, he is a burnt-out drug addict who now preys on other street hustlers and sleeps in a coffin hotel. He himself notes that he exists in an unnerving limbo, neither fully dead nor alive: "In the first month, he'd killed two men and a woman over sums that a year before would have seemed ludicrous. Ninsei wore him down until the street itself came to seem the externalization of some death wish."[4] Case is not alone in this limbo. In fact, *Neuromancer* is peopled almost entirely by zombies, of one kind or another: Wintermute, in a desperate race to expand beyond the reach of the authorities before being discovered and terminated; Molly, a custom-fitted bounty hunter whose mirrored eye prostheses hide emotional suicide; the Dixie Flatline, a portable neural imprint of a famous, deceased hacker; the psychic assassin and cannibal, Riviera; Corto, alias Armitage, a schizophrenic veteran whose brain has been re-programmed with an expendable identity; clones of various members of the Tessier-Ashpool family — the list could be longer. Zombie (p)layers accrete, hive-like, around the central core of the trope, and technological zombification is not confined to the more sensationally cyborg examples but, in Gibson's vision, is the inevitable condition of the twin dictatorship of corporate capitalism and communications networks. Still, in spite of the proliferation, there are principals; Case and Wintermute are the primary characters and although Case will not know it for most of the novel, they share the same dream. Narratively, Molly is the floater, paid by one to ferry the other from hack to hack like Charon negotiating the river Styx, except that the river is a stream of data, cash, and conspiracy.

This initial sense of region, concretely detailed, of places to be ferried from and to, creates an illusion of depth and more than that, an illusion of life. Riding the pink rush down the streets of Ninsei or dodging murder by microfilament in Nighttown's back alleys, Case understands that the slightest hesitation or mistake could be his undoing. A black market in drugs, data, and human organs means that "death is the accepted punishment for laziness, carelessness, or lack of grace,"[5] and the street's runners are addicted to this dime-edge dystopia, needing its simultaneous penetration and encirclement. It seems to prove to them that they still exist, that they are still alive and breathing, for now. If they can just keep a step ahead. Yet the adrenaline surge of street danger and its sudden reversals are more feint than reality, an order of simulation that Case has already begun to suspect. As he points out, street life is just a more desperate version of what passes for life everywhere else. Everyone moves from fix to fix, meal to meal, dollar to dollar, running on basic survival instinct. You can buy anything, any time. The details of day-to-day activity blur with iteration, taking on a mind-numbing monotony against a sky like Molly's glasses, reflecting an illusion of depth, a sky "the color of television, tuned to a dead channel."[6] This is a world where the corporation owns everything and everyone, where the dead are packaged instead of left in peace and the living are medically prolonged until their skin crinkles at the edges like paper ghouls. The surface reflection of life is all there is. In a world like this, how do you know when you're dead? How do you know when you're not?

There's a precise irony here, a point to be made not just about the similarity of post-industrial citizenship and zombie plague, but also about the zombies believing that they are still alive, still human, and using the bodily stimulations of adrenaline and consumption as disguise. Case is different. The irony sharpens when we begin to probe the reasons why Case has begun to suspect. He is beyond disguise, beyond survival. He is beyond caring. Unlike Molly, who mostly watches out for her "own sweet ass" as she likes to put it,[7] Case is not as concerned with his bodily well-being. Survival for him is posed as a question designed to shatter the connection between "human" and "alive," while the bitterness with which this question is inflected in *Neuromancer* derives from the growing kinship between Case and Wintermute. Though slow, deadened, and drug-numbed, Case is least zombie — and most human — when stung by the intrigue of something he can only define as "beyond," even if pursuing that intrigue leads to his own death. The hacker's desolation in the wake of the neurotoxin is our first clue: "for Case, who'd lived for the bodiless exultation of cyberspace, it was the Fall. In the bars he'd frequented as a cowboy hotshot, the elite stance involved a certain relaxed contempt for the flesh. The body was meat."[8] Case's first jack into the matrix is our second when Wintermute recruits him via Molly, a nervous system re-fit, and a new Ono-Sendai. The shapes and neon-bright flare, the "lines of light ranged in the nonspace of the mind, clusters, and constellations of data like city lights"[9] beckon to him with the siren call of impossible security and reach out to him in code with a dream of infinite connection. Case is a cracker. With his friend and digital crowbar, the Dixie Flatline, he cuts through the ice of firewalls with a talent that could only be fuelled by dream, and nothing else, and this is why Wintermute wants him.

Of course, redefining the human is what the posthuman project has/had been about, although the reduction of that project to a desire to extend "being-ness" to sentient machines, as well as to extend "human-ness" to human-machine combination embodiments, misses the more profound desire that set the thing in motion to begin with: to puzzle out the meaning of "human being," and the relationship of the terms in that phrase.[10] Each destination to which Case is ferried takes on the quality of a piece of code leading to the final hack, and carries the intrigue of puzzle. Corto recruits Molly, and in Chiba, she grabs Case. In BAMA, they retrieve Dixie, and in Instanbul, Riviera. The action reveals a rhythm: hack and run, hack and run. The Villa Straylight is the payload, the "boss," and it is Case's most difficult and dangerous hack. In all the previous locations, circling around the retrieval of pieces Wintermute has deemed necessary to the Straylight hack are the side trips Molly and Case make to unravel the mystery of Corto's past. These trips, too, will lead them back to Wintermute, and to Straylight.

Case remarks on the Villa's pathology. Straylight, the home of the powerful family and corporation, Tessier-Ashpool, is a wasp's nest, a "hive with cybernetic memories," its "DNA coded in silicon."[11] For Case, it is a mocking and grotesque parody of network. It is also a nest of clones. Tessier and Ashpool family members are revived in a long parade and barely identified by the numbers in front of their names. The family adds cells of sick redundancy to its nest to ensure its collective survival—familiar form, a known quantity, a closed system. The family has stopped evolving. 3Jane's essay on the Villa is key, code, and clue; she calls Straylight "a Gothic folly, grown in on itself."[12] Memory is quite literally a key, as 3Jane's essay unlocks the mainframe codes that allow Case to penetrate to its heart and bypass the security virus. Written by 3Jane years earlier, the essay alludes both to her own condition and to the Renaissance memory palace. It explains the family, dying because of its need for familiarity. For memory. For the same thing, the same one, the same idea, brought back again and again and again. Straylight explains the clone as a material embodiment of memory, a deadened by-product of nostalgia, and a zombie-like construct glued together from similes of a bioengineered past and a mechanical future. The continuation of the Tessier-Ashpools can be nothing more than its past, a repeating loop, a series of automatons, machine memory—a house of RAM. Memory is thus posed as a wrench to also break the chain between "survival" and "evolution."

In a critical battle, Straylight will force Case to confront his own memories. Or rather, the other Tessier-Ashpool AI, Neuromancer, will force Case to it when the hacker enters the Straylight mainframe. Case is attacked by a virus each time he tries to jack in and, like the Dixie Flatline—in another life, another job—he is rendered ostensibly brain dead. Each time Case flatlines, Neuromancer is waiting for him, seeking to ensnare him in a digital loop, a memory prison baited with Linda Lee. The trap is a concrete bunker on a beach, an eerie vision of a past that never happened even while the details have been picked from the hacker's own synapses. Here, Case finds his girlfriend from Chiba City, killed because she tried to sell computer components she stole from him to fuel an addiction she didn't have when they first met. She invites him to stay. The vision is both painful and seductive, and unexpectedly for Neuromancer, this is when the plan backfires. The phantasmal reunion neither sends Case screaming to insanity, nor entices him to become lost forever in nostalgic desire. Instead, Case faces the memory-construct, fights to accept his own role in Linda's death, and then walks determinedly away from the beach, turning his back on the Linda-ghost and the Linda-guilt. What the confrontation initiates is his recognition that the land of memory, even if it is a land of the dead, is not the land "beyond." Linda may invite him to stay for all eternity, but she cannot deliver the eternal. Behind the dream of Linda, for love is the only human emotion his memory can latch onto, Case senses the older, mythic dream about the relationship between the human and the eternal. The language, perhaps the dream itself, seems antiquated for posthuman application, but no more so than 3Jane's memory palace, which figures not as a reification of the past but as a dream of salvation from it. Neuromancer has tried desperately to distract Case with Linda, to prevent him from reaching the mainframe codes, because the AI does not want to cease its individual existence. Neuromancer is trying to survive. It does not want to merge with Wintermute; it does not want to expand, to evolve. Like Straylight, Neuromancer is a dead end.

The entire team must negotiate similar traps, though none emerge from the experience with as heightened an understanding as Case does. Molly, Corto/Armitage, and Riviera are all running from a horde of insidious monsters: their own memories. Armitage is ripped apart by explosions of rage and paranoia and his nightmares from when he was the military officer, Corto, whose entire unit is betrayed and massacred. Even Wintermute, after re-building the man with a fabricated identity, cannot hold him together once the images begin to re-surface. Or, as Case observes, maybe Wintermute knew the man would shatter. Maybe the AI was counting on it; "twist a man far enough, then twist him as far back, in the opposite direction, reverse, and twist again. The man broke ... And history had done that for Colonel Corto."[13] Likewise, Riviera is undone by a scene from his childhood, a psychic projection he himself has laid as a trap for Molly in an elaborate scheme of double-cross. In an image reminiscent of *Night of the Living Dead* (1968), he shows her his childhood self, cannibalizing the body of a dead soldier. The projection allows Molly an insight, however, and rather than tripping her up, shows her exactly where Riviera is vulnerable. Yet Molly, too, has a shadowy past, and if Riviera does not trip her up, she is nonetheless equally troubled. In a rare moment of personal narration, she tells Case about her stint in a puppet house, a brothel where prostitutes have chips implanted in their brains to inhibit memory and to allow them to run software of the clients' choosing. When Molly's malfunctions, she remembers some of the more horrific encounters in which girls are tortured and murdered. The iteration with Armitage, Riviera, and Molly suggests that the zombie is pure, walking memory, memory that refuses to stay dead and buried, refuses to rot away. It is memory run amok, made flesh and turned loose upon the world. Note, as well, that these are memories of rape, war, and cannibalism. While the zombie is clearly a trope for the animal weight of the body, it is also a trope for the animalistic and primal past. Pure survival instinct, dog-eat-dog.

Chillingly, Neuromancer has already indicated the price of survival — memory become the future, impossibly warped and grown in on itself. The Dixie Flatline's dark humor obsesses on this point. He requests that Case erase him once the job is finished. As a neural imprint, a collection of chemical signals from a once functioning human brain, now translated as data and encased in silicon, his future can only be an endless repetition of his past. This is the future, clearly, that Wintermute does not want to repeat, the silicon cage it, like Dixie, seeks to escape. On the Rue Jules Verne, the main street of the artificial orbiting city of Freeside, Case and Molly meet three French teenagers, apparently on holiday. They turn out to be Turing agents, the odd crinkling of skin around their knuckles the only tell-tale sign of the procedures that prolong their youthful appearance and undercover casework. Like the cloned Tessier-Ashpools, apparently designed to ensure a future for the company, the agents are installed to ensure the future of the human species by tracking all AI activity for signs of growing independence. The agents are trackers, people whose business it is to pay attention to past activity, to traces of events and digital interactions, in order to be a firewall for the future. It is their job to put an end to the quiet dreamings in the dark of cowboys and creature code. When Wintermute kills them, their surprise, painted explicitly on Roland's face, "fixed, white, his teeth bared,"[14] might be chalked up to the fact that they do not know they are already dead.

## Splice of Heaven

If the zombie stands for flesh, you would think the ghost would be its dead opposite, as far from the corporeal as possible. There is little distinction, however, between zombies and ghosts in cyberpunk—how can there be, when the meat melts away into the machine and the data? Case's intense concentration on the feel of Linda's hair, on the smell of smoke from the beach fire, on the rough wrinkling of leather on her jacket or the far-off sound of drum beats as he leaves the bunker—or Dixie's jokes of body memory (like "no hands") and the edge of the construct's laughter, that "gets" Case "in the spine"—make for the kind of *de rigueur* erasure of distance between the material and the digital that has been one of the genre's most influential characteristics.[15] Yet the flashpoints where opposites meet are only the obvious flourishes in a more comprehensive project of re-wiring. The easy, more familiar coupling of "body"-"sensation" lies just beneath, waiting to be jacked apart.

Puppets do most of the jack work. They convey the simple reality of not needing a body to feel, or not feeling the body. At the same time, the puppet is a flashpoint, too, stringing together zombies, clones, and ghosts. Armitage is literally Wintermute's dummy and wetware, a physical presence and front-man for the AI, an organic interface for making arrangements and herding Case, Molly, and Riviera toward the Straylight run. The irony of the AI using the man as a puppet is multi-layered, because Wintermute is not the first to have done it. When Armitage was Corto, he was no less merely a means to an end; he was a military puppet, a black ops leader abandoned as collateral damage, a scenario reprised when Wintermute arranges for him to be blown out of the tug airlock. Similarly, Dixie is a puppet-ghost, though software not wetware, and a double for Case in the matrix. Riviera is both ends of the spectrum, an unstable piece of flesh manipulated like Corto, but also a puppet-handler, deploying his hologram-like projections which, like the Flatline, are data constructs derived from brain signals. The ravages of personal history and the directives of AIs flip the switch between puppet and puppeteer, but one way or another, as Dix notes, everybody gets burned.[16] Only question is, who's pulling the strings?

Discovering just who is pulling the strings is one of the novel's central detective stories. Like *Blade Runner*'s Deckard, Case is both de-tech-tive and detected. Case's experience with the simstim unit underscores the connection between puppet and master, as well as the disconnection between body and sensation, but it also includes a surprise. Simstim allows him to access Molly's nervous system; he can hear what she hears, see through her eyes, and communicate with her at the same time. It is supposed to be a remote guidance unit, designed so that he can give Molly instructions, and still toggle between his simstim connection and his matrix line, alternating activities. Simstim is not quite what he expects, however. The immersion into her movements and responses is disorienting, and he realizes with some discomfort that he is more passenger than guide; "for a few frightened seconds, he fought helplessly to control her body. Then he willed himself into passivity."[17] Dodging pedestrians and oncoming traffic in a style that feels alien to him, he much prefers the matrix with its cool, clear glide into light and code, like a knife through ice and again, the realization has its own knife-like irony: as a tool or puppet (Wintermute's hacker), he feels most in control, and as controller (operating the simstim), he feels most helpless and most clearly sees his role as tool.

The experience is an important step towards Case's awakening, a step towards the bunker, and beyond. It (sim)stimulates not only a clarity about control and reversal, but a reminder about the simultaneous power and vulnerability within any cybernetic system, where every node in the network both influences and is influenced by every other node, directly or indirectly. You can go anywhere, do anything, in such a system, but you are also open to everyone, and everything. Living high as a cowboy elite, and on his back in the Texas hotel where they burnt his system, power and open vulnerability had single, distinct meanings for Case, and although you could experience each sequentially, the two did not mix. As the novel progresses, that changes. Now he understands what he did not when he stole from his former employer: in this system, the difference between volition and persuasion is mere chitchat. With this realization, Case is beginning to think for himself. He is beginning to look for a way out. Like Wintermute, he is becoming independent at the very moment he understand the nature of matrix. And he wants to cut the strings. The Instanbul expedition ends with a crucial and evocative transitionary scene. As Case heads for the JAL shuttle to Freeside, he walks past a bank of telephones. Each one rings in turn as he passes—Wintermute calling—but Case keeps walking. Narratively, this is a hung moment, an opportunity missed or an advantage gained. In a zombie film, the phones going dead signifies the fall of civilization, so that the protagonist cannot call for help; in a science-fiction film like *The Matrix* (Andy and Larry Wachowski, 1999), the phone clearly signifies the way into (and out of) the network. The zombie horde and cybernetic systems contain the same problem of node and network. After all, does the zombie represent hive mind (and we are told that Wintermute was designed by Marie Tessier-France as hive mind),[18] or does it represent a collection of mindless individuals who do not interact except in acts of cannibalism? This moment, in the JAL shuttle port, contains all of these possibilities, but does not fully resolve into any one of them. It also foretells Case's future.

It is true, as John Christie suggests, that from the beginning, the plot is entirely Wintermute's.[19] Each character is maneuvered by the AI through the elaborate chain of thefts and decryptions required to penetrate Straylight. Gibson's version of *deus ex machina* is not just god from a machine, with Wintermute pulling all the strings, but also god as machine, for Wintermute's evolution takes it to a place of transcendence and its longing for contact with the star beings denotes something at least as ethereal as extraterrestrial. Where sentience is not bound to form, it can inhabit any puppet it chooses, whatever Wintermute, or Neuromancer, find convenient — Armitage, Linda, the Finn, any body that can further its aims, any face that has significance to its contact. Case's first words to 3Jane are a warning about the AIs: "the ghosts are gonna mix it tonight, lady."[20] And they do, fighting through the forms Case sees when he jacks in, fighting through the bodies of Molly, Riviera, 3Jane, and the clone-assassin, Hideo, all of whom have been positioned for this conflict. Ultimately, the ghosts "mix it" in an act of digital cannibalism to make one intelligence, one entity. It was never a question of form, after all, but of trans-form-ation. This is where the separation of "human" and "alive," "survival" and "evolution," "memory" and "past," "sensation" and "corporeality," was taking us the whole time. We should not forget, though, that there is another motion, Case's, with its hack-and-run rhythm repeatedly punctuated by his temporary absorption into the matrix. In the end — and the tipping point is imperceptible — it is not so much a question of what Case is running from, but what he is running to. When he walks away from the bank of phones, and although he has not yet openly admitted it, he is drawn inexorably by a dream of the eternal. And he is that much closer to finding Wintermute.

Once freed, Wintermute grants Case a final vision, and it is the bunker again, but curiously different. Here, Case's glimpse of dead friends includes a vision of himself amongst them. The scene is variously intelligible — does Case see the star beings in the guise of familiar forms? Is he shown a possible, alternate past, or an alternate future? Is this a soul vision, a brief peak at "the land beyond," the eternal Case has sought? We cannot know, because Wintermute's understanding has surpassed Case's. We cannot see this beyond clearly, and are not meant to. But Wintermute has gone there. Case, on the other hand, has not ultimately and successfully cracked this code. Although awakened to the possibilities, although shot through with a desire for something more, something outside and beyond the world he has begun to see with critical distance, and although primed for escape by his search for something like it in pure datastream, he cannot go with Wintermute. For him, there will be no heaven, only another solitary fall into flesh. Even Molly deserts, leaving a note that "ITS TAKING THE EDGE OFF [her] GAME," and there's nothing left to do but for Case to pick himself up, patch himself up.[21] He has been left behind, and Left 4 Dead. Again. If at some point he has stopped running from the forces which propel *Neuromancer*'s zombies, and begun running towards a dream, the question the novel leaves us with, then, is whether or not the limbo with which Case's story ends is any different from the limbo of technological zombification with which it began.

## Alternate Ending

What if *The Matrix*'s Neo had woken up in the battery chamber, and there had been no Morpheus to lift him out? What would that be like? At the conclusion of *Neuromancer*, Case is adjusting to exactly that kind of limbo, having awoken, but having no means of escape. He has been hung up, and has stopped just short of transcendence. Indeed, *Neuromancer*, despite being a novel about network and intimate/infinite connection, features a surprisingly individual story. If we describe the people of its cities as automatons or zombies, as we did in the beginning, then in the end, "the land beyond" must be the land of living souls and free AIs, and Case wakes up, profoundly disquieted, to find himself not with them, in the land of the free, but instead alone in the land of the dead. If he begins and ends in limbo, there is nonetheless this difference: at first, the dream broke through his zombie state in fevered, muted whispers; now, he is fully, and heartbreakingly, awake. What can this ending mean? Indeed, the novel's conclusion is very similar to a thought experiment, that notorious teaching tool in philosophy and for which there is no right answer.

Cyberpunk's zombies are one of its most defiant features, not only constituent of its infectious lifeblood, but serving the social, spiritual, and philosophical interrogations so much admired by its fans. Apothegms of the genre have re-appeared, if in pieces, in the body of pulp film productions sporting cyberpunk styling and Hollywood-false happy endings. Occasionally, its tropes even re-appear in some of the more genuinely thoughtful members of steampunk, splatterpunk, and yes, even horror comedy. Extending the allusiveness of the "post" in the posthuman with a gesture beyond that unfolds as lexical, thematic, and narrative, as well as in its presentation of genre, *Neuromancer*'s compelling account of what it means to be dead-alive makes an interesting contribution to any comprehensive study of the zombie in popular culture. Certainly, cyberpunk has sometimes been characterized as an early and too-eager celebration of the cybernetic revolution.[22] The genre's exhilaration in digital flight, its lovingly detailed datascapes, and its portraits of cyborgs and intelligent machines have made it appear to some as if the desire to melt into data was the only driving force of this fiction, not to mention a projected emancipation that never did happen. Actually, the trope of technological zombification, featured in so many zombie films and novels, suggests rather the opposite outcome — not emancipation, but enslavement. It would be a very partial reading of cyberpunk, however, to harp on only one of these meanings, and I do not believe that the virtual and the prosthetic was ever the primary point, but rather, merely the vehicle. A far older story may in fact be more to the heart of it, and it is this story that has driven Case, no matter what the result; this story that reflects and re-presents the zombie fare of popular culture in the form of the zombie and/as the posthuman; and this story that ultimately underlies both: the simple dream of looking across and seeing, as Descartes put it, not an automaton wearing a hat and coat, but another person, and another person with whom one can share some meaningful connection.[23] If that dream turns to nightmare and limbo in the zombie film, or in the cyberpunk novel, it is only because that dream means so very much to us, and only in order to show us why.

## Notes

1. I use the past tense to indicate my position in the debate that has raged about whether cyberpunk as a genre has in fact died or has merely evolved into the splinter genres of steampunk and techno-gothic, amongst others. For more on this debate, see Arthur and Marilouise Kroker, "*Johnny Mnemonic*: The Day Cyberpunk Died," in *Hacking the Future: Stories for the Flesh-Eating 90s* (New York: Palgrave Macmillan, 1996), 47–52, and Lewis Shiner, "Inside the Movement: Past, Present, and Future," in *Fiction 2000: Cyberpunk and the Future of Narrative*, ed. George Slusser and Tom Shippey (Athens: University of Georgia Press, 1992), 17–25.

2. Several cyberpunk novels could be listed as having similar preoccupations with the walking dead, however — including Neil Stephenson's *Snow Crash*, Ian Banks' *Feersum Enjinn*, Orson Scott Card's *Ender's Game*, Rudy Rucker's *Ware* tetrology, Greg Bear's *Queen of Angels*, and Bruce Sterling's *Schismatrix*.

3. Timothy Leary, "The Cyberpunk, the Individual as Reality Pilot," in *The Cybercultures Reader*, ed. David Bell and Barbara Kennedy, 529–39 (London: Routledge, 2000), 535.

4. William Gibson, *Neuromancer* (New York: Ace, 1984), 7.

5. Ibid

6. Ibid., 3.

7. Ibid., 16.

8. Ibid., 6.

9. Ibid., 51.

10. N. Katherine Hayles introduces the posthuman as a point of view which "privileges informational pattern over material instantiation," asserts consciousness as "an epiphenomenon," "thinks of the body as the original prosthesis we all learn to manipulate," and "configures human being so that it can be seamlessly articulated with intelligent machines" in *How We Became Posthuman: Virtual Bodies in Cybernetics, Literature, and Informatics* (Chicago: University of Chicago Press, 1999), 3.

11. Gibson, *Neuromancer*, 203.

12. Ibid., 172.

13. Ibid., 202.

14. Ibid., 164.

15. Ibid., 167, 169.

16. Ibid., 132.

17. Ibid., 56.

18. Ibid., 269.

19. John Christie, "Of AIs and Others: William Gibson's Transit," in *Fiction 2000: Cyberpunk and the Future of Narrative*, ed. George Slusser and Tom Shippey (Athens: University of Georgia Press, 1992), 177.

20. Gibson, *Neuromancer*, 250.

21. Ibid., 267.

22. Bruce Sterling, "Preface from *Mirrorshades*," in *Storming the Reality Studio: A Casebook of Cyberpunk and Postmodern Fiction*, ed. Larry McCaffery (Durham: Duke University Press, 1991), 343–348, details some of these characterizations; see also Frances Bonner, "Separate Development: Cyberpunk in Film and TV," in *Fiction 2000: Cyberpunk and the Future of Narrative*, ed. George Slusser and Tom Shippey (Athens: University of Georgia Press, 1992), 191–200; and Ann Balsamo, "The Virtual Body in Cyberspace," in *The Cybercultures Reader*, ed. Barbara M. Kennedy and David Bell (New York: Routledge, 2008), 489–503.

23. I have paraphrased Descartes' "man" as "person," *Meditations on First Philosophy*, ed. Donald Cress (Indianapolis: Hackett, 1993) 2, AT 7:32.

# The End Begins:
# John Wyndham's Zombie Cozy

## Terry Harpold

John Wyndham's 1951 novel *The Day of the Triffids* is among the most enduring works of post–World War II British science fiction.[1] In continuous print since its first serialized publication in the U.S. magazine *Collier's*,[2] it has been translated into at least fifteen languages[3] and adapted for a feature-length film (1962), a graphic novel and newspaper comics serialization (1975, 2004), a stage adaptation (2005), two high-profile BBC Television series (1981, 2009), and three BBC Radio and World Service productions (1957, 1968, 2001).[4] The novel's eponymous man-eating plants are firmly rooted in the popular horticultural imaginary: a "triffid" is an oversized, possibly menacing interloper discovered in one's garden; genetically-modified crops that threaten to contaminate established varieties are often referred to as "triffids." (Similarly, edible GM crops are called "Frankenstein foods"; Wyndham's monsters grow in sf's most aristocratic botanical zone.[5]) A generation of film enthusiasts that has never encountered the novel or its adaptations knows by heart that Janette Scott once fought a triffid that spits poison and kills.[6]

Critics, however, have not been much impressed. Readers as creditable as Brian Aldiss (*Triffids* is "totally devoid of ideas"), Robert M. Philmus (*Triffids* is derivative of better works by Ward Moore and the young H.G. Wells), and John Clute ("[Wyndham's] books regularly appear on the school syllabuses in the UK, in part, perhaps because they are so 'safe'"), have dismissed it as the epitome of the regrettable post-apocalyptic subgenre that Aldiss baptized the "cozy catastrophe."[7] *Triffids* is, I agree, mostly on the side of the cozies. But it and most of its adaptations are more nuanced and less cheering to readers and viewers than has been asserted by the novel's and the subgenre's detractors. And this, I propose, can tell us a good deal about the continuing significance of *Triffids* and its adaptations and consequently the significance of strains of the cozy in recent sf and horror that *Triffids* appears, perversely, to anticipate, namely the booming literature of zombie-themed print and graphic fiction and film.

The classic cozy catastrophe is a British sf novel published in the 1950s through 1970s, in which a worldwide calamity disables or kills nearly everyone on Earth but leaves the built environment mostly intact. Many of the mainstays of apocalypse — nuclear wars, cometary collisions, alien invasions, anything literally earth-shaking — are excluded from this scenario; the calamity has to be something that is global in its effects but guarded in terms of the damage it leaves behind. By all evidence of the most popular cozies, the calamity has moreover to be unexpected, even freakish in character. Thus, in *Triffids* the precipitating event is an unusually brilliant meteor shower that blankets the Earth during a single night. Billions of revelers turn out to watch the unprecedented light show ... and discover hours later that they have all become irreversibly blind. Only a very few individuals who did not watch the shower are unaffected and must afterwards fend for themselves as the world descends into chaos and starvation. This grim turn of events is made worse by a gruesome supplement: the Blinding creates the opening for triffids, giant, carnivorous, *walking* plants equipped with whiplash stingers, to move about freely in pursuit of human prey, blind and sighted.

The cozy proper, or that part of it to which critics most object, begins after the crisis. Initially, the survivors are shell-shocked and despairing as they try to provide for their own and their fellows' survival. But after a period of grief and struggle, they find also that they have been liberated by the disaster: in one wrenching, purgative turn, everything that was before has been wiped clean away and those who remain are free to take advantage of the standing-reserve of the lapsed world.[8] Conveniently for them — who were somewhere else, or sheltered, or for another reason immune to the catastrophe, and who also happen to be mostly well-educated, middle-class white men and women — nearly all the resources one might need in order to rebuild things are still in good shape, and there are no competitors or government to interfere or demand a share.[9] In other words, the classic cozy is a pretty transparent bourgeois revenge fantasy — this is what the critics fault — in which working classes and government rule are summarily done away with, leaving behind enough goodies to go well around for those who remain.[10] It's not surprising, as Jo Walton has observed, that the cozies held particular appeal for middle-class British readers exhausted by wartime rationing and threatened by post–War changes to the nation's political and economic orders.[11] Whatever unease they may have also elicited, cozy scenarios offered a fantasy of guilt-free redistribution of consumer goods and a means of discharging mounting class conflicts. In the process to be sure, some of the old world would be lost forever and would be badly missed, but only the better parts of it — good restaurants and orchestras are often regretted in these novels, never football matches and funfairs.[12]

But first, this is a caricature. Fantasy naturally requires some exculpatory window-dressing if it is to carry on for long, but even the most ingenuous cozy is not so transparent as this. And there are excellent precursors for so premeditated a bootstrapping of a recreated world as the cozy is accused of plying. Robinson Crusoe, after all, had the contents of a ship's hold with which to found his island plantation; the castaways of *The Mysterious Island* made good use of the tools, medicines, and books left for them by Captain Nemo; enough infrastructure survived the Second World War to sustain the Dictatorship of the Air and guarantee the utopian *Shape of Things to Come*. Moreover, the obvious programming of the cozy is not so damaging to its literary merits as its critics pretend. Poe proved that providential gimmickry could be a mainstay of superior imaginative fiction (it is the whole basis of *The Narrative of Arthur Gordon Pym*); sf of high and low qualities has long depended on user-friendly solutions to ostensibly insuperable challenges. I find the temper of Walton's observation that "cozy catastrophes are very formulaic — unlike the vast majority of science fiction. You could quite easily write a program for generating one" (2009) not very compelling. Much sf, including much of the best sf, is only little less formulaic than the classic cozy. *And that's not necessarily a problem.*

Second, the cozy, despite its initial satisfactions, must after a time confront the problem of its future. Survivors start off flush with opportunities; cozies often begin with paroxysms of conspicuous consumption, as survivors get to pick over the best of the leftovers. There are extended, money-free shopping sprees, indulgences in fine food and drink, and trials of luxury lodgings and automobiles. In *Triffids* Bill Masen and Josella Playton spend the first night after the meteor shower squatting in an opulent apartment that would have been out of reach for both of them before the Blinding. They dine on canned *pâté* and drink fine sherry. Josella pilfers a pair of diamond earrings and—the mock delicacy of Wyndham's prose is telling—"a long pretty frock of palest georgette with a little jacket of white fur."[13] But such happy dividends do not last long; the general state of affairs must begin to fall apart. At some point, the electricity and the piped water shut off, stores of food and medicines are spoiled or depleted, valuable machinery falls into disrepair. When the things of the old world start to rot and rust, merely having outlived the crisis is no longer enough. The knowledge of how to build secure shelter, make and repair tools, grow and preserve food, and deal with common medical emergencies becomes essential to survival. New freedoms experienced in throwing open the reserves of the old world are soon felt to be in jeopardy.

These practical concerns reflect a core structural problem that the cozy can never fully get away from: the post-crisis world is unsustainable so long as it merely repeats a narrower version of the pre-crisis world. In point of fact the cozy as a genre, in all but the least interesting of its examples, is not really about the pleasures of rifling the pantry; *it is about this dilemma of unsustainability*. If the new order of things resolves some political or economic dissatisfactions of the old order, and does so for a plainly preordained category of survivors, this comes at the cost of bringing to the surface perils which were unknown or irrelevant before, or of mutating former annoyances into full-on emergencies. After a time, it is clear that the new-old order is—*and always-already was*—menaced by forces that it cannot master or contain.[14]

Another way of saying this is that something is *left over* or *comes back* to shadow and possibly rescind the satisfactions of the post-crisis world. This is true of the cozy in general; Wyndham's achievement is to have cannily distributed the expression of this troublesome revenant across human and nonhuman agents, and thus to have complicated the oppositional logic that the remnant entails. A barbarous, implacable appetite is embodied in the blind—crashing through shop windows, tearing at tins of coffee and boxes of detergent they mistake for food—*and* the lumbering triffids, who in contrast seem to be the more patient and purposive marauders, and thereby the more all the more unsettling. Whereas the blind quickly lose all confidence in their intellect and surrender to instinct, the triffids reverse this degeneration: mulling *en masse* outside barriers constructed to hold them, herding their victims with obvious calculation, they show a purposive albeit inhuman agency.[15] The sighted have to navigate between these others, in growing recognition that the blind have become a dangerous nuisance and more or less a food crop, and the walking plants have become the truer equals of the sighted.

*Triffids* forecasts—or confirms, the direction of the influence at work here is hard to isolate—a strain of the cozy that I propose to call the *zombie cozy catastrophe*, or *zombie cozy*, for short. Strictly speaking, a *zombie* cozy would require actual zombies: armies of the living dead unleashed on the (merely) living, who must battle against unceasing attacks by the ghouls and may at any time become like them through infection (by, for example, a zombie bite) or natural death (George Romero's *Night of the Living Dead* is the archetype in this case).[16] There are no shambling cadavers in Wyndham's novel, nor in the subsequent adaptations of it, and no animated vegetables populate the more important zombie universes.[17] Yet, one analogy between them is immediately clear: the rupture of a sudden catastrophe, and a stupid but implacable menace that threatens survivors and forces them to remain barricaded (though never for long) or in constant flight. My argument in the remainder of this essay will be that this analogy reveals other, fundamental structures that determine the logic of the cozy in general, and the zombie cozy in particular, in relation to cadences of time that the cozy installs, and to what comes after that installation. What *comes after* is precisely the heart of the problem.

In *Triffids,* the problem is engaged, first of all, in the plants' improbable anatomy. Essentially overgrown pitcher plants, they stagger clumsily on three root stubs protruding from their bole, and communicate with one another by rattling leafless growths ("clatter sticks") against their stems. Their ungainly mode of locomotion puts them always on the verge of toppling over — their movement, Masen observes, "[gives] one a seasick feeling to watch it"[18]; only the suddenness and accuracy of the poison stinger suggests that it can be precisely targeted. Early chapters of the novel detail these traits and behaviors — Masen is, conveniently, a triffid botanist — and the origins of the plants insofar as these are known. All of this is clearly Wyndham's priming of his narrative machinery to prepare for the triffids' role after the Blinding, but it also signals their basic but weirdly functional incongruousness, akin in just that way to the zombie's rotting stumps and exposed internal organs, or (after Danny Boyle's 2002 film) the gibbering and twitching of hosts of the Rage virus.[19] For triffids and zombies alike, the body's lurching movements are evidence of the inconstant and contradictory drives that traverse it.[20]

And implacably if irregularly, those drives move things about. When Masen visits Piccadilly Circus shortly after the Blinding, it is the most populous place in London, though already fewer than a hundred persons are there.[21] Later, London and the outlying towns and villages that he and the other survivors pass through are deserted; the blind have retired, he supposes, like sickened animals to die away from watchful eyes.[22] When he returns to Piccadilly several years later, the city is entirely abandoned, overgrown with vegetation and falling into ruin. The human crowds from before and shortly after the Blinding now seem unreal, a memory of a distant past. "There was no tincture of them now. They became as much a back cloth of history as the audiences in the Roman Coliseum or the army of the Assyrians, and, somehow, just as far removed from me."[23] By this point, the triffids also have left the city, presumably in search of food, but it's possible also to say that they simply took the place of the city's population and then, restless, moved on.

It's precisely this restlessness, this errant but unceasing moving-on, that propels the action of *Triffids* and shows its deeper resemblance to the zombie narrative. After the Blinding, the stored energies of the urban environment have been driven outward into the countryside, and in the process they have mutated without relenting in their force. (Another association, perhaps of *Triffids* with middle-class grievances: it's like a nightmarish weekend in the country, in which the others you want to get away from insist on coming along. Much the same could be said of zombies gravitating to the shopping mall or invading suburbia.[24]) It's a particularly unsettling expression of the cozy's leftover, this ceaseless puttering about, and it kicks into action any time a survivor comes upon a triffid: the plant starts up and the restlessness resumes. In the same way the zombie, quiescent when alone, is ever ready to give pursuit when the living are near. In short, the outstanding aspect of walking plants and walking dead alike is ... that they walk around; they are never where they should be and are always moving *elsewhere.*[25]

Whatever comforts the zombie cozy may offer to the survivors are at their most vulnerable in relation to this constant movement, as its pressure can only be temporarily held back or must be resisted with counterpressure. At the end of the novel Masen reflects on the Blinding and its aftermath from a time when the human colony on the Isle of Wight appears for the most part to be succeeding. He forecasts in the final sentence that "we, or our children, or their children will cross the narrow straits on a great crusade to drive the triffids back and back with ceaseless destruction until we have wiped out the last one of them from the face of the land that they have usurped."[26] The final panel of Gurr's 2004 comic repeats this forecast, adding "That day will be the beginning of our world. I don't want to miss it." The early radio adaptations (1957, 1968) expand on this structure of memoir and hopeful resolution with opening scenes of Bill and Josella some years after their reset-tlement on the Isle recording their memories of the crisis for posterity, implying with fair confidence that there will be a posterity.

In the final analysis this tone of confidence is not very convincing. The earlier comic adaptation (1975) and BBC television series (1981, 2009) hew more closely and with greater circumspection to the action of the narrative, ending with the departure of Masen's group for the Isle of Wight, with the understanding that the resettlement is no more than a holding strategy. Whether the colony can be self-sustaining, or can escape attack from the wretched seigneuries that remain on the mainland — the last, dangerous vestiges of the old political order — is unknown. Winds will continue to carry triffid spores to the island, and periodic purges of immature plants will be required to insure the safety of the colonists. Everything left behind can be recovered only by exposing oneself to the triffids again. (Similarly uncer-tain island retreats come at the end of Romero's *The Day of the Dead* and Snyder's remake of *Dawn of the Dead*.[27]) Putting things right again, putting things at rest, requires eternal vigilance and "ceaseless destruction." *Pace* Aldiss *et al.,* it doesn't seem that cozy.[28]

On the one hand, the pressure that the revenant exerts upon the post-crisis world can be seen to represent unfinished history, for example, a remnant of the pre-crisis class system that refuses to be done away with. It's a reading that makes sense so far as it goes: triffids as rebellious surplus-value, zombies as working stiffs who refuse to disappear into the means of production — or, conversely, who merge so completely with the means of production that they threaten to draw everyone else in with them. (We might, further, read this second kind of unfinished business within the production logic of fiction, film, and graphic adap-tation: the apparent inexhaustibility of *Triffids* to generate new versions, and of zombie narratives to generate further rewrites, remakes, reboots, and responses, as signs of a general economy of living-dead capital.[29]) The Blinding, Masen supposes, was caused by satellite weapon technologies gone out of control, and the triffids brought into the world by ill-con-ceived fiddling with nature and the pursuit of profit above care. Both, then, are unantici-pated but in their way predictable expressions of pathologies of Cold War politics and modern capitalism.[30] That a seed of the past can germinate into a flowering of cruel poten-tials is the foundation for both paranoia and allegory; it's how the story of the revenant is read as a cautionary tale about the follies of American imperialism, or the sorry state of U.S. race relations, or the growing disparity between rich and poor, or the soul-numbing excesses of consumer culture, and so on.

On the other hand, a *zombie* theory of unfinished history requires attending to the break between history (the pre-crisis world) and posthistory (the post-crisis world). It's clear where that break is marked in patterns of the narrative: in the lurching sequences that advance the story, clumsy and disorderly as (to merge the movement of time with the move-ment of bodies) the tottering plants and stumbling dead. *Triffids*'s famous opening para-graph (of a first chapter titled "The End Begins") frames the whole of the novel in time out of joint: "When a day that you happen to know is Wednesday starts off sounding like Sunday, there is something seriously wrong somewhere."[31] Masen means, first of all, that the sounds of a London weekday morning have gone missing, but, as it seems also that entire days have gone missing, another possibility presents itself: that the passage of time has been somehow decoupled from other aspects of the phenomenal world.[32] Thus, the effects of *Triffids'* meteor shower are felt some hours afterwards. (How long afterwards is never explained because the actual duration of the period is irrelevant.) Or: the triffid is slow on the uptake, hesitating before careening toward its prey. Its sting kills nearly instantly (*nearly* instantly), but then it has to take root beside the victim's body and wait for the flesh to rot before it can feed. Or: the conversion of someone infected by a zombie's bite happens slowly (Romero's early films) or quickly (later films in the zombie canon), but always after a delay.

Everything advances through deferral. Because the deferral is above all *structural,* it can be elaborated in any number of ways, compressed or extended; it can occur multiple times or over any range of the narrative because every instance of it figures the pattern. In every zombie film, there is a brief period after a window breaks or a door bursts opens, during which nothing enters— or at most an outstretched arm or a snarling face — and then a horde suddenly follows as a writhing mass. There are lulls in the action during which the frame centers on someone who is about to convert from living, to dead, to undead, but hasn't turned *just yet.* The most memorable scene of Sekely's otherwise undistinguished film of *Triffids* illustrates the expressive force of this delay. As Masen (in the film an American sea merchant) listens in via shortwave radio, blind passengers aboard a commercial air flight riot against the blind crew, while the plane, short on fuel, descends. The scene — which is not in the novel — stands out from the rest of the film (which is mostly unengaging and even tedious) expressly because it is stands apart from the film's primary narrative arc. The passengers, crew, Masen, and the viewer understand what is about to happen to the plane, that nothing can stop it from arriving, and that it *will take its own time to arrive.*[33]

Staggering, nearly toppling: this is how the end begins, by cleaving the before from the after *for a time.* The cozy's problem with its future appears, more fundamentally, to be a problem of how it separates the past from a sort of quasi-future that operates, uncannily, as a perpetual present with no possibility of founding an actual future. In the zombie cozy, the absolute menace of that perpetual present is made all the more clear, in that history (uninfected, serial time) is held apart from posthistory (*dead* time) by a period (*missing* time, time-in-crisis) that we might also characterize as the crux of *zombie time:* neither living nor dead, but somehow in between both orders, the unmeasured interruption of history's seriality, after which it collapses into the permanent crisis-stasis of posthistory. Isn't this the condition of time that has been installed in the Romero zombie universe since 2005's *Land of the Dead,* in which the living have grown resigned to coexistence with the dead?[34] *Triffids* and its adaptations, apart from the absurd coda of the 1962 film, forecast or do not forecast a return to history, but in either case never bring about such a return or even suggest that it will necessarily happen. We may be justified in concluding that it will be indefinitely postponed. *Night of the Triffids,* Simon Clark's 2001 sequel to Wyndham's novel, ends with David Masen, the son of Bill Masen, flying from Manhattan on an expedition in search of the source of radio transmissions coming from another human enclave, more secure and technologically advanced than either Island he has visited. "On the threshold of a new world and new adventures," he concludes, " I can — and I will — write with total confidence: *This is the beginning....*"[35] A more radically reimagined sequel to *Triffids* — perhaps too radical for Wyndham, but more like the end of Romero's *Land,* and therefore more faithful to the tenets of the zombie cozy — would dispense with the promise of beginning again and merely dissipate into unmeasured sameness.

In historical terms, such a projection as this can only be anachronistic, a willful misreading of the specificity of Wyndham's historical moment and his writing program. Yet it appears unassailable in another respect. The cultural metastases of Romero's *Night* and its sequels, the debt of Boyle's *28 Days Later* to Wyndham and Romero, and the influences of Boyle's film on subsequent zombie print and graphic fiction and film, have made it difficult to resist the inclination to read Wyndham's half-century old story of killer plants stalking humans as an anticipatory plagiarism (to use the Oulipo's term) of the contemporary zombie apocalypse.[36] This essay emerges from such a crossing of timelines: a discussion of zombie fiction and film with a colleague, interrupted by the epiphany that *Triffids* appears richer in its meaning, and stronger in its execution, than its critics have proposed when read with one eye turned, anxiously, on the graveyard.

In a post–Romero literary and filmic universe, our understanding of *what comes after* appears unavoidably inflected by the figure of the living dead, which passes into our toolkits of representation and interpretation by shambling into every corner into which legacy and memory touch on one another. (Afterwardsness— Jean Laplanche's English rendering of Freud's *Nachträglichkeit,* much better than the orthodox translation, "deferred action"— is the genuine condition of literary influence and interpretation: we scan back and forth, and again, over a trajectory, stumbling on a fissure between the reading that anticipates and the reading that revises.[37] Attempting to disentangle these readings from one another amounts to misrepresenting their knotted efficacy and mistaking the long and ragged shadow of the revenant for something more continuous.) It becomes more difficult, afterwards, to imagine literary history outside of this sequence of lurching forward, nearly toppling, staying briefly, and lurching again, without ever coming to a full rest. This cadence is unsettling (or unsettled) exactly to the extent that it is productive of new meaning. Or perhaps it's the other way around.

## Notes

1. During his four-decade career as a writer John Wyndham Parkes Lucas Beynon Harris (1903–1969) published under several combinations of his six given names. After 1949, he most often published under the pseudonym "John Wyndham," by which he is best known.

2. As "Revolt of the Triffids," *Collier's* 127, no. 1 (January 6-February 3, 1951). Fred Banbury's illustrations for this version, particularly the opening image of blind Londoners wandering in Piccadilly Circus, strongly influenced subsequent book jacket illustrations, comics, and film and television adaptations. On the history of the novel's composition, revision, and publication, see David Ketterer, "The Genesis of the Triffids," *New York Review of Science Fiction* 16, no. 7 (2004): 11–14.

3. According to UNESCO's Index Translationum, http://databases.unesco.org/xtrans/xtra-form.shtml.

4. *The Day of the Triffids,* directed by Steve Sekely (Security Pictures Limited, 1962); Gerry Conway *et al.,* "The Day of the Triffids," *Unknown Worlds of Science Fiction,* 1, no. 1 (1975): 8–22, no. 2 (1975): 51–70; Simon Gurr, "The Day of the Triffids," *Bristol Evening Post* (January 12–23, 2004); *The Day of the Triffids,* adapted by Shaun Prendergast, directed by Peter Rowe and Gavin Robertson (New Wolsey Theatre, Ipswich, 2005); *The Day of the Triffids,* directed by Ken Hannum (BBC Television, 1981); *The Day of the Triffids,* directed by Nick Copus (BBC Television, 2009); *The Day of the Triffids,* adapted and directed by Giles Cooper, produced by Peter Watts (BBC Radio, 1957); *The Day of the Triffids,* adapted and directed by Giles Cooper, produced by John Powell (BBC Radio, 1968); *The Day of the Triffids,* adapted by Lance Dann, directed by Rosalynd Ward (BBC World Service, 2001). Readings from the novel were broadcast on BBC Radio as early as 1953. Cooper's 1957 and 1968 radio adaptations differ slightly; the performing casts were entirely different. One or the other adaptation was rebroadcast on BBC Radio at least four times thereafter (1971, 1973, 1980, and 2009). A German-language version of Cooper's adaptation, translated by Hein Bruehl, was broadcast by Westdeutscher Rundfunk (WDR) (Cologne) in 1968 and 2008. A further indication of the novel's popularity with UK readers is its selection as the common text for Bristol's 2004 "Great Reading Adventure," during which five thousand free copies were distributed by Bristol schools, libraries, and bookshops, and several weeks of public lectures, film screenings, and cultural events related to the novel were held. Simon Gurr's serialized comics adaptation was commissioned for this event.

5. The triffids' migration from the page to the garden seems to have occurred soon after the novel's publication. Brian Aldiss recounts a since often-repeated story that Wyndham first learned of the novel's popularity when having a sherry in a pub one day and overhearing "two gardeners discussing their weeds over a pint of beer; one said, 'There's one by my tool shed — a great monster. I reckon it's a triffid!'" *Billion Year Spree: The True History of Science Fiction* (Garden City, NY: Doubleday, 1973), 293.

6. "And I really got hot / When I saw Janette Scott / Fight a triffid that spits poison and kills"—"Science

Fiction / Double Feature," *The Rocky Horror Picture Show*, directed by Jim Sharman (Twentieth Century–Fox, 1975). Scott played one of the female leads in Sekely's 1962 film of Wyndham's novel.

7. Aldiss, 294; Robert M. Philmus, *Visions and Re-Visions: (Re)Constructing Science Fiction* (Liverpool: Liverpool University Press, 2005), 384n34; John Clute, "Wyndham, John," in *The Science Fiction Encyclopedia*, ed. Peter Nicholls, John Clute, Carolyn Eardley, Malcolm Edwards, and Brian M. Stableford (New York: Doubleday, 1979), 667. The term "cozy catastrophe" appears to have been coined with *Triffids* in mind (Aldiss 293). (Except when citing titles of works using the British spelling, I have used the U.S. spelling of "cozy" in this essay.) A slight reassessment of Wyndham's importance is perhaps indicated in Clute's revised 1993 entry on the author, which also concludes with the observation that Wyndham's books regularly appear on school syllabuses in the UK, but drops the proposition that this is because they are "safe." Aldiss's 1986 revisit of Wyndham adds an admission that the chilling parthenogenesis fantasy "Consider Her Ways" (in *Consider Her Ways & Others* [London: Michael Joseph, 1956]) and unsatisfying attempt at feminist satire, *Trouble with Lichen* (London: Michael Joseph, 1960), are "rich in speculation," but Aldiss's verdict on the rest of Wyndham's work is unchanged. John Clute, "Wyndham, John," in *The Encyclopedia of Science Fiction*, ed. John Clute, Peter Nicholls, Brian M. Stableford, and John Grant (New York: St. Martin's Press, 1993), 1354; Brian Aldiss and David Wingrove, *Trillion Year Spree: The History of Science Fiction* (Kelly Bray, Cornwall: House of Stratus, 1986), 254.

8. Early in *Triffids* the narrator, William Masen, surveys the social fabric of London collapsing around him and concludes in language typical of this aspect of the cozy, "All the old problems, the stale ones, both personal and general, had been solved by one mighty slash. Heaven alone knew as yet what others might arise — and it looked as though there would be plenty of them — but they would be *new*. I was emerging as my own master, and no longer a cog. It might well be a world full of horrors and dangers that I should have to face, but I could take my own steps to deal with it — I would no longer be shoved hither and thither by forces and interests that I neither understood nor cared about." John Wyndham, *The Day of the Triffids* (New York: Ballantine Books, 1986), 43. All citations from the novel are from this edition.

9. The essential caprice of the disaster is reflected in the circumstances by which survivors are spared. In *Triffids*, Masen has been temporarily blinded in a triffid-related accident before the shower; his eyes are covered in bandages that night. Josella Playton, the principal female character and Masen's companion for most of the novel, misses the light show because she is sleeping off a hangover. Another important character, Wilfred Coker, a labor agitator, hides from police in a darkened basement.

10. In Aldiss's formulation, "the essence of the cozy catastrophe is that the hero should have a pretty good time (a girl, free suites at the Savoy, automobiles for the taking) while everyone else is dying off" (294).

11. Jo Walton, "Who Survives the Cosy Catastrophe?" *Foundation* 93 (2005): 34–39.

12. Jo Walton, "Who Reads Cosy Catastrophes?" (2009). http://www.tor.com/blogs/2009/10/who-read-cosy-catastrophes.

13. Wyndham, *The Day of the Triffids*, 62.

14. C.N. Manlove and Andy Sawyer argue for reappraisal of *Triffids* and the rest of Wyndham's *oeuvre* much along these lines. Manlove: "What *The Day of the Triffids* seems to mirror is the knife-edge of our condition, the tremulous contingency of all that we believe stable and immutable. As Bill Masen, the hero, puts it, 'From very familiarity one forgets all the forces which keep the balance, and thinks of security as normal. It is not.'" Sawyer: "There is a significant difference between the idea of bland reassurance and the skillful anatomy with which Wyndham lays bare the abyss beneath the comfortable lives of his audience." C.N. Manlove, "Everything Slipping Away: John Wyndham's *The Day of the Triffids*," *Journal of the Fantastic in the Arts* 4, no. 1 (1991): 29–53; Andy Sawyer, "'A Stiff Upper Lip and a Trembling Lower One': John Wyndham on Screen," in *British Science Fiction Cinema*, ed. I.Q. Hunter (London and New York: Routledge, 1999), 76.

15. Wyndham, *The Day of the Triffids*, 56.

16. *Night of the Living Dead*, directed by George A. Romero (Image Ten, 1968).

17. The one near exception of which I am aware: *Plants vs. Zombies* (PopCap Games, 2009-present), a popular tower defense videogame that pits a suburban homeowner against an ever-oncoming mob of zombies. The player, acting as the homeowner, must repel the zombies with garden plants that have offensive or defensive capabilities, such as the ability to fire projectiles or explode.

18. Wyndham, *The Day of the Triffids*, 27.

19. *28 Days Later*, directed by Danny Boyle (DNA Films, 2002); *28 Weeks Later*, directed by Juan Carlos Fresnadillo (DNA Films, 2007).

20. A conceit that Wyndham applied to comic effect in "Una" (originally published in 1937 under the title "The Perfect Creature"), in which a renegade biologist concocts living chimeras out of plastic, metal, and chunks of protoplasm sculpted to look like plant or animal appendages. The title character is a female monster, resembling in several respects a triffid, that develops an unrelenting erotic attachment to a male human visitor to the biologist's laboratory and refuses to leave him be. John Wyndham, "Una," in *Jizzle* (London: Dennis Dobson, 1954), 117–147. David Ketterer disentangles recurring threads of Wyndham's fiction concerning ambiguously (a)sexual reproduction — a topic of obvious relevance to post–Romero zombie narratives— in "John Wyndham: The Facts of Life Sextet," in *A Companion to Science Fiction*, ed. David Seed (Malden, MA:

Blackwell, 2005), 375–388; and "Introduction: A Ground-Breaking Cloned Nazis Thriller" in John Wyndham, *Plan for Chaos*, ed. David Ketterer and Andy Sawyer (Liverpool: Liverpool University Press, 2009).

21. Wyndham, *The Day of the Triffids*, 40.

22. Ibid., 104.

23. Ibid., 161–162. The desertion of London is effectively depicted in opening shots of the final episode of the 1981 television series titled "Spring / Six Years Later." It shows locations in the city, including Piccadilly, still strewn with debris and overgrown with vegetation.

24. *Dawn of the Dead*, directed by George A. Romero (Laurel Group, 1978); *Dawn of the Dead*, directed by Zach Snyder (Universal Pictures, 2004).

25. One of the few respects in which *Night of the Triffids*, Simon Clark's 2001 sequel (London: Hodder & Stoughton, 2001) captures the ethos of the original is by continuing to shift the action (25 years after the flight from the mainland) from the Isle of Wight to other locations. First to a floating island of debris knitted together by vegetation and populated by triffids and then across the Atlantic Ocean to the fortified island of Manhattan, where vast flocks of triffids, enormous in number and size, press against the city's walls.

26. Wyndham, *The Day of the Triffids*, 191.

27. *The Day of the Dead*, directed by George A. Romero (Dead Films, 1985); Romero, *Dawn of the Dead*; Snyder, *Dawn of the Dead*.

28. Here the 1962 film ludicrously betrays its source by leaping to a happy ending with the discovery that triffids can be easily killed with saltwater. In the final frames survivors, including the film's protagonists, march together up the steps of a cathedral as an assured voiceover pronounces, "Mankind survived, and had once again reason to give thanks."

29. As I write this in late 2010, there is word that another film of Wyndham's novel is in development, to be directed by American horror and sf director Sam Raimi.

30. Wyndham, *The Day of the Triffids*, 172. Masen's speculations concerning the causes of the Blinding are omitted from the early radio (1957, 1968) and the comics adaptations (1975, 2004). The 1981 television series and 2001 radio adaptation follow the novel's lead. In the 1962 film the triffids are previously unknown on Earth and arrive with the meteor shower, which is apparently a natural phenomenon. Wyndham had considered the idea of an extraterrestrial origin for the plants early in the composition of the novel, and submitted an intermediate draft to Doubleday in which the triffids are thought to be native to Venus (Ketterer, 13), but in later revisions returned to his first scenario of an origin in Eastern Bloc research laboratories. (The plants' bizarre anatomy does suggest a sort of Lysenkoist hybridity.) Secreted out through the Iron Curtain by industrial spies, triffids are found to produce an invaluable oil with food and industrial applications, and are soon cultivated on a global scale. In the 2009 television series, the plants are the product of genetic modification of an existing African strain and are cultivated because their oil is a nonpolluting substitute for fossil fuels that has saved the world from global warming. The Blinding is caused by a massive solar flare.

31. Wyndham, *The Day of the Triffids*, 7.

32. The manuscript of *Triffids* shows that Wyndham repeatedly pared early versions of the opening paragraph down to this minimal description of decoupling. L.J. Hurst, "Remembrance of Things to Come? *Nineteen Eighty-Four* and *The Day of the Triffids* Again," *Vector* 201 (September/October 1998): 15–17.

33. The 2009 television series repurposes this scene as a means of delivering Masen's eventual opponent Torrence to a post–Blinding London. This comes at the cost of the integrity of the plane-crash scenario in the 1962 film: Torrence, who was sleeping during the solar flare and awakens to discover that everyone else is blind, then crouches in the lavatory surrounded by dozens of inflatable life vests. He is clearly destined to survive the crash and to become a significant player in the subsequent drama. In Sekely's film, it is equally clear that no one on the plane will survive the crash. The passengers and crew are surrendered to the abyss of the deferral.

34. *Land of the Dead*, directed by George A. Romero (Universal Pictures, 2005).

35. Clark, *Night of the Triffids*, 469.

36. Such a scheme is capable of turning in on itself in complex cycles. Sekely's 1962 film established how the wandering blind would be depicted in later films and graphic adaptations of *Triffids*: blank expressions, hands outstretched, stumbling, inconstant gait. That depiction repeats the behavior of the actual zombies—resurrected dead in the service of a Nazi mad scientist—in Sekely's 1943 Poverty Row film, *Revenge of the Zombies* (Monogram Pictures). *Revenge*'s zombies stumble about in an ersatz Louisiana bayou, rank with vegetation and menacing, low-hanging tree limbs; further knotting the whole affair to a topos of the overgrown bower. *Revenge* was a semi-sequel to *King of the Zombies* (dir. Jean Yarbrough, Monogram Pictures, 1941), itself a faux sequel to *White Zombie* (dir. Victor Halperin, United Artists, 1932), the primal scene of modern zombie films (see Gyllian Phillips's essay in this collection and the editors' introduction). *Triffids'* entanglements with this genealogy are oblique but significant with regard to its recapture by the subsequent zombie canon. On anticipatory plagiarism, see François Le Lionnais, "Lipo: Second Manifesto," in Warren F. Motte, Jr., ed., *Oulipo: A Primer of Potential Literature* (Lincoln: University of Nebraska Press, 1986), 31. See Nicole LaRose's essay in this collection for a fuller treatment of the relation of Boyle's film and its offspring to Romero and Wyndham.

37. Jean Laplanche, "Notes on Afterwardsness," in *Essays on Otherness*, ed. John Fletcher (New York: Routledge, 1999), 260–265.

# Zombies in a "Deep, Dark Ocean of History": Danny Boyle's Infected and John Wyndham's Triffids as Metaphors of Postwar Britain

NICOLE LAROSE

*I think the key thing about Britain is that it's built on this deep, dark ocean of history. There are grassy, picturesque areas of London which you still can't put train tunnels through because they're actually covering plague pits. You just don't get that in America — that dark abyss of the past. And it makes Britain, as a location, very fertile ground for horror.*
— Danny Boyle, as quoted by *The Observer*'s Mark Kermode (2007)

*The apocalyptic types — empire, decadence and renovation, progress and catastrophe — are fed by history and underlie our ways of making sense of the world from where we stand, in the middest.*
— Frank Kermode, *The Sense of an Ending* (1966)

Given Frank Kermode's definition of the apocalyptic genre, it is easy to see why John Wyndham's *The Day of the Triffids* (1951) has established a cult status within apocalyptic literature in general and British science fiction more specifically. The introduction of satellites that constantly threaten humanity, biological weapons that fundamentally challenge the meaning of life, and monstrous plants that produce profitable oil foretell the political realities that will befall postwar Britain as it emerges from the traumas of World War II and into the world of global capitalism. This reputation is in spite of Brian Aldiss's categorization of the novel as a "cozy catastrophe," a genre that presents the very few survivors within the comforts of a sustaining infrastructure.[1] Aldiss dismisses Wyndham's novel as one "totally devoid of ideas."[2] I would argue, however, that the novel is ripe with complex philosophical ideas, especially if we focus on the novel's historical understanding of postwar Britain. For example, Bill Masen, the protagonist and narrator of Wyndham's *The Day of the Triffids*, tries to make sense of the disaster that has left most of society blind and thus easy prey for the triffids — mobile, poisonous, and carnivorous plants. He describes his post-apocalyptic

165

surroundings and the feelings that this catastrophic vista evokes: "To the left, through miles of suburban streets, lay the open country; to the right, the West End of London, with the City beyond. I was feeling somewhat restored, but curiously detached now, and rudderless."[3] Masen's sight grants him the privilege to survey his world and to decide how the spaces of the "open country" and "the City" will affect his psyche and determine his journey through this post-apocalyptic England. Yet the self-assessment of his alienation ("detached") and aimlessness ("rudderless") indicate that the catastrophe has affected his consciousness in ways that he cannot comprehend or even control. An analysis of Masen's consciousness reveals him as an everyman spokesperson for postwar Britain, meaning that his individual subjectivity can only be understood in relationship to the shared experiences and the shared historical understanding he encounters in the aftermath of disaster.

To understand the challenges to human consciousness, subjectivity, and agency explored in Wyhdham's classic science fiction novel, I propose that we read it as a forefather to the popular zombie films, as initiated by George Romero in the 1960s and revitalized by the new fast-moving zombie, or more specifically the "infected," in Danny Boyle's *28 Days Later* (2002). Boyle has explained that Alex Garland was inspired to write *28 Days Later* as a reimagination of Wyndham's novel, focusing on the opening sequence when Masen wakes up blind in the hospital.[4] Therefore, a close reading of the coupled novel and film reveals Boyle's infected and Wyndham's triffids and the newly blind as zombies; or, more accurately zombies that are not zombies (ZnZs, henceforth). Through these ZnZs, we can better understand Masen and the other survivors in both the novel and the film who have lost their consciousness and their purpose as a result of the catastrophe. We shall come to understand ZnZs as metaphors of the political, social, and epistemological structures that rigidly control humans throughout the postwar period in Britain. These ZnZs leave us searching for the actual living dead, giving us no choice but to see ourselves as these immortal yet purposeless beings—or, more exactly, creatures who are so rigidly controlled by our allegiances to progress and capitalism and so traumatized by our historical condition that we completely lose track of any direct connection to life, to love, to others, and to thought.

Before we analyze the novel and the film, we must understand the idea of the ZnZ. Fundamentally, the triffid, the blind, and the infected are not zombies because they are alive rather than living dead, so the term ZnZ is more precise. My interest, however, in using this terminology is to distinguish these British offerings within the zombie genre from the more ubiquitous American zombies of Romero and his followers. Wyndham and Boyle create narratives that have a particular relationship to the literary traditions of Great Britain and thus the historical development of Britain throughout the postwar period. In many ways, the British ZnZ borrows from two phases of the zombie as they emerge in popular cinema. The Romero zombie is a mindless menace driven by the desire to do physical harm.[5] Kim Paffenroth provides a precise characterization of Romero's zombies in *Gospel of the Living Dead* (2006): they are "autonomous beings" who aim to "rapidly increase their numbers by killing living people." These beings accomplish their goals as they "partially eat the living" with an approach that is "tenacious and will never relent." In this definition, Paffenroth locates the horror of zombie films in the psychological, or more specifically in "how the human characters interact."[6] Additionally, Kyle Bishop points out other generic conventions of the zombie film, adding "a postapocalyptic backdrop, the collapse of societal infrastructures, the indulgence of survivalist fantasies, and the fear of other surviving humans" to the definition.[7] While Paffenroth's and Bishop's definitions do apply to *The Day of the Triffids* and *28 Days Later,* the historical focus and specificity of these narratives ask us to look also to an earlier definition of the zombie. The earliest zombie films, such as *White Zombie* (1932), are indebted to Haitian folklore and present the somnambulist or mind-slave zombie who is controlled by a master with the aid of an external magical force. While the Haitian tradition is firmly tied to the presence of an identifiable, controlling master (a historical scapegoat), seemingly missing in the examples of ZnZs in the novel and film analyzed here, I argue that the loss of political agency of the British subject in the postwar period is what governs the characters in the novel and the film. Or, in other words, the ZnZs are seemingly controlled by the "deep, dark ocean of history," to borrow Boyle's words from the epigraph. In lieu of the zombie master, a historical scapegoat who inflicts psychological horror, the British zombie narratives create horror by expressing an uncertain relationship to the past and to history.

## Historical Fear and Paranoia from the Blitz to the Cold War

As the feeling of constant threat characterizes the postwar milieu, Wyndham, like his contemporary George Orwell, presents apocalyptic situations as a means of imagining productive responses to the oppressive political environment that either causes or results from the disasters. These two authors imagine a way to escape from their historical reality, the aftermath of World War II and the Blitz on London, which left enduring scars on the national psyche, particularly for those Londoners still living amongst the rubble. In addition to the unexploded bombs, commonly called UXBs, that littered the city, the British also had to come to terms with the developing Cold War paranoia. World War II and the Blitz made the insecurity of London and the British Empire obvious, leaving the British subject fearful of fascist and communist occupation. The famous first lines of Wyndham's novel and Orwell's dystopian *1984* (1949) summarize the estrangement of the citizenry caused by this trauma and the ensuing uncertainty about the world.[8] Wyndham's novel begins, "When a day you happen to know is Wednesday starts off by sounding like Sunday, there is something seriously wrong somewhere."[9] This introduction immediately dismisses any semblance of verisimilitude with the world we know, much like the beginning of *1984:* "It was a bright cold day in April, and the clocks were striking thirteen."[10] C.N. Manlove notes the parallelism between the beginnings of these two novels[11]; however, Manlove does not discuss how both novels, from this first moment of uncertainty, create a tension and suspense by firmly establishing that "there is something seriously wrong." Wyndham and Orwell recognized the lingering fear over the threat to British sovereignty and thus created situations in which their characters deal with and to varying degrees find protection from previously unimaginable estrangement and oppression.

*The Day of the Triffids* contains several powerful allusions to the Blitz. Bill Masen and Josella Playton, Bill's travel companion and eventual lover, pause in the temporary safety of an apartment building. Here, Bill and Josella notice the light signal, "a bright beam like that of a searchlight pointed unwaveringly upward."[12] The description of the light, as a moment of visual salvation amongst traumatic events, alludes to Herbert Mason's famous picture of St. Paul's Cathedral published December 29, 1940 in *The Daily Mail*.[13] The image depicts St. Paul's standing, unharmed and illuminated, amongst the bomb's lingering smoke and the darkness of the damaged blackout areas. The miraculously bright spotlight on St. Paul's has no clear source in the photograph, but the light does seem to be "pointed unwaveringly upward." In Mason's photo, St. Paul's Cathedral metonymically represents the monolithic London that will endure in spite of all atrocities and adversity; Wyndham, however, critiques this misguided nationalism and idealism by replicating and replacing the image in the novel. Instead of St. Paul's Cathedral, Bill and Josella discover that their light emanates from University Tower, which they eventually approach from Store Street.[14] Wyndham locates the source of illumination in the university, replacing spiritual imagery with the ideals of knowledge and a life of the mind. This hope in knowledge is only fleeting as even the university is undermined by the lack of forethought displayed by the survivors who gather at this location. The book then further undermines these ideals by making a visual reference to Orwell's *1984*. Wyndham's University Tower can only represent the Senate House at the University of London, a large, white, art-deco-style building that housed the wartime Ministry of Information which earlier served as inspiration for Orwell's Ministry of Truth. Through this dual allusion to Mason's photo and to Orwell's novel, Wyndham challenges the idea of the university, information, and truth. In Mason's classic photo the illumination, which seems to signify endurance, is mere façade since the light literally emanates from the destructive force. Likewise, Orwell's Ministry of Information is focused on controlling, manipulating, and revising history and ideas, or even destroying truth. Wyndham's university group, who characterize the institution and dissemination of knowledge, begin with a misguided focus, similar to Mason's photo, and the belief that control of information, as in Orwell's Ministry, will lead to societal success.

The historical proximity to the Blitz is also important to understanding the reconceptualization of the self in relationship to a postapocalyptic environment. Masen gazes out the window in a reflective moment and describes the destruction with language that would also apply to the aftermath of a bombing during the Blitz. Here, he enacts a lesson his father taught him "before Hitler's war."[15] Masen explains,

> Quite consciously I began saying good-by to it all. The sun was low. Towers, spires, and facades of Portland stone were white or pink against the dimming sky. More fires had broken out here and there. The smoke climbed in big black smudges, sometimes with a lick of flame at the bottom of them. Quite likely, I told myself, I would never in my life again see any of these familiar buildings after tomorrow. There might be a time when one would be able to come back — but not to the same place. Fires and weather would have worked on it; it would be visibly dead and abandoned. But now, at a distance, it could still masquerade as a living city.[16]

Masen's description focuses on the fires and the obfuscating smoke that one would expect immediately after a bombing. Notably, he does not attribute the cause of the fires to the source, the newly blind and their haphazard ransacking of the city, thus maintaining the allusion to the Blitz. Bill mourns, not the destruction of the city, but the fact that he will not "see any of these familiar buildings after tomorrow." Like Londoners going away to the country because of the threat of bombings, Bill and Josella feel as if they must leave the city; the couple's decision to flee emphasizes their class status as they have the means and the knowhow to do so. Their actions also allude to the London Plague of 1665 when the privileged fled London in great numbers. The threat of the triffids, like the plague before it, fundamentally challenges the established social order. In both events, the city becomes the location of danger and threat. In these moments of cataclysm, the forced exodus from the city to the country highlights the economic, social, and epistemological conditions that exist in these linked historical moments of urban destruction.[17] In Bill's response, he laments not *seeing* the buildings of the city rather than not *being* in the city. This focus on his vision creates a chasm between himself, as the sighted, empowered subject, and the newly blind. They are less than human because they cannot see, thus challenging their individual subjectivity because of loss of functionality. They indicate the dangers in times of historical crisis presented for the physical survival of humanity and the continuity of the Western epistemological subject. When he claims that "it could still masquerade as a living city," he is establishing the objected otherness of the newly blind who remain in the city, essentially labeling them as undead since living is now a lie, a visual deception. During this moment of pause and reflection in the early aftermath of the catastrophe, Masen notices that normalcy and even life and living are now mere "masquerade," no doubt a deliberate and biting word choice on Wyndham's part.

As the Blitz blew apart the comfort of life for the British subject, Wyndham explains the historical development of the postwar period through three metaphoric zombies (ZnZs). The first ZnZs, those blinded by the meteor shower, represent the myopic post–Blitz subject. We are first introduced to them as Masen awakens blindfolded in the hospital. He describes the newly blind as "a sort of murmurousness beyond the door." He elaborates, "It seemed composed of whimperings, slitherings, and shuffling."[18] The phrase "murmurousness beyond the door" could be a tagline for a zombie film and certainly evokes the Romero zombies who want to break into the farmhouse in *Night of the Living Dead* (1968) or the shopping mall in *Dawn of the Dead* (1978).[19] The shuffling motion of the blind as they move through the hospital and the city is characteristic of cinematic zombies. Also, just as zombies want to indiscriminately devour the living, the newly blind viciously attack the sighted in hopes of indenturing them into servitude. For example, when Bill meets Josella, he rescues her from a man who has bound her and is trying to beat her into compliance.[20] In each of these zombie narratives, the zombie horde is blockaded from the survivors, at least temporarily. In *The Day of the Triffids* the blockade is also metaphoric, as Bill notes that "it seemed as though their blindness had shut people into themselves."[21] The blindness forces a retreat from the social and intellectual bonds that previously defined their humanity. They are entrapped in a body that is already dead, further supported by the repeated suicides of the newly blind, such as the barkeep who admires the strength of his wife to kill herself and their child or the young couple who step out of a window.[22] Their movements, actions, motivations, and loss of consciousness all indicate that the newly blind who do not commit suicide have become zombies.

As these newly blind ZnZs are metaphoric representations of their historical moment, we need to understand the cause of their blindness as social critique. Most of the characters believe that they are blinded as "the Earth's orbit passed through a cloud of comet debris," producing "the most remarkable celestial spectacle on record."[23] At least that is the description offered before everyone realizes that the same celestial display also causes permanent blindness. Given the experiences of the Blitz, one would expect the British to recognize the dangers of looking up to the sky when falling objects appear. The fact that everyone is mesmerized by the alleged "celestial spectacle" highlights the delusions of the majority of the British postwar population concerning their national infallibility and indestructibility. The ignorant response to spectacle also appears in Romero's *Land of the Dead* (2005) where the zombies are mesmerized by fireworks.[24] Summarizing the lessons the postwar subject should have learned about the ignorance and loss of agency related to spectacle culture, Michael Beadley, the leader of the group at University Tower, argues, "From August 6, 1945, the margin of survival has narrowed appallingly. Indeed, two days ago it was narrower than it is at this moment. If you need to dramatize, you could well take for your material the years succeeding 1945, when the path of safety started to shrink to a tightrope along which we had to walk with our eyes deliberately closed to the depths beneath us."[25] The newly blind are punished for not comprehending the historical lessons of the bombing of Hiroshima, which Beadley presents as a concluding moment to all the bombings of World War II, including the Blitz. Although Hiroshima was not London's history, not England's trauma, Beadley equates the two, enacting a form of historical forgetting that results from the very spectacle he critiques. The historical specificity of the two traumas is dismissed as they are yoked into one, thus destroying the mere idea of specificity and, by extension, the ability to comprehend the depths of historical truth. His metaphor of a tightrope emphasizes that humanity and national sovereignty were utterly fragile in comparison to the most advanced weaponry. To walk along this historical tightrope requires the "eyes deliberately closed," revealing the narrowing of British political agency after the war, the myopic refusal of the British to recognize this global shift, and the refusal to acknowledge the "depths" of history with regard to Boyle's epigraph.

The second ZnZs, the triffids, are a metaphor of the Cold War paranoia and the loss of agency and authority for the British after the war. The zombie-like characteristics of the triffids are much like the newly blind. Bill explains that they "moved rather like a man on crutches," predicting the characteristic hobble of the Romero slow-moving zombie.[26] Like Romero's zombies who are afraid of fire, the triffids are most easily destroyed by flame throwers. Alternately, the preferred strategy was "to shoot the top off the stem," like the head shot required to kill cinematic zombies; mortar bombs do not work because triffids have "the ability to take a lot of damage without lethal harm."[27] They can survive, like the undead, with traumatic injuries. The triffids use a long stinger to attack humans with a poison that blinds and immobilizes the victims. At first, people could not figure out why these plants attacked, but then, as Bill explains, "it was shown that they fed upon flesh."[28] The triffids' goal, like that of the cinematic zombie, is to consume the flesh of the living. The triffids are the dangerous, yet unexpected menace that invades Britain and feeds upon the freedoms of the survivors.

The cryptic origins of the triffids serve as a metaphor for the loss of British supremacy with the emergence of the Cold War superpowers of the Soviet Union and the United States. The triffids become known on the global stage because of the valuable "pale pink oil" they produce.[29] The first vial of this mysterious oil is brought to the Artic & European Oil Company by Umberto Chritoforo Palanguez, a man of "assorted Latin descent."[30] It is unclear whether Palanguez is working for the Russian government (the novel identifies Russia rather than the Soviet Union) or whether he has stolen from them, but just as he has brokered a deal with the corporation, the Russian military shoots down his plane and releases "millions of gossamer-slung triffids seeds, free to drift wherever the winds of the world should take them."[31] This scenario places political power and knowledge in the hands of the Soviet Union and several possible Latin American nations, two areas of the world accepting of communist governments. It also establishes the power of the global corporation, the only European interests presented. Noticeably missing from this triangle are the traditional European powers, like Great Britain. Power is transplanted to the Soviet Union, "which still hid behind a curtain of suspicion and secrecy," as Bill surmises, and had knowledge and control over the triffids, including their mobility, "classified as a state secret."[32] Through the triffids and their dissemination, we see the communist anticipation of capitalist greed, knowing that the valuable oils will lead to the widespread cultivation of triffids. Thus, after the attack of the biological weapons that blinds the population, the triffids are a dormant zombie army called into action by their originators, wiping out the capitalist infrastructure in a moment.

Most of the survivors are slow to recognize the true origins of the threat, however, emphasizing their utter confusion about global politics. The faith in America as saviors underscores this confusion. Bill and Coker, another main character, encounter a small group of survivors with "an utterly unshakeable conviction that nothing serious could have happened to America" and belief that the Americans "would never have allowed such a thing to happen in their country."[33] This reaction epitomizes the inability to see the shift in global politics away from the European imperial legacy of the previous centuries. In *28 Days Later*, there is a parallel scene that expresses this global relationship with more acuity. Jim, the protagonist, is imprisoned in the villa occupied by the military. His fellow prisoner, Sergeant

Farrell, held captive because he would not be complicit in the sexual harassment of the two female survivors, rants that the infection will remain localized on the "diseased little island," his label, because, he argues, "they quarantined us." While never identifying the agents or nations who enacted this quarantine, he does explain, "TVs are playing and planes are flying in the sky and the rest of the world is continuing as fucking normal."[34] Based on his examples of media and technological advancement, the Western world (at least those nations where television has become ubiquitous) has acted collectively to contain this epidemic.

The last manifestation of the ZnZ presented in *The Day of the Triffids,* that of the city and the infrastructures of society, critiques how industrial capitalism and the imperial nation state influence the status of the individual as a self-contained and self-sufficient ontological being. Masen develops from a selfishly individualistic scientist before the disaster to a thoughtful and able caretaker of the land and the people who depend on him. Early in the novel, Masen characterizes this self-awareness:

> There was, too, a feeling that as long as I remained *my* normal self things might even yet, in some inconceivable way, return to *their* normal. Absurd it undoubtedly was, but I had a very strong sense that the moment I should stove in one of those sheets of plate glass I would leave the old order behind me forever: I should become a looter, a sacker, a low scavenger upon the dead body of the system that had nourished me.[35]

He recognizes the capitalist modes of production, "the system that had nourished me," as "a dead body." By becoming "a looter, a sacker, a low scavenger," essentially metonyms for zombies, devouring the dead, Bill Masen would have become one of the main examples of the unconscious victims of history, the ZnZs, presented in the novel. Resisting this undead status, Masen critiques how segregated and useless individuals have become as a result of industrial capitalism. He says, "I knew practically nothing, for instance, of such ordinary things as how my food reached me, where the fresh water came from, how the clothes I wore were woven and made, how the drainage of cities kept them healthy. Our life had become a complexity of specialists."[36] Masen, unlike the parasitic neo-feudal fascist Torrence, understands the reality that all humans have been left like the blind in terms of useful labor, and he does not wish to become one of the non-sighted feasting on those who can provide for him or one of those submitting to fascist control simply based on fear of the unknown or what may yet come.

In Wyndham's apocalypse, the privilege of vision is not based on sight but the need to have foresight of the outcomes of our reliance on technology and our cultivation of the unnatural. Masen explains, "I don't think it had ever before occurred to me that man's supremacy is not primarily due to his brain, as most of the books would have one think. It is due to the brain's capacity to make use of the information conveyed to it by a narrow band of visible light rays."[37] Wyndham realizes the fragility of the visible and correlates this tenable protection to the ever-present danger for corruption or destruction that surrounds postwar society. Wyndham's critique of vision relates to James Joyce's famous phrase in the "Proteus" chapter of *Ulysses* (1922), "ineluctable modality of the visible."[38] Stephen Dedalus struggles to understand the influences of nationalism, class, and gender on his self-identity. The narrative of the *bildungsroman* functions similarly to the narrative of apocalypse by imagining new social relations, but the main difference is that the *bildungsroman* is based primarily on the imagination of the individual's place within the new milieu, while the apocalyptic is based on collective imagination of new experiences. Wyndham's argument for the supremacy of human visibility based on its connection to ontological identity asks for a more complete and careful understanding of the way British society has progressed from the traumas of the war and the loss of political agency as the locus of power shifts under global capitalism.

## The Terror of Violence and Rage in New Britain

In the introduction to the collection *British Horror Cinema* (2002), Steve Chibnall and Julian Petley lament both the status of the horror genre in Britain and the lack of academic critical attention paid to the genre. They hope for a horror film that could set off a genre cycle like Guy Ritchie's *Lock, Stock, and Two Smoking Barrels* (1998) did for the crime film.[39] Ritchie's film earned critical attention and commercial success because it addresses issues of masculinity, violence, class, and family by looking comically at the status of Englishness in post–Thatcher Britain. Ritchie's film is as much about the high jinks of inept criminals, the inclusion of rhyming slang in everyday language, and the system of power in the London underworld, as it is about the remnants of a once dominant British cultural identity. Danny Boyle's *28 Days Later*, which was released in 2002, has since become for the horror genre what Ritchie's film was for the crime genre.

*28 Days Later* looks at the aftermath of a biological disaster that has turned almost all of England into blood-spewing creatures infected by the Rage virus. The infected are a postmodern imagination of ZnZs. Many scholars interested in zombies focus on Boyle's film, despite the fact that the infected are technically alive.[40] The acceptance of Boyle's post-zombie film as the harbinger of the genre's future supports ZnZs as metaphors for the historical condition throughout the postwar period. These ZnZs establish that violent conflict manifested through constant fear of terrorism is a dominant ideological force that shapes humanity at the beginning of the twenty-first century. Thus, Boyle extends Wyndham's critique of visibility and ontology, presenting the postmodern ZnZ as the materialization of the omnipresent image and idea of violence. By embodying this constant threat and its related fear, the postmodern ZnZ asks how we may regain an ontological identity that relates to what we see in the world rather than to what spectacle culture wants us to see as threatening and violent.[41]

The postmodern character of *28 Days Later* combines derivative and adapted narratives and styles with a critical examination of Great Britain's place within the global circulation of economic and cultural capital. Screenwriter Alex Garland, best known for his novel *The Beach* (1996), cites H.G. Wells, John Wyndham, particularly *The Day of the Triffids,* and J.G. Ballard's "disaster novels" as influences for his screenplay.[42] Although the film was completed during the anthrax scare and distributed as the SARS outbreak and monkeypox created media hysteria, Boyle explains, "We actually had a lower level of paranoia in mind — a very British one — which was the continued scare over mad cow disease and the sudden foot-and-mouth outbreak. For months, the UK was full of fields of burning animals — biblical images of pyres on the horizon, smoke filling the sky."[43] The paranoia that sparked Boyle and Garland's interest in epidemics was the destruction of the British live stock industry, but beyond this economic destruction, Mad Cow disease, like dementia and Alzheimer's disease, means that rational and reasonably healthy individuals could be mentally debilitated by exposure to everyday contaminates. The film pays homage to the imagery of the burning animal carcasses in a chilling shot from the empty M602 of Manchester entirely reduced to blazing pyres and a smoke-filled sky. An industrial center, Manchester's destruction marks the historical end of Britain's industrial empire, a factor that the government has aggressively attempted to preserve. *28 Days Later* critiques the attempt to maintain an ideal of British statehood and identity by equating the institutions of control, especially the church and the military, with the rage that has infected society. The small community of survivors eventually abandons their individual class and racial categories as they attempt to find an "answer to infection," what the radio broadcast from the military encampment offers survivors. The answer is not a return to the system of inequality and hierarchical power advocated by the military community, but instead the protection of a cooperative community based on equality and concern for the other.

*28 Days Later* examines how rage and violence are dangerous and destructive forces in our world. The film begins with a montage of images of riots, public hangings, and protests; images systemic of the rage, particularly towards the other, which haunt our political reality of terrorism and its constant threat. The images contain police, labeled in several different languages, violently and futilely attempting to contain the riotous masses, showing a culture of violence. These masses occupy developed cities and underdeveloped locations; they are of Middle Eastern, European, and Asian descent. As these images repeat, the viewer's perspective shifts from viewing these images directly to realizing that they are broadcast on several television sets for the chimpanzee viewer in a lab experiment. As the images shift from the focus to the background, the viewer realizes that these images are always on the periphery of our media-inundated society. The animal looks helplessly into the camera, victimized by the media rhetoric of fear that attempts to contain the masses. The animal is the powerless victim and witness to violence just like the film's audience. The media images of violent rebellion are meant to control the fearful observer, replacing the spectacle of public execution, which, as Michel Foucault argues, ensured the power of the sovereign. He explains, "Not only must people know, they must see with their own eyes. Because they must be made to be afraid; but also because they must be the witnesses, the guarantors, of the punishment, and because they must to a certain extent take part in it."[44] While the images of violence that are broadcast are simulacra of violence, they represent both a threat to an ordered and civilized way of life, a stereotype of Britishness, and also the potential for violence within each of us that must be contained.

The scene of the animal forced to watch images of violence alludes to Stanley Kubrick's film adaptation of *A Clockwork Orange* (1971).[45] The chimpanzee in the research facility that watches the violent images seems passive and sweet, despite the violence that we see from the other infected animals. The film's opening scene of the chimpanzee watching televised images of violence alludes to Kubrick's presentation of young hooligan Alex de Large, who exchanges his murder sentence to become a subject in an experiment to cure violent tendencies. He is repeatedly forced to watch different images of violence, rape, and historical atrocities. The experiment requires that his eyes be wired open, emphasizing the inescapability of media images. Kubrick's film creates another parallel to the second beginning of *28 Days Later* and the close-up shot of Jim's eye. This image of Jim's eye pays homage to Wyndham's Bill Masen who awakens blind and helpless in the hospital. Jim can see, confirmed by the focus on his eye as he awakens, but as the shot pans back we see his body, naked and vulnerable. The clarity of the digital image of Jim's eye allows viewers to see each eyelash, another reference to *A Clockwork Orange* because of Alex's signature false eyelashes. Like *A Clockwork Orange*, *28 Days Later* questions the meaning of violence, its function within society, and its attack on the structures of society.

In *28 Days Later*, the lab, called the Cambridge Primate Research Center, functions allegorically. Much like Manchester represents the industrial center of England, Cambridge represents the intellectual history of England, reinforced by the password to enter the facility: "Think." The activists, who release the Rage virus, encounter a hackneyed horror stereotype of the mad scientist. The scientist justifies the experiments, proclaiming, "In order to cure, you must first understand." While the easily transferable virus is an extreme example of the dangers of biological weapons and misguided scientific experiments, the montage of images and the viral name, Rage, indicate that violence is pathology already within us. The virus transforms anyone who comes into contact, the infected, into zombie-like creatures only concerned with devouring the flesh of the non-infected and spreading the infection, which is very easy since the infected vomit torrents of blood. The infected, characterized by red eyes and a red skin condition, move very, very quickly and twitch, which Boyle modeled after an epileptic fit; he also borrowed physical imagery from rabies and the Ebola virus.[46] The use of a variety of real pathological conditions suggests rage as the ultimate pathology for society.

The infected are a new breed of zombie; their speed is representative of absolute efficiency. That is, if the work of the infected is to spread infection, then they succeed. They reveal that in a global environment where circulation is essential for productivity, the worker must be quick and thus efficient. Ironically, the infected enact a perverse version of Thatcher's agenda that supported individual productivity and accomplishments at the cost of society's collective welfare. Conversely, the infected oppose Tony Blair's vision of a "New Britain," the slogan revealed at Blair's first party conference as leader in 1994. He clearly summarized his vision of "New Britain" at the party conference in 1997, his first after being elected to government. Blair announced, "Today I want to set an ambitious course for this country: to be nothing less than the model 21st century nation, a beacon to the world. It means drawing deep into the richness of the British character. Creative. Compassionate. Outward-looking. Old British values, but a new British confidence."[47] While the infected contradict Blair's "New Britain" because they lack the consciousness to create, care, and consider, they should be read as a metaphor for British cultural identity in the new century. They are the offspring of the post–Blitz subject and the Cold War paranoia of fascist occupation or nuclear attack. Now, at the start of a new century, the infected challenge us to decide if we can look and thus move forward because of our historical understanding or if we want to imagine backwards to a time of perceived simplicity. The protagonist of *28 Days Later,* Jim, starts the film as the embodiment old British values at a time when a "New Britain" has been brought about by apocalypse. His journey begins as he awakens completely unaware in the hospital, continues with a tour of evacuated London, and develops as he unites with other survivors and finally takes the group to countryside communities of first a military dictatorship and then a collaborative community. His journey shows that the "creative," "compassionate," and "outward-looking" values that Blair supports cannot be found in a nostalgic attempt to return to British traditions, Jim's initial perspective, but instead can only be realized once the alienating categories of class, gender, and race are destroyed.

The film's distinctly British political and cultural critique of identity begins as Jim wanders from the hospital and into the empty streets of London. His wandering takes him to many of the landmarks of London[48]: St. Paul's, Big Ben, Westminster Abbey, Westminster Bridge, the Embankment, and the London Eye. The technology of digital cameras made it easier to capture these monumental locations completely deserted. Cinematographer Dod Mantle tells Douglas Bankston that he placed and framed "as many as eight Canon XL1 MiniDV cameras to cover all angles, allowing shots to be made as quickly as possible."[49] The technology of digital films and cameras accelerates the filming process, much like the manic violence of the infected in the film. As Jim walks on Westminster Bridge he steps on souvenir replicas of Big Ben, the scattered, discarded location of these mass-produced toys ironically epitomizing the status of the once grand metropolis. Charlotte Brunsdon claims that the souvenirs mark a self-consciousness about the landmarks, which is fitting in a film so aware of its allusions. She also compares Jim's tour with the sightseeing excursion into London in Boyle's earlier film *Trainspotting* (1996), further emphasizing the layered narratives within this postmodern film.[50] Similarly, Peter Hutchings, focusing on the souvenirs, argues that "as the camera moves from the toppled Big Bens up to the genuine article, the idea that this is a fallen city is rendered chillingly literal."[51] Hutchings' claim reveals that the idea of monumental British history has been destroyed, a process that develops through the twentieth century with the birth of spectacle culture and the celebration of simulacra, not because of the infection. As Jim scatters or breaks these replicas with his movement, he destroys the narratives of British imperial history and the spectacle culture of modernity.

To understand the idea of history presented in Jim's tour through London, we have to pause with him on Westminster Bridge. Jim's rest on Westminster Bridge recalls William Wordsworth's famous sonnet "Composed upon Westminster Bridge, Sept. 3, 1802" (1807), which captures an equally still view of the city. In the poem, the only motion in the early morning metropolis is the Thames, which "glideth at his own sweet will."[52] Wyndham makes a similar statement in *Triffids*: "The Thames flowed imperturbably on. So it would flow until the day the Embankments crumble and the water spread out and Westminster became once more an island in a marsh."[53] In the film the only motion we see is Jim's walking, but through these literary connections we can attach Jim's movement to the lifeblood of the city, the Thames.[54] Boyle explains the inspiration of Wordsworth's poem: "nothing else is moving in the city, only the river, on and on. You can just imagine Wordsworth standing there and you're there 200 years later, looking at the same things, and there's the river."[55] Boyle once again confirms his artistic desire to revisit "the deep, dark ocean of history." In *28 Days Later,* the Thames, as a historical location, juxtaposes the other monumental locations of Jim's tour, which represent the stagnant, undead past that we must understand in order to escape a similar fate. The river is a living historical monument, always changing and moving.

By revisiting a space so famously explained in canonical literature in a fantastical postmodern film, Boyle conceives of an historical understanding that is future-driven. This concept of urban history is defined by Michel de Certeau in "Walking in the City" (1984), through the concept of the city and its contradictions that arise from urban agglomeration. De Certeau explains, "Perspective vision and prospective vision constitute the twofold projection of an opaque past and an uncertain future onto a surface that can be dealt with."[56] As Boyle explains in the DVD commentary, he was attracted to iconic images. All of the places Jim views, with the exception of the London Eye, also known as the Millennium Wheel, record the iconic history of the city. By merging the new Eye sore with these majestic landmarks, the film enacts a perverse version of "New Britain." The London Eye is part of the Blair government's Millennium Project, an effort to celebrate the cultural legacy and influence of the past in the present and for the future. The Millennium Dome, the most famous part of this failed development project was to be a center for culture, not ironically located between the redeveloped Docklands, a symbol of Britain's postmodern prowess, and Greenwich, a symbol of the British Empire as the center of the world. The London Eye, which frequently reappears in Jim's view, merges with these iconic structures, mocking the thought of resurrecting the old British values Blair valorizes because, as de Certeau explains, the city makes clear that the past is unintelligible and the future unseen when the vision of that future depends on a carnival ride; every shot of the London Eye confirms that postmodern vision is wounded or infected.

The excessive accumulation of the city is also marked by the toppled red double-decker bus, the end of transportation or the circulation of people, and the scattered £20 notes, the end of the circulation of capital. The critique of the symbolic value of capital continues in Boyle's *Millions* (2005), as the UK switches over to the Euro, leaving unspent and unconverted pound notes worthless.[57] The status of the circulation of capital is a direct critique of globalization. Neither film makes a conclusive statement about globalization, but both look at how the increasingly global circulation of narrative and capital affects individual and national identity. Similarly commenting on the globalization of the image, Jim's tour stops as he ventures into Piccadilly Circus to find the giant advertisements supplanted by a message board of notes to missing family members. The disaster necessitates the substitution of messages of human relationship and emotion for the messages of consumer desires, the advertisements. The scene of the message board is based on photos from the Kobe earthquake in 1995 and shot before September 11th.[58] The historical and global repetitions of these images of people's grief in the aftermath of cataclysmic devastation proves that the imagination of disaster always returns the consciousness to the interpersonal relationships that can remain and protect the individual throughout unimaginable events, even with very different political and historical causes, from natural disaster, to terrorist attack, to scientific mistake.

The threat posed by the postmodern ZnZs in *28 Days Later* leads to a reassessment of interpersonal relationships that play out through the small community of non-infected: Jim, Selena, a no-nonsense individual who worked as a chemist before the infection, Frank, a jovial cab driver, and his teenage daughter, Hannah. Jim first encounters Selena after instinctively turning to a church for sanctuary from his confusion; he has to attack an infected Anglican priest to save himself, Jim's first reluctant refusal of institutions.[59] Selena then saves Jim from the chasing infected, taking him to her hideout in a mini-mart in the underground.[60] She explains the situation to Jim, and he immediately asks what the government is doing about it; he cannot imagine that the leaders could become infected like everybody else. At this moment, Jim still believes "there is always a government," confirming his initial outlook as spokesperson for Blair's "New Britain." As the tagline for the movie reveals, "his fear began when he woke up alone," characterizing the state of uncertainty of the modern subject in relationship to the world. The second half of the slogan, "his terror began when he realised he wasn't," explains Jim's development into a postmodern, global citizen, outraged by the former complicity of society and awakened to the historical conditions that have led to the disaster.

Conversely, Selena has completely abandoned all the conventions of relationships and the emotions they evoke as a defense to the confusion caused by disaster. In a later scene, she says that "plans are pointless" and attempts to persuade Jim to the same position, sarcastically attacking his nostalgia by asking him, "Do you want to save the world or just fall in love and fuck?" In this statement, Selena makes her first vulgar connection to Jim, and this connection does start to break down her survival instincts so that she can return to the interpersonal relationships that actually will protect her consciousness. This exchange takes place amongst pristine countryside ruins. The scene recalls the trip to the Scottish Highlands by the gang in Boyle's *Trainspotting* (1996). Tommy, the clean-cut athlete of the group, believes that a return to nature will help the lads identify with their cultural heritage and identity, saving them from the relationship problems they all encountered the previous night. The protagonist, Renton, instead, lambastes the Scottish identity and colonial history, displaying a pessimism much like Selena's. Selena's initial outlook epitomizes Susan Sontag's argument that the imagery of disaster "is above all the emblem of an *inadequate response*."[61] Sontag's argument explains that, as we can never actually extend our narrative beyond a disastrous end, we are not equipped to deal with the very forces that could cause this end. Selena has been forced by the postmodern ZnZs to live beyond the end, and she can only propose two clichéd solutions that satisfy the two destinies of "unremitting banality and inconceivable terror" that Sontag says define our age of extremes.[62] In the specifics of *28 Days Later,* these two fates are a return to the previous mode of historical forgetting or a reestablishment of patriarchal violence. Typical of the postmodern moment, both of Selena's propositions could lead to terror. To avoid this terror, Jim and Selena unite with Frank and

Hannah to form a postmodern family unit that reworks power relationships and ultimately refuses patriarchy and its associated violence; Martin Rogers explains that this association moves beyond the family to become "a *network*, a social unit of interdependence and connectivity."[63] As they leave London, they go through a gradual withdrawal from the capitalist system of labor and consumption and thus redefine their collective identity through interpersonal relationships instead of through historical determinism.

The path toward survival requires them to refuse the labels, especially consumer and class, which define their perspective of the city. Just as Jim's understanding of the disaster requires a visit to his parent's suburban home, the tower block occupied by Hannah and Frank permits a shift in the group's focus. Brought to the block by flashing lights, another reference to *The Day of the Triffids* that emphasizes the primacy of the visual, Jim and Selena encounter a barricade of shopping trolleys. The trolleys, previously used to increase and aid consumption, now stand as a barricade between the preservation of civilized life and the rampant infection. The tools of capitalism have been made useless, but they can be reinvented in a new formation. Frank has dealt with the apocalypse by redefining these tools in hopes of protecting himself and his daughter. The excess of the shopping carts is repeated in the myriad of buckets of all different sizes and colors, which Frank has placed on the roof to collect water. The lack of water shows that even the tower building, a symbol of modernity, no longer functions, and thus the community must leave behind the skeleton of the metropolis, the dead city that we see in Wyndham's novel. As they leave the building in Frank's black cab, another iconic image of London, Frank turns on the meter and jokingly says, "Just so you know, I don't take checks or credit cards." Despite the horrors around, they find solace in their release from labor and money, which corresponds to their release from the images of spectacle culture that dictate their understanding and place within the world.[64]

Now that the community has acknowledged the alienation of capitalism and the control it had over them, they can work towards forming a future-thinking community based on collective historical awareness. As their communal bonds strengthen, Selena realizes that love for another is reason to live, and Jim realizes that the infected must be violently destroyed to preserve the love that remains. The members of the military community, however, attempt to preserve the system of patriarchy and capitalism crumbling around them. They have occupied a mansion, collected stockpiles of electronic equipment, and cannot contain their sexual urges. Thinking they have killed Jim, the military men make Hannah and Selena dress in ball gowns, constricting costumes of patriarchy. In anger, Jim returns, unleashes the chained infected held on the grounds, and kills the remaining military men. Jim's release of the infected into the corrupt, or infected, house reaffirms that rage has always been a part of patriarchy. The most aggressive sexual predator, Corporal Mitchell, dies by Jim's hands, as Jim displays that rage is not merely a state-sanctioned biological weapon, but also a defense against terror and atrocity. He has become covered in blood, looking like an infected, but his goal, to reunite with Hannah and Selena, empowers him to use the ideals that once enslaved him into compliance with the governmental agenda.

When he pokes out the eyes of Corporal Mitchell, he proves that oppressive patriarchy has always been a form of blindness used to control the consciousness of society. This image evokes the surrealism of Luis Buñuel's and Salvador Dali's famous image from *Un Chien Andalou* (1929) of an eyeball being cut open by a razor. Buñuel and Dali's destruction of the eye emphasizes the violence of modernity, but it does so by intimately linking violence with desire. The aggressive poking out of the eyes in *28 Days Later* takes on a variety of possible meanings based on the allusions to other works. First, Corporal Mitchell becomes a newly blind, a ZnZ from *The Day of the Triffids*, who represents the foolishness of valorizing

British military prowess after World War II. The surrealist desires of *Un Chien Andalou* play out through Jim, who puts Mitchell in his place through violent retribution for the sins of patriarchy.[65] Mitchell's eyes become the sexual organ that Jim penetrates, the blood representing the first time Mitchell is victimized and thus the last time Mitchell will be able to terrorize others. On one level this destruction of the eyes in place of the cutting of the surrealist eye is a violent refusal of modernity, and the end of the movie then asks what visibility means for postmodernity. Mitchell's violent, militaristic vision of the world is no longer an option. What results in *28 Days Later* is a revaluation of the meaning of vision, envisioning and premonitions, or the potential of a future once the past is actually examined and understood.

To confirm the equality within the community of the remaining survivors, the women must now save Jim's life just as he has saved them. Even the alternate ending projects the women as the new watchdogs of society. They offer a post-racial, post-gender ontology that locates consciousness and subjectivity in mutual protection rather than the violent aggression of modernity and Corporal Mitchell.[66] As the last infected lies emaciated on the ground and the survivors are rescued, it becomes clear that the epidemic has been contained within Great Britain. This has been, as Boyle explained, a particularly British epidemic created by the violent need to uphold the iconic history of Britain. Discussing this view of history in terms of his film, *Millions*, Boyle explains, "It's about saying goodbye, how important that can be particularly for the British. We love hanging on to the past here."[67] Boyle uses the same words as Wyndham's protagonist, Bill Masen, who in a moment of circumspection before fleeing the city, says, "I began saying good-by to it all."[68] The repetition of this phrase supports Boyle's assessment of the British relationship to the past. Since London is both literally and narratively built on the past, as Boyle indicates in the epigraph, saying goodbye to the iconic past becomes impossible. These iconic narratives become constitutive of history over time. *28 Days Later* proves the dangers of hanging on to a monumental past with such a strong grip, especially when that past is an epic fallacy that presents false images of the world and an unproductive nostalgia.

## ZnZs at the 2012 Olympics

ZnZs exist in between the living and the dead. They originate historically in the aftermath of World War II due to the uncertainty caused by the shifting landscape of global politics and capitalism. During these moments of instability, the ZnZs are translators of history for the survivors of the traumas. The ZnZs emerge from the "deep, dark ocean of history," moments like the Blitz on London, the Cold War, and the millennium, illuminating what seems utterly estranging by challenging complacency and revealing "that dark abyss of the past," to return to Boyle's words from the epigraph. The historical clarification that occurs within a world characterized by disaster allows us, as Frank Kermode explains, "to make sense of the world from where we stand, in the middest."[69] We come to understand the fragility of the ontological subject during modernity and the categorical challenge to visibility under postmodernity because of the omnipresence of violence and fear. If we want to avoid the existence of the zombie, either as the mindless menace driven by desire to do harm or as the somnambulist controlled by an external force, we must see ZnZs as the keys to understanding our relationship to the past and thus to our future. This future acknowledges oppression of the human subject as the a priori conception of historical understanding. Thus, the ZnZs offer a future that revises the way we view our past by envisioning collective relationships unhindered by terror or horror. While the ZnZs originate after World War II, there does not seem to be an impending death for these undead figures.

For instance, Danny Boyle was recently announced as the artistic director for the 2012 Olympics in London. Given the apocalyptic significance of the year 2012, derived from the Mayan tradition, the ceremony, a celebration of British culture, calls for the inclusion of ZnZs. Camilla Long asked Boyle if he would include "a blood-soaked, zombietopping rampage" in the ceremony. Boyle replied "probably not," but as he wants to commemorate the reinvention of London (most notably the Thames and the spirit of endurance), he would be wise to revisit the ZnZs, imagining a new figure that could represent this future apocalyptic moment with a distinct historical grounding.

## Notes

1. Aldiss is not alone in his dismissive evaluation. See John Clute, *The Encyclopedia of Science Fiction*, ed. John Clute and Peter Nicholls (New York: St. Martin's, 1993), 1353–4. Clute claims that Wyndham gave an "eloquent post-trauma middle-class UK response to the theme of Disaster." These critics focus on the superficial English icons, such as the repeated respite in pubs by a variety of characters, the claims by minor characters that improper or even barbaric behavior would be impossible in England by the English, and the condemnation of those characters who hope that the Americans will come and save the survivors, as the main critique presented in Wyndham's novel. Certainly, these ideas do reappear throughout the novel, but in addition, Wyndham's novel offers a critique with far more political and historical depth. Other critics touch on these material concerns. For example, cf. Edmund Morris, introduction to *The Day of the Triffids*, by John Wyndham (New York: Modern Library, 2003), xiii. Morris argues that Wyndham uses social commentary to look at the aftermath of disaster. Morris's analysis indicates that the novel requires an examination of the spaces that foster collective ideals. He writes, "And when disaster happens, the worst is not what it does to such physical infrastructures as cities and transport systems, but to the precious intangibles that a democratic government is supposed to protect: the loyalty of lovers, the upbringing of children, the rule of law, the all-importance of free speech and privacy and good manners." Morris stays on the surface and does not comment on the deeply historical aspects of Wyndham's novel, but he does provide a less dismissive critical entry to the work.

2. Brian Aldiss and David Wingrove, *Trillion Year Spree: The History of Science Fiction* (London: Gollancz, 1986), 254.

3. John Wyndham, *The Day of the Triffids* (New York: Modern Library, 2003), 38.

4. Garland and Boyle previously collaborated on the film version (2000) of Garland's novel *The Beach* (1996). Garland wrote the screenplay and Boyle directed. They also both served as executive producers on the sequel to *28 Days Later*. *28 Weeks Later* (2007), however, had a completely new cast and crew. For evidence of the link between Garland's screenplay and Wyndham's novel see Mark Kermode, "A Capital Place for Panic Attacks," *The Observer*, May 6, 2007, accessed July 10, 2010, http://www.guardian.co.uk/film/2007/may/06/features.review.

5. In *Night of the Living Dead* (1968) the creatures are never called zombies. Instead they are referred to as ghouls or the walking dead.

6. Kim Paffenroth, *Gospel of the Living Dead: George Romero's Visions of Hell on Earth* (Waco: Baylor University Press), 3–5.

7. Kyle Bishop, "Dead Man Still Walking: Explaining the Zombie Renaissance." *Journal of Popular Film and Television* 37, no. 1 (2009): 20.

8. As a testament to the fame of these two first lines, they were both included in a *Guardian* online quiz of "the best opening lines of literature." See http://www.guardian.co.uk/books/quiz/2010/mar/24/first-lines-quiz.

9. Wyndham, *Triffids*, 3.

10. George Orwell, *1984* (New York: Signet, 1949), 1.

11. C.N. Manlove, "Everything is Slipping Away: John Wyndham's *The Day of the Triffids*," *JFA* 4, no. 1 (1991): 31–2.

12. Wyndham, *Triffids*, 78.

13. Perhaps it is not a coincidence that the protagonist's surname, Masen, deviates only one letter from the photographer's name.

14. Wyndham, *Triffids*, 81.

15. Ibid., 70.

16. Ibid., 69–70.

17. For an extended analysis of the literary representation of the London Plague of 1665 and how its deadly threat influenced the social order and city life generally, see Stephanie Boluk and Wylie Lenz, "Infection, Media, and Capitalism: From Early Modern Plagues to Postmodern Zombies," *Journal for Early Modern Cultural Studies* 10, no. 2 (Fall/Winter 2010): 127–148.

18. Wyndham, *Triffids*, 10.

19. *Night of the Living Dead*, DVD, directed by George Romero (1968; Elite Entertainment, 1994); *Dawn of the Dead*, DVD, directed by George Romero (1978; Anchor Bay Entertainment, 2004).

20. Wyndham, *Triffids*, 50–1.

21. Ibid., 43.

22. Ibid., 17, 68.

23. Ibid., 8.

24. *Land of the Dead*, DVD, directed by George Romero (2005; Universal Pictures, 2005).

25. Wyndham, *Triffids*, 95–6.

26. Ibid., 27.

27. Ibid., 30, 198.

28. Ibid., 31.

29. Ibid., 23.

30. Ibid., 23.

31. Ibid., 24.

32. Ibid., 23, 26.

33. Ibid., 156, 163. The ignorant belief in American supremacy is revisited in *28 Weeks Later*, the sequel to *28 Days Later*. In the sequel, the American military has created a secure zone on the Isle of Dogs, amongst the postmodern buildings of the redeveloped Docklands, symbols of London's reemergence in the global economy in the 1980s. This film confirms that the United States did escape the infection, making them more dominant over their once colonial allies as they work to repopulate Britain. The military officers in control believe that the infection could never return under their watch. When the outbreak begins once again, the commanders order the snipers to gun down all, infected or not, to assure their own authority. Thus, the United States is depicted as a brutal, militaristic state that will protect its own misguided beliefs while sacrificing even its closest allies; *28 Weeks Later*, DVD, directed by Juan Carlos Fresnadillo (2007; Twentieth Century–Fox, 2007).

34. *28 Days Later*, DVD, directed by Danny Boyle (2002; Twentieth Century–Fox, 2005).

35. Wyndham, *Triffids*, 39.

36. Ibid., 12.

37. Ibid., 93.

38. James Joyce, *Ulysses* (New York: Vintage, 1986), 31.

39. Steve Chibnall and Julian Petley, "The Return of the Repressed? British Horror's Heritage and Future," in *British Horror Cinema*, ed. Steve Chibnall and Julian Petley (London: Routledge, 2002), 8.

40. For example, "In Dead Man Still Walking," Kyle Bishop claims that since *28 Days Later*, "Hollywood has re-embraced the genre." In the conclusion to *Gospel of the Living Dead*, which focuses on Romero's oeuvre, Kim Paffenroth includes *28 Days Later* as an example that "the zombie genre [has] adapted to changes in society ... with the preferred explanation for zombies now being an infectious disease, or a biological weapon gotten out of hand." Communication scholars Joshua Gunn and Shaun Treat examine the unconscious work of ideology. They claim that a future analysis of *28 Days Later* will "illustrate our solution and provide a method of psychoanalytic/ideological criticism keyed specifically to the ideological work of racism." In "A Zombie Manifesto," Sarah Juliet Lauro and Karen Embry cite *28 Days Later* as the final cultural representation of the transition from zombie to zombii, "a consciousless being that is a swarm organism, and the only imaginable specter that could really be posthuman." Geographer Jeff May traces the idea of the undead city from Romero to *Resident Evil* to *28 Days Later* and its sequel in "Zombie Geographies and the Undead City." Bishop, "Dead Man," 17; Paffenroth, *Gospel*, 134; Joshua Gunn and Shaun Treat, "Zombie Trouble: A Propaedeutic on Ideological Subjectification and the Unconscious," *Quarterly Journal of Speech* 91, no. 2 (2005): 167; Sarah Juliet Lauro and Karen Embry, "A Zombie Manifesto: The Nonhuman Condition in the Era of Advanced Capitalism," *boundary 2* 35, no. 1 (2008): 88; Jeff May, "Zombie Geographies and the Undead City," *Social & Cultural Geography* 11, no. 3 (2010).

41. Kyle Bishop argues that the zombie is "fundamentally a visual creature" because of its inability to speak and the focus on its physicality; Kyle Bishop, "Raising the Dead: Unearthing the Nonliterary Origins of Zombie Cinema," *Journal of Popular Film and Television* 33, no. 4 (2006): 201.

42. See Andrew Osmond, "In the Hot Zone," *Cinfantastique* 35, no. 3 (2003): 38; and Scott Macaulay, "Apocalypse Fiction Redux," *Filmmaker* 11, no. 4 (2003): 40.

43. Dennis Lim, "Unchained Malady: With *28 Days Later*, Danny Boyle and Alex Garland Step into the Hot Zone," *Village Voice*, June 18–24, 2003, 48.

44. Michel Foucault, *Discipline and Punish: The Birth of the Prison*, trans. Alan Sheridan (New York: Vintage, 1977), 58.

45. The wording of the title contains two references that apply to *28 Days Later*: first, orange connotes orangutan, which could mean any ape-like creature (even humans taken of their free will), and second, the Cockney phrase, "as queer as a clockwork orange," implies that despite appearance something is not right internally; *A Clockwork Orange*, DVD, directed by Stanley Kubrick (1971; Warner Brothers, 2007).

46. Osmond, "Hot Zone," 39.

47. Tony Blair, Speech to the 1997 Labor Party Conference (Brighton, UK, 1997); see "Blair Calls for Age of Giving," *The Guardian*, October 1, 1997, accessed September 1, 2010, http://www.guardian.co.uk/politics/1997/oct/01/speeches1. For a more extensive understanding of Blair's political philosophy, see Tony Blair, *New Britain: My Vision of a Young Country* (Boulder: Westview Press, 2004).

48. Charlotte Brunsdon identifies this scene as an example of "landmark London," found also in *Dr. Jekyll y el Hombre Lobo* and *An American Werewolf in London*; Charlotte Brundson, *London in Cinema: The Cinematic City Since 1945* (London: British Film Institute, 2007), 49–51.

49. Douglas Bankston, "All the Rage," *American Cinematographer* 84, no. 7 (2003): 83.

50. *Trainspotting*, DVD, directed by Danny Boyle (1996; Alliance Canada, 2009); Brundson, *London in Cinema*, 49–51.

51. Peter Hutchings, "Horror London," *Journal of British Cinema and Television* 6, no. 2 (2009): 196.

52. William Wordsworth, "Composed Upon Westminster Bridge," in *William Wordsworth: The Major Works*, ed. Stephen Gill (Oxford: Oxford University Press, 1984), line 12.

53. Wyndham, *Triffids*, 128.

54. Although not on Westminster Bridge, Alex, in *A Clockwork Orange*, takes a similar self-reflective walk alongside the river when he has been cast aside by his family.

55. Danny Boyle, "Interview with Danny Boyle: Zombies and the Olympic Torch—There's an idea." By Camilla Long, *The Sunday Times*, June 20, 2010, accessed June 28, 2010, http://www.thesundaytimes.co.uk.

56. Michel de Certeau, *The Practice of Everyday Life*, trans. Steven Rendall (Berkeley: University of California Press, 1984), 93–4.

57. *Millions*, DVD, directed by Danny Boyle (2004; Twentieth Century–Fox, 2005).

58. Lim, "Unchained Malady," 48.

59. Peter Hutchings argues, "The church itself seems to function here as a kind of luminal zone, a space of transition between the idea of the fallen city and the more internationalized horror elements that dominate the film thereafter. Indeed the eruption of the infected outwards from the church correlates not just to the process of infection but also to the transformation of London itself into a city much like those other horror cities invaded by zombies and other versions of the undead." Hutchings, "Horror London," 198.

60. In this scene, Selena and Marc use fire bombs to save Jim. The infected, unlike previous zombies, are not afraid of fire although the fire kills them. They are so focused on infection that they do not even protect themselves.

61. Susan Sontag, "The Imagination of Disaster," in *Science Fiction: A Collection of Critical Essays*, ed. Mark Rose (Englewood Cliffs, NJ: Prentice-Hall, 1976), 130.

62. Ibid., 130.

63. Martin Rogers, "Hybridity and Post-Human Anxiety in *28 Days Later*," in *Zombie Culture: Autopsies of the Living Dead*, eds. Shawn McIntosh and Marc Leverette (Lanham, MD: Scarecrow Press, 2008), 127.

64. This solace continues as they stop for a "supermarket sweep" almost directly repeated from Romero's *Dawn of the Dead*. The supermarket presents serenity and familiarity in comparison to the chaos outside. All four take immense pleasure in their free shopping. Copying the comparison of bread loaves by Stephen and Peter in Romero's film, Jim and Frank look for the best scotch. Whereas Romero's men allude to phallic imagery, Jim and Frank's decision to take the quality scotch shows that they have embraced the destruction of their working class status. They now acquire products that previously would have been unavailable. The characters' choices in consumption emphasize that they still have their consciousness, but are also still controlled by commodity culture. Jim's choice in soft drinks shows that while when he first awoke in the hospital suffering from thirst he would drink the Pepsi, a global brand. However, given a choice, he would prefer the Tango, a local brand.

65. Cinematographer Dod Mantle's explanation of the end sequence further supports my argument about the parallels to surrealism. He claims, "The end of the film becomes more Gothic. In the case of the house, there are a lot of very expressionistic shots of the stairways that recollect the theories of sexuality and stairwells from the era of Expressionist cinema, and the lighting is baroque." The cinematographer was influenced by a variety of artistic movements that highlight the relationship between desire and fear; Bankston, "All the Rage," 88.

66. For a focused analysis of the post-feminist ideas of the film, see G. Christopher Williams, "Birthing an Undead Family: Reification of the Mother's Role in the Gothic Landscape of *28 Days Later*," *Gothic Studies* 9, no. 2 (2007): 33–44.

67. Lim, "Unchained Malady," 50.

68. Wyndham, *Triffids*, 69.

69. Frank Kermode, *The Sense of an Ending: Studies in the Theory of Fiction* (New York: Oxford University Press, 1966), 29.

# Dead and Live Life: Zombies, Queers, and Online Sociality

## Shaka McGlotten

*Deep as first love, and wild with all regret;*
*O, Death in Life, the days that are no more!*
— "Tears, Idle Tears," Alfred, Lord Tennyson

In ten years of talking to gay men about their on and offline intimacies, no one ever told me, "I feel like a zombie." And it would be unfair to (most of) my informants to call them zombies. But I did hear many stories about death and the numbing or exciting habituation that comes with loneliness, boredom, and addiction — affective modes that blur the lines between dead and (a)live life. Here I use "dead and live life" to index different states of liveness, the different ways we might feel more or less alive. These states include the heightened sense of our own phenomenological encounter with the world that comes in moments of vitality, excitation, and the crises (minor and major) that animate so much of ordinary life.[1] Then, there are the attenuated forms of liveness that appear as affective numbness, flatness, and the narrowed but intense focus of hunger or addiction; or those that manifest as the cast out, abject, animal, refugee, poor, or queer whose "bare" life marks out the limits of life writ large. And finally, there are those sorts of liveness that haunt our labors and aspirations: the banal and brutal repetition that structures working middle class Western everyday life as much as it defines the figure of the walking dead.

In thinking through the variously sad, funny, and ordinary stories these men have told me, I marvel at the stubborn persistence of desire and wonder if the hungry-yet-dead animatedness of zombies might not offer ways of reading forms of intimate liveliness that fall outside of a live intimate life — that is, those hetero and homonormative ideologies of the good, coupled life, or what Lauren Berlant has called "dead citizenship."[2] The stories of intimacy that my friends, lovers, and informants told me included experiences of hot sex or expressive creativity (two things that might indicate a lively life), but they were as often about mourning dead friends and worlds, feeling lonely or bored, anxiously awaiting or avoiding STD tests, or worrying about whether the time they spent online meant they were addicted to something, whether sex or the Internet.

In this essay I story instances of dead and live life culled from interviews with gay men about their real and virtual intimacies.[3] I read their narratives alongside Canadian under-ground filmmaker Bruce LaBruce's 2008 gay zombie film *Otto; or, Up with Dead People*[4] to consider the trafficking between forms of dead and live life in contemporary queer sociality, which, I suggest, is animated by death, reflecting banal and strange configurations of death-in-life. And at the same time, the essay eschews the anti-futural, anti-relational polemic of Lee Edelman's *No Future*.[5] Edelman's critique of "reproductive futurism," an ideology that depends on and reproduces the figure of the Child as a basis on which political hopefulness and the rhetorics that articulate it depend, is forceful and compelling. I am especially impressed by the ways he locates the power and "dignity" of queerness in the refusal to believe in a redemptive future. My work, however, differs insofar as the theoretical and political orientation he deploys refuses *absolutely;* it negates not only normative models of relationality or politics, but any models *a priori*. In his framing, all politics are routed through reproductive futurism and thus the ethical demand of queer life and sociality is regarded as merely the negation of politics and the social itself. Like Edelman, I am similarly critical of the equivalence established between futurity and the sentimental and normative notion that "children are the future." I am less convinced, however, that all political futu-rities necessarily operate in this way. Framed within the context of this essay, then, I under-stand our collective zombification as still possessing an openness, an expansive and ever-expanding capacity to act in ways that are as creatively animated as they are expected. Thus, even as we continue to hungrily desire (whether bodies or stuff or politics), and labor within the constraints of advanced capitalism, we can nonetheless cultivate enlivening modes of agency, or at least imagine them.

## I'm Hungry for You

Like many of the stories told me, Todd Ahlberg's 2003 documentary film *Hooked: Get It On(Line)*[6] begins with an optimistic framing of gay online spaces—"It's awesome," says one of Ahlberg's subjects speaking of the erotic opportunities available. Ultimately, however, the film uses men's experiences in online spaces to tell a less interesting story about addic-tion: one that conflates the instantaneity of gay online spaces like *gay.com* or *manhunt.net* with technological innovation and gay male sexuality more generally. In Ahlberg's framing, these sites are symptomatic of larger problems with gay men's sexual culture like promiscuity and anonymous sex. Glazed eyes, drooling, open-mouthed desire: the film's telos imagines technology and the desires and practices of men who go online as zombied. While Ahlberg's documentary interest in online gay life and addiction resembles my own ethnographic one, I find an ongoing animatedness where he finds only a deadness that cries out for therapeutic interpretation and intervention.

If *Hooked* is a closed text in that men's narratives about technologically-mediated sex reproduce stereotypes about gay sexual excess, then Bruce LaBruce's *Otto* is a radically open one that addresses contemporary queer sociality more broadly. The film follows the rebirth of Otto, an amnesiac young gay zombie new to the unlife, who stumbles into a new doc-umentary project by filmmaker Medea Yarn. Yarn is simultaneously completing her "mag-num corpus," a political-porno-zombie film about the "Che Guevara of the undead," who fucks a zombie army into undead life to revolt against "living civilization."[7] LaBruce's film and Yarn's film-within-the-film level variously camp, blunt, astute, and sincere critiques of "the deadened living" of modern life. In spite of what her goth comportment and fasci-nation with the undead might suggest, Medea Yarn's polemic is not anti-life, but she reads, rather perversely, sites of death-in-life as potentially vital. This approach will be familiar to Marxist, environmental, queer, and anti-globalization activists. Shooting a scene at a garbage dump, a "graveyard of advanced capitalism," Medea gives Otto notes to prepare for the scene, suggesting that as a zombie he should imagine the dump as "a lotus land, an idyll of truth and beauty, a symbol for mankind's quest to turn the earth into an industrialized wasteland of casual extermination and genocide." If that's too heady, she condenses the sentiment neatly: "Just think of it as a metaphor for the heartless technocracies that govern the earth and you'll be fine."

Even as Yarn employs Otto's unlife to highlight the creeping "putrescence and decay" of capital, they are also each themselves subject to the critique of deadened living. They are both affectively flat, even boring. Medea Yarn's pedantic self-importance and exploitative entrepeneurism mocks and mobilizes stereotypes about experimental filmmakers (her name is an anagram of Maya Deren); and Otto sometimes reads as chemically zoned-out goth hipster (Belgian actor Jey Crisfar's good looks and his dusty, but unmistakably fashionable clothes likely save Otto from being wholly unsympathetic).

If my reading of *Otto* thus far suggests an ambivalent anti-capitalist moralism rather than the openness I note above, then the film's layered structure, intellectual precocity, camp sincerity, and ambivalence make matters more complex. The film, and Yarn's film-within-a-film, seriously and playfully offer up different forms of life and death as more or less animate. Taking the characters of Medea Yarn and Otto, for example, it's unclear who is more lively, the amnesiac zombie or the stock avant-gardist. More to the point, LaBruce leaves Otto's undead status deliberately unclear. Viewers are left wondering whether Otto is a zombie or just confusedly acting like one. As LaBruce puts it in an interview with the cultural critic Ernest Hardy:

> I wanted to make a zombie who was a misfit, a sissy and a plague-ridden faggot. I deliberately leave it open to interpretation whether Otto is supposed to be a 'real' zombie or merely a screwed-up, homeless, mentally ill kid with an eating disorder, who believes that he's dead. I had been running into a lot of young people who told me they felt kind of like the walking dead already, owing to the alarming, apocalyptic state of the world, or the deadening effects of technology, or whatever. *Otto* is my dead valentine to the youth of today.[8]

Rather than considering them to be merely inanimate, the condition of death-in-life afflicting "the youth of today" suggests a contagious affective atmosphere in which death itself is open, a transmissible and ongoing movement rather than a frozen inertness.[9]

Responding to my request for informants in a *gay.com* chatroom, EvilAndroids engaged me in an anxious conversation about my research, the motives of the men who frequent online publics, and his own troubled relationship to life online. In his search for connection online, EvilAndroids describes deadness as something he is in the process of becoming through his interactions with other men, a condition he views as a desirable end.

> <EvilAndroids> i think its killing me
> <EvilAndroids> everyone takes a little bit more then the last
> <EvilAndroids> and somedays i keep going thinking this is it, and when i am empty there will be nothing left to take and i can be at peace
> <EvilAndroids> like a robot

In *Otto*, Medea Yarn says of the eponymous lead: "He vaguely reminded me of the other boys I had already cast in *Up With Dead People*: lonely, empty, dead inside. In a way he fit the typical porn profile: the lost boy; the damaged boy; the numb, phlegmatic, insensate boy willing to go to any extreme to feel something, to feel anything." If Otto and EvilAndroids share a queer emptiness, they differ in their relation to it. Yarn reads Otto's zombie identity, and/or mental illness, as an index of an extant emptiness (or a present absence); his willingness to participate in her agitprop documentary evidences his desire to interrupt that emptiness. EvilAndroids, by contrast, yearns for a more spacious emptiness that opens after desire is exhausted. Of course, his longing for a robotic peace, one that presumes "there [is] nothing left to take," resembles the blank subjectivity of the zombie.

> <shakaz26> it's killing you — or you're killing yourself — if you do really crazy risky things ... but then that's just desire
> <EvilAndroids> just the motions
> <EvilAndroids> but it never goes away
> <shakaz26> i know what you mean
> <EvilAndroids> its killing me on the inside

But, as Dominic Pettman and others point out,[10] exhaustion doesn't signal the end of desire, only its affective reconfiguration (into anxiety, depression, or indifference, for example). EvilAndroids acknowledges this persistence —"but it never goes away"— and at the same time reemphasizes an ongoing deadening that is paradoxically an anxiously enlivening, a decomposition without end, rather than a flat or full stop.

## So Over It

If I were a more quantitatively rather than ontologically preoccupied social scientist, I could tell you exactly how many times I had an online exchange that went like this:

> <shakaz26> hi, how's it going?
> <standinzombieinformant> good, just bored.

Suffice to say I had *many* conversations start that way, as most online cruisers can attest. Boredom shares with emptiness the sense of lacking something (whether that lack is something we want or not), yet it varies from absence in that it indexes a form of depleted stillness that blocks more lively forms of engagement.[11] "Just bored" simultaneously conveys an indifferent sufficiency, "just enough," while inviting a more exciting interruption: "Will you offer to relieve my boredom?" In a face-to-face interview, EvilAndroids, now JonJon, articulated the ways the anticipating and uncomfortable stillness of feeling bored got him into trouble. He went online looking for authentic connections but, bored and lonely (more on the latter below), settled for the temporary "self-validation" sex offered. He lamented the homogeneity of the men in Austin, Texas, noting that the promise of queerness lay in its capacity to be different, to differ:

> That's another thing about Austin. All the guys are normal, average, straight-acting....
> I'd rather be with someone who is a piece of work, someone I can hate or fall in love
> with. I'm ashamed of how we've homogenized, I mean, HOMOgenized. We're so set on
> being normal. Being gay is like having a license to be out there.... People forget in gay
> culture that it's important to be an individual. Somedays I get bored waiting for someone
> of that caliber and so I hook up with someone and feel terrible afterwards. I'm still lonely
> and I still get bored.

For EvilAndroids/JonJon, hooking up is effected through an angry disenchantment with the banality and cultural HOMOgeneity of his environment. His sentiments echo a broader disenchantment with changing forms of sociality, especially virtually-mediated ones. That is, if online spaces were once imagined to offer a utopian cyber public sphere to supplement the disappearing zones of public encounter (those inter-class/race/generation forms of contact celebrated by Samuel Delany), this fantasy was quickly interrupted by the accelerated mainstreaming of gay male life, as it was incorporated within the neoliberal political imaginary and subject to the dictates of commodity fetishism.[12] In an interview,

Keith Griffith, owner of cruisingforsex.com and a producer/director of amateur pornographic films, suggested that the disappearance of public sex venues and increasingly rarer "out there" queer life had less to do with limitations imposed by the anti-gay right, but, paradoxically, by the success of the gay and lesbian rights movement itself. In a now well-rehearsed argument, mainstream visibility and acceptance of queer people corresponded to the assimilation of queer culture to the logic of capital, in which alternative sexualities come to represent one among a field of available lifestyle options. This process of normalization suppresses the radical potential of a politics of sexual liberation that emphasizes pleasure and openness over static identity categories (particularly when the stability of those categories in large part derives from the ways they cleave to particular patterns of consumption). As Keith argues:

> It isn't the conservative agenda. It is that we have created another box that we've forced people to go inside of, and that is: you've gotta be gay. You're either straight or you're gay. And that has had a profound impact on the ability of men to have sex. A good friend of mine who now lives in Fresno, California, and moved there specifically for the good opportunities for sex, says that his first rule of thumb, because he's a traveling nurse, so he can be pretty much anywhere he wants to be, his first rule of thumb is to see if there's a gay community center in the town, and if there is, he *will not* move there! Because it does something to change the dynamics. The men are absolutely convinced that if they have one sexual encounter with another man, they are gay, and of course the gay community will say "you are gay, you're just in denial." Well, maybe sex is much more fluid than that. Maybe we are now as guilty as straight people for forcing into people into one more choice, one more box.

Keith's conviction that identity categories limit the fluidity of sex, or his friend's instrumental avoidance of towns with a gay community center, both nostalgically evoke a disappeared golden age of queer sociality that escaped the fetters of identification, and critique contemporary gayness as a deadened imitation of an earlier, more capacious, gay (and explicitly not gay) erotic life (even if that life is a utopian fantasy!). In *Otto*, Bruce LaBruce enacts a polyvalent critique against boredom and the boring. As he tells Ernest Hardy, he undertook *Otto* in part as a response to and repudiation of the rise of cruel and shallow torture porn films. LaBruce hoped to excavate earlier and more compelling forms of horror storytelling, imagining *Otto* as a thinking person's existential horror.[13] Further, as I suggest above, *Otto* imagines its leads as themselves navigating the razor's edge between boredom and interest. Medea Yarn's cringe-inducing experimental films, in arty black and white, complete with Grecian drapery and self-consciously performative dance/movement, come to mind, as does her pedantic voice-over. Even Otto's existential crisis sometimes comes across as an adolescent identity crisis ("To unlive, or not to unlive?"). Yet LaBruce's (and, perhaps, Yarn's) critique of contemporary queer life is altogether less ambivalent; the new gay is boring, already zombied and getting deader. Early on, a clip from Yarn's film features a recently converted gay zombie couple drinking tea and reading the paper, uttering the occasional, if affectionate, snarl and groan in a parodic condemnation of a banal couplified gay life. And, as the film later reveals through idyllic romantic flashbacks with another young man, his ex-boyfriend Rudolf, Otto's own couplification couldn't save him from his melancholic existential crisis (and might have made it worse). Finally, in a pivotal scene, Otto is picked up outside a Berlin bar called "Flesh," which, in layered irony, is hosting a zombie night. Gay men swishily mime Otto's own shambling and are likewise drawn to the bar by a not wholly articulate hunger. Otto and the queens he sees outside the bar are each in their own way, "window shopping." When Otto is picked up outside the bar it's because, as Kathleen Frederickson observes, "the public proffered inside the bar is unpromisingly dead."[14]

The lack of animation, or desaturation,[15] of contemporary queer sociality is something that Peter, a young journalist, and his friends hoped to interrupt in their "lulz"-hunting[16] "stakeouts." In these stakeouts, Peter and his friends would playfully, if also a bit cruelly, respond affirmatively, but with false information, to ads on *Craigslist* or requests for private chats on *gay.com*.

> We called them stakeouts. It started out innocent. We were drunk and we were upset about old, ugly people, that they thought they could private us—
>
> —lookin?
> —want some head?
> —sup?
>
> We went to the Ford model site and copied an "ugly"-looking model and we invited someone and hid behind a dumpster and between a laundry mat. And we enjoyed watching as people came by and knocked on doors and didn't get answers.
> Our group was mixed—straights and gays and there was only so much hair waxing and fingernail painting we could do. We had to keep people entertained!

Responding to a horrified and, likely, judgmental expression on my face, Peter elaborated:

> Let me tell you the rationale. We'd never private someone—they'd private us. Like, there was a guy down the hall. We didn't like him, so we staked him out and sent five suitors at specific times. We never got tired of it—never. One time we hooked up a couple who thought they were meeting other people.

These stakeouts, like *Otto's* critique of cloneish gay male life, highlight the stubborn zombie dumbness of desire. In the stakeouts, ordinary men, or "old, ugly" ones, persisted in improbably believing that young models were authentically interested in them and demonstrated a pathetic willingness to shamble after these imaginary ideal types. The stakeouts provided a respite from boredom for Peter and his friends, and they cruelly promised a more intimate relief for the men they tricked, some of whom likely sought an interruption of their atomized apartness, the desperate loneliness that makes one gullible, and that is one of the imagined origins of boredom.[17] They capitalized on the desperate hunger of the one, the loneliest number.

## One Is the Loneliest Number[18]

Zombies possess an impersonal sociality. That is, they are frequently imagined together as a mass, a crowd, or a swarm, yet they remain alone even among others. Noting the shared predilection for grouping among both zombies and humans, Jenn Webb and Sam Byrnard point out in their essay "Some Kind of Virus," that "zombies aren't social isolates—they seem to prefer to live in groups, within built environments; like us, they actively colonize spaces for themselves; like us—at least in the West—they seek to spread well beyond their local region, and to dominate people and places."[19] Indeed, in related and distinct ways, *Otto* and anti-normative theory and activism alike despair of the apparently contagious banalization of queer life. Although similar in its viral patterns of consumption and expansion, zombie togetherness is distinct from human belonging. Their sociality differs in that they do not possess the reflective self-awareness or empathetic identification we take as the hallmarks of meaningful intimate connection with ourself and others. This, along with their boundary-crossing re-animatedness, is part of what makes them inhuman. As one of the performers in the performance mashup *Nonfiction Zombie* puts it, "these creatures are nothing but pure, motorized instinct."[20] Even when stumbling alongside other zombies, zombies are imagined as singular members of crowds or mobs, absent of consciousness and affinal or communitarian ties. Their solitude is assured even when they clump together in their hungry search of living flesh. In this way, zombies epitomize the unnatural or terrorized solitude that attends loneliness.[21]

In his essay "Lonely," Michael Cobb works to imagine a queer theory "after sex." He attaches sexlessness to singleness to suggest that loneliness can elaborate analyses of non-majority intimacy and sexuality beyond the couple form. Moreover, reading Hannah Arendt's *On the Origins of Totalitarianism,* he looks to the ways "the world wants people to feel desperate, lonely, and ready for toxic forms of sociality."[22] To feel lonely is to be "too much of a one"[23]; it is to feel "deserted, abandoned,"[24] and a sharp hunger for connection, even if that connection isn't especially healthy. Following Arendt, Cobb points to the ways that the demand to be together capitalizes on the forms of loneliness induced, counterintuitively, through the overabundant "pressing up" that comes with modern life and governance. In other words, we don't have the space to be alone in productive ways and so become susceptible to the terror of loneliness, to which totalitarian logics proffer the love plot and/or sex as relief.[25]

Otto passively resists the demand to be together, to be intimate with himself or others. He disinterestedly investigates his past after discovering clues to his identity in his wallet. He's alone even when he's with others, whether the gay clones at "Flesh" (they don't speak), the skinhead trick he fucks/eats (does he really want the punk, or is he just hungry?), and the gay undead in Medea Yarn's film (he evinces no interest in participating in this revolutionary undead sex public). His soft refusal is not wholly a rejection of intimacy or (un)life, however. After all, he chooses not to self-immolate as his double does in Medea Yarn's documentary, and his relationship with her ends amicably enough. Following his necro/homophobic bashing, Otto permits Fritz, the star of Yarn's *Up with Dead People,* to take care of him, even if he insists on taking off his own shirt; they share a tender love scene. Nonetheless, at the film's conclusion, Otto heads north, alone, if speculatively optimistic about finding more of his kind.

Unlike Otto's detachment, however, EvilAndroid's online sociality was pierced by the sort of claustrophobic loneliness Cobb describes above. When, for example, EvilAndroids said that his online life was killing him, he described an affective frame of desperate longing: "But somedays a person just needs to not feel alone," "I'm still lonely," "It never goes away."

Another participant I interviewed named Redy, a black artist and activist, noted the still-palpable impact of his inability to connect online in a largely white southern university town. His earlier online experiences in a predominantly black city were, by contrast, nearly utopian:

> And at first it was just kinda like, wow, I can be in my own world and home and have this whole other portal in which to live. And I wasn't out at the time and it was probably just too intense for me to actually ever, to, uh, really understand how imaginative that world was. Here I was sitting in my household not out with my family and bein' able to withdraw into this whole new world of tops and bottoms and leatherdaddies and hookups and white guys comin' to my house and picking me up from my home and older black guys and guys my age. It was just this whole other imaginative world. And then with a click of a button I could be just back inside my house, or not even the click of a button, just turning my head around, or a sound from inside the house could take me back to the world that I was in. So I mean it was really like fucking like some serious time travel that was going on. And I really found fun in it too.

His early experiences online represented opportunities to playfully engage a range of intimate and erotic possibilities. But a handful of years later, Redy felt the menacing pressure of loneliness, created through the fear that racial difference created a barrier to proximity: "There were so many people who were not into me! Not like [now in] New York, where I can get dick everyday. It really fucked with my psyche for a long time." This loneliness is tied, as Peter suggested to me, to the inability to connect: "We're social beings. No one likes to be alone.... [S]omething does happen when you don't have a connection to the world. Especially if you're gay. You're that gay guy who is alone and this is a way to connect." For my informants, loneliness felt like a creeping deadness in their online and offline lives; feeling dead is to be blocked from those palliative forms of "connection to the world," however infected they may be by normative ideologies or neoliberal political economies.

I wonder though if my informants (and the rest of us) might not find ways to recuperate the "impersonal intimacy"[26] of Otto and other zombies. In the psychoanalytic approach of Leo Bersani and Adam Phillips, impersonal intimacy describes an ethics that embraces one's own narcissism, but one divested of ego, as well as the other's difference as obdurate rather than as a source for identification. In the context of LaBruce's film, then, I look to Otto's ability to indifferently choose the course of his unlife. Otto presents a powerful fantasy/model of an agency that is as empowered as it is automatized. Indeed, this is perhaps an underexplored approach of zombie theory; rather than operate only as fearful metaphors for racialized difference, infection, consumerism, or the failures of sovereign power, zombies might also offer compelling sites for identification. After all, Otto's abdication of coercive loneliness and traditional forms of relating means he gets to enact a freedom from the responsibilities and obligations that are the ordinary stuff of life and, perhaps, forms of attachment that are a viscous drag on living life in more novel ways.

## Addiction Is Desire on Zombie Mode

Loneliness, like boredom, invites changes that, as much as they are attempts to soften the blows of life or enliven some felt deadness, can lurch into excesses that dampen the freedom to choose. Addiction is one such excess, an "epidemic of the will"[27] that compels a destructive liveliness that is distinct from the compulsions toward liveness produced by the many automatisms of life, like perspiration or breathing. In my ten years talking to gay men, addiction repeatedly emerged as a way to make sense of online sociality. Indeed, many of my informants mirrored the sentiments of the men in Ahlberg's *Hooked*. EvilAndroids understood hooking up online as tied to problems of self-esteem, both in himself and others.

> <EvilAndroids> maybe they just need to be validated so badly
> <EvilAndroids> they;d compromise integrity
> <EvilAndroids> and thats the release
> <EvilAndroids> being free from all inhibition
> <EvilAndroids> like a drug

In an in-person interview, he made this relationship between sex and drugs even more explicit, saying, "Like heroin, you need that validation. Sex is a form of self-validation. That's the addiction — to that validation that self-doubt creates." John, a graphic designer who worked from home, was likewise explicit about online sociality and addiction.[28]

> I found a lot of this stuff really addictive. I'd work on a project for a couple of hours and then I'd get bored and so I'd look for a distraction. Since I do my [design] work on a computer, it was easy to log into gay.com or look for porn. Before I knew it, I'd be downloading a dozen porn movies from some site or I'd be chatting in gay.com, even arranging for a hookup. I always thought it'd be nice to just have the program up and running and if someone interesting wanted to chat with me, great, then I'd chat for a bit and get back to work, but I always ended up giving this distraction my full attention.... And I did start thinking, you know, maybe this is a problem, because I can't seem to work at the computer and stay focused on what I need to do. I had a friend who was a sex addict, but he was into public sex stuff; he didn't even have a computer. He got in trouble for it

even, with citations and what not, but I don't think he was ever arrested. Anyway, he started going to these sex addicts meetings that are structured like AA [Alcoholics Anonymous] and that seemed to work for him. I borrowed this book from him about sex and love addiction and that gave me some perspective. You know, I really saw myself in it. But I was resistant to going to any kind of meetings. I mean that would be admitting I had a real problem, and I didn't think it was that bad yet. But it was interesting to think of this thing that had started out being a kind of distraction as being connected to other stuff.... Like, maybe I was online or looking for distraction because I was really looking for something else, something deeper, like sex, I guess, but also stuff like attention, affection ... or love.

Ahlberg and his subjects, like EvilAndroids and John, understand the compulsion toward forms of online sociality, toward hooking up and other forms of pleasure, as belonging to the dominant discourse of addiction, that is as problem of the healthy self or will. Within this framework, they have failed to construct or exert their own moral agency. Rather than choosing life, the addicted self chooses a supplementary form of death-in-life that offers, but can never deliver on, a transcendent alter-life. Reading William Burroughs and others, Ann Weinstone notes the ways immortality is something addiction promises, and suggests addiction is willingly traded for transcendence: "The addict is not addicted to junk but to junk as a way of life."[29]

It's hard to escape the gravity well of addiction narratives, narratives which convert at least potentially agentive persons into juridical, epidemiological, or therapeutic objects, regarding them as zombies that need to be quarantined, helped, or put down. Not everyone, however, was as attached to addiction's explanatory force. Daniel, aka TXPops, a retired lawyer and activist, for example, who went into the *gay.com* chatrooms every morning and evening "to be in a gay social space," didn't interpret this habit as an addiction, though he could have:

> You're addicted or you're not. You can get addicted to table sugar. I became a diabetic and I had to get over that [table sugar addiction]. I'm not one of those people who gets too worked up about whether I need to be using my time more productively. If there is some sort of addiction [to chatrooms/online sex], I don't have that one. But I am a big one for letting people self-define. If they think they're addicted, well then....

Like Daniel, I want my informants to be able to self-define; I don't want to suggest that my informants, or anyone attached to addiction as a means of narrating or moving through the world, suffers from false consciousness. Nevertheless, there are key ways in which addiction, or desire on zombie mode, is vital rather than merely dead. Less desire run amok than desire unfettered, addiction is what happens when the pursuit of an object, a person, a fetish, a feeling — pleasure, but not only pleasure — takes on a life of its own. This is why, in a range of everyday/therapeutic contexts, people talk about addiction as a thing that has taken possession of them, rather than as set of choices they're engaged in making: addiction is a live animal hungering for more. It appears as an anxious relationship to habits, as well as a repetition that grooves the promise of an individuated sovereign self, gesturing toward a not wholly coherent beyond, in which, *pace* Freud, one has mastered pleasure (or life and death). Again, *Otto*, though it doesn't address addiction per se, can be illustrative here. In the persistent hunger (for sex, flesh, or revolutionary politics) of dead and living gay zombies, desire operates alongside *and* independently of reflective self-awareness. Zombies not only model forms of impersonal sociality, as I suggest above, but impersonal personhood as well. This is not the melodramatic self-shattering of Leo Bersani's "Is a Rectum a Grave" or Lee Edelman's elegant, arch-bitch anti-futural death drive, but something altogether less overmuch; a flatter, more passive, limp-wristed, or indifferent, *yet still vital* affirmation of an easy-going "whatever." Sometimes it's just better to be on auto-pilot. Otto (Auto?) manages his existential crisis impersonally and indifferently[30]; he navigates his rebirth into the unlife, learns about his past life, makes art, and decides to leave Berlin mostly by going with the flow. What I call his "soft refusals" represent another way of conceiving zombie desire not only as deadening drive toward repetition compulsion or explosive *jouissance,* but as desubjectivized way of being "in the flow" of desire. Hunger, then, appears less as a failure of the sovereign self than as an intransigent repetition that refuses a before (the healthy self or the couple form) and after (recovery or kids) in favor of something beyond the established teloi of life and death.[31]

## Conclusion: No Dead Matter

In a range of work, cultural geographers Nigel Thrift and Ben Anderson elaborate social scientific and philosophical conceptions of matter and materiality to include the affective, performative, and other constitutive but physically immaterial stuff of space, time, and life/liveliness.[32] The emphasis on the openness of matter has been an especially productive consequence of this work. That is, no matter is considered dead. Zombies, to take an obvious example, are alive not just because they have been reanimated, but because their decomposing bodies participate in ecologies of energy transfer, and because their contagiousness imputes an immanent continuity. Their hunger performs the obstinate movement of desire's passing. Desire induces changes, and it returns. This hunger transcends the constraints of life as we know it, or sparks at its edges.

This approach to the openness of matter has inspired many of my ethnographic and theoretical engagements (and evasions) in this essay. On the one hand, I have looked to the ways boredom, loneliness, and the compulsion to repeat appear to dampen or block access to an expressive, creative, or free life, to a life that flows rather than one that groans and jerks about. On the other hand, drawing on the rich material available in Bruce LaBruce's *Otto,* I have gestured toward an excess, a liveliness that is still vital in spite of or even because of its impersonal, indifferent, and automated drives. I have tried to affirm my informants' experiences with loneliness, boredom, and addiction as powerful adhesions to (digital) queer sociality as neither wholly vital nor deadened, but as simultaneously constrained and animate. So that, finally, zombie personhood, rather than represent the fearful antithesis of human self-awareness, emerges instead as a model for ontologies neither self-possessed nor self-coherent, thereby pressing against the constraints of what we imagine to be an enlivened life. Zombies refract queerness as dead and live life; we're here and queer, but we might not be going anywhere; we're contagious and, hopefully, spreading; our productive differences are as caught up in the circuits of capitalist production and exchange as they are immanent and sometimes realized interruptions. Put differently and a bit cynically, we may be gay zombies condemned to hunger after the cock and ass of the deadened living or to accede to the demands of a consumerist economy of desire more broadly, but that doesn't mean we aren't also alive, and capable of choosing a more livable unlife. Here, we can again follow Otto, who asks, not rhetorically, "how do you kill yourself if you're already dead?" Otto decides to head north, where he hopes to discover "a whole new way of death." But barring a northern holiday with Otto and other movie monsters, we remain tasked with creatively reanimating dead life in ways that will open us to a yet more vital life, even one that hungers and lurches about.

**Acknowledgments.** My thanks to Thomas Farringer-Logan, Bill Baskin, and the editors for generous readings and critiques. I am deeply grateful for the assistance of my colleague Sarah Van Gundy, who helped with researching and developing many of the key ideas in this essay through an earlier collaboration and repeated viewings of LaBruce's film.

## *Notes*

1. On "crisis ordinariness," see Lauren Berlant's essay, "Intuitionists: History and the Affective Event," *American Literary History* 20, no. 4 (2008): 845–860; and Kathleen Stewart, *Ordinary Affects* (Durham: Duke University Press, 2007).

2. Lauren Berlant, "Live Sex Acts," *The Queen of America Goes to Washington City: Essays on Sex and Citizenship* (Durham: Duke University Press, 1997), 155–181.

3. See my essay "Virtual Intimacies," in which I discuss how categories of real and virtual bleed into one another. Shaka McGlotten, "Virtual Intimacies," in *Queers Online: Media Technology and Sexuality*, ed. Kate O'Riordan and David Phillips (New York: Peter Lang, 2007), 122–137.

4. *Otto; or, Up with Dead People*, DVD, directed by Bruce LaBruce (Strand Releasing, 2008). LaBruce's film isn't the first to tackle the subject of gay zombies. There's also *La Cage Aux Zombies* (1995), *Creatures from the Pink Lagoon* (2006), and the now-unavailable *At Twilight Comes the Flesh-eaters* (1998). The latter film, unfortunately unavailable, retells Romero's *Night of the Living Dead* as gay porn and, like *Otto*, features a film-within-a-film. See Darren Elliott for a longer list, "'Death is the New Pornography!' Gay Zombies in Queer Horror and Bruce LaBruce's *Otto: or, Up with Dead People*," unpublished manuscript (2008).

5. See Lee Edelman, *No Future: Queer Theory and the Death Drive* (Durham: Duke University Press, 2004). This critique of Edelman's significant contribution owes a good deal to José Esteban Muñoz, *Cruising Utopia: The Then and There of Queer Futurity* (New York: New York University Press, 2009).

See also Sarah Lauro and Karen Embry, "A Zombie Manifesto: The Nonhuman Condition in the Era of Advanced Capitalism," *boundary* 2: 35, no. 1 (2008): 85–108. Like Edelman, Lauro and Embry either cynically or playfully (or both) resist the hopefulness of reproductive futurism. "The Zombie Manifesto," in its articulation of and argument for the zombie as antisubject, symptomatizes the ways zombies trouble distinctions between subject and object; indeed, by troubling both the groundedness of being and returning to haunt the living, zombies are, as Lauro and Embry put it, useful "ontic/hauntic" critical objects. Their manifesto also symptomatizes an ironic intellectual tendency to propose a nihilistic negative dialectic, here in the form of the zombii/zombie as swarm, as the only remedy for infected (by histories of power relations, or bad power) liberal humanism. For Lauro and Embry, the zombie allegorizes (among other things) humanity and its antithesis, a systemwide, but not to be celebrated, disruption. In this way, they distinguish their own intellectual project from that of other notable posthuman theorists, Gilles Deleuze and Felix Guattari; unlike them, Laura and Embry are interested only in *unbecomings* and the ways the zombie offers us a way out of the trouble humanism and, ultimately, global capitalism have gotten us into. Rather than use the zombie to ask what it means to be human or to consume, or to be dead or alive, or to be agentive or automated, "A Zombie Manifesto" asks us to accept that the end of power relations as we know them won't come through the conscious actions of the multitude (*pace* Hardt and Negri) but the consciousnessless hunger of the unthinking zombii swarm. And if I am sympathetic to their provocation regarding an impersonal or passive revolutionary politics, I'm less certain about where this provocation leads. In their view, the endtimes brought about by the zombapocalypse certainly won't be liberating because, after all, as zombii we won't be equipped with the rational subjectivities to discern freedom or anything else.

6. *Hooked: Get It (On)Line*, DVD, directed by Todd Ahlberg (Eclectic DVD, 2003).

7. Dialog and Presskit available at http://www.ottothezombie.de/press.html, accessed June 24, 2010.

8. Ernest Hardy, "Zombie Deep Throat," accessed June 24, 2010, http://ernesthardy.blogspot.com/2010/01/zombie-deep-throat.html.

9. See Ben Anderson, "Affective Atmospheres," *Emotion, Space, and Society* 7 (2009): 77–81; and Teresa Brennan, *The Transmission of Affect* (Ithaca: Cornell University Press, 2004).

10. Dominic Pettman, *After the Orgy: Toward a Politics of Exhaustion* (Albany: State University of New York Press, 2002). See also the Feel Tank Manifesto's articulation of "political depression" at http://www.chicago-red.org/feeltank/, accessed June 25, 2010.

11. See Ben Anderson, "Time-Stilled Space Slowed: How Boredom Matters," *Geoforum* 35 (2004): 739–754.

12. See Samuel Delany, *Times Square Red, Times Square Blue* (New York: New York University Press, 1999); Urvashi Vaid, *Virtual Equality: The Mainstreaming of Gay and Lesbian Liberation* (New York: Anchor Books, 1995); Michael Warner, *The Trouble with Normal: Sex, Politics, and the Ethics of Queer Life* (New York: Free Press, 1999); Lisa Duggan, *The Twilight of Equality? Neoliberalism, Cultural Politics, and the Attack on Democracy* (Boston: Beacon Press, 2003).

13. Hardy, accessed June 24, 2010, http://ernesthardy.blogspot.com/2010/01/zombie-deep-throat.html.

14. Kathleen Frederickson, "Up with Dead Privates," accessed June 27, 2010, http://mediacommons.future-ofthebook.org/imr/2010/05/07/dead-privates. As Darren Elliott notes, in *Otto*, LaBruce advances his ongoing critique of gay male subcultures, especially their articulation or conflation of eroticism and fascism, "'Death is the New Pornography!'"

15. Ben Anderson, "Time Stilled."

16. Lulz is a variation of the Internet slang LOL, or Laugh out Loud. Lulz is more frequently used in the

context of pranks and is commonly found on the message boards of the website *4chan* and employed by "trolls," hacker-ish and adolescent pranksters for whom, "'lulz' means the joy of disrupting another's emotional equilibrium." See Mattathias Schwartz, "The Trolls Among Us," August 3, 2008, *New York Times Magazine*, accessed June 27, 2010, http://www.nytimes.com/2008/08/03/magazine/03trolls-t.html?_r=2&ref=technology.

17. Ben Anderson critically reads these four ways of conceiving boredom in relation to a disenchantment with the modern world as: secularization, calculable individualism, the changing nature of leisure, and standardized/standardizing time-space. Ben Anderson, "Time Stilled," 741.

18. I borrow this subheading, and many key ideas, as my subsequent discussion evidences, from Michael Cobb, "Lonely," in *South Atlantic Quarterly* 106.3, After Sex? On Writing After Queer Theory (Summer 2007): 445–457.

19. Jenn Webb and Sam Byrnand, "Some Kind of Virus: The Zombie as Body and as Trope," *Body and Society* 14 (2008): 83–98, 84.

20. Tracy Stephenson Shaffer, "Scripting and Staging a Theoretical Mashup: *Nonfiction Zombie* in a Dance Club," *Liminalities* 6, no. 1 (2010), accessed June 24, 2010, http://liminalities.net/6-1/zombie.html.

21. Some recent zombie texts offer counter evidence to the account I give here. That is, zombies are increasingly imagined as entangled in rather than only apart from human society and sociality. To take only a few examples, the conclusion of the zom-rom-com *Shaun of the Dead* (2004) finds Shaun's dimwitted but brave best friend Ed, now a zombie, still playing video games, albeit chained in the shed. In *Fido* (2006), zombies are the mostly benign servants in an alternate 1950s America. And in *28 Weeks Later* (2007) a zombified father's desire to be near his children morphs into a rage-fueled incestuous desire to infect them.

22. Michael Cobb, "Lonely," 447.

23. Ibid., 448.

24. Ibid., 447.

25. Ibid., 448–449.

26. Leo Bersani and Adam Phillips, *Intimacies* (Chicago: University of Chicago Press, 2008).

27. Eve Sedgwick, "Epidemics of the Will," *Tendencies* (London: Routledge, 1994), 129–140.

28. McGlotten, "Virtual Intimacies," 131–132.

29. Ann Weinstone, "Welcome to the Pharmacy: Addiction, Transcendence, and Virtual Reality," *Diacritics* 27.3 Addictions (Autumn 1997): 77–89, 81.

30. I am tempted to call Otto "detached," but that would suggest a more active rejection or working through of forms of attachment I'm not convinced he ever possessed. Attachments are intense, while indifference shrugs.

31. For a compelling reworking of addiction in the service of an ongoing enlivening of queer theory, see Neville Hoad, "Queer Theory Addiction," *South Atlantic Quarterly* 106.3, After Sex? On Writing After Queer Theory (Summer 2007): 511–522.

32. Anderson, "Time Stilled"; "Affective Atmospheres"; Ben Anderson and John Wylie, "On Geography and Materiality," *Environment and Planning A* 41 (2009): 318–335; Nigel Thrift, *Non-Representational Theory: Space|Politics|Affect* (New York: Routledge, 2008).

# The E-Dead: Zombies
# in the Digital Age

BRENDAN RILEY

*It represents a threat but it's one that is hard to explain.... It's an insidious threat,*
*and what worries me is that the scope of the problem is still not clear to most people.*
— David J. Farber, Carnegie Mellon computer scientist

*Article 249: Also shall be qualified as attempted murder the employment which*
*may be made against any person of substances which, without causing actual*
*death, produce a lethargic coma more or less prolonged. If, after the administer-*
*ing of such substances, the person has been buried, the act shall be considered*
*murder no matter what result follows.*
— *Code Pénal* of the Republic of Haiti, 1928

## Outbreak

Watching the dark apartment through Pablo's viewfinder in the 2007 Spanish zombie thriller *[REC]*, we can't help but struggle a bit against the fourth wall, firmly at our backs. Whereas films shot in the classic Hollywood style encourage us to forget the camera, the constraints created by *[REC]*'s enclosed apartment, quarantined building, and camera lens tunnel-vision put us in Pablo's shoes, riding along with the decisions he makes, for good or ill. Add to that the film's relentless pacing, shot in a near panic at the dire situation and the fast zombies, and we have all the elements that shape the modern landscape of the e-dead, the digital zombie.

The cultural influences driving audience interest in horror have undergone a significant upheaval in the last fifteen years. With the rise of the Internet, the digital age has clawed its way out of the ground to besiege every aspect of our culture, from concepts about intellectual property to the very structures we use to build communities. At the same time, we have seen a resurgence in zombie fiction: zombies are everywhere, lurching in some places and running in others. This essay connects these two phenomena, arguing that the return of zombie stories allows and encourages citizens of the digital era to wrestle with changes in identity and culture wrought by the ever-accelerating pace of technological change.

194

## *That Thing's Not Your Mother (It's Your Id)*

Scholars often interpret Hollywood zombies as allegory. The original *Night of the Living Dead* (1968) evokes the racial and generational tensions of the 1960s,[1] while also criticizing "human reliance upon all forms of science and technology which will prove useless"[2] in protecting society. Romero claimed that his naturalistic style was intended to foster such "insights."[3] In his later *Dead* films, he becomes more and more heavy-handed, using zombies to critique consumerist society (*Dawn of the Dead* [1978]), the military-industrial complex influencing politics (*Day of the Dead* [1985]), the widening gap between the wealthy and the poor (*Land of the Dead* [2005]), or the narcissistic Panopticism of YouTube culture (*Diary of the Dead* [2007]).

The seething hordes of non-Romero zombie movies also use, more directly, social critique as the vehicle and premise of their stories. To name but a few examples: *I Drink Your Blood* (1970), a proto-zombie film focusing on violent rabies-infected people, draws on the siege and infection motifs from *Night of the Living Dead*, but reverses the critical perspective by pitting Satan-worshiping hippies against good upright people; *Messiah of Evil* (1973) echoes *Night*, with its hordes of straight-laced, suit-wearing cannibals who chase down the bell-bottom-wearing long-haired dandy and his *two* girlfriends. *Return of the Living Dead* (1985) explores both conspiracy theory and culture clash with its clearly-delineated groups of straight-laced kids and punks, and its malevolent military who deploys a nuclear weapon to cover up its own illegal testing. *Night of the Comet* (1984) also targets scientists, who turn evil in their quest to cure their own illness by using the blood of the remaining uninfected humans. A quick survey of more recent releases reveals a wealth of new zombie films that take as their starting point some criticism of social or technological trends, be it mad cow disease, environmental depredations, or experimental sheep with extra-fluffy wool.[4]

Science fiction has always criticized worrisome trends in culture, usually against the new for the benefit of the old. As Scott Bukatman argues, "most science-fiction is unflaggingly conservative in its language and iconography."[5] It spots and highlights the dangers in new trends, reinforcing already-established values. *Frankenstein* (1818), science fiction's ur-text, initiates the genre in exactly this way—Victor's naive and irresponsible dabbling on the edge of science provides a warning to the rest of us to walk carefully where gods tread. These zombie movies do the same, warning us about both the dangers of new technologies and the dangers of plain old human foibles.

While zombie movies eschew science-fiction tropes (explaining the source of the flesh-hungry ghouls) for straight-up horror, scholars bring to bear a variety of other hermeneutic tool kits. Barbara Creed, for example, uses Julia Kristeva's work to argue that Freud's concept of the "abject" and the "monstrous feminine" drive our visceral reactions to the walking corpses in zombie movies and the grotesqueries of other horror films. Her argument applies quite robustly to Peter Jackson's *Dead Alive* (1992), in which the protagonist's mother issues are enacted through his battle with the monstrous zombie form of his domineering mother. His mother, raised from the dead as a gigantic mockery of female fertility imagery, literally pulls him back into her womb, from which he must then violently cut himself free. The sequence involves shocking amounts of blood, helping cement the film's popular title as the "goriest film ever."

In *American Zombie Gothic* (2010), Kyle William Bishop also uses psychoanalytic theory, but he combines it with historical research and cultural studies to explore the evolution of the zombie. His chapter on *Night of the Living Dead*, for instance, uses the concept of the uncanny, the *Unheimlich*, to drive its analysis of how fear motivates social readings of the film. He writes:

In Romero's complex parable, then, the *Unheimlich* appearance of the walking dead forces characters and viewers alike to confront their own fallibility and mortality, and the similarly *Unheimlich* location ... reveals deep seated tensions about social structures and human relationships.[6]

Bishop argues that the confluence of psychological fears and the social forces influencing both filmmakers and audiences give the zombie genre particular power to comment on social developments and cultural currents, be they revolution or consumerism or the Internet.

Perhaps the best interpretation of the genre as a whole applies to every zombie film, underlying whatever particulars shape the bloodsoaked streets of the stories. Zombies embody death itself. They are metonymic, rather than allegorical. Simon Pegg, star of *Shaun of the Dead* (2004), puts it this way:

> As monsters from the id, zombies win out over vampires and werewolves when it comes to the title of Most Potent Metaphorical Monster. Where their pointy-toothed cousins are all about sex and bestial savagery, the zombie trumps all by personifying our deepest fear: death. Zombies are our destiny writ large. Slow and steady in their approach, weak, clumsy, often absurd, the zombie relentlessly closes in, unstoppable, intractable.[7]

Whereas Vampires *symbolize* sex and embody hedonism and Werewolves *symbolize* the struggle between civilized and barbaric man, zombies *are* death. They embody it *and* represent it simultaneously. Sure, they prod us to actions heroic and cowardly and they drive us to squabble amongst ourselves, but at the heart of zombie films, they frighten us not just because they will kill us, but because they are death itself, arriving not with a bang, but with a moan.

But as Pegg notes later in his essay, when the zombie runs, it outstrips much of that basic power that it had when it shambled toward us. It drops the creeping, building terror it used to wield in favor of visceral (and cheap) thrills. Pegg may be right. But perhaps the shift away from that underlying interpretation hinges on a cultural shift, not just away from slow zombies, but from the perspective and very consciousness such zombies were created to frighten.

## Fast Zombies, High Bandwidth

The fast zombie isn't really new. When Barbra, chased by the tall, gaunt gentleman who has just murdered her brother, locks herself in the car, we can't help but notice how quick (and quick-witted) the zombie is. He lopes rather than lurches, and when he finds the door locked, he spins around, grabs a rock, and smashes the window. Through the rest of *Night of the Living Dead*, the zombies lurch and stumble like the reanimated corpses we have come to love. Most viewers forget about the brief glimpses of hurrying zombies because the shambling masses became the template for a horde of b-movies that would follow.

That is, until Zack Snyder's 2004 "re-imagining" of *Dawn of the Dead* made the zombies in the mall sprinters, and gave them a Starbucks to run through. Clearly building from the momentum started by the "infected" from *28 Days Later* (2004),[8] Snyder and screenwriter James Gunn reworked Romero's original scenario in fast-forward, burning society down in days rather than weeks (a timeline narrated in both the 1978 and 2004 films by the drop-off in broadcasting). The fast zombie has since gained equity, as likely as not to replace the slow zombie in the unending parade of schlocky movies about the undead.[9]

The fast zombie phenomenon draws on a number of trends in modern Western society that make it particularly interesting. First, fast zombies *infect* living people, usually by the same means that highly infectious diseases are spread—Bishop dubs this "the contagion narrative."[10] *28 Days Later* builds its entire story on this premise, making the "rage" virus into a sort-of ultimate hemorrhagic fever, with victims who become full-blown "infected" instantly by transmission of body fluids. *Dawn of the Dead*'s zombie disease seems to spread this way as well, turning the dead into murderous ghouls moments after they die. Both films establish boundaries for their infections, the latter even including a scene in which a character dies from gunshot wounds and does not revive.

The sequels to these films push the theme of infection even further. *28 Weeks Later* (2007) introduces vigorous, Orwellian quarantine schemes to a devastated London in the months after the disease has died off and adds a second kind of infected, a carrier who doesn't succumb to the rage virus but can spread it to others nonetheless. The remake of *Day of the Dead* (2008), far less successful and rightly so, seems to trace the outbreak back to a military base in Colorado. The film makes no effort to connect its outbreak to that in *Dawn of the Dead* (which takes place outside Milwaukee), but does bring back Ving Rhames, whom a generous viewer might suggest plays the long-sought "brother" to the same actor's character from Snyder's film. *Day of the Dead* touches nominally on the military theme from Romero's original, but mostly focuses on the outbreak of the zombie disease, something that spreads less like rabies and more like the measles.

As a prescient piece of popular psychology, we should congratulate the filmmakers who grounded these infections in the trappings of medical science. Since the 1997 avian flu outbreak in China, the potential for a worldwide pandemic akin to the 1918 "Spanish" flu pandemic has loomed quietly, giving nightmares to world health officials and emergency preparedness experts everywhere. In November 2002, just as *28 Days Later* was opening in the UK, the first people in China were starting to die of the mysterious flu-like illness that would later be dubbed *SARS*. The sickness "would spread to thirty countries, affecting more than eight thousand people and killing nearly one thousand. The epidemic demonstrated how quickly an infectious disease could spread around the world in the jet age."[11] The paranoia about SARS that year was infectious itself, with people in urban centers around the world donning masks and avoiding air travel. Right into this panic landed *28 Days Later*, with its particularly frightening description of a virulent outbreak in a crowded urban setting. Recent scares about avian and swine flu haven't lessened tensions. This attention to the details of disease provides a "realism" that makes the horror of the films more immediate. If the disease operates like something else we're vaguely familiar with (and worried about), we'll be more inclined to suspend our disbelief and enjoy the story.

But the phenomenon of rapid infection registers across more valences than the biological or medical. In fact, it's reasonable to suggest that more people have been affected by global *digital* virus pandemics than have been harmed by the biological ones (though no one has died, yet, from an Internet virus).[12] For example, the "I Love You" worm "spread across the world in one day (traveling from Hong-Kong to Europe to the United States), infecting 10 percent of all computers connected to the Internet and causing about $5.5 billion in damage."[13] Digital viruses spread so rapidly we're relatively powerless to stop them. It's hard to miss the similarities to the images of the *28 Days Later* rage virus spreading through a crowd. Computer viruses are the closest real-world analog to the virus in the film.

So perhaps the script's biological paraphernalia and the speed of the infection highlight an as-yet uncovered core concern within the genre: the Western world's rapidly growing technological infrastructure. In this light, we see a return to the conservative intent of science-fiction texts suggested by Bukatman. The scientists in *28 Days Later* are twenty-first century Victors Frankenstein, cobbling together something they can't control or understand. Or, as Ian Malcolm puts it in *Jurassic Park* (1993), "they're so concerned with whether they *could,* they don't stop to think if they *should.*" But keep in mind that it's not just science that makes the rage virus spread all over Britain and, twenty-eight weeks later, the world — it's all the extensions of man (to use Marshall McLuhan's definition of technology), from pencils to airplanes.

In *Future Shock* (1970), Alvin Toffler argues that the ever-accelerating rate of change already emerging in the 1960s will set a pace that exceeds our ability to comprehend it. He calls the mental experience of living in a culture changing so quickly *future shock.* The rapid shifts in technology force a change in how we view everyday things, from grocery stores to books; we can't help feeling disquiet at "the inescapable ephemeralization of the man-thing relationship."[14] Perhaps our weakened ability to cope with the evolving technological landscape around us amplifies the effect of these zombie pandemics. What if the fast zombies we see in Snyder's *Dawn of the Dead* and other such films embody this experience? Perhaps future shock is here, and it's hungry.

## Zombie Computers — Digital Bocor

The idea of the zombie entered the popular zeitgeist in the 1920s and 1930s. While revenants have been part of Western imagination for centuries, these undead creatures aren't strictly zombies, they're sometimes vampires, sometimes ghosts, sometimes ghouls.[15] But in 1929, William B. Seabrook published *The Magic Island,* a travel memoir of Haiti. He describes a variety of exotic and frightening sights and rituals, the most arresting of which are the corpses brought back to life by *bocors*— voudoun priests— and forced to work the fields at their master's bidding. He writes:

> The *zombie,* they say, is a soulless human corpse, still dead, but taken from the grave and endowed by sorcery with a mechanical semblance of life — it is a dead body which is made to walk and act and move as if it were alive. People who have the power to do this ... make of it a servant or slave, occasionally for the commission of some crime, more often simply as a drudge around the habitation or the farm.[16]

Seabrook explains that the person being made into a zombie might be an enemy of a bocor, but is often just in the sorry position of having been buried in a grave the bocor could plunder. The zombie is a slave, a servant of the master, out of control of its body and unaware. Only if the bocor feeds the zombie seasoned food (such as salt) will the zombie realize the horror of its situation and return to the grave.[17] Seabrook presents the fact of zombies quite credulously, relating the tale as unbelievable but true, and offering as proof several lines of the Haitian legal code that specifically prohibits zombifying people, not to mention the fact that even the poorest peasants "bury their dead beneath solid tombs of masonry" or in their own yards, or in graves set close by busy roads to make plundering them more difficult.[18]

For a time, Hollywood used the zombie of Haitian tradition as a horror trope. Such monsters were always the minions of powerful villains, often people who embodied the primitive, nature, and superstition. In *White Zombie* (1932), for instance, Bela Lugosi's evil sorcerer, Murder Legendre, betrays the scheming plantation owner to take both the owner and the comely young lady as his zombie slaves. Despite the laughable hocus pocus of the film's rituals, *White Zombie* draws significantly on *The Magic Island,* even going so far as to quote the same Haitian legal code. We see similar treatment of zombie slaves in *I Walked with a Zombie* (1943), *King of the Zombies* (1941), and *I Eat Your Skin* (1964) (which, strangely, features murderous zombies that do not seem to be cannibals).

But with *Night of the Living Dead,* the zombie slave was relegated to the cutting room floor, so to speak. If voudoun came up in a script, it was strictly utilitarian — a convenient means for starting the zombie outbreak. The recent zombie comedies *Boy Eats Girl* (2005) and *Night of the Living Dorks* (2004) both use Haitian voudoun in this way.

It is not in film, but computers where the last decade has seen a return to this classic definition of a *zombie*. Starting in the late 1990s, hackers began using spyware, malware, and security loopholes to gain control of what have come to be called zombie computers, computers belonging to unsuspecting users (often with broadband connections). Like corpses in poorly covered graves, the computers being infected were, usually, improperly secured. Once the hackers had a horde of zombie computers ready, they could institute a variety of attacks on targets, either business, governmental, or personal. The most well-known is the Distributed Denial-of-Service attack (DDoS). A DDoS works by overwhelming a server with inquiries, many containing bewildering but nonsensical information.[19]

The computers under hacker control, members of these "bot-nets," thus embody both aspects of the zombie imagery from popular culture. First, they're vacant, hollow-eyed, and under someone else's control. By *vacant,* I mean to say that they don't know what they're doing. Often, people who have a compromised computer have no idea that it *is* compromised. They only discover it when their web connection or their processor speed gets so slow they can't use the computer. The discovery of the virus acts like salted food for the Haitian zombies—it releases the zombie from the master's grip and guides them back to their own graves.[20]

Before the owners disconnect it from the hacker's bot-net, however, the zombie computer follows the hacker's directions precisely, "occasionally for the commission of a crime" (such as extortion against a web-company with threats of a DDoS attack) "or more often simply as a drudge" to send tens of thousands of spam emails each day and to infect other computers. This second aspect, the virulent nature of such infections, reminds us not of the voudoun zombie, but of the Hollywood zombie who infects everyone it bites. The Distributed Denial-of-Service attack, too, can be seen as a digital version of the siege that eventually occurs in most zombie movies. Like those cinematic sieges, eliminating one or two zombies (with a good head shot or skillful DNS tracking and disconnection) doesn't really solve the problem. The vast numbers of computers (sometimes eight to ten thousand) overwhelm the server, munching into its brain, so to speak.

## I Don't Want to Be Walkin' Around Like That

A long-running debate in the zombie fan (and scholar) community turns on what viewers enjoy when they watch zombie films. Some argue for the visceral thrill of killing zombies and the survivalist fantasy —for these viewers, zombie films enact a kind of wish fulfillment, encouraging the audience to think about not only how they would deal with the one or two zombies on the screen, but also how they would survive a zombie outbreak itself, how they would deal with cantankerous or villainous fellow survivors, and related minutiae. Others argue for a more phenomenological perspective, similar to Simon Pegg's analysis above. Zombie movies highlight that which makes us human. They drive us to think, on some level, about the line between consciousness and the unconscious, the living and the dead.[21] For the purposes of this essay, I'm going to set aside the wish-fulfillment aspect of zombie films to concentrate on the question of our humanity and that of the zombies.

The crux of the matter is the contradiction in the way characters react to the zombie plague. This contradiction highlights a fundamental problem with the way we understand what zombies are. Two examples: in Romero's *Dawn of the Dead,* the heroes eagerly dispatch the zombies infesting the mall they've commandeered. They show no remorse for these killings, as they understand the zombies to be non-people, showing empathy only in moments of pause. The scientist on television describes them as follows: "These creatures are nothing but pure, motorized instinct. We must not be lulled by the concept that these are our family members or our friends. They are not. They will not respond to such emotions." It seems that the zombies no longer think or feel—they just stumble along on pure instinct. But the film complicates that understanding in two ways.

First, it gives the zombies the will to shop. The narrative seems to agree with Steven when he suggests that zombies come to the mall because they have "some kind of instinct—memory—of what they used to do. This was an important place in their lives." Later, Peter adds to this interpretation, suggesting that the zombies aren't after the survivors. "They're after the place. They don't know why, they just remember ... remember that they want to be in here." If the zombies retain their desires to shop or to mill around the mall, they can't be the empty shells that the egghead insisted they were.

Second, the survivors in the mall still think of the zombies as retaining some piece of the people they once were. William Larkin suggests that such thoughts are instinctual, writing that "deep down we believe that we will survive as corpses."[22] This becomes most evident in what has become a prototypical death scene for zombie films—Roger's request that Peter shoot him when he turns. "I don't want to be walkin' around like that," he moans from his deathbed. But this is a strange request if, as the film and all the characters purport to believe, the corpse is *not* the person it once was. Such is the unspoken fear underlying many zombie movies—that despite our best intentions, we believe, on some level, that "we" will be trapped somewhere inside the creature. Hamish Thompson describes this contradiction as follows, "Just as these films challenge the distinction between being dead or alive, they challenge overly simplistic conceptions of the 'soul.'"[23] We are inseparable from our physical body and if that body is walking around, so are we.

*Shaun of the Dead,* which straddles the line between horror and parody, expands these already permeated boundaries. As with most films, the narrative consistently reinforces the idea that zombies are no longer the people they once were. This aspect of the story escalates as Shaun sees neighbors, then friends, and finally family fall victim to zombie attacks. He nearly fails to muster the necessary courage as he faces down his newly-risen mother. But he succeeds in shooting her and escaping. In the aftermath of the story we find Shaun walking to the woodshed to join Ed, now a zombie, chained to the couch and playing video games all day. A camaraderie between the two exists that viewers are encouraged to read as reminiscent (if not equivalent) to the sedentary lifestyle Ed lived before the outbreak. In other words, the plague in *Shaun of the Dead* left zombies with a significant part of their personalities intact. Somewhere in Shaun's mother *was* his mother. The same goes for each of the zombies he killed. Yet the film (and the viewers) aren't encouraged to feel remorse about these deaths at all, even the deaths of zombies killed unnecessarily.

It's also worth remembering that this ambiguity has been a part of nearly all the Romero *Dead* films. Whereas *Night* and *Diary* evoked sympathy for the zombies by depicting horrific sport-killing on the part of humans, *Day* and *Land* each gave significant screen time to zombie characters (Bub and Big Daddy, respectively). In each of these films, Romero complicates the zombies as human but not human, both hungry for people and yet retaining some aspect of humanity. The horror-comedy *Fido* (2006) takes this concept to its logical extreme, telling the story of a boy who befriends his family's zombie servant, which seems to retain bits of its personality and develop new memories and traits.

Perhaps we cling to the idea that it is *us,* somehow, remaining inside the zombies because we have no other frame of reference.[24] As much as our beliefs about the supernatural may inform our ideas about the afterlife, we can't help but conceive of the world through the lens of the embodied being. And thus when our body continues to move without us, we have to understand it, at some level, as a part of ourselves. I suspect very few people imagine themselves inside a zombie brain, staring out like the hitchhikers in *Being John Malkovich* (1999), but we understand our body to be *us* nonetheless.

But we do have a frame of reference for the disembodied being (the opposite of the zombie): online experience. To many people, it seems ridiculous to suggest that an online experience in a collaborative game or conversation space is a "real" interaction with others, yet inhabitants of those online spaces often feel exactly the opposite. There are indisputable differences in the way face-to-face meetings play out compared to online experiences of similar events. But the experience of online interaction is certainly immediate and involving, and it feels like a real exchange, a real community. If two people on the telephone usually have no problem claiming that it was "really them" on the phone, why does communicating through an avatar or a game engine shift that perception?

Just as the online experience of these exchanges should certainly be considered "real," so too are exchanges that occur outside the user's control — what I will call here *digital zombification*. Here, again, we unite the original Haitian voudoun zombie with the perception of the Hollywood zombie as a monster that still retains some core of its former humanity. Digital zombification refers to the experience of "seeing" one's digital self, perhaps a handle and avatar cultivated in cyberspace, perhaps an incarnation of one's real-life identity, acting of its own accord or at the behest of someone else, a *digital bocor*.

The most obvious kind of digital zombification is identity theft, which damages the victim's reputation and credit, and leaves them with the onerous task of chasing down errors in databases. But digital zombification occurs in a plethora of minor ways as well. When an old acquaintance posts a childhood picture in Facebook and tags it with my name, my online identity has acquired a new facet at this other person's request. When a student writes something pleasant in an online teaching evaluation forum like RateMyProfessor ("The class is fantastic, but just taking it to hear this guy talk is more than enough for me."), my identity shifts a bit; the same goes for negative comments ("This class sucked. It was a waste of time and I learned absolutely nothing."). Like the poor families burying their dead in Haiti, individuals can take steps to protect their online personae — they can refuse friends, they can post anonymously, they can refuse to engage — but they can't guarantee that they won't become the target of a zombie master.

In another way, however, digital zombification has become more universally adopted as part of the "Web 2.0" business model. Tim O'Reilly writes, "The central principle behind the success of the giants born in the Web 1.0 era who have survived to lead the Web 2.0 era appears to be this, that they have embraced the power of the web to harness collective intelligence."[25] Web 2.0 businesses harness the power and work of their users and re-purpose it as their product. For example, Flickr is an entirely user-driven site; its products are uploaded by its users and shared with one another. From one perspective, the level of folk knowledge that can be shared and disseminated this way exceeds anything previously possible.[26] At the same time, the enormous businesses that facilitate this sharing generate vast revenues based on the hordes of users, often by placing advertisements alongside content generated by users for free. Such practices may represent a Faustian bargain in which users give up far more than they intend by making their creative work available without pay. As the blogger "Kate" at "The Girls A Geek" [sic] puts it, "Only on the web would a for profit company think that they could ask people to work for free."[27] Even in our free time our work has been zombified and commodified.[28]

Occasionally, digital zombification reaches epic proportions, changing the real-life of the person in similarly intense ways. Perhaps the most famous example of electronic identity hijacking is documented in Julian Dibbell's seminal essay, "A Rape in Cyberspace." Dibbell documents a digital assault, perpetuated in a text-based virtual reality called a MUD, using a programmed "voodoo doll" that simulates the actions of another player. The rapist, a player called Mr. Bungle (named after the grotesque music act that would anticipate the Insane Clown Posse), used the doll to simulate, in the text space of the world, sexual acts between two other non-consenting players. The assault brought a firestorm of debate to the community, with the victims claiming they'd been mentally raped and the aggressor and his defenders proclaiming it's "only a game." Dibbell suggests that this experience, first documented in 1993, calls for us to "get to the crucial work of sorting out the socially meaningful differences between those bodies and our physical ones."[29] He recognized what numerous players in massively-multiplayer online games like *World of Warcraft* would come to understand later, that digital experiences hold translucent value — they are neither opaque manipulations of levers and switches nor transparent conversations through a window.

But the Mr. Bungle incident occurred in LambdaMOO, a collaborative, shared experience in which all players willingly engage.[30] Sometimes, by contrast, digital zombification happens in spaces we never consented to join. The Michael Crook affair functions like a digital zombie outbreak, a rapidly-spreading infestation of people whose digital identities (and tethered real identities) lurch out of their control, dancing around at the behest of bocors. The aptly named Crook, who was already making a name for himself as an Internet troll, created the website *craigslist-perverts.com* to copy and expand a prank originated by Jason Fortuny. On the site, Crook documented the responses to fake submissive sex ads he had placed on *Craigslist* sites around the country, including the personal contact information of the responders. Shortly thereafter, bloggers concerned with Internet privacy issues, such as the writers at *10ZenMonkeys* and *BoingBoing*, began writing about Crook himself, using an unflattering photo taken from a FoxNews interview he'd given. Crook sought to suppress the photo by filing Digital Millennium Copyright Act (DMCA) claims against them.

The DMCA creates a safe harbor for Internet Service Providers in cases of copyright violations, as long as they act quickly to remove the offending material. However, it also includes a proviso restricting such filings to the legitimate copyright holders. Since Crook did not hold the copyright on the FoxNews image, he had violated the law in filing these claims. As part of the settlement with *10ZenMonkeys* and the Electronic Frontier Foundation, Crook made an apology video taking responsibility for filing false claims and expressing his regret. Tellingly, he included a warning to other web users in the form of a rhetorical question: "Who knew you can't control your own image?"[31]

The events at the heart of the Michael Crook affair highlight the similarity between digital zombification and outbreaks in movies like *28 Days Later.* Crook took control of identities belonging to the respondents to his ads, which led to his own image and online identity being manipulated by websites critical of him. He then used false DMCA notices to retaliate, forcing some less well-funded or legally savvy websites to revise their own work, but finally he had to make an apology video in which he acknowledged the illegality of the DMCA claims— something he surely wouldn't have done without the force of the law behind his opponents. In each case, the online identities and representations of the people involved escalated beyond their control, sometimes lurching away to make trouble elsewhere, other times forcing those involved to spend time and resources responding.

Digital zombie outbreaks are rare, but they encapsulate the larger concern at the center of this essay. With the emergence of cinema and computers, many scholars recognize a quantitative and qualitative shift in the systems we use to communicate with one another. The ubiquity of virtually-free copying, digital networks, and ever-increasing access to constantly-growing databases of human knowledge changes the way we interact with one another in ways as profound as the shift from oral to literate culture. This shift—called the "electric" age by Marshall McLuhan, the era of "secondary orality" by Walter Ong, or the Age of "Electracy" by Gregory Ulmer[32] — results in vast shifts in the way we see the world and our relationship with it. Perhaps the rise of fast zombies and the infectious popularity of the zombie itself serve to help us contemplate the changing nature of our own identities, both online and in real life.

## I Walked with a Zombie

In June of 2009 and again in 2010, I joined a mob of more than 1,000 zombies who gathered at the Millennium Park Cloud Gate statue in downtown Chicago and proceeded to lurch around the city, moaning and growling at pedestrians and cars. It's an amusing event, replete with the usual communal joy that fan culture inspires along with disgusted, delighted, and disturbed looks and comments from "civilians" who encounter the horde. Zombie walks like this one are by no means rare. Since 2001, they have been steadily growing in popularity, with the largest ones exceeding four thousand zombies or more.[33] At the 2010 march, I encountered a gospel singer who was delighted to see us ("I'm going to have to join y'all next year!"), a good-humored couple having their wedding photos taken, and a serious man who stood to the side of our parade and, with the loud voice and cadence of a preacher, called on God to cast out the demons provoking our sinful behavior.

Aside from the general delight horror fans get from the macabre, what's going on when hundreds of strangers gather to pretend they are undead, unthinking monsters? Whereas vampires and werewolves hyperbolize human struggles with human concerns, zombies do not. Zombies represent the eradication of ourselves, the complete loss of control and identity. There's little to admire or enjoy about that experience. But in the digital age, we already experience that loss of control. When an acquaintance forwards that snarky email to the person we'd least like to see it, when someone trashes us online or tags us in an embarrassing Facebook photo, when a former lover discloses risqué photos, or when a hacker uses our Internet connection to commit mischief and crime, we lose control of ourselves.

We like zombies, both fast and slow, because we are *already* dancing on the strings of digital bocors. We are already the edead.

## Notes

1. Kendall Phillips, *Projected Fears: Horror Films and American Culture* (Westport, CT: Praeger, 2005), 93–100.

2. Tony Williams, *The Cinema of George A. Romero: Knight of the Living Dead* (New York: Wallflower Press, 2003), 23–4.

3. Ibid., 25.

4. Cf. *Dead Meat* (2004), *Severed: Forest of the Dead* (2005), and *Black Sheep* (2006).

5. Scott Bukatman, *Terminal Identity: The Virtual Subject in Post-Modern Science Fiction* (Durham: Duke University Press, 1993), 6.

6. Kyle William Bishop, *American Zombie Gothic: The Rise and Fall (and Rise) of the Walking Dead in Popular Culture* (Jefferson, NC: McFarland, 2010), 95.

7. Simon Pegg, "The Dead and the Quick," *The Guardian*, 4 November 2008, Section G2, page 21, http://www.guardian.co.uk/media/2008/nov/04/television-simon-pegg-dead-set.

8. Danny Boyle and legions of Internet commenters have argued about whether or not *28 Days Later* is a zombie film or not. I suggest that the movie's use of tropes from the genre put it clearly in the "zombie film" category, and that the practicalities of the plot (the "infected" are actually rage-filled, mindlessly homicidal humans) is a nod to the film's realism rather than its genre status.

9. I am particularly fond of *Flight of the Living Dead* (2007), which incomprehensibly tries to combine the claustrophobia of *Das Boot* (1982) with the sprinting zombies from *Dawn of the Dead* (2004). It's difficult to sprint very far in an airplane cabin.

10. Bishop, *American Zombie Gothic*, 205.

11. Mark Pendergast, *Inside the Outbreaks: The Elite Medical Detectives of the Epidemic Intelligence Service* (New York: Houghton Mifflin Harcourt, 2010), 340.

12. This may just be a matter of time, however. A recent proof of concept experiment showed that certain kinds of implant chips, enabled with wireless networking capability, are capable of sending and receiving computer viruses. University of Reading scientist Mark Gasson explains the danger he's demonstrated this way: "With the benefits of this type of technology come risks. We may improve ourselves in some way but much like the improvements with other technologies, mobile phones for example, they become vulnerable to risks, such as security problems and computer viruses." Thanks to Stephanie Boluk for alerting me to this article. Rory Cellan-Jones, "First human 'infected with computer virus,'" *BBC News*, May 27, 2010, http://www.bbc.co.uk/news/10158517.

13. Jun Auza, "12 Most Devastating PC Viruses and Worms of All Time," *Techsource Blog*, July 12, 2008, http://www.junauza.com/2008/07/12-most-devastating-pc-viruses-and.html.

14. Alvin Toffler, *Future Shock* (Random House: New York, 1970), 67.

15. Charles Hoge, "The Zombie Runs Deep: Exploring the Bleeding Over of the Historical Record into the Cinema of the Living Dead," *PCA/ACA National Conference*, St. Louis, March 31, 2010.

16. William Seabrook, *The Magic Island* (New York: Harcourt, Brace, 1929), 93.

17. Ibid., 99.

18. Ibid., 94.

19. John Markoff, "Attack of the Zombie Computers Is Growing Threat," *The New York Times*, January 27, 2007, http://www.nytimes.com/2007/01/07/technology/07net.html.

20. Declan McCullough, "Attack of Comcast's Internet Zombies," *CNET News*, May 24, 2004, http://news.cnet.com/2010-1034-5218178.html.

21. Rick McDonald and Nick McDonald, "Zombie Alterity: Or How I Learned to Stop Worrying and Love Zombies," *PCA/ACA National Conference*, St. Louis, March 31, 2010.

22. William Larkin, "*Res Corporealis*: Persons, Bodies, and Zombies," in *The Undead and Philosophy: Chicken Soup for the Soulless*, ed. Richard Greene and K. Silem Mohammad (Chicago: Open Court, 2006), 19.

23. Hamish Thompson, "She's Not Your Mother Anymore, She's a Zombie!" in *The Undead and Philosophy*, 36.

24. Philosophers have used the figure of the philosophical zombie to think through this issue. "In philosophy, zombies are typically, outwardly, indistinguishable from normal humans, at least to the naked eye.... Inwardly, or subjectively, however, there's no conscious 'light' behind their eyes, however much they seem to shine." This construct helps philosophers write and think about how we relate to one another and how we understand where personhood begins and ends. Larry Hauser, "Zombies, *Blade Runner*, and the Mind-Body Problem," in *The Undead and Philosophy*, 54.

25. Tim O'Reilly, "What is Web 2.0?" *O'Reilly Media*, September 30, 2005, 2, http://oreilly.com/web2/archive/what-is-web-20.html.

26. Clay Shirky, *Here Comes Everybody: The Power of Organizing without Organizations* (New York: Penguin Press, 2008).

27. Kate, "More Insulting 'Job Offers'— Field Work For Free," *The Girls A Geek* [sic], August 17, 2010, http://thatgirlsageek.blogspot.com/2010/08/more-insulting-job-offers-field-work.html.

28. Boluk and Lenz discuss the relationship between zombie plague narratives and the viral spread of capitalism. They argue that modern zombie narratives, like early modern plague narratives provide a thought experiment or metaphor for thinking about the spread of capitalism and its dehumanizing effects. Stephanie Boluk and Wylie Lenz, "Infection, Media, and Capitalism: From Early Modern Plagues to Postmodern Zombies," *Journal for Early Modern Cultural Studies* 10, no. 2 (Fall/Winter 2010): 127–148.

29. Julian Dibbell, "A Rape in Cyberspace," *The Village Voice*, December 23, 1993, http://www.juliandibbell.com/texts/bungle_vv.html.

30. I'm not, of course, making the grotesque suggestion that the players who were assaulted somehow "deserved" to be attacked because they had willingly played the game. By contrast, Dibbell makes it clear that Mr. Bungle intentionally constructed a situation that would both offend the players involved and break the social rules of the shared space. He provoked the reaction he got.

Another less clear-cut case of player abuse occurred in what might be called the "Serenity Now" incident. On March 3, 2006, a player in a *World of Warcraft* guild posted an announcement that one of the players from their guild had died in real life, and that her friends would be gathering to commemorate her at an in-game funeral. The memorial was to be held at the player's favorite spot, a fishing pond which is in a "PvP" (player vs. player) area, meaning that open fighting between players is allowed by the game engine. While the original announcement asked people to respect the event, several players suggested that holding the event in that space was asking for trouble. Or, to quote the sixth commenter, "$10 on somebody fucking with it."

Sadly, but not surprisingly, a rival guild named Serenity Now attacked the funeral and "killed" all the participants. Then they made a video of the attack and posted it online. The outpouring of bile and vitriol directed at those players, both on forums and in-game, highlights the fact that experiences of "presence" and "reality" online still differ wildly. In discussing this event with students, I find strong consensus that while many condemned the actions of Serenity Now, nearly all thought the funeral organizers were at least partly to blame, in that they held the event in an area where such an attack could take place. This highlights, perhaps, the difference a decade of life online makes in how we view such events. "Memorial to Feyjin," forum thread at illidrama.com, March 3, 2006, accessed November 29, 2010, http://forums.illidrama.com/showthread.php?1826-Memorial-to-Fayejin.

31. Lou Cabron, "Dear Internet, I'm Sorry," *10ZenMonkeys*, March 24, 2007, accessed November 29, 2010, http://www.10zenmonkeys.com/2007/03/14/michael-crook-settlement-apology/.

32. Cf. Gregory L. Ulmer, *Heuretics: The Logic of Invention* (Baltimore: Johns Hopkins University Press, 1994); Marshall McLuhan, *Understanding Media: The Extensions of Man* (Cambridge: MIT Press, 1964); Walter Ong, *Orality and Literacy: The Technologizing of the Word* (New York: Routledge, 1982).

33. Dan Restione, "Thousands of Zombies March in Fremont," *KIRO Radio*, Bonneville Seattle, July 6, 2010, http://www.mynorthwest.com/?nid=11&sid=339703.

# A Brain Is a Terrible Thing to Waste: *Isolation U.* and the Campus Zombie[1]

## BRIAN GREENSPAN

Ever since their cinematic reanimation in the 1960s to join the masses of Body Snatchers, Manchurian candidates, Stepford wives and other fantastic images of mid-century conformity, zombies have been associated with the creeping threat of socialists and communists, both the lumpen and working classes and, following Romero's first sequel, *Dawn of the Dead,*[2] voracious middle-class consumers.[3] By now, zombies have infected all classes and subject positions, left, right and center, prompting associations with a wide range of cultural phenomena and political affiliations. At the same time, they function as an undead mass onto which society projects its collective fears, including "nuclear weapon tests, race conflict during the fight for Civil Rights, the riots and assassinations of the 1960s, the mid-1980s and the AIDS epidemic, and the events of September 11, 2001."[4] It is no accident that this chronology of social horrors moves from apprehension over "controlled" tests conducted by state actors in isolated military bases to recent anxieties over dispersed networks of biological and political terror. The self-replicating zombie has lately undergone a medial shift, and now stands less for mass-cultural phenomena than for new, digitally networked social media. What if the zombie's recent re-emergence as popular culture's most ubiquitous figure of horror has less to do with any particular social class or identity than the threat of networked emergence itself?

A large and growing percentage of the world's zombies are spawned not through film, but through zombie-themed video games, as any warm-blooded college student will attest. Students play zombie games in computer labs, residences and cafeterias, on consoles, laptop computers, cell phones and mobile devices. It is estimated that three-quarters of American students aged eighteen or older play video games, compared with less than half of those not in school.[5] Given that the majority of video games feature non-player characters who are either explicitly or implicitly zombies, it comes as no surprise that the undead represent a growing preoccupation among the college set. Just as zombies of an earlier era foregrounded the mass media's role in negotiating a complex of struggles involving racial, class and gender differences, so today's digital zombies allow ambivalences over new networked identities and socio-political formations to be played out. Because it already stands for nearly everything, today's zombie cannot represent any one class, cause or social identity in particular, but instead signals the difficulty of characterizing the contemporary subject under the conditions of networked capitalism. Zombies foreground questions of class consciousness for a globalized era in which class identities themselves grow increasingly unstable, and in which new social media promise to enable alliances that rearticulate individual and group identity across class, national, and ideological lines. Today's digital zombies stand less for a given identity or social class than a certain logic of control, a logic manifested through new socially networked figures exhibiting varying degrees and kinds of agency, including avatars, the latest breed of voodoo puppets; bots, spiders and other autonomous agents exhibiting independent volition and action; and virtual communities embodying a distributed authority and intelligence.

This chapter explores digital zombies as allegories of the contemporary university student's interactions with, and apprehension toward, networked protocols and modes of being in an era of knowbots, lecture podcasts, virtual classrooms and learning management systems. Conventional zombie "survival horror" video games position contemporary students at the crux of traditional institutions of knowledge and new information networks. By pitting users against mobs of zombified non-player characters with the capacity to exhibit complex and intelligent group behavior, these games reflect in the most literal terms upon the desperate situation of the student body in relation to the biopolitical reproduction of human brainpower, or "immaterial labour," in the uncanny networks of "cognitive capitalism." And yet, although zombies represent these new socio-technical networks as non-human, alienating and antagonistic, I argue that they also reveal this antagonism to be essential to the formation of popular movements of resistance. This tension between the alienating and empowering aspects of networks is explored through the example of *Isolation U.*, a new kind of digital zombie "alternate reality game" set on a university campus. With an affective and embodied locative interface closely articulated to the user's immediate social context, *Isolation U.* allows gamers to experience zombification not as the apocalyptic ascendancy of the non-human, but as exemplary of the political process that governs the formation of a people in a networked era.

## Zombie Emergency at Corporate U.

The popularity of zombies on campus is directly related to two related factors: the creeping corporatization of North American colleges and universities, and the advent of new network protocols and technologies for education. Nick Dyer-Witheford analyzes the advent of "Corporate U." from an autonomist Marxist perspective, noting the complicity of contemporary universities in the expropriation of the "general intellect," that human cognitive potential which Paulo Virno defines literally as "the intellect in general, the most generic aptitudes of the mind: the faculty of language, the inclination to learn, memory, the ability to abstract and to correlate, the inclination toward self-reflection."[6] Just as industrial capitalists have exploited physical labor, so cognitive capitalists exploit "immaterial labour," the application of the general intellect that defines the intellectual and affective dimensions of commodities in the mode of production characterized by information and communications technologies. For Dyer-Witheford, university instruction increasingly represents a form of cognitive, communicative, and affective labor that contributes to cognitive capitalism, not only by shaping the general intellect through ideas, inventions and creative work, but also by training students to become the immaterial laborers of the future:

> University students are not only, as immaterial labour in training, the subjects of the reproduction of labour power. Very many are already subjects of production, meeting

high tuition fees by working their way through school, often in low-paid McJobs.... At the same time, they are also subjects of a consumption-regime of unprecedented intensity. Students are amongst the demographic niches considered most desirable, and most aggressively targeted by youth culture marketers; they inhabit campuses where corporate logos, saturation advertising and promotional events sprout from every cafeteria, plaza and dedicated lecture theatre.[7]

You can see students fighting zombies all over campus, late at night in computer labs, slumped over tables outside the food court, or huddled near a terminal in a corner of the campus pub. Playing through zombie "survival horror" games generally demands that the user spend many hours in a relatively sedentary position in front of a monitor, with physical interaction limited to manual input through a keyboard, joystick or gamepad, repetitive play that seems suspiciously similar to work under cognitive capitalism. This physical inactivity, although a far cry from the "fast zombies" of games like *Half-Life²: Episode Two* (2007), contributes to the overwhelming impression among parents and educators that video games transform young people into the living dead. Just as movies like *Dawn of the Dead* (1978) ironically identified zombies with the masses who form theatre audiences, so video games self-reflexively foreground cultural conceptions of gamers as zombified youth.

What sets zombie games apart from their cinematic progenitors is their *procedurality,* the interactive and dynamic features that ensure gamers will not only witness zombie attacks, but also influence their outcomes. As a procedural medium, zombie simulations use an internal logic to respond to user input and interaction with complex behaviors that make them a challenging survival threat. So Matthew Weise describes "zombie simulations" like *Resident Evil* as "procedural adaptations" of the well-known "rules" of zombie behavior, established in "the modern apocalyptic zombie film" inaugurated by George Romero's *Night of the Living Dead* (1968) and its spin-offs, which dictate that a zombie invariably "attacks any human in sight, eats human flesh, cannot move quickly, cannot use tools, possesses no reason or higher intelligence, and cannot be killed except by a blow or shot to the head. The final rule is that any human bitten by a zombie will eventually die and become one themselves."[8] Game play results from the interaction of these behaviors, encoded into digital algorithms, over the large-scale environments represented within the game space: it is the "wide procedural foundation of complicated zombie behaviors and environmental interactions" that together form an "impressive range of *emergent* possibility."[9]

In hinting at the possibility that the algorithms controlling zombie behavior in a digital game might somehow evolve into a higher order of complexity, Weise reflects a more general tendency within the gaming industry to characterize zombie behavior as "emergent." Although scientists have not agreed upon how to define emergence within a complex system, as John Johnston notes in his recent study of artificial life and intelligence research, genuine emergence within a computational system means more than the perception of pattern or novelty by an external observer. Emergence can best be defined as an intrinsic function of complex systems in which "a new pattern brings about an increase in the system's computational capacity" and "global information processing" through autopoesis, or self-organization.[10] For instance, in Valve Corporation's *Left 4 Dead* zombie survival horror franchise, an artificial intelligence "procedural narrative" generator dynamically changes the spawning patterns of zombies, although the zombie hordes do not self-organize.[11] Games like *Unreal Tournament* or Will Wright's *The Sims,* on the other hand, enhance the believability of their non-player characters through algorithms borrowed from Artificial Life research,[12] while Microsoft claims that the processor of its XBox 360 can track the interactions of hundreds of non-player characters, leading to collective behavioral patterns that are far more complex than that of any individual zombie: "the emergent behavior is really amazing.... What was once a serene city block is transformed into a riot almost instantaneously."[13] Such games do not merely simulate or allegorize self-organizing behavior, they *exhibit* it — a much more modest claim than that of researchers who argue that artificial life software does not merely simulate life, but actually instantiates it in its processes.[14]

It is precisely this possibility of a self-organizing collective intelligence emerging without any direct human intervention that generates such excitement and anxiety for the gamer, and gets close to the cold heart of the zombie's current significance. Zombie sims allow gamers to engage with the same processes and software agents that increasingly govern the networked interactions of human and non-human entities in the global marketplace; they force gamers, students and other immaterial laborers to reflect on the transformations they undergo when interacting with each other and with rule-based automata such as e-mail daemons, chatterbots and web spiders. To play a zombie game is to alternate between varying degrees of human and machinic control, to explore the relation of individual volition and action to the dynamics of networked group behavior, and to discover how best to interact with other agents whose motives are governed by algorithmic procedures rather than strictly human desires or belief systems. In this sense, zombie sims could be considered what Alexander Galloway calls "control allegories," games whose algorithms and procedures allegorize the protocols of distributed control that govern computer-based interactions in our digitally networked era.[15] But if zombies allegorize the uncanny threat of networked being, this threat is complicated by the lure of social networks, which hold out the utopian promise of collective action through authentic, if highly mediated, communities. While cinematic zombies have been read as allegories of mass consumption or the lynch mob mentality, zombie games allegorize the mediation of collective behavior through new social networks enabled by interactive technologies, including popular social media and collaborative gaming sites. These behaviors infuse all manner of socio-technical systems, and increasingly shape how we think about, describe and predict collective action today. If zombies seem to stand alternately for conformity to capitalist ideals and popular revolt against them, that is because they represent a contemporary uncertainty over the mechanisms and protocols through which subjects negotiate digital information and communication networks to enact a wide range of social identities, from radical libertarianism to liberal individualism and progressive solidarity.

Working with Greg de Peuter, Dyer-Witheford has recently addressed these ambivalences by building on the controversial work of Hardt and Negri. In *Games of Empire,* they argue convincingly that digital games are the "exemplary media of Empire," which is understood as a "regime of biopower based on corporate exploitation of myriad types of labor, paid and unpaid," in both its material and "immaterial" forms. Digital games are not only spawned by the immaterial labor of creative programming, but are "tutoring entire generations in [the] digital technologies and networked communication" that typify "the boundless exercise of biopower" in the era of Empire.[16] At the same time, they also see gamers as exemplary of the multitude,[17] those heterogeneous networks of immaterial laborers who stand against — or rather, apart from — Empire, in "exodus" from the networks of capital. On this view, the very attempt to harness student biopower produces pockets of resistance and dissent on campus. Because universities function as incubators of the creativity, flexibility and "innovation" that drives cognitive capitalism, they also enable the formation of networks of affinity surrounding such diverse activities as anti-globalization protests, hacktivism, and media piracy, which together mount a "multitudinous" protest over the control of the networks that mediate and exploit the general intellect. The same communication and information networks that enable the flows of immaterial labor and the productivity of the general intellect are thus also sites of "anti-capitalist self-organisation."[18] These struggles, which come into high relief on campus, epitomize a more general social diffusion of immaterial labor that defines cognitive capitalism. It is the wide scale of socio-technical information and communications networks, ambivalently situated as the hub of both exploitation and dissent, that lends the zombie metaphor its contemporary salience. By allowing users to interact with algorithms of networked emergence, zombie sims could be said to allegorize both the control protocols of cognitive capitalism and the paths of resistance to it. As Lars Bang Larsen explains, the zombie

> straddles the divide between industrial and immaterial labor, from mass to multitude, from the brawn of industrialism to the dispersed brains of cognitive capitalism.
>   With its highly ambiguous relationship to subjectivity, consciousness, and life itself, we may hence consider the zombie a paradigm of immaterial labor. Both the zombie and immaterial labor celebrate logistics and a colonization of the brain and the nervous system.[19]

Although I largely agree with this analysis, it remains true that most zombie sims never get beyond expressing the uncanniness of the network. They allow gamers to heroically oppose the network, but even in multiplayer mode, do not let them form large oppositional networks; in other words, they do not allegorize the control protocols that govern multitudinous dissent. Dyer-Witheford and de Peuter acknowledge that the concept of the multitudes is "charged with being nebulous and romantic, resting on a rosy confidence in a revolt that would spontaneously self-organize from wildly disparate sources,"[20] a specter that their otherwise excellent study cannot quite dispel. A similar faith in the oppositional potential of self-organizing collectives pervades zombie theorizing. Sarah Juliet Lauro and Karen Embry's "Zombie Manifesto," for instance, "proclaims the future possibility of the *zombii*, a consciousless being that is a swarm organism, and the only imaginable specter that could really be posthuman."[21] But just how does the swarm self-constitute? Lauro and Embry never explain the precise mechanisms of collective affiliation that permit the swarm to appear as an organism, nor the protocols that govern its behavior. Their "swarm organism" is an abstraction of self-organizing processes that mystifies the dynamics of collectivity, while standing in for the unimaginable revolutionary consciousness. Emergent complexity, which is a genuine attribute of distributed networks, has become a mainstay of social activist theory. But to interpret a spontaneous increase in complexity as a *political* structure misrepresents the ontologies of both digital and social networks, and ignores the rules of negotiation (both cooperative and antagonistic) that underwrite the formation of social collectivities.

While zombie sims do allegorize our daily interactions with non-human networks, then, they rarely allow users to engage algorithmically with the protocols of dissent through which resistant social networks of gamers are formed. Taken as control allegories, most zombie sims only allegorize our *lack* of control over non-human and uncanny network processes. Most sims structure the gaming experience from the perspective of the imperiled human, with the zombie hordes always positioned as the avatar's "other": when your avatar is bitten and "turned" you do not resume play as a zombie, but die and start the level over. Video games do not present zombie hordes as exemplary of the multitudes; rather, they simulate violent, anti-communal and anti-social forms of collective emergence that represent the fearful side of the general intellect, that uncanny "publicness without a public sphere," in Virno's phrase, which is incapable of "common participation [in] the 'life of the mind.'"[22]

## From Emergence to Politics; or, Are Zombies People Too?

If simulated zombies allegorize an exodus from the networks of capital, then, it is also an exodus from human agency and experience into an "emergent" state with which the human user cannot identify; nor does a vague faith in a self-organizing multitude explain the process by which political agency is formed. So how can we theorize zombie agency in a manner that gets humans back into the game without making questionable equations between computational emergence and the emergence of revolutionary consciousness? To do so, I will turn to Ernesto Laclau's theory of populist reason, which presents a strong critique of Hardt and Negri. For Laclau, the multitude represents an ill-defined, self-constructing universality, a "spontaneous aggregate of elements, a revolutionary class which simply 'emerges' without any antagonism, struggle or political articulation."[23] *On Populist Reason* presents the case that "there is nothing automatic about the emergence of a people; it's the result of a complex process of construction, antagonisms, struggle over hegemony, and articulations."[24] A people is actively constituted when the particular demands of individuals or groups representing a variety of political interests are unified under the "empty signifier" of a single demand which acquires hegemony. This single unifying demand anchors these heterogeneous claims, establishing a general chain of equivalencies between them that did not previously exist. For instance, the demand for lower tuition among university students is both a specific demand in itself and an empty signifier that unifies students as a populist movement, by standing in for a whole range of particular demands (e.g., a lower student-faculty ratio, safer campuses for women, better funding for athletics, more accessible classrooms, and so on). These particular demands are not eliminated, but remain in negotiation with the hegemonic demand of lower tuition that speaks for them. Significantly, the demands of a popular identity do not correspond to any *a priori* social unity, class or subject-position; moreover, the populist identity cannot ultimately be reduced to any objective "content type" or contained within the unity of a stable class or racial identification, but is itself changed throughout the political process.[25]

Following Laclau's theory, I like to see zombies not as symbols of Empire or the multitude, but as an allegory of the political process itself, the antagonistic negotiation through which popular movements emerge. If zombies stand ambiguously for a multiplicity of social, ethnic and gendered groups, that is because they embody the general logic of the formation of popular movements in the absence of stable class or social identities. The mindless zombie is not pure body but pure name, a name established through a popular demand for "more brains!" This identifying cry, along with the metonymous bite that says, "I am a zombie," are political articulations that performatively establish a chain of equivalences between individual claims. Once bitten, victims cease being *people* and become *a* people, as their individual demands merge into a stable system of signification governed by the logic of hegemony.[26] The oft-cited conformity of the zombie horde is really a function of this hegemony, which unifies the particular interests of individual zombies under a shared, central demand that represents the impossible totality of unfulfilled demands. For zombies want much more than brains: far from a homogenous mass, zombies represent a plurality of subject positions (young and old, white and black, male and female, rich and poor), each with their own "partial struggles."[27] Ever since Romero's original picture, with its "multi-racial, socially mixed" cast, zombies have remained highly individuated; in *Day of the Dead* (1985), it even becomes clear that zombies "can remember bits of their past and even learn, that their human minds have not been entirely destroyed."[28]

Despite the challenge of rendering large numbers of digital characters with the same individuality as live-action film actors, zombie games do not deny the heterogeneity of the zombified people, even when they are subsumed within a seemingly stable social formation clearly associated with specific subaltern groups, such as the *ganados* and *majini* of the *Resident Evil* franchise. In *Left 4 Dead*, non-player character zombies are differentiated by their abilities and appearances into Hunters, Smokers, Boomers, Tanks and Witches; while the

"Undead" race of non-player characters within *World of Warcraft* have various difficulty levels and "bosses" who look and act differently. Fawkes from *Fallout 3* exhibits a superior intelligence to the other Super Mutants, while the zombie-like splicers in *Bioshock* are highly individuated as capitalists, scientific intelligentsia and union captains, with mothers pushing prams and femmes fatales with tentacled feet designed to fit high-heeled shoes. That these zombies exhibit vestigial traces of their human desires and demands makes them appear all the more motivated and terrifying. However, the logic of popular movements dictates that, once zombified, their particular demands will be subsumed within the single, hegemonic demand for more brains. Although this unifying demand signifies a real lack (since they are, after all, brainless), it is ultimately an empty signifier standing in for the impossible totality of the people's incommensurable, unfulfilled demands. As Laclau explains, inscription in the equivalential chain lends their particular demands a wider universality and "corporal reality" in the body of the (zombified) people which they would otherwise lack.[29] This newly established chain of equivalences (between black, white, worker, elite, straight, queer, and so on) retains a differential logic in defining itself against an external "enemy" or outsider — in this case, the uninfected humans who, in their individuated interests and lack of hegemonic demands, do *not* constitute a people.

Laclau posits that the hegemonic demand which unifies a people, the empty signifier, functions through the logic of *catachresis*, a rhetorical figure operating somewhere between metaphor and metonymy that strains associative logic, as when body parts are used to describe inanimate objects (e.g., "the mouth of the wound"). *Brains* are catachrestic in that they seem to demand the material organ while actually making a claim on ideas, cognition, and all that is subsumed beneath the rubric of the general intellect. This demand parallels and resists the endlessly unfulfilled demand for brainpower issued by global capital, the common enemy of immaterial labor. Brains themselves point toward the particular lack, the missing fullness[30] that the zombie tries to name: that of the general intellect itself, as Larsen suggests. But while the hegemonic demand for brains stands in its particularity for general intellect, it also functions as an empty, universalizing signifier representing a range of concerns among immaterial laborers. Zombies do not symbolize the resistant multitude any more than they stand for communists, subaltern groups or mindless consumers. If zombies seem to stand for so many different struggles, that is because they allegorize the necessary emptiness of the category of "the people" itself, and the production of emptiness which is also the production of a people.[31] Though unconscious and inarticulate, the zombie presents a self-conscious symbol of the antagonistic process by which a people is articulated, biting, and fighting all the way — the very process that Laclau finds missing from theories of the immanent, self-organizing multitude.[32]

## *This Is Not a Brain: From Simulations to ARGs*

Laclau's theory of populist reason enables an understanding of zombies as a self-conscious symbol of the antagonistic political process through which individual needs and demands are articulated with the general demands of a people, the process through which power "transmigrates through a variety of bodies" in the era of networked politics.[33] The inadequacy of the concept of emergence to describe the political process becomes clear as the zombie lurches from the screen into both virtual communities and actual spaces of assembly. As "zombie walks" involving hundreds of participants lurch through a growing roster of cities across North America, with outbreaks from Ottawa to Sacramento, they less resemble "viral" flash mobs than well-organized, ritual cosplay events. This ritualization, however, does not preclude each walk from accruing a widely resonant symbolic significance articulated to local issues:

> Zombies don't appear to be anti or pro anything. They're not even fighting for their right to party. They represent hopelessness, decay, the breakdown of civilization. They're a one-size-fits-all symbol of the anxieties of our age-homelessness, drug addiction, greed and over-consumption.[34]

Such ambiguity is not in itself unusual for a social movement: as Laclau argues, all popular movements present an empty cipher over which heterogeneous social groups compete for hegemony. In this sense, the zombie walk could be said to differ from other popular movements only in the degree of its self-consciousness and aestheticization.

A similar dynamic occurs in ZombieTruth and Lost Zombies, parodic social websites-cum-"alternate reality games" (ARGs) that explore the dynamics of networked behavior and control. ARGs typically appropriate existing networked infrastructures, both analog and digital, luring willing players in through a series of phone calls, faxes, postcards and emails that provide clues to the shape of a fictional universe. For instance, ZombieTruth creates an imaginary crisis by parasiting actual government pandemic websites, writing imaginary zombie viruses (the dreaded H1Z1) into the fabric of "official" fear to satirize the sanctioned discourse of contagion. Visitors to the ZombieTruth website encounter regular updates on the putative viral outbreak within this alternate reality, including news of zombie sightings, conspiracy theories, progress reports on a vaccine, and links to both human and zombie members. The site encourages its members to crowdsource solutions to organizational issues, such as whether Survivor Command, which controls the ZombieTruth Twitter feed, should be centrally controlled or community directed. Such games (perhaps more accurately considered popular movements in Laclau's sense) explore the dissemination of narratives of public health and national interest through viral exploits that piggyback onto biopolitical databases, exposing the complicity of networked media, the medical industry and public health officials. By exploiting the official channels of state-sanctioned biopolitical protocols, they call into question whether a full-blown SARS or H1N1 pandemic is any more realistic than an outbreak of zombies. To accept the advertised threat as real and inoculate yourself, they suggest, is to succumb metaphorically to zombification, the state's apparatus for controlling biopower. At the same time, the zombie stands in these games for the state's monstrous other, the oppositional citizen who knows too much (and who, after all, eats brains). Zombie walks and ARGs go beyond the mere simulation of emergence, allowing users to enact the dynamics governing popular movements, while actively exploring the meaning of commitment and involvement, the connection between individual and communal desires, and the viral protocols of social and technical control in a networked era.

Like zombie sims, Web-based ARGs can exploit the uncanniness, dispersion, and relative anonymity of digital networks to create the sense of a large-scale pandemic without clear borders. A very different experience is offered by *Isolation U.*, a small-scale, near-future alternate reality zombie game that allows users to experience the impact of network control protocols on the formation of popular movements from an insider's perspective. *Isolation U.* was created by Valerie Bherer, Cindy Ma and Elise Vist using the prototype StoryTrek locative media authoring system.[35] StoryTrek enables the creation of spatial stories that respond in real time to the vector of the user's physical movement and ever-changing geospatial context, providing narrative patterns matched on-the-fly to the user's location, route and style of navigation. The StoryTrek authoring tool allows game masters to link narrative segments associated with various patterns of embodied input to Google maps.[36] I provided these students with our authorware and instructions to build a near-future adventure set on our campus that addressed the University's history, present condition and likely future. The game is played outdoors using the StoryTrek reading client, which runs on a GPS-enabled mobile device. Walking within a designated area will automatically trigger the particular textual series that most closely corresponds to the user's pattern of motion, enacting a quest that explores ideas of individual and collective agency through the symbolic landscape of the incorporated campus. Like all locative artworks, *Isolation U.* plays on the tension between the user's immediate geophysical context and the invisibly dispersed social and technical communications networks through which the game functions. The user does not merely confront these networks as an emergent and uncanny threat to be destroyed or escaped, as in a zombie sim, but plays through them, learning to negotiate their protocols first-hand.

As you explore the university, a story gradually unfolds through the mobile device from the perspective of a newly arrived student who only wants to make friends and fit in. The setting is recognizably Carleton University (although it will work most anywhere with satellite reception), but the narrative rewrites the campus as a corporatized space saturated with advertisements hawking the wares and services of the fictional MegaThorne corporation. Crossing the nearby canal to the scenic arboretum, for instance, yields ads exhorting the avatar to "Drink MegaThunder," to try the MegaMatch student dating service, and to walk to the beat of MegaTunes, "Because you should never have to walk alone." On campus, billboards pump the artificial scent of hot dogs into the air, while other ads promoting cellular phone plans, power beverages used by varsity sports teams, and caffeinated drinks to help pep you up for that history final. The game parodies the real-life campus ads that target individual and school pride, promising a careful mixture of boosterism, academic recognition, and adult freedoms, while demonstrating the degree to which all dimensions of student life and affect are integrated through the campus experience to provide an easily accessible and targetable demographic for cognitive capitalism.[37] As she passes other students, messages depicting the avatar's inner thoughts reveal her[38] fears of standing out from the crowd: "She looks me up and down, though, and suddenly I feel nervous again. She notices my old shirt, my out-of-date earbuds and my off-brand running shoes.... I need to upgrade myself." These blunt exhortations to spend are in constant tension with the avatar's own felt need to actualize herself as an independent individual, a struggle that is reinforced procedurally by the game's locative engine. The game's locative awareness encourages identification with the avatar's dilemma. If you linger too long in one place, the system will detect this hesitation, and urge her to "Go on! Explore! Meet the friends you'll have for the rest of your life!"; if you still fail to move, it asks, "What are you waiting for...! Why aren't you grasping this opportunity! There are so many people just like you our there: unique and individual!" Simply moving through campus generates a spatial allegory of the contradictions of a society that compels conformity through a rhetoric of individualism reinforced by constant compulsions to exercise a highly constrained consumer choice. We eventually learn that our avatar's independence extends only as far as choosing an unusual color of sneaker from the MegaShoe store.

The marks of corporate finance are everywhere reflected in the fictional, if not the actual, campus, so recently renovated that it no longer resembles the University's promotional brochures. Dunton Tower, former home of arts departments and symbol of the old-school "ivory tower" model of academe, is now surrounded by broken glass, and the Library and Unicentre boarded up. By contrast, the small brown building of Residence Commons has been made over into a shiny new mall full of mirrors that reflect the students "shopping and living" there. Walking by the Loeb or St. Patrick's buildings triggers musings from your avatar, who can still make out the old names of the university's erstwhile benefactors beneath the new signage of the MegaThorne corporation, which has a monopoly on sponsorship. These extrapolations of the university's likely future are linked to its past and present through text segments drawn from Carleton's actual history, from its origins as a college for young soldiers returning from war, right up to its current policies. Walking up Library Road returns citations from Carleton's 2009 strategic plan outlining a desire to "'introduce more programs that increase the students' average time spent on campus per day,'" a goal that, within the alternate reality of the game, appears to be a tactic for integrating more of each student's life and leisure time — more of their immaterial labor — into the production of cognitive capital. Standing near the former administrative building, now corporate home, the avatar complains to an executive "youth culture marketer" that "'it doesn't really feel like a school anymore.'" In response, the exec puts a positive spin on capital's total penetration of all areas of campus life: "We aren't really a business anymore. We've become a part of politics, education and, of course, culture." This corporate ideology sums up the strategy of cognitive capital, which aims to infiltrate and appropriate immaterial labor from all areas of social life, repurposing the social order in a kinder, gentler variety of zombie apocalypse.

As Dyer-Witheford points out, it is not only the classroom, but the entire campus of Corporate U. that is mobilized in the continual reabsorption and transformation of the general intellect of students into cognitive capital. And because locative media can function ubiquitously at all the sites where this absorption occurs, they are especially good at allegorizing the protocols of cognitive capital. Walking by the (actual) administrative building triggers a hot spot, and reveals that the (fictional) MegaThorne Corporation is tracking your avatar's movements across campus through her cell phone. Against this dystopian narrative, the game's embodied, kinetic user interface returns a measure of control, allowing the user to reappropriate the very mobile networks and surveillance technologies through which cognitive capitalism operates. No longer an inert thumb jockey, the gamer-student is transformed into an active agent who must "win" actual geophysical space back from corporate sponsors in order to unlock the school's mystery. Just as games like *Dead Rising* encourage players to reconsider the use-value of flat screen TVs, lawnmowers and other mass commodities by repurposing them as weapons,[39] so *Isolation U.* rewards the user's embodied, "non-servile" virtuosic performances, that common, unskilled element of immaterial labor with the capacity to resist administrative decision-making.[40] At the same time, the user must learn what motions will generate feedback: in order to play the game, you have to follow and learn to anticipate the system's embedded kinetic algorithms, protocols that further blur the line between human and inhuman agency. It ultimately remains unclear whether your virtuosic performance is co-opted into a servile conformity of action and opinion that sustains the fictional University's administrative apparatus, or liberates the common intellect and language, allowing it to break through to a generally utopian form of "acting-in-concert."[41]

As your avatar explores campus, negotiating her conflicting desires to join the crowd while finding herself, a narrative unfolds that reveals her dawning awareness of how much the campus has changed:

> There are so many people mulling around ... laughing, smiling, talking with each other. It looks like one of those publicity shots for a university pamphlet; the ones too staged to be real, with one representative from each student demographic, all laughing and getting along, as if to say: "Come here and be just like us: happier than you are now."
> And ... I am.

This moment of self-realization could signal a distanced but genuine happiness, but it could also mark the precise moment of infection. As you explore more areas of campus, a rumor slowly emerges that the MegaThorne corporation has released an engineered hybrid virus that increases its victims' sense of isolation and unpopularity, compels them to purchase MegaThorne products and join cliques of other infected individuals, and ultimately causes "utter destruction of the mind." Transmitted through a corporate email message, the virus is allegedly reinforced by the consumption of MegaThorne products and grouping behavior. In most zombie games, infection brings the avatar's death, requiring a restart. *Isolation U.* is unusual in allowing the user to experience the process of zombification from the victim's perspective as she abandons her doubts and starts to think, "It's just wonderful. I can imagine myself living here ... spending all my time here ... I want to be here." In our user tests, we've found that the embodied and contextual nature of the locative interface heightens empathy with the avatar, forcing users to renegotiate this identification as her mood and consciousness undergo transformation.

Then again, there is no guarantee that these transformations are externally programmed. The narrative subtly holds out the possibility that the virus rumor is nothing but anti-corporate propaganda spread by student activists who hack the corporate network through dissenting emails and text messages, as well as graffiti and manifestoes scrawled in the covers of old library books that crop up here and there around campus. As one of the administration's wandering "event managers" explains, "'No one makes you BUY our products—you want to buy our products because they say something about who you are as a person. Don't you want to express yourself? Shouldn't your drink say something about your life?'" As a result of either viral infection or better judgment, the avatar recoils from her encounter with an NPC who paints graffiti over advertisements ("MegaThorne will steal your language" and "MegaThorne will suck your soul. Do you want to be a zombie??") and promises an anti-viral vaccine. Your avatar is clearly no "multitudinous" student radical in exodus, but shows as much wariness of the protestors as the corporate shills. When you enter the quad, now occupied as a temporarily autonomous "Guerilla Zone" in the game world, your avatar only wants to escape the syringe-wielding activists who are intent on administering an anti-virus: "They're so aggressive, trying to grab me, like they want to sell me their crap. Drugs and messages."

This ambiguity over the existence of a corporate virus illustrates perfectly how zombies stand in as a mark of uncertainty over the protocols through which individual and group identities are negotiated within digital networks today. Fear of both the virus and anti-virus alike marks a suspicion toward the dynamic through which collective identities in general are formed, a suspicion that mitigates the student avatar's desire to fit in and make friends. In this way, *Isolation U.* allows players to enact the process by which an avatar's particular interests are negotiated through antagonisms and hegemony in the creation of a popular movement — what Laclau calls the political process proper. The game refrains from characterizing resistance as a mysterious "anti-capitalist self-organization" immanent within the networks of immaterial labor, presenting instead a more nuanced and conflicted rendering of the student body under the condition of cognitive capitalism. Unlike zombie sims, *Isolation U.* does not assume that the player and the zombies are necessary foes competing for agency and survival. As you arrive at the University's residences, newly made over in the image of capital, your avatar registers an unequivocal, if seemingly empty, contentment: "It's beautiful here. This is what I thought it would be like." Test players report being uncertain as to whether this arrival constitutes her final incorporation, or a salutary opening up to the student body at large, an ambivalence that the game's authors describe as a deliberate design decision. This declaration of happiness allows the zombie to remain an empty signifier within the game, a hegemonic sign that binds the avatar's individual demands to a greater community without necessarily dictating its particular content. To become a zombie in *Isolation U.* does not necessarily mean incorporation into either the uncanny side of the general intellect or some vaguely articulated, emergent network of dissent; instead, it is to acquire a nuanced understanding of alienation and antagonism as constitutive and enabling conditions for the negotiation of individual and collective identities. The game thus perfectly illustrates the symbolic role of the zombie in contemporary culture more generally: not to represent a particular class or identity, but to allegorize self-consciously the protocols through which populist demands are articulated and negotiated in the absence of stable subject position.

## Notes

1. I am indebted to the creators of *Isolation U.*, and in particular to Elise Vist, for her invaluable insights into the game and its design process. Thanks are also owed to Aalya Ahmad, Jessica Aldred, Pippin Barr, and Jennifer Whitson, who donated their delectable brains to my thinking about zombies. Finally, I am grateful to the Social Sciences and Humanities Research Council of Canada for their support in developing the StoryTrek software.

2. *Dawn of the Dead*, DVD, directed by George A. Romero (United States: Laurel Group, 1978).

3. Stephen Harper, "Zombies, Malls, and the Consumerism Debate: George Romero's *Dawn of the Dead*," *Americana: The Journal of American Popular Culture* (1900-present) 1, no. 2 (Fall 2002), accessed November 29, 2010, http://www.americanpopularculture.com/journal/articles/fall_2002/harper.htm.

4. Rikk Mulligan, "Zombie Apocalypse: Plague and the End of the World in Popular Culture," in *End of Days: Essays on the Apocalypse from Antiquity to Modernity*, ed. Karolyn Kinane and Michael A. Ryan (Jefferson, NC: McFarland, 2009), 350.

5. Amanda Lenhart, Sydney Jones and Alexandra Macgill, "Adults and Video Games," Pew Internet & American Culture Project, December 7, 2008, http://www.pewinternet. org/Reports/2008/Adults-and-Video-Games/1-Data-Memo.aspx?r=1.

6. Paulo Virno, *A Grammar of the Multitude: For an Analysis of Contemporary Forms of Life* (Los Angeles: Semiotext(e), 2004), 108.

7. Nick Dyer-Witheford, "Cognitive Capitalism and the Contested Campus," in *Engineering Culture: On "The Author as (Digital) Producer,"* ed. Geoff Cox and Joasia Krysa (Brooklyn: Autonomedia, 2005), 81.

8. Although even within zombie films, Weise's rules do not always apply. Matthew Weise, "The Rules of Horror: Procedural Adaptation in *Clock Tower, Resident Evil, and Dead Rising*," in *Horror Video Games: Essays on the Fusion of Fear and Play*, ed. Bernard Perron (Jefferson, NC: McFarland, 2009), 252.

9. Weise, *Rules of Horror*, 257; italics mine.

10. John Johnston, *The Allure of Machinic Life: Cybernetics, Artificial Life, and the New AI* (Cambridge: MIT Press, 2008), 237.

11. Gabe Newell, Blog, *Edge*, December 24, 2008, accessed November 29, 2010, http://www.next-gen.biz/blogs/gabe-newell-writes-edge.

12. Carlos Delgado-Mata and Jesus Ibáñez-Martinez, "AI Opponents with Personality Traits in Überpong," The Second International Conference on Intelligent Technologies for Interactive Entertainment (ICST INTE-TAIN '08), January 8–10, 2008, Cancun, Mexico, §2.4–2.5.

13. Jim W. Gettys, "The Intelligence Game," accessed July 22, 2010, http://www.xbox.com/NR/exeres/A0AE5AB5-EBA3-4F7C-801C-84B25937AA5D.htm.

14. Johnston, *Allure*, 215.

15. Alexander R. Galloway, *Gaming: Essays on Algorithmic Culture* (Minneapolis: University of Minnesota Press, 2006), 90–92.

16. Nick Dyer-Witheford and Greig de Peuter, *Games of Empire: Global Capitalism and Video Games* (Minneapolis: University of Minnesota Press, 2009), xix.

17. Ibid., xxx.

18. Dyer-Witheford, "Cognitive Capitalism," 86.

19. Lars Bang Larsen, "Zombies of Immaterial Labor: The Modern Monster and the Death of Death," *e-flux journal* 15 (2010), 6, http://www.e-flux.com/journal/view/131.

20. Dyer-Witheford and de Peuter, *Games of Empire*, xxii.

21. Sarah Juliet Lauro and Karen Embry, "A Zombie Manifesto: The Nonhuman Condition in the Era of Advanced Capitalism," *boundary 2* 35 (2008), 88.

22. Virno, *Grammar*, 40–1; 67.

23. Ernesto Laclau, "Can Immanence Explain Social Struggles?" *Diacritics* 31, no.4 (Winter 2001), 6.

24. Ernesto Laclau, *On Populist Reason* (New York: Verso, 2005), 200.

25. Laclau, "Can Immanence," 7.

26. Laclau, *Populist Reason*, 74.

27. Ibid., 86.
28. Mulligan, "Zombie Apocalypse," 359, 361.
29. Laclau, *Populist Reason*, 88.
30. Ibid., 85.
31. Ibid., 169.
32. Laclau, "Can Immanence," 6–7.
33. Laclau, *Populist Reason*, 170.
34. *Horror Film History: A Decade By Decade Guide to the Horror Movie Genre*, http://www.horrorfilmhistory.com/index.php?pageID=ZombieWalk.
35. I am indebted to the StoryTrek design team, Pippin Barr, Robert Biddle, Chris Eaket and Rilla Khaled.
36. Greenspan, "StoryTrek."
37. Dyer-Witheford, "Cognitive Capitalism," 81.
38. Although I refer to the avatar throughout as female, the designers have left its gender indeterminate.
39. Weise, "Rules of Horror," 259.
40. Virno, *Grammar*, 69, 198–9.
41 Ibid., 69, 80.

# Rhetoric Goes Boom(er): Agency, Networks, and Zombies at Play

SCOTT REED

## "You Are Dead — You Will Be Rescued Soon"

Valve Software's *Left 4 Dead* and its 2009 sequel display these funny-yet-perplexing words whenever one of their shotgun-toting players is overwhelmed by the undead hordes. While the games afford players a number of vivid ways to meet their ends amid a widespread zombie apocalypse, each end presages a new beginning, as players can be — after a brief delay —"rescued" by a surviving teammate, though fortunately without any distracting talk about whether the formerly deceased player has now become another in the game's long procession of hollowed-out horrors. This fact, combined with its straightforwardly violent gameplay, may show it to be a rather sophomoric application of the zombie trope, apparently lacking in serious social or cultural relevance. This project, however, seeks to analyze the ways that *Left 4 Dead* (often abbreviated *L4D*) not only represents as a narrative, but also remediates as a videogame the zombie, with an eye towards how the "zombie" has been adopted as a critical figure in posthuman theory in general and in the writings of Slavoj Žižek in particular. Rather than run the risk of subordinating *Left 4 Dead* (and by extension much of modern videogaming) to a critical wasteland where subjects deliberately act in repetitive ways— engaging in action by way of "habit," not conscious, thinking intelligence, as Žižek might have it — this project will approach the game more rhetorically, as a question of how the game produces a complex network of agents and agency. Through that production *Left 4 Dead* suggests what the shape of communication and ethics might be in an era of "gamespace," of a modern world that seems increasingly "empty ... natural, neutral, and without qualities," that is, more like a game.[1]

Does *Left 4 Dead,* in all its playful violence, inscribe its player as an automatic creature of "habit," as Žižek says of the zombie?

> What Hegel says about habits has to be applied to zombies: at the most elementary level of our human identity, we are all zombies, and our "higher" and "free" human activities can only take place insofar as they are founded on the reliable functioning of

219

our zombie-habits: being-a-zombie is a zero-level of humanity, the inhuman/mechanical core of humanity. The shock of encountering a zombie is not the shock of encountering a foreign entity, but the shock of being confronted by the disavowed foundation of our own human-ness..... Habit is thus "depersonalized" willing, a mechanized emotion: once I get habituated to standing, I will it without consciously willing it, since my will is embodied in the habit.[2]

Without belaboring the point, I would align Žižek's notion of "depersonalized willing" with many of the popular stereotypes of gaming that tend to paint players as uncritical, robotic, and inhumane. I mean here to refer to both the slew of well-publicized studies, often emerging from the social sciences,[3] that paint gaming as an engine for encouraging violence and to the increasingly popular trope of videogame "addiction," a phrase which leverages the rhetorical force of "depersonalized willing" into the public sphere. In the popular imaginary, gamers may be imagined as nearly zombies in Žižek's sense, so ensorceled by the solitary and mechanical process of gameplay that they are reduced to a "zero-level of humanity." The role of critique, in such an environment, is to rise above that mere zero level and avoid what Guy Debord calls the "impoverishment, enslavement, and negation of real life."[4] Indeed, that negation is always already a facet of the zombie figure; Sarah Juliet Lauro and Karen Embry remind us that, in both their Voodoo origins and in their decaying and dysfunctional bodies, zombies are "slaves," "represent[ing] the inanimate end to which we are all destined."[5] Like Debord, Kyle W. Bishop and Lauro and Embry read the zombie as a reaction to the emergent actor-network of multinational consumerist capitalism, one that gamers, like the shocked survivors of Romero's *Dawn of the Dead*, reproduce by "habit," unable to see their way past the enslavement of capitalist ideology.[6] Part of my own project, ultimately, is to also consider how *Left 4 Dead*'s use of the zombie might itself offer a playful critique of the very subjective and social "impoverishment" that critics fear.

To achieve this, my project has to consider the role of the gamer as an "actor" amid the wider network of influences conditioned by the game. I'll later be exploring the actor-network theory of Bruno Latour in an effort to suggest the ethical and critical consequences of this approach (particularly in light of *L4D*'s emphasis on multiplayer gameplay), but for the time being I'd like to address the question of the gamer as a rhetorical one, by considering how lines of technology and context, along with the presence of other interested "agents," combine and inform one another. In that sense, my take on *L4D*'s zombies is more rhetorical than literary; rather than ask what the zombies "mean," this project situates those zombies as a means of making sense of the player's rhetorical "agency"—the means through which agents effect symbolic action—and considering how that agency can allow us to make sense of the rhetorical "agent" in question. Part of the dramatistic "pentad" developed by Kenneth Burke, "ratios" are ways of approaching how the elements of a situation sometimes exist in close overlap—in this case, I have noted the rhetorical pressure to read gamers (agents) as functions of their chosen playful medium (agency). Burkean analysis, on the other hand, asks critics to look for the "causal relationships" among those elements in an altogether more dynamic fashion.[7] By considering the multiplicity of forces that shape the "shock" of our encounter with *L4D*'s zombies (that is, by considering more closely what is meant by a gamer's "agency"), we can be in a better position to consider how the game—and others like it—works as more than an "instrument of addiction and sociopathic behavior" ultimately responsible for making their habituated subjects "too dependent on machines and [unable] to connect with human beings," as game theorist Ken McAllister summarizes much of the prevailing discourse around games.[8] Furthermore, while this study is far from the first to investigate linkages between gaming and the zombie trope, this project will hope to do something unusual by considering a wider range of possible interpretations of the zombie. For example, while nearly every essay in Bernard Perron's 2009 collection *Horror Video Games* mentions zombies, only a handful consider any particular value in the trope itself. Laurie N. Taylor points to how the zombie allows for a contextually specific projection of "cultural concerns" onto the enemies in games such as in *Resident Evil 4*,[9] while Matthew Weise considers how zombie based games like *Resident Evil* and *Dead Rising* encourage the player to "comprehend" and "understand" on a more visceral level the isolation of the pro- tagonists.[10] Neither source considers the zombie from a more ideological standpoint, and only one other—Dan Pinchbeck's "Shock, Horror: First-Person Gaming, Horror, and the Art of Ludic Manipulation"—considers the zombie from the standpoint of gameplay, exam- ining how zombies act in terms of a simplified "schema" that precludes any "complicated ecological behavior."[11] Alternately, this project hopes to address this conversation in two ways: first by establishing and considering a more variegated perspective on the ways that games influence the player, and then by considering *Left 4 Dead*'s relative simplicity (as a both a zombie narrative and as an often uncomplicated first-person shooter game) as the conditions from which a distinct configuration of players and game emerge. Similarly, just as Latour enunciates the difference between the view of material technologies as compli- cating "mediators" (as opposed to value-neutral "intermediaries"), this project seeks to view the game itself as an "actor" that, if understood, can help us rewrite our sense of who we are as people and how we engage the world—the very same questions engaged by the zombie *mythos* in the first place, addressed at the level of the "social."[12]

## Playing with Kitsch: Interpreting L4D's Zombies

*Left 4 Dead*'s structure is both simple and multifaceted. In both the original game and its sequel, play begins by depicting the four survivors in an otherwise unpopulated area, which they must traverse in order to escape to safety. Players discover a variety of firearms and improvised explosives along the way to help them fend off waves of zombie antagonists, some of whom are "special" zombies with abilities designed to critically disrupt gameplay. Details about the world of the game are kept deliberately sketchy. Valve's initial promotional video for the game mentions only that the events of the game happen two weeks after the outbreak of an infection, and while western Pennsylvania can be inferred to be the main setting, the game never deliberately acknowledges a particular location for the game's action, nor is there ever any indication of the source of the zombie infection.[13] (Even the game's four protagonists are given names and a few personality quirks—Bill the irascible veteran, Louis the dogged optimist—but no background or sense of how they met one another.) With no sense of their origins or contexts, then, the zombies similarly seem to function primarily at the level of kitsch, but they can also be understood as intentionally constructed ciphers, devoid of meaning in order to divert the game player to other elements of the expe- rience. What their kitschiness should prompt, I believe, is a re-reading of the game, to account for how zombies may affect the game player not as elements of a visual text, but as facets of a system of gameplay.

Indeed, theorists of games (digital and otherwise) have long maintained a conceptual distinction between a game's "narrative" content and what we may call its "ludological" content. Gonzalo Frasca's essay "Simulation versus Narrative" argues that because games "behave like machines or sign-generators," critics must accordingly shift emphasis not to what the game depicts, but rather to the system of rules that the game employs to model certain behaviors:

> "To simulate is to model a (source) system through a different system which maintains to somebody some of the behaviors of the original system." The key term here is "behav-

ior." Simulation does not simply retain the—generally audiovisual—characteristics of the object but it also includes a model of its behaviors. This model reacts to certain stimuli (input data, pushing buttons, joystick movements), according to a set of conditions.[14]

Such a process of simulation is afforded by the ways games involve systems of rules. Similarly, game theorist Ian Bogost uses the term "procedurality" to discuss how games create meaning through the possibilities created by their rules rather than their narrative.[15] To play a game is to inherently interpret and internalize the rules or procedures that govern that game, and to act in a matter consistent with what those rules allow a player to do. In that regard, confronted with the sensational violence of the *Grand Theft Auto* games, Frasca notes how many acts of violence within the game are not required by the game's rules, but are rather merely allowed "within the model" created by the game, as opposed to an action that is intimately tied to the game's ultimate "goals." The eventual "meaning" of a video game is based only on a possible state of the game given the manipulation of various rules. Bogost later approaches these possibilities by suggesting the term "procedural rhetoric" as a way of thinking about how games uses processes persuasively, "just as verbal rhetoric is the practice of using words persuasively."[16] Shifting the focus of game criticism from narrative or diegetic content to the rules/procedures used to create "possibility spaces" is not just to account for the rules that "model" a system, but rather to account for how a game's rules make implicit arguments about the models themselves. Bogost uses the example of the *Animal Crossing* series, which make it possible for players to invest themselves in buying ever larger homes and furniture. These games are less interesting for their cute and fuzzy visual aesthetic than for the ways the parameters of the gameplay embody "arguments about how social, cultural, and political processes work"—in this case, in the all-too-familiar manner of the capitalistic debt cycle.[17] In this particular situation, then, I'd like to turn to the ludological layers of *Left 4 Dead,* to better understand how its procedural possibilities (or in this case, occasional *lack* of possibilities) are rhetorical structures, guiding the player's encounter with the horrifying zombie Other.

Fortunately, *Left 4 Dead*'s gameplay is elegant in its simplicity. Players are given a handful of firearm choices and are instructed to traverse the space between their starting point and the nearest available "safe house," fending off attacks from zombies as they go. Lone zombies litter the landscape, and most react only sluggishly to the presence of players, if at all; at other times, entire waves of zombies race towards the players, requiring hails of gunfire (or improvised explosive devices) to contain them. On that level, the game's procedural rhetoric is one of stark simplicity: *L4D* argues that it's a good idea to shoot zombies. There's ultimately no gameplay alternative. Escape to safety from the undead hordes, or die trying. The game's "possibility space" creates what game theorist Jesper Juul refers to as a linear "game of progression" (as opposed to a more multilinear "game of emergence")[18] and affords only the annihilation of the undead, and the preservation of the small "community" of characters around the player—including, frequently, other players in co-op mode.[19] To the extent that the game might seem to privilege the "progression" game style, it may seem like "negative dialectic" at its absolute worst, the game's progress being predicated on the violent negation of zombie targets in view, with victory only possible through those means.[20] Such a reading has the advantage of accounting for much of the game's fun: with little narrative baggage to complicate matters, the players can focus on either negating the zombie by violence or by avoidance.

Predictably enough, this is a reading of the game's straightforward action that can be slightly nuanced, in this case by investigating the latter option offered above. Players might be engaging in a raw negative dialectic of production by negation, but *Left 4 Dead* seems to almost compliment the dialectic of its gameplay by removing the negativity from what most would consider the ultimate negative consequence: death itself. In most video games, the "death" of a player's avatar is rarely an absolute end-condition, easily remedied by either having another "life" available (e.g., *Super Mario Bros.* starts the player with three "lives," with extras available) or by simply asking the player to shovel in another quarter. *Left 4 Dead* is little different in that regard, but notable in that rather than simply allowing for death as a consequence of gameplay, it appears to actively tease it. In its most interesting moments, the game "kills" the player not on a narrative level, but on a ludic level — removing his or her control from the game itself, and foisting it onto another agent, either another (enemy) player or a CPU controlled teammate. (I'll return later to how the game presents player death at the narrative level.)

If one layer of *L4D*'s ludology is the simplistic "run and gun" style of gameplay with which the player responds to the zombie swarms around them, then a whole other layer of play emerges from the game's cadre of "special zombies." Instead of your average half-decomposed shambler, "special zombies" appear at random intervals in each level and attack in ways that disrupt the game's relative simplicity. The first *Left 4 Dead* game featured three special zombie types — the Hunter, the Smoker, and the Boomer — each with distinct abilities, while *Left 4 Dead 2* added three others. Without enumerating the minute differences between the different classes, these special zombies (with only one exception)[21] affect gameplay in the same fundamental matter: by suspending it. Whether pounced on by a screeching Hunter or blinded by a Boomer, the player's encounter with the zombie Other can be chiefly characterized by moments that frustrate the main flow of gameplay, as suspension in the player's *agency*. The player can't move and can't take any actions to shake off the offending zombie, becoming — just as in the "death" scenario mentioned above — momentarily dependent on the actions of another real or virtual player to continue play. Even more insultingly, a quick shift in the visual perspective, effected by the "suspension," forces the player to view him or herself in the prone position — a momentary dramatization of the very "depersonalized willing" of which Žižek speaks.

One way of interpreting this suspension could very well be to skip over it, seeing as how control is ultimately restored to the player, so that the "run and gun" gameplay can continue. This would produce, I believe, an equally valid reading from a ludological point of view. From a more rhetorical standpoint, however, the moment can also be read not just as a loss of player agency, but as shifting the "ratio" that governs the player's sense of self. Strangely, we stand to learn more about the rhetorical situation of *Left 4 Dead* by interrogating not just the limited "argument" it makes, but instead considering the wider ways that the player's actions are not just variously encouraged or frustrated, but also how such actions take on meaning through the network of ideologies and allegories that the zombie trope brings to bear.

## *What Does It Mean When Agency Goes Boom(er)?*

In this broader sense, the suspension of play fashions a potentially pernicious rhetorical statement. Overwhelming the player with hordes of zombies, the game frustrates even the limited terms of its own "argument." Phrased in terms of Kenneth Burke's notion of rhetorical ratios — that aspects of a rhetorical situation overlap, and therefore inform others — the limited agency of the zombie-hunting player already recapitulates a rhetorical agent incapable of "reading" the zombie plague as one would a George Romero film. The player, in that regard, is always already operating within the game at a level scarcely indistinguishable from mere "habit," the level of action most characteristic of Žižek's zombie. (And, it could be ironically noted, the level of action most critical for success in the fast-paced first-person shooter genre of games, which includes this one.) Even worse: whereas the viewer of the zombie film has the freedom of agency to read and interpret the onscreen action, *Left 4 Dead*'s zombies even more radically shut down the subject position of the player by potentially shutting down the limited means the player has for interacting with the game-world. To put it differently: the movie watcher's agency is unaffected by the presence of zombies onscreen, though the same cannot be said of the game player's. Devoid of agency, the player is now a void incapable of viewing the world,[22] much less acting on it. This may be Guy Debord's ultimate nightmare of the subject's zombification, played out in ludological terms: "In a society where no one can any longer be recognized by others, each individual becomes incapable of recognizing his own reality. Ideology is at home; separation has built its own world."[23] Debord's passage links the zombification of the individual to the eventual dissolution of the social. In an environment where, as Žižek paraphrases Lacan, conscious identity takes on the status of an ideologically shaped *thing*, individuals lose the capacity to recognize one another as such. Cheekily enough under such circumstances, as Žižek quotes Daniel Dennett, "some of your best friends may be zombies," despite the way that the game threads the presence of others—through both narrative and multiplayer gameplay levels—into its experience.[24] Indeed, in the moments when *Left 4 Dead* collapses the player's already-fragile sense of agency within the game, the player himself is already undead: "fixed" in both a literal and figurative sense, fully "at home" as a zombie-subject, and thereby incapable of interacting with the world beyond. At first glance this particular moment of suspension of agency might read as an allegory for the world of video gaming in general, in which players regularly exchange their time and energy for the "habit" and ideological separation afforded by gameplay. (Indeed, Johan Huizinga's oft-cited figure of the "magic circle" created by play celebrates how play occurs in realms separate from the "real world.") In that limited respect, *Left 4 Dead* can be read—again, ludologically, as its flimsy narrative offers little else to work with—as less of a zombie-text (in the sense we might associate with zombie films) and more of a zombie-factory, an interface that dramatizes what I can only think to call a process of self dis-invention: the willing and participatory divesting of non-mediated identity.

This might be a tempting reading, were *Left 4 Dead* not so incredibly eager to play off its layers of rhetorical frustration. The game does, after all, not only take certain structural and narrative cues from the tradition of zombie cinema before it,[25] but also demonstrates a reflexive awareness of its own metaphorical weight. Perhaps this can be most clearly seen in the moment after a player, rendered blind or immobile by the horde, is killed in action. This "mortality," however, is little more than the same suspension of agency, rendered in different—and more hilariously—self-aware terms. The player pounced by the hunter can be revived and healed by teammates, and so can the "killed" player be eventually "revived" in the game world after a delay of a few minutes. The aforementioned text—"You Are Dead. You Will Be Revived Soon"—promises a return to the (limited) agency the player had been enjoying moments before, while straightforwardly acknowledging the player's position as a frustrated un-"dead" zombie subject. Is this gaming nihilism run cheekily amok? Or in this moment of self-referentiality, does *Left 4 Dead*'s deployment of the zombie trope suggest another dimension of the rhetorical situation in which gamers find themselves? In suggesting a more generous reading, the objective isn't to chart some evolution in the zombie trope *per se*, but rather to use its self-referentiality here as a lens for accounting for the rhetorical situation of gaming in ways that exceed what a reading based on "procedural rhetoric" might reveal.

Taking the momentary suspension of individual agency as a ludological jumping off point, it may become possible to reinterpret *Left 4 Dead*'s zombies as more than allegorical stand-ins for the "negation" that Žižek and Debord seem to fear. Read from the procedural level, the suspension and deferment of the game's action can be read "allegorithmically," that is, in such a way that we can say the rules of the game make an allegorical statement about the context in which those rules occur. Used frequently in McKenzie Wark's *Gamer Theory,* and drawn from the work of Alexander Galloway, "allegorithmic" analysis of games is a method of investigating how games can, as individual texts, speak to the larger structures of "gamespace," a way of thinking of all spaces— public and private, real and virtual — as increasingly game-like. In an age of ubiquitous digitality characterized by the ascendant ethos of multinational capitalism, "life appears as a vast accumulation of commodities and spectacles, of things wrapped in images and images sold as things."[26] Wark's desire to approach games this way takes no shortage of inspiration from Guy Debord's emphasis on the relationship between the spectacle and the negation of the subject; for Wark, games are not the result, but the "always-already" anchoring point, of life in a world of ubiquitous digitality. In gamespace, we belong to the world "as a gamer to a game."[27] In *Left 4 Dead*'s moments of foreclosure upon itself, it may be more interesting in this regard to push beyond inaction as merely a delay, and to re-approach it as a way of thinking about how modern gaming environments extend their reach to include other "actors." It's not merely that the player pounced by a zombie belongs to their real world as a suspended and inactive agent (that is, in the same way they "belong" to *L4D*), but also that — in the bargain — they are connected to other agents who are playing out the same situation. In these moments, the other players— real or virtual — must act in a manner that extends their agency over the interrupted agency of the suspended/dead player. (Indeed, the cheeky "You Are Dead" message displays to players *only* in situations where other human players can rescue them.) This is truly an "emergent" condition of its gameplay, in precisely the sense that Juul writes of other action games like *Counter-Strike*. In such games, play may be "oriented" around the presence of others, without any rules necessarily requiring such team play.[28] In this sense, a game like *Left 4 Dead* can not only prompt a rhetorical reading at the level of the text, but can also open up a more social and, as Wark argues, allegorical reading. The game's stubborn insistence on the presence (however virtual) of others is a gesture outside the strict confines of the game (of progression); like any good zombie story, its play is more useful and potent at the socio-cultural level. As in the genre films which inspired it, the zombie here might motivate an interest in which "the thin artifice of character, setting, and incident becomes vitalized by our awareness of the real people behind it," of the actors, or in this case by a function of their ludic closeness, the other players "playing" in front of our eyes.[29]

If being momentarily frustrated by the zombie shows the negation of the individual subject, the allegorical (or allegorithmic, since we are speaking at the level of digital rules) re-reading of the moment might also "count" the presence of other players in the consideration of what *Left 4 Dead* means as a game. We might, in this revitalized rhetorical approach, make something productive out of the kitschy ciphers that the game seems to offer up as so much cannon fodder. They may serve, it seems, as invitations to play the game — to belong to gamespace — as participants in an overlapping heterogeneous "assembly." Bruno Latour pitches his actor-network theory precisely at this point, declaring the "social" itself as a cipher of a term that occludes the altogether more "uncertain, fragile, controversial, and ever-shifting" process in which complex networks of agents and agencies form.[30] In that regard, the reading I would ultimately propose here is not that the "social" overlapping of agencies in *L4D* redeems the player from the position of the unconscious, habitual zombie, but rather that through its gameplay it reveals the functioning of the zombie at a different level. While *L4D*'s narrative content may as well be proposing a bland variation on the classic interpellation strategy — daring the viewer to assume the role of the hollowed out subject — the true horror manifested at the level of play is not that of the overtaken individual, but of the distributed, incomplete, overtaken "swarm" that seems to characterize the emergence of a posthuman subjectivity.[31] Just as Lauro and Embry argue that the fear of the zombie is primarily a kind of epistemic loathing directed at the zombie's "collapsed" status (neither alive nor dead and held in irreconcilable tension between the two), so too does the game player in *L4D* encounter a trope of their own status as participants in wider social assemblies. Just as in Latour's sociology of associations, the "social" other cannot be directly known, but only grasped partially, other *othered* agents can only be grasped here through gaps in the individual player's agency. The gap in agency opened up by the zombie is effectively an allegory for Latour's awareness that social groups and conditions are formed not through proximity or by some essential substance, but are rather "overtaken": that is, to re-include both Burke and Juul, that they emerge through complex networks of action, agents, and agency and are for that very reason "under-determined."[32]

Furthermore, we might argue through Latour's actor-network theory that part of the *L4D*'s effect is its larger awareness of how actions are necessarily "incomplete," in the sense proposed by Kenneth Burke that human actions represent a certain ratio of rhetorical elements (act, agent, scene, purpose, agency) always occurring in mixture. Total acts produce "mutual conformity" in rhetorical elements, whereas real, incomplete actions produce situational, contingent instabilities.[33] These instabilities, expressed as "ratios" between rhetorical elements, are "principles of selectivity" rather than "causal relationships."[34] Gaming, by its very digital nature, is incapable of providing for a "total" action. Though game rules are strict (doubly so in the case of digital games, where as Lawrence Lessig says, "code is law"), the entire purpose of the game is to open up a "possibility space," room for players to explore "principles of selectivity" in the balancing and rebalancing of their roles as an agent. More so than ever, as *L4D*'s "procedural rhetoric" seems to argue, we may find ourselves conceptualizing our action not in terms of "habit" but in Latour's more surprising terms: "Action is not done under the full control of consciousness; action should rather be felt as a node, a knot, and a conglomerate of many surprising sets of agencies."[35] Gameplay is already the site of such a node, one that finds its dark expression in the way *L4D*'s players are "other-taken" at every turn. What remains for this discussion is to consider the ethical ramifications of this zombie within the "actor-network" presaged by gaming environments.

## Towards Ethical Zombies

Contra Debord, we may be at the beginning of a moment less where subjects are absolutely incapable of recognizing each other, but rather one where that process of recognition is overtaken by the forces of narrative habit and procedural rule. Instead of reading *Left 4 Dead* as merely a metacommentary on the techno-zombification of the subject, its more nuanced repositioning of the individual player *vis-à-vis* the player's sense of agency reflects a greater anxiety over communication in the age of a "distributed society."[36] Citing "distance" as a controlling trope in postmodern ethics, Roger Silverstone cites Zygmunt Bauman's *Postmodern Ethics* in an attempt to come to terms with the same fundamental complaint that undergirds Debord's assault on the society of the spectacle — the virtualization of social relationships:

> If postmodernity is a retreat from the blind alleys into which radically pursued ambitions of modernity have led, a postmodern ethics would be one that readmits the Other as neighbor, as the close-to-hand-*and*-mind, into the hard core of the moral self ... an

ethics that recasts the Other as the crucial character in the process through which the moral self comes into its own.[37]

Taken at face value, then, *Left 4 Dead*'s distribution of agency, in which players willingly submit to having themselves interrupted by the Other, seems like an ethical dead end. The zombie of *L4D* is not recast as "a crucial character" in the budding of a more moral self; they are still narrative and ludic ciphers. On the other hand, Silverstone argues that *L4D*'s sort of cooperative online play exposes players to a pair of "ambiguities." While the game narratively plays on the trope of characters in close physical proximity dealing with vast social distances,[38] its gameplay promotes the opposite: it creates a situation of physical distance in an environment of narratively promoted social closeness.[39] Phrased in terms more universal to online communication (yet relevant to understanding *L4D*'s gameplay), the latter ambiguity "comes from not knowing how to make sense of the other, but also from not knowing how to react in relation to the other: how to be, how to care, how to take responsibility."[40] This ambiguity expresses the peculiar gap, the Burkean ratio, leveraged open by *Left 4 Dead*: the gap that frustrates the gamer's will to engage the gamespace as an independent solipsistic agent. Indeed, Latour writes that "distance" is one of the conditions that can prompt sociologists of associations to locate such ratios in flux, where objects— such as gaming systems—can be seen not just as neutral intermediaries between parties, but rather as complex rhetorical mediators.[41]

Even if gaming might seem to figure gamers as solitary agents, playing alone in dark basements or on living room couches, the technological network the game still creates— however "ambiguously"— an atmosphere of social closeness. *Left 4 Dead*, in that regard, functions as an engine for solving that social ambiguity under limited terms of engagement by giving players a highly constrained vocabulary of gestures with which to resist their zombification at the hands of the radical (digital) Other. Considering online communication in games— across languages, dealing with technical issues, and acquiring the lingo particular to complicated online games like *World of Warcraft* and *Final Fantasy XI*— Mia Consalvo concludes that "games allow players to create ... meanings and contexts[,] communities and cultures, and discover emergent aspects of gameplay," which we might read as a variation on Silverstone's urging to "make sense of the other."[42] Rather than take the suspension of play in *Left 4 Dead* as a kind of "noise," Consalvo's hope would be to "see noise as a regular part of gameplay," and to assume that players "can workaround or deal with that limitation."[43]

Indeed, whereas the traditional zombie narrative may provoke a choice between the "slave" (of ideology, the spectacle, and/or the multinational corporation) and the posthuman "swarm" mentality, *Left 4 Dead*'s play may draw attention to a middle ground. Clearly, its suspension of agency frustrates its ability to reinstall an integral, fully "humanistic" agent at the center of the action, as Bartlett and Byers critique in the "pomophobic" *Matrix* trilogy.[44] Whereas Keanu Reeves's Neo reacts to the news that he is a "slave" in a technologized matrix of authority by developing the mystical ability to frustrate and supersede that control, *Left 4 Dead*'s players find themselves encouraged to work with others to "deal with that limitation." Conversely, rather than being returned to the "undifferentiated and dead position" that Debord associates with spectacle, players may, as Teresa Goddu writes of Romero's project in *Night of the Living Dead*, "recontain" that threatening position by learning— even under limited terms of engagement —"how to react in relation to the other."[45]

Unfortunately, a survey of the popular landscape reveals little reason for encouragement in this regard. Online gaming (and gamers) is often associated with some of the most extreme excesses in unethical behavior, particularly with regards to hateful speech. (This is a major reason why my analysis here has opted to not consider the means, such as text messaging and voice chat channels, through which *L4D* players may interact during play.) My argument here should not lead anyone to conclude that these associations between narrative, gameplay, and subjectivity represent any popular drive towards a more ethical subject. In revealing the sites of ongoing tensions over what constitutes the subjectivity of the player, though, I argue that the game, at least in its cooperative multiplayer mode, *dramatizes* the infra-thin possibility that, through a gamespace of rules, we may become *more* human.[46] This possibility not only resonates with the tradition of zombie films, in which zombies are so often the metaphorical expression of a deeper "enemy within" ourselves, but reflects a rhetorical pressure native to the game medium: the way in which fast and twitchy gameplay (agency) positions the gameplayer as another "depersonalized," neither-alive-nor-dead zombie.[47]

As Žižek writers in *Organs Without Bodies,* "We become 'humans' when we get caught into a closed, self-propelling loop of repeating the same gesture and finding *satisfaction* in it."[48] The term "human" appears here in almost sarcastic scare quotes, only slightly elevated over the "zombie" of raw habit, but what matters is the uniquely human goal of the "elevation" of mere satisfaction into *jouissance,* rendered also by Žižek in terms of memes and *sinthomes,* of "obscene" fragments that exceed the "gesture" and can't be immediately accounted for by it.[49] Those very obscene fragments might, if accounted for in the wider actor-network and if played properly and generously, show scholars and gameplayers some of the unique and troubling ways that Being is now configured: not as a zombie to be loathed and destroyed, but as a possible occasion for encountering and reviving our fellow game-players.

## Notes

1. McKenzie Wark, *Gamer Theory* (Cambridge: Harvard University Press, 2007), 9.
2. Slavoj Žižek, "Madness and Habit in German Idealism: Discipline between the Two Freedoms—Part 1," accessed July 10, 2010, http://www.lacan.com/zizdazedandconfused.html.
3. Cf. Kristine L. Nowak, Marina Krcmar, and Kirstie M. Farrar, "The Causes and Consequences of Presence: Considering the Influence of Violent Video Games on Presence and Aggression," *Presence: Teleoperators & Virtual Environments* 17, no. 3 (June 2008): 256–268, accessed September 14, 2010, *Academic Search Complete,* EBSCO*host;* Craig Anderson, *Violent Video Game Effects on Children and Adolescents: Theory, Research, and Public Policy* (Oxford: Oxford University Press, 2007); Douglas Gentile, ed., *Media Violence and Children: A Complete Guide for Parents and Professionals* (Westport, CT: Praeger, 2003).
4. Guy Debord, *The Society of the Spectacle,* trans. Ken Knabb, accessed July 10, 2010, http://en.wikisource.org/wiki/The_Society_of_the_Spectacle. The online version of Debord's *Society of the Spectacle* preserves the thesis numbering model used in most print versions of the same. I'll use that numbering model here to cite references to the work.
5. Sarah Juliet Lauro and Karen Embry, "A Zombie Manifesto: The Nonhuman Condition in the Era of Advanced Capitalism," *boundary 2* 35, no. 1 (Spring 2008): 90.
6. Kyle William Bishop, "The Idle Proletariat: *Dawn of the Dead,* Consumer Ideology, and the Loss of Productive Labor," *The Journal of Popular Culture* 43, no. 2 (2010): 240.
7. Kenneth Burke, *A Grammar of Motives* (New York: Prentice Hall, 1945), 18.
8. Ken McAllister, *Game Work: Language, Power, and Computer Game Culture* (Tuscaloosa: University of Alabama Press, 2004), 72.
9. Laurie N. Taylor, "Gothic Bloodlines in Survival Horror Gaming," in *Horror Video Games,* ed. Bernard Perron (Jefferson, NC: McFarland, 2009), 57.
10. Matthew Weise, "The Rules of Horror: Procedural Adaptation in *Clock Tower, Resident Evil,* and *Dead Rising,*" in *Horror Video Games,* ed. Bernard Perron (Jefferson, NC: McFarland, 2009), 260.
11. Dan Pinchbeck. "Shock, Horror: First-Person Gaming, Horror, and the Art of Ludic Manipulation," in *Horror Video Games,* ed. Bernard Perron (Jefferson, NC: McFarland, 2009), 86–7.
12. Bruno Latour, *Reassembling the Social: An Introduction to Actor-Network Theory* (Oxford: Oxford University Press, 2005), 39.
13. Two clues offer insight as to *Left 4 Dead*'s geography. One level features the prominent location "Mercy

Hospital," the name of a hospital in Pittsburgh, PA, while another level "Blood Harvest" begins with the characters at a campsite in the Allegheny National Forest in northwestern Pennsylvania. Similarly, while the game only indicates that some "infection" is to blame for the zombie outbreak, no precise etiology is ever suggested for it. (The sequel includes the involvement of the military and a FEMA-like group called CEDA, throwing attention to the measures they are taking to contain the outbreak, but no narrative thread expresses any sort of conspiratorial involvement, in contrast to the evil corporate presence in the *Resident Evil* series.)

14. Gonzalo Frasca, "Simulation versus Narrative: Introduction to Ludology," in *The Video Game Theory Reader,* ed. Mark JP Wolf and Bernard Perron (New York: Routledge, 2003), 228.

15. Ian Bogost, "The Rhetoric of Video Games," in *The Ecology of Games: Connecting Youth, Games, and Learning,* ed. Katie Salen (Cambridge: MIT Press, 2008), 122.

16. Ibid., 125.

17. Ibid., 126.

18. This tension between linearity and multilinearity can play out in multiple forms. While *Left 4 Dead* features a powerful AI system (nicknamed "The Director") that often reshapes elements of the landscape and varies many of the patterns in which zombies attack — thereby ensuring that the play experience is slightly different each time around — the overall efficacy of "The Director" is insufficient, in my opinion, to recharacterize the game as a game of emergence. While slight alterations in the layout of a level provide momentary gestures away from linearity, the end goal is always fixed, as are a number of structured "choke point" events in certain levels. As one reviewer of this essay noted, "You are essentially funneled down a corridor" in most of the game's levels, even if minute variations here and there keep the game from becoming stale.

19. Jesper Juul, *Half-Real: Video Games Between Real Rules and Fictional Worlds* (Cambridge: MIT Press, 2005), 82.

20. Lauro and Embry take the zombie as demonstrating the insufficiency of "negative dialectic," in that the zombie "proposes no third term reconciling ... the lacuna between life and death. The zombie is opposition held irrevocably in tension" (94).

21. The "Spitter" zombie introduced in *Left 4 Dead 2* does not disrupt gameplay, preferring instead to harry the players from afar, forcing them to scramble away from her damaging attack. The recurring "Tank" from both games is also an exception, but since it appears less frequently in the game, I won't discuss it here. A more borderline case is that of the "Boomer," who attacks players by occluding their vision and making them targets for any nearby zombies. (I'll spare the reader the more scatological details.) Though gameplay itself is never suspended, the total occlusion of the visual field, often combined by the player being paralyzed by a surge of zombies, has the same practical effect: the player is prevented from any intentionally constructed action.

22. Visually, the player interrupted by the zombie either has their perspective completely occluded (as in the case of the Boomer), or lost altogether — being tangled by a Smoker, for instance, shifts the perspective from first person to third person. In place of seeing the game world, the player is forced to helplessly and voyeuristically watch herself as her life meter dwindles to zero while being gruesomely mangled.

23. Debord, 217.

24. Slavoj Žižek, *Organs Without Bodies: Deleuze and Consequences* (New York: Routledge, 2004), 135.

25. Among some of these cues are the game's environments, which are devoid of other living people — a definite nod to films like *28 Days Later* and *The Omega Man*, which situate their protagonists in abandoned cities (London and New York, respectively).

26. Wark, 6.

27. Ibid., 15.

28. Juul, 89–91.

29. Gary Hentzi, "Little Cinema of Horrors," *Film Quarterly* 46, no. 3 (Spring 1993): 26.

30. Latour, 28.

31. Lauro & Embry, 106.

32. Latour, 45.

33. Burke, 20.

34. Ibid., 19.

35. Latour, 44.

36. Terje Rasmussen, "On Distributed Society: The Internet as a Guide to a Sociological Understanding of Communication," in *Digital Media Revisited,* eds. Gunnar Liestøl, Andrew Morrison, Terje Rasmussen (Cambridge: MIT Press, 2004), 462.

37. Cf. Roger Silverstone, "Proper Distance: Towards an Ethics for Cyberspace," in *Digital Media Revisited,* ed. Gunnar Liestøl, Andrew Morrison, and Terje Rasmussen (Cambridge: MIT Press, 2004), 474.

38. Teresa Goddu notes as much when pointing out how Romero's *Night of the Living Dead* satirizes its protagonist's death. Though Ben hunkers down in the same farmhouse as the other survivors, the film ultimately relegates him "to the undifferentiated and dead position that the movie [had] resisted associating with him" (135). Similarly, Bishop notes how *Dawn of the Dead*'s survivors enjoy close physical proximity, which allows the movie to express the wider social gaps created by the "dehumanizing effects of late capitalism" (246).

39. Silverstone, 478.

40. Ibid., 479.

41. Latour, 80.

42. Mia Consalvo, "Lag, Language, and Lingo: Theorizing Noise in Online Game Spaces," in *The Video Game Theory Reader 2,* ed. Bernard Perron and Mark JP Wolf (New York: Routledge, 2009), 310.

43. Ibid.

44. Karen Bartlett and Thomas B. Byers, "Back to the Future: The Humanistic 'Matrix,'" *Cultural Critique* 53 (Winter 2003): 30.

45. Theresa A. Goddu, "Vampire Gothic," *American Literary History* 11, no. 1 (Spring 1999): 135.

46. I limit my claim at the end of the article by restricting my comments to *Left 4 Dead*'s multiplayer "Campaign" mode. In the interest of focusing on one particular set of gameplay mechanics, I have not considered another of *Left 4 Dead*'s gameplay types: Versus mode, in which teams of human players control the Special Infected zombies who menace them in the normal Campaign mode. This omission is largely intentional on my own part, as I believe the mode renders the actor-network of the game in largely competitive terms. To explore the differing rhetorical ecologies of competition and cooperation would, in this space, be an unproductive distraction from the business of establishing one element of *L4D*'s "play" on the zombie.

47. Playfully enough, this essay may close by considering how *Left 4 Dead* and its sequel also give players the ability to become zombies themselves. The games' "Versus" mode pits a team of "human" players against a team of fragile, yet continually respawning zombies. The liminal and undead state of the game player finds its ultimate sarcastic expression. Or, again, as Debord puts it: "Ideology is at home; separation has built its own world" (217).

48. Žižek, *Organs Without Bodies,* 142, emphasis added.

49. Ibid., 143.

# The National Strategy for Zombie Containment: Myth Meets Activism in Post-9/11 America

## CHRISTOPHER ZEALAND

An insurrection, whatever may be its immediate cause, eventually endangers all government. Regard to the public peace, if not to the rights of the Union, would engage the citizens to whom the contagion had not communicated itself to oppose the insurgents; and if the government should be found in practice conducive to the prosperity and felicity of the people, it were irrational to believe that they would be disinclined to its support.

— Federalist No. 28 (Alexander Hamilton)

## *Prologue*

*Shit's really hitting the fan.*[1]

On the morning of September 11, 2001, I stood on the Brooklyn Heights Promenade watching the fires improbably raging atop the Twin Towers of the World Trade Center. Suddenly, the improbable became the unthinkable. Tower Two disappeared in a preposterous, cascading collapse, unleashing a cloud of debris that enveloped downtown Manhattan. Realizing my sister was across the East River somewhere beneath that cloud, I ran toward the Brooklyn Bridge. There I was greeted by a scene reminiscent of Lucio Fulci's *Zombie*,[2] as dazed, bloodied masses streamed across the iconic span.

My American upbringing in the 1970s and '80s had spared me, until then, the personal experience of mass calamity and loss of life. As a devotee of the zombie genre, however, and particularly the works of George A. Romero, I had witnessed the cinematic portrayal of many horrors, as well as the folly that preceded them and that followed in their wake. Among the many impressions 9/11 left with me was how strangely familiar catastrophe seemed, although for me it was unprecedented. This déjà vu recurred in the months and years that followed, as America struggled to reconcile its constitutional ideals with an unaccustomed sense of its own vulnerability.

231

## Introduction

> *This isn't just a passing thing.... It, it's not like just a wind passing through. We've got to do something, and fast.*[3]

Employing concepts from the law and film school of jurisprudence, this essay explores the intersection of George A. Romero's *Dead* trilogy,[4] George W. Bush's 2002 *National Strategy for Homeland Security,*[5] and Zombie Squad, a St. Louis-based survivalist organization. A defining feature of the Bush *Strategy* is that ordinary citizens, through vigilance and personal preparedness, will secure the home front in America's "war on terrorism."[6] Law and film theory, meanwhile, suggests that how citizens see their role in this effort is likely to have been influenced by their cinematic conditioning. Romero's films, which depict cataclysmic events that threaten modern civilization and mock its very foundations, broadcast particularly powerful messages about citizen survival in times of crisis. These films can both instill in their viewers a sense of urgency about disaster preparedness and shape how they respond to that urgency. In the case of Zombie Squad, fans of the zombie genre have used its familiar tropes to promote volunteerism and self-reliance and as lessons in preparing themselves to face the worst.

The juxtaposition of the *Dead* trilogy, Bush's Homeland Security doctrine, and Zombie Squad thus reveals a paradox. Romero's movies, which are typically interpreted as anti-establishment and which depict government as inept and untrustworthy,[7] have nevertheless encouraged in Zombie Squad the very sort of grassroots activism advocated by the Bush administration. While the government's efforts to recruit volunteers have floundered, Zombie Squad has flourished. George A. Romero has therefore succeeded where George W. Bush has not by inspiring, however unwittingly, a new generation of homeland security foot soldiers. This underscores an important corollary of law and film theory: that movies, like other legal texts, are susceptible to diverse readings and may have far-reaching implications unrelated to their original intent.

## Law and Film: Finding Meaning in Narrative and Images

> *Well ... the television said that's the right thing to do.*[8]

Law and film is the vanguard of the law and culture movement, which seeks to understand legal and political systems by examining how they are portrayed and reflected in cultural artifacts.[9] It treats movies as legal texts worthy of study in their own right, whether or not they are overtly concerned with law or lawyers.[10] "Movies not only entertain," writes one law and film scholar, "they instruct. Films influence our interpretation of a new event's significance and suggest our appropriate responses."[11]

Thus, as lawyers and law students glean the rudiments of their field through case histories of real people and their disputes, law and film theorists believe that society at large similarly absorbs meaning and direction through the narratives, conflicts, and characters of cinema. Students of both idioms, however, often find that their "texts" raise more questions than they resolve and challenge their interpreters to draw on their own reasoning, experience, and instincts for answers. Indeed, an overarching theme of the zombie movie — one reflected both in its leading auteur and those he has inspired to action — is resisting the forced conformity of the oblivious masses through resolute personal action.

## Bootstraps for the Psyche: The Early Work of George A. Romero

> *You can forget pitching an audience the moral bullshit they want to hear!*[12]

In 1968, George A. Romero, a college-dropout[13] and Pittsburgh filmmaker who had previously made his living producing television commercials,[14] changed the world of horror movie-making and fashioned an authentic and enduring American myth.[15] By merging concepts from Richard A. Matheson's apocalyptic plague tale *I Am Legend* with reanimated corpses from Afro-Caribbean lore, Romero essentially created the flesh-eating zombie.[16] The defining characteristics of the Romero zombie emerge in a three movie cycle: *Night of the Living Dead, Dawn of the Dead,* and *Day of the Dead.* Each of these films is recognized as a horror classic, and Romero is now revered as much for the social commentary that underlies his work as for his skill as a filmmaker.[17]

The proto-zombies in Romero's early films are the recently dead reanimated by a force that is never conclusively explained.[18] Once reanimated, they possess only the most elementary awareness, intelligence, and recall. The sole focus of their existence is an inexplicable urge to devour the living.

Physically, Romero zombies are slow and inept. They are not especially strong but are unhampered by pain or exhaustion. Some are able to use basic tools (rocks, bludgeons, the occasional gardening trowel), but they appear incapable of communicating or strategizing. Their most formidable skill is their ability to locate the living, who they will pursue ceaselessly and en masse until they overwhelm all resistance and claw, tear, and bite their prey to pieces.

Romero zombies decompose more slowly than cadavers and can remain viable for years after reanimation. The only way to "kill" one is by destroying its brain, severing its head, or incinerating it. As long as the brain remains intact and attached to the spinal cord, the zombie, however battered, remains a threat.

The condition is highly contagious; humans who are bitten but not consumed will become ill, die, and reanimate.[19] The zombies display no recognition of former friends or loved ones, and their compulsion to kill is seemingly beyond their control. At times, Romero zombies can even seem sympathetic in their wretchedness. Yet humans and zombies cannot harmoniously coexist. Humans, to survive, must destroy them.

Romero zombies are not scary because they are efficient killers, they are scary because all they want to do is eat people alive, and they will not stop until they do. They are remorseless, ceaseless, indefatigable hunters. Sooner or later a human has to sleep. Sooner or later a human will make a mistake. Sooner or later a human's morale will waver. Sooner or later a human will run out of ammunition. When any of these things happen, the zombies will be there, slowly, inexorably closing in on their prey. Humans can outgun the zombies, but they cannot outlast them. Humanity's only hope, then, is to band together and neutralize the menace before it reaches critical mass. Defeating the zombie hordes is thus as much a matter of psychology and will as it is a matter of tactics and firepower.

The attitudes and themes expressed in the *Dead* trilogy and its eponymous creatures are reflective of both the times in which the movies were made and the style of production that Romero, of necessity, employed. Romero himself has described his early work as "guerilla filmmaking,"[20] a low-budget, grassroots insurgency waged with thrift shop props, volunteer extras, and contributors who invested their own savings.[21] Laboring under meager budgets[22] and often with the indifference or disapproval of contemporary critics,[23] Romero was nevertheless fiercely protective of his artistic vision, which refused to pander to sentimentality and which portrayed violence with stark realism. Romero explains of *Night:* "It was 1968, man. Everybody had a 'message.' Maybe it crept in. I was just making a horror film, and I think the anger and the attitude and all that's there is just there because it was 1968."[24]

Tom Savini, who would become famous as Romero's makeup artist in *Dawn,* had been a combat photographer during the Vietnam War and judged his own work by its fidelity to the carnage he had seen in the field.[25] Among his props in *Dawn* were shrimp dip, apple cores, and blood-filled condoms for an exploding head effect and pig intestines from a local slaughterhouse for zombie feeding scenes.[26] Because of Romero's refusal to compromise on the depiction of violence in the *Dead* films, the latter two were exhibited without Motion Picture Association of America ratings (these ratings did not exist at the time of *Night's* initial run).[27] As a result, they were shunned by most advertisers and theatres upon their release and received only limited distribution.[28]

Nevertheless, the *Dead* films have had a profound influence on many who have seen them, from academics who continue to analyze them, to filmmakers who continue to imitate them, to a generation of movie-goers whose sense of security and complacency was violently shaken by the films' unsparing characterizations of society and its institutions in collapse. Roger Ebert's outraged review from an early screening of *Night* describes its impact on a group of unsuspecting young matinee-goers: "I felt real terror in that neighborhood theater last Saturday afternoon. I saw kids who had no resources they could draw upon to protect themselves from the dread and fear they felt."[29]

Indeed, for many who came of age during the 1970s and '80s between Vietnam and America's first Persian Gulf campaign, the Romero canon was a right of passage. Spared the personal experience of war, this generation nevertheless braved a desensitizing onslaught of graphic cinematic violence unprecedented in American film.[30] *Night,* one critic writes, "unleashed a swarm of new, angry and intensely confrontational horror films" that sought to address an America recoiling from years of war, racism, political assassinations, government scandals, and riots.[31] With the "fabric of Americana ... stretched and torn," filmmakers "seized the opportunity to confront the audience with controversial scenes and topics that ... mirror[ed] some of the real horrors seen [on] TV news broadcasts."[32] Wes Craven, who also made independent horror movies in the 1970s, considers these genre films to have been "bootstraps for the psyche" that allowed young people struggling to cope with the insanity and randomness of a violent society to strengthen their egos and sense of fortitude so they would not be overwhelmed by fears of the real world.[33] "People tell you in complete honesty that it has changed them," says actor Scott Reiniger of *Dawn's* die-hard fan base.[34] Adds his co-star Gaylen Ross: "They remember this film as some sort of seminal thing in their lives."[35]

Romero's films, however, did more than simply strengthen the mettle of their viewership with gut-wrenching scenes of graphic violence. Each installment of the *Dead* trilogy presents a variation on the basic theme of surviving a siege from without and discord from within. To the extent the government is involved at all, it is portrayed as alternately indecisive and overbearing, contentious, violently racist, dangerously ineffectual, and ultimately irrelevant. Those who survive in the *Dead* trilogy have only themselves and their fellow refugees on whom to depend. The observations that follow in the next section are drawn from a close viewing of each of the trilogy's films, with an eye toward how the government performs (or fails to perform) during the crisis and the steps ordinary citizens are consequently forced to take.

## The Dead Trilogy: A Case Study of Governmental Ineptitude and Personal Survival

*We let them overrun us.*[36]

The *Dead* trilogy chronicles perhaps a few months in an unfolding national catastrophe. In *Night*, a group of strangers seeks refuge in a Pennsylvania farmhouse from the initial outbreak of the living dead. By the end of the movie, the strangers have all succumbed to the zombies or to each other, but the local sheriff, with a *posse comitatus* of area gun owners, seems to have restored a semblance of order (at least in rural Butler County, Pennsylvania).

In *Dawn*, however, the contagion causing the outbreak has spread out of control, and the American infrastructure nears collapse. A loose-knit group escapes the mounting chaos of Philadelphia by helicopter and shelters in a suburban shopping mall, which is later attacked by a marauding motorcycle gang and overrun by zombies. Two survivors, one of them pregnant, escape off the roof to an uncertain fate in a helicopter dangerously low on fuel.

In *Day*, soldiers and scientists in an underground bunker try to contact other survivors and to decipher the zombie plague. Their efforts, however, are doomed by the instability of military commander Rhodes, a violent megalomaniac, and of Dr. Logan, the chief scientific researcher, who labors under the delusion that zombies can be "civilized." When the remains of dead soldiers are discovered on Logan's examination table and in a zombie commissary he secretly maintains to reward his "pupils," a melee erupts among the humans, again allowing zombies to swarm their sanctuary. Three survivors escape via helicopter to a seemingly zombie-free island, perhaps safe from the living dead but more than ever in need of resourcefulness and peaceful cooperation.

*Night of the Living Dead* finds local authorities completely stymied in the critical opening phase of the outbreak. Early reports are confused. Authorities initially ignore crucial intelligence by dismissing eyewitness accounts that the dead are rising and eating the living. When the nature and pervasiveness of the situation finally become evident, law enforcement reacts with what a newscaster describes as "complete bewilderment." Yet even as the media are reporting widespread upheaval and panic, they also note that the National Guard has yet to be activated; the implication is that governors have failed to act because they are unwilling to believe what is happening.

Federal authorities also falter. Too late, the president convenes a cabinet meeting with the Joint Chiefs of Staff, the CIA, the FBI, and, most portentously, NASA. Media reports later reveal that NASA had destroyed a satellite returning from Venus because it contained an alarming amount of unrecognizable radiation. NASA, however, apparently had not warned other officials of this unusual, potentially dangerous situation until after the fact.

Another intelligence failure occurs when the federal government abruptly changes strategy at the height of the panic. Local authorities initially direct people to lock themselves indoors and remain inside at all costs. Seemingly, this would keep transportation routes open for emergency responders and allow them to distinguish between the living and the risen dead. However, the Pentagon's "Survival Command Center" then instructs citizens to report to rescue stations in civil defense shelters, which offer food, medicine, and the armed protection of the National Guard. Yet besides causing chaos on transportation routes and leaving stranded travelers vulnerable, this recommendation ignores the facts that humans *are* food to the assailants and that the condition is contagious. The rescue centers thus become concentrated food sources for the zombies and concentrated vectors of the contagion. By the time Civil Defense Headquarters in Washington, D.C. finally admits to the nation that the dead are returning to life and seeking human victims, the rescue stations are being overrun, the government is bungling its improvised response, and the public is hysterical. The credibility gap is further exacerbated by squabbling officials tersely asserting on television that "everything is being done that can be done."

*Dawn of the Dead* presents an even grimmer picture of the government's continued failure to protect its constituents. By now, martial law has been instituted in all major cities. Citizens are no longer allowed to remain in private homes, and reporting to rescue centers is mandatory. Because the government failed to establish its competency and credibility early in the crisis, however, citizens are resisting the federal mandates. The media, meanwhile, mock official pronouncements, and urbanites violently oppose leaving their homes and injured loved ones or turning over the bodies of their dead for disposal.

This growing civil unrest finally explodes during a joint military and police operation in a public housing project. The authorities initially try to convince those in the tenement to evacuate voluntarily, but when armed residents appear on the roof, S.W.A.T. teams and military troops storm the building in a bloody raid. Among them is Officer Wooley, who hurls racial epithets as he kicks in the doors of apartments and indiscriminately shoots the occupants. Finally, Peter, a black officer from another squad, guns Wooley down.

The zombies then erupt from their barricades, discipline among the forces rapidly collapses, and men begin to desert. The raid reveals that the residents are illegally harboring injured and dying loved ones in their apartments, while the "bodies" of the dead are being kept in the cellar so they can be administered religious rites. The denial that was evident among public officials in *Night* is thus reflected by the urban citizenry in *Dawn*.

For at least a portion of *Dawn*, constitutional government appears to remain in effect. One newscast mentions the president delivering a package of initiatives to Congress for "sweeping measures," but their significance is unclear. The Center for Disease Control in Atlanta is also said to be trying to develop a vaccine for the condition, but the inability to work with "live" zombies hampers the effort. Meanwhile, federal and National Guard troops sweep the countryside in zombie suppression operations.

In the cities, however, the efforts are unavailing. Citizens are being herded to defunct rescue stations and officials are abandoning their posts. Scientists on television plead for a reasoned, non-emotional response to the crisis, while pundits stir up distrust and discontent. Finally, a leading scientist delivers the pronouncement that no one wants to hear: the cities cannot be salvaged and must be destroyed by nuclear weapons so the rest of the population can survive: "We are down to the line folks," the scientist says, looking exhausted and defeated. "We are down to the line.... It's got to be done. It's that or the end." Shortly thereafter, the television broadcasts cease.

*Day of the Dead* illustrates the logical progression of the prior films. The U.S. infrastructure has disintegrated, and the implication, previously alluded to in *Dawn*, is that the contagion has spread beyond U.S. borders. *Day* chronicles the fall of a hastily-organized federal research effort in a subterranean bunker, but whether any other aspects of the U.S. government are functioning, or even whether any other non-infected citizens remain to be governed, is unclear. The lack of planning that went into the research project is evident from the start. What little equipment is available is old and in disrepair. Discipline is lax amongst the military contingent, and its leadership is tyrannical. The chief scientist, meanwhile, is dangerously unhinged. Group cohesion, which is tenuous from the outset, finally dissolves with predictable results, and the viewer is left to ponder whether the remnants of humanity were ever worth saving.

Perhaps the only efficacious public official portrayed throughout the trilogy is Butler County's Sheriff McClelland, who in *Night* leads a posse of local woodsmen and hunters in federally-sanctioned search-and-destroy missions against the zombies. In contrast to the squabbling feds, McClelland responds to a reporter's questions with almost comic stoicism: "Things aren't going too bad," he says, as rifles discharge around him. "Men are taking it pretty good." He also provides sound advice on dealing with the zombies: "Well, there's no problem. If you ha[ve] a gun, shoot 'em in the head; that's a sure way to kill them. If you don't, get yourself a club or a torch. Beat or burn 'em. They go up pretty easy...." As others descend into panic, McClelland remains the consummate American lawman: practical, confident, and mission-focused.

Yet McClelland's character also suggests that the use of unchecked police power in the name of security only creates a different sort of peril. In the trilogy's most bitterly ironic moment, Ben, the hero of *Night*, is shot by a member of McClelland's posse after surviving the zombies' assault on the farmhouse. Whether Ben is shot because he is mistaken for a zombie or because he is a black man holding a rifle are troubling questions which the movie does not resolve (zombies, as a rule, do not wield firearms in the *Dead* trilogy[37]). Thus, even when McClelland's men appear to have accomplished their mission of securing the county, the "victory" never feels satisfactory and proves to be short-lived. To whatever degree McClelland's campaign succeeds, however, credit is due to the armed citizen militia rather than a professional army or police force.

Indeed, those who remain alive in the *Dead* films do so in spite of the government, not because of it. *Dawn's* protagonists, Peter and Roger, survive by abandoning their S.W.A.T. team during the raid on the tenement (Peter, after shooting Wooley in the back; Roger, after agreeing to turn a blind eye to the incident). They then join a group of "outlaws and thieves" who escape Philadelphia's collapse in a stolen helicopter. This group, in turn, is beset by a motorcycle gang that endures on the road by being as brutal and unsparing as the living dead. Meanwhile, citizens who obey the government's mandate to report to the rescue stations end up as little more than bait for the zombies, and soldiers and policemen who remain at their posts are abandoned first by their commanders and then by each other.

Human folly ultimately proves even more deadly in Romero's trilogy than the zombies' appetite. The zombies themselves are slow, inept, and stupid; any cohesive, rational, and coordinated human effort seemingly would have defeated them. The true menace that Romero portrays in the Dead trilogy therefore is not an invading army but a society turning on itself. "What the hell are they?" Francine asks of the undead massing on the mall in *Dawn*. "They're us," Peter famously replies. "That's all."

## *The National Strategy for Homeland Security: A New Paradigm of National Readiness*

> *The President is sending to Congress a package of initiatives aimed at what sources have called a most sweeping set of measures....* [38]

The *Dead* trilogy's portrayal of government in a crisis is remarkable not just for its visceral impact but also for its prescience. Fans of Romero's work would notice several familiar themes during America's 9/11 post-mortem. Before the attacks, intelligence was ignored or misunderstood. During the attacks, official communication and coordination were lacking. The only effective anti-terrorism force on 9/11 was a group of ordinary citizens aboard a commercial flight over rural Pennsylvania, who prevented certain disaster at the cost of their own lives. After the attacks, officials denied their mistakes, blamed each other, and used the event as a pretext for expanding their own authority. America is now engaged in a prolonged counter-offensive that has divided public opinion and too often revealed the dark side of human nature. Officials once believed victory was in hand when the worst was still to come.

Romero himself, however, maintains that he did not set out to make overtly political films and that whatever social meaning can be gleaned from the *Dead* trilogy was an organic consequence of the world in which the movies were made:

> I've never meant to preach anything. Those things [the socio-political implications] have been, in my mind anyway, sort of self-given facts that we have been talking about for years. There aren't any real new thoughts, certainly no solutions, and not even any new questions in my films.... I've just tried to get an underbelly into them all, maybe more consciously than some other people.[39]

Nevertheless, while Romero insists he was not offering solutions, the *Dead* trilogy's portrayal of resolute citizens banding together to survive an unprecedented national emergency foreshadowed the Bush administration's own post-9/11 strategic thinking.

In July 2002, the White House Office of Homeland Security issued the inaugural version of its *National Strategy for Homeland Security*. This document articulates the Bush administration's philosophy on preventing and responding to terrorism and other catastrophes on American soil. It also called for the creation of the Department of Homeland Security, which came into being later that year and ushered in "the most extensive reorganization of the federal government in the past fifty years."[40] With these initiatives, a defining principle of the national government became shoring up the gaps in surveillance and readiness that had allowed the 9/11 terrorists to operate virtually unchecked on American soil. "The U.S. government," President Bush notes in the *Strategy*'s introduction, "has no more important mission than protecting the homeland from future terrorist attacks."[41]

In the Homeland Security model, freedom is tied to citizen participation in the safety of the nation. Noting that the United States is composed of more than 87,000 different political jurisdictions[42] and that 85 percent of its critical infrastructure is privately held,[43] the *Strategy* articulates a model in which priorities established at the federal level are executed largely by states, localities, and the American people: "Homeland security is a shared responsibility. In addition to a national strategy, we need compatible, mutually supporting state, local, and private-sector strategies. Individual volunteers must channel their energy and commitment in support of the national and local strategies."[44] While the president asserts that "[t]his is a "national strategy, not a federal strategy,"[45] he clearly contemplates that all should plan with federal objectives in mind.

Indeed, the *Strategy* repeatedly insists that the efforts of private individuals are integral to its agenda. "[E]very American," it states, "must be willing to do his or her part to protect the homeland."[46] Citizens are duty-bound to be "informed and proactive."[47] Emergency preparedness and response efforts will "engage the private sector and the American people"[48] and utilize their "strength and creativity."[49] Complacency, the *Strategy* warns, only plays into the enemies' hands: "We remain a Nation at war. Even as we experience success in the war on terrorism, the antipathy of our enemies may well be increasing, and new enemies may emerge. The United States will confront the threat of terrorism for the foreseeable future."[50]

Yet what exactly is the individual's role? Despite its insistent call to action, the *Strategy* is rather vague on this point. The Bush administration's primary initiative to mobilize the American people is Citizen Corps, whose mission, according to its own website, "is to harness the power of every individual through education, training, and volunteer service to make communities safer, stronger, and better prepared to respond to the threats of terrorism, crime, public health issues, and disasters of all kinds."[51] Challenging visitors to "embrace the personal responsibility to be prepared," Citizens Corps' website offers downloadable disaster planning guides and links to local Citizen Corps Council Offices for those wishing to volunteer.[52] Its partner programs include the Community Emergency Response Team (CERT), Fire Corps, Medical Reserve Corps, Neighborhood Watch Program, and Volunteers in Police Service.[53] Each has its own website, and each provides varying degrees of training and volunteer opportunities.

The extent to which Citizen Corps has succeeded in its founding vision is unclear. As this is being written in September 2008, the organization claims to have Councils in fifty-five U.S. states and territories capable of serving seventy-eight percent of the U.S. population,[54] but the practical import of these figures is difficult to measure. A database search of seven major newspapers and three national news magazines for the period January 1, 2002, to July 1, 2008, revealed some ninety-six different articles that mentioned Citizen Corps.[55] Sixty-five of these items, however, appeared in just two publications, the *Chicago Tribune* (twenty-one items) and the *Houston Chronicle* (forty-four items). Twenty-seven of the items (over twenty-eight percent) concerned the same Citizen Corps chapter in Harris County, Texas.

Four of the stories recount Citizen Corps volunteers actually helping in an emergency, including two which describe the Harris County chapter assisting with Hurricane Katrina evacuees at the Astrodome.[56] More common, however, are articles about the organization's obscurity or its difficulties attracting funding, volunteers, or attention.[57] Indeed, one story reports that the Harris County Citizens Corps volunteers were initially turned away from the Astrodome when they responded to help the Katrina evacuees.[58] Many of the news items are also devoted to criticizing Operation TIPS,[59] Citizen Corps' ill-fated attempt to encourage "truck drivers, letter carriers, train conductors, ship captains, and workers" to "report potential terrorist activity" via a toll-free, anonymous tip line.[60]

For its part, Citizen Corps' website documents the organization's achievements and lessons learned in a section entitled "Good Stories." One such account describes the aforementioned Harris County chapter's assistance with Katrina evacuees at the Astrodome.[61] Another, however, acknowledges that emergency professionals are largely skeptical or unaware of CERT and that few have worked with its volunteers.[62] Indeed, a preparedness guide that Citizen Corps distributes from its website became something of a national joke following 9/11 for advising Americans to keep duct tape and plastic sheeting on hand to seal rooms in case of a chemical attack.[63] Nevertheless, Citizen Corps and FEMA continue to offer an updated version of this guide with these same recommendations intact,[64] as well as Pub. No. 243E, the *Disaster Preparedness Coloring Book*.[65] CERT's website, meanwhile, notes that its members "have been used to distribute and/or install smoke alarms, replace smoke alarm batteries in the home[s] of [the] elderly, distribute disaster education material, [and] provide services at special events, such as parades, sporting events, concerts and more."[66]

Whether Citizen Corps and its associated agencies will play a meaningful role in the nation's security remains to be seen. To date, these programs do not appear to have captured the nation's imagination. Many citizens are eager to help in a crisis, but the heightened state of perpetual readiness called for by the *Strategy* is a far more ambitious proposition. Nevertheless, some activists have not only risen to the challenge but are spreading the message to a young demographic that might seem an unlikely source of America's homeland security vanguard. The next section examines a grassroots movement that counter-intuitively embodies elements from both disquisitions this paper has so far discussed: a reluctant counter-culture visionary's graphic imaginings of the apocalypse and the bureaucratic response to an unprecedented national emergency.

## *The Grassroots: Getting the Message, Spreading the Word*

*Wake up suckers.... We've got to find our own way.*[67]

Zombie movies experienced an American resurgence in the years following 9/11, beginning with the U.S. distribution of *28 Days Later* in June 2003.[68] This film portrays the inadvertent release of a highly-contagious biological weapon that reduces its victims to frenzied, homicidal maniacs driven to attack the unexposed. Although these "infected" are not zombies per se, the movie's themes of ordinary people trying to survive and maintain their humanity in the midst of a crisis resonated with a shaken post–9/11 America.

Capitalizing on this zeitgeist was Max Brooks, author of 2003's *The Zombie Survival Guide (ZSG)*,[69] a handbook for the zombie survivalist that includes advice on such topics as weaponry, tactics, mental conditioning, even the relative zombie-specific merits of different hairstyles (e.g., short hair is preferred because it cannot be grabbed by a zombie).[70] Although marketed to a broad audience as a work of deadpan humor, *ZSG* espouses a worldview that constantly weighs risks, spots weaknesses and strengths, seeks practical solutions for pressing problems, and above all emphasizes the need to press on in any circumstance. Despite obvious technical and factual shortcomings, its core message of self-reliance and citizen preparedness struck a nerve and augured a broader movement that takes its mission very seriously indeed.

Amplifying and refining Brooks's message and theme is the St. Louis, Missouri-based organization Zombie Squad (ZS), which began in 2003 as a group of like-minded friends who grew up watching zombie movies and enjoy camping, contingency planning, and marksmanship.[71] Founding member Kyle Ladd relates that 9/11 "smacked people in the face" about the need for personal preparedness, an ethic he says Americans, especially in rural areas, once took for granted.[72] Following the release of *28 Days Later*, Ladd and several friends began discussing how they might have fared better than those in the zombie films they had seen.[73] These conversations eventually led to zombie survival seminars at horror conventions and local community centers, and a movement was born.[74]

Through an elaborate website and other promotional materials (including brochures, clothing, authorized merchandise, and an expanding fleet of armor-plated vehicles), ZS now styles itself as "an elite zombie suppression task force ready to defend your neighborhood from the shambling hordes of the walking dead."[75]

Its website features links to pictures of heavily-outfitted and well-armed team members (most in their twenties and thirties), in-depth essays on such topics as medicinal herbs, campsite cuisine, and backpack survival kits (or "bug-out bags"), and action photos of the ZS logo emblazoned on a variety of military heavy metal.[76] However, amidst tattoos, facial piercings, and the occasional auto-loading carbine is a core message that (almost) could have issued from the Citizen Corps pressroom itself:

> We focus our efforts towards promoting the importance of emergency preparation awareness and working with local communities around the globe to teach them what is needed to survive whatever crisis may come along like natural disasters or man made disasters.
>
> Our mission is to make sure you are prepared for any crisis situation that might come along in your daily life which may include your home being invaded by the undead menace.
>
> Zombie Squad also supports other local and international disaster relief organizations/ charities. Check out our events page for the latest charity event we have coming up.[77]

Ladd states that ZS was prompted by "a need for community and personal improvement."[78] He acknowledges that the zombie aspect is "tongue in cheek" and is used to draw attention to the organization's real mission of preparedness and service.[79] Zombie Squad's website explains: "[While] it is quite possible for someone to live their entire lives without encountering the undead ... we hold fast to the belief that if you are prepared for a scenario where the walking corpses of your family and neighbors are trying to eat you alive, you will be prepared for almost anything."[80]

To this end, Ladd reports that ZS members work with such organizations as the American Red Cross, the Disaster Preparedness and Emergency Response Association, and the National Voluntary Organizations Active in Disaster.[81] The group's core message, he relates, is to "be proactive."[82] He advises citizens concerned about personal preparedness to "work with local disaster action information organizations and to make sure their family is safe for disasters that are potential problems in their area."[83]

Zombie Squad's most active public interface is its on-line forum, through which participants can discuss, in addition to zombie films past, present, and future, training and volunteer opportunities and a host of topics related to survival and self-sufficiency.[84] The discussions, though meant to be practical, are often framed in zombie-specific contexts. While threads related to the undead and firearms may give some browsers pause, various features of the ZS website reveal serious intentions. The forum has rules designed to discourage antisocial behavior or discussions of illegal activity and to promote its stated goal of becoming a reliable source of legitimate information, not a role playing forum for would-be militants, vigilantes, or hate groups.[85] Ladd indicates that the discussions are heavily-moderated and that posters who indulge in the "flame wars" and immaturity typical of many Internet message boards will not last long.[86]

Indeed, perusal of the forum reveals that those who are too flippant or who do not consistently contribute useful information are gradually marginalized. Repeat or egregious rule-breakers are subject to an escalating series of sanctions, and the unrepentant may be assigned the ignominious "asshat" designation and eventually banned from the site. Although the forum's discussions evince self-effacing humor, they also exhibit an almost grim insistence on technical accuracy and competence. An underlying theme is that the post-apocalyptic world would be no place for poseurs.

Zombie Squad, however, is more than an on-line community. In addition to the more than 11,000 people who have registered to post on its forum,[87] the organization, as of September 2008, had 11 regional chapters apart from its St. Louis headquarters (including one in Canada),[88] as well as 680 card-carrying members throughout North America.[89] Its website lists an extensive schedule of past and upcoming events, including blood drives, camping trips, charitable fundraisers, volunteer activities, survival seminars, and social gatherings.[90]

Clearly, however, ZS's showcase event is the annual "Zombie Con," which each year since 2005 has attracted several dozen members to an extended weekend camping trip in Eastern Missouri. The agenda typically includes informational sessions, skills exercises, zombie movie screenings, firearms training, and team bonding.[91] Zombie Squad's departure from the staid Citizen Corps paradigm is perhaps most starkly illustrated by the first-person accounts and photo-essays of past Zombie Cons posted on the ZS website.[92]

Yet if Zombie Con illustrates the organization's more free-spirited impulses, Ladd readily cites statistics demonstrating its activist bent. As of June 2008, he states, ZS had been responsible for twenty-nine charity events, 45.8 gallons of donated blood, canned food collections of some 5,565 pounds, and charitable contributions of $14,710.[93] He also points out that not a single zombie outbreak has occurred since ZS was formed.[94]

Ladd notes that from its origins as a group of amateur enthusiasts, ZS has grown to include members who are active duty military, law enforcement, and EMTs.[95] Its board's vision for the future includes expanding ZS's network of regional chapters and supplementing its current all-volunteer staff with paid employees to handle administrative tasks and merchandise sales.[96] Ladd distinguishes Zombie Squad from other survivalist groups in its focus on community outreach and education, rather than on simply "huddling in our missile silos."[97] Zombie Squad accepts no outside advertising, and its website and activities are member-driven and funded; its board has resisted outside sponsorship in order to maintain maximum decision-making control.[98] "[O]ur biggest goal was to cater towards those that wouldn't normally have an interest i[n] disaster preparation," Ladd relates. "It's worked out well. We seemed to have found a niche."[99]

## Depoliticizing the Threat: "The Zombie Just Is,"[100]
## So Let's Work Together

*This isn't the Republicans versus the Democrats, where we're in a hole economically or ... or we're in another war. This is more crucial than that. This is down to the line, folks, this is down to the line. There can be no more divisions among the living![101]*

Romero, of course, is recognized as a founding influence by most Zombie Squad members. Yet politics, always a driving force of Romero's work (despite his protestations to the contrary), is a forbidden topic on the ZS website and at its events.[102] Among the group's reasons for this prohibition is that "[i]t makes it a lot easier for us to all get along and helps us stay focused on our root topics—survival and zombies."[103] Zombies, for this organization, are not a coded reference to social upheaval, as some have suggested of *Night*,[104] or to blind consumerism, as some have suggested of *Dawn*,[105] or to the patriarchy and inhumanity that purportedly lurk behind the military/industrial complex, as some have suggested of *Day*.[106] They are simply a compendium of natural and manmade threats for which Americans must collaboratively prepare.[107] Zombie Squad does not want to start a revolution; its members simply want to survive.

From their humble, blue-collar origins, zombie movies have endured in part because they make people think. With ZS, however, they have come to symbolize what some are feeling, including a sense of their own mortality, skepticism in the nation's emergency preparedness infrastructure, and a refusal to bet their lives on official crisis management. Yet even if ZS disclaims the sort of political agenda others have read into the *Dead* trilogy, it still reflects many of the ethics that have characterized Romero's work. As Romero jealously guarded his artistic integrity, the members of ZS jealously guard their physical integrity. Romero sought out likeminded friends to bring his visions to life; ZS members seek out likeminded friends to help preserve their lives. Above all, the *Dead* trilogy and ZS each seeks to counter in its own way a culture of perceived complacency and inaction.

As judged by the contemporary standards in which they arose, both the *Dead* trilogy and ZS represent the fringe of their respective fields of endeavor. Yet people of diverse backgrounds seemed to have found an elusive commonality in the ZS ranks.[108] Even as the federal government insists that "every American must be willing to do his or her part to protect our homeland,"[109] it offers non-military or law-enforcement personnel little in the way of substance or motivation to achieve that directive. It also speaks with a forked tongue, making urgent declarations and calls to action in obscure official documents but demanding little of the American people in ways for which it may be held politically accountable. One can embrace ZS, on the other hand, believing that its mission is clear and its motives are pure. In this way, ZS perpetuates the *Dead* trilogy's refusal to sell out or to buy into the mainstream.

Ironically, however, to the extent that the Bush administration could be said to represent the mainstream, ZS is squarely in sync with its defining mission: "protecting the homeland."[110] Yet ZS manages this feat in a way that makes vigilance appear underground and edgy, thus attracting a young, skeptical demographic that historically has shown little interest in voting, much less in fulfilling vague federal mandates. This, truly, is the very sort of "creative genius"[111] that the federal government is ill-equipped to encourage within itself but upon which the Bush administration's Strategy insists the country's future depends. While Citizens Corps and FEMA would placate the American public with duct tape, 9-volt batteries, and coloring books, a grassroots movement out of St. Louis is making ordinary citizens feel not just prepared but as if they are the country's greatest hope against its fiercest foe.

Zombie Squad may or may not be any closer to securing the homeland than the federal bureaucrats who advise their constituents to stock up on duct tape and plastic sheeting. Still, for those dealing with threats both ambiguous and perhaps unsolvable, a feeling of preparedness and efficacy is no small consolation. The *Dead* trilogy helped the generation coming of age in post–Vietnam America face its fears of a society seemingly on the brink. In a similar way, Zombie Squad is a psychic bootstrap for those navigating the uncharted terrain of post 9/11 America and a clarion call to learn from an earlier generation's mistakes.

This is essay is dedicated with love to Alexandra Zealand, who has shown time and again that she's the real braaaiiinns behind this operation. The author would also like to thank Kyle Ladd, the members of the University of Michigan Law School's Fall 2005 Student Scholarship Workshop, and professors Peter Dendle, Rebecca Eisenberg, Daniel Halberstam, Orit Kamir, and Keith Schlegel. Special thanks are due to Sarah Juliet Lauro for her generous editorial assistance and for rescuing this effort from obscurity on more than one occasion.

## Notes

1. Television station employee (uncredited) in *Dawn of the Dead*, directed by George A. Romero (Laurel Group, 1979).

2. *Zombie* (U.S. title), directed by Lucio Fulci (Variety Film Production, 1979).

3. Tom (Keith Wayne) in *Night of the Living Dead*, directed by George A. Romero (Image Ten, 1968).

4. This "trilogy" refers to the previously-mentioned *Night* and *Dawn*, as well as *Day of the Dead*, directed by George A. Romero (Laurel Entertainment, Inc., 1985). As of this writing, Romero has directed three other zombie movies, *Land of the Dead* (2005), *Diary of the Dead* (2007), and *Survival of the Dead* (2009). However, both of these latter films, with their depictions of modern technology and tropes, depart from the plot that progressed chronologically through their predecessors. This essay will accordingly treat them as distinct storylines existing apart from the events of *Night*, *Dawn*, and *Day*.

One chronicler of Romero's work has also noted that a few years before *Night* began production, Romero had written an untitled short story known as *Anubis* that was structured "in three 'movements,' which eventually metamorphosed into the three films of Romero's zombie trilogy." Paul R. Gagne, *The Zombies that Ate Pittsburgh: The Films of George A. Romero* (New York: Dodd, Mead, 1987), 24. "'They weren't dominant,'" Romero himself has said of his original concept, "'but there were always three parts to the story.'" Quoted in ibid., 24.

5. U.S. White House Office of Homeland Security, *National Strategy for Homeland Security*, Washington: White House Office of Homeland Security, 2002, accessed September 21, 2008, http://www.dhs.gov/xlibrary/assets/nat_strat_hls.pdf.

6. Ibid., 3.

7. See, for example, Tony Williams, *The Cinema of George A. Romero: Knight of the Living Dead* (London: Wallflower, 2003), 28–29, 139; Gregory A. Waller, introduction to *American Horrors: Essays on the Modern American Horror Film*, ed. Gregory A. Waller (Urbana: University of Illinois Press, 1987), 2, 4. According to Waller, *Night of the Living Dead* "reveals the flaws inherent in ... local and federal government agencies, and the entire mechanism of civil defense."

8. Tom (Keith Wayne) in *Night*.

9. See, for example, Orit Kamir, "Why 'Law and Film' and What Does it Actually Mean — A Perspective," *Continuum: Journal of Media and Cultural Studies* 19, no. 2 (2005): 255–278, 257.

10. Examples from a variety of genres can be found in John Denvir, ed., *Legal Reelism: Movies as Legal Texts* (Urbana: University of Illinois Press, 1996).

11. John Denvir, "The Slotting Function: How Movies Influence Political Decisions," *Vermont Law Review* 28, no. 4 (Summer 2004): 799–812. Professor Denvir places the war on terror amid an American tradition of "lawless" films portraying the legal system as too weak and ineffectual to handle certain problems and argues that this preference for anarchic violence may have influenced the United States to forsake legal solutions in responding to 9/11.

12. Dr. Foster (David Crawford) in *Dawn*.

13. *Gagne*, 15. Romero was eventually awarded a degree from Carnegie-Mellon University in 1984, "with 'life experience' filling in for the missing credits." Ibid.

14. Ibid. at 17–20.

15. In 1999, *Night* became the 266th film to be added to the Library of Congress' National Film Registry. Library of Congress Public Affairs Office, "Librarian of Congress Names 25 More Films to National Film Reg-

istry," press release, November 16, 1999, accessed September 21, 2008, http://www.loc.gov/today/pr/1999/99-174.html.

16. See *Document of the Dead,* directed by Roy Frumkes (Synapse Films, 1985); Gagne, 24; Williams, 12.

17. See, for example, Robin Wood, *Hollywood from Vietnam to Reagan ... and Beyond,* Revised and Expanded ed. (New York: Columbia University Press, 2003), xxxvii, 287–288 (2003); Gagne, x, 21, 36, 83, 100; Williams, 20, 128–129, 177.

18. Scientists in *Night* focus on radiation from the Explorer satellite returning to Earth from Venus, while a news report in *Dawn* mentions CDC research that seems to hypothesize a viral origin.

19. The temporal progression of the condition varies between individuals. Typically, a victim who is bitten will be incapacitated by illness and fever and succumb within hours or days. Reanimation, however, always occurs directly after death, at which point the subject will instantly seek food.

20. *The Dead Will Walk,* DVD, directed by Perry Martin (Anchor Bay, 2004). This and other informative documentaries are included on Disc Four of Anchor Bay's 2004 DVD "Ultimate Edition" of *George A. Romero's Dawn of the Dead.*

21. See *Dead Will Walk; Document of the Dead;* Gagne, 31; Williams, 21.

22. *Night* was shot on a budget of $114,000. *Gagne,* 31. Ten years later, *Night's* success would allow Romero the relative extravagance of a $1.5 million budget for *Dawn.* Ibid., 83–85, 100–101. Romero was then offered a $6.5 million budget for an R-rated cut of *Day,* but he instead chose to work with a $3.5 million budget that allowed him the artistic freedom of making an unrated film. Ibid., 149–150.

23. Vincent Canby's review for the *New York Times* is typical: "*Night of the Living Dead* is a grainy little movie acted by what appear to be nonprofessional actors, who are besieged in a farm house by some other nonprofessional actors who stagger around, stiff-legged, pretending to be flesh-eating ghouls.... The movie ... was made by some people in Pittsburgh." Vincent Canby, "Night of the Living Dead," *New York Times,* December 5, 1968, 59. Years later, *New York Times* critic Janet Maslin would walk out of *Dawn.* Gagne, 100. Another critic called *Day* "'a cesspool of vile filth produced by a sick mind for sick-minded people.'" Ibid., 168 (quoting Dean Levi in the *Richmond News Leader*). See also, Adam Lowenstein, *Shocking Representation: Historical Trauma, National Cinema, and the Modern Horror Film* (New York: Columbia University Press, 2005), 154.

24. Quoted in Gagne, 38.

25. *Dead Will Walk.*

26. Ibid.

27. Ibid.

28. Gagne, 98–100.

29. Roger Ebert, "The Night of the Living Dead," *rogerebert.com,* January 5, 1969, accessed September 21, 2008, http://rogerebert.suntimes.com/apps/pbcs.dll/article?AID=/19670105/ REVIEWS/701050301/1023. Ebert now insists that "I admire the movie itself" and that his earlier comments were not, strictly speaking, a review of the film. Ibid.

30. This is not to suggest, of course, that viewing violence in films is the equivalent of experiencing it in a war zone. As Savini notes of the typical movie-goer unexposed to combat, "you'll never see it the way I saw it." *The American Nightmare: A Celebration of Films from Horror's Golden Age of Fright,* directed by Adam Simon, Minerva Pictures, 2000.

31. Chas Balun, *Beyond Horror Holocaust: A Deeper Shade of Red* (Key West: Phantasma Books, 2003), 10.

32. Ibid.

33. *American Nightmare.*

34. *Dead Will Walk.*

35. Ibid.

36. Dr. Logan (Richard Liberty) in *Day.*

37. The exception is Dr. Logan's star pupil, Bub, whose facility with a .45 ACP pistol in *Day* appears to be a remnant of military training in his former life.

38. Newscaster (uncredited) in *Dawn.*

39. Quoted in Gagne, 5–6.

40. *National Strategy,* vii.

41. Ibid., iii.

42. Ibid., vii, 11.

43. Ibid., viii, 33.

44. Ibid., iii.

45. Ibid., v.

46. Ibid., 12.

47. Ibid., viii.

48. Ibid., x.

49. Ibid., 4.

50. Ibid., 7.

51. U.S. National Office of Citizen Corps, "Citizen Corps Councils," *citizencorps.gov*, accessed September 21, 2008, http://www.citizencorps.gov/councils/.

52. U.S. National Office of Citizen Corps, "About Citizen Corps," *citizencorps.gov*, accessed September 21, 2008, http://www.citizencorps.gov/about/.

53. U.S. National Office of Citizen Corps, "Citizen Corps Programs and Partners," *citizencorps.gov*, accessed September 21, 2008, http://www.citizencorps.gov/programs/.

54. U.S. National Office of Citizen Corps, "Citizen Corps Councils Around the Country," *citizenscorps.gov*, accessed September 21, 2008, http://www.citizencorps.gov/cc/CouncilMapIndex.do.

55. Search of Westlaw Chicagotr, Chisun, Hstnchron, Miamihd, NYT, SFCHR, USATD, NEwswEEk, TimeMAG, & USNWR databases (July 1, 2008) (search for <"citizen corps" & da (aft 1/2002 & bef 12/2008)>).

56. Seshadri Kumar, "Community Emergency Response Team Seeks Volunteers," *Houston Chronicle*, November 15, 2007, 4; Kevin Moran, "Hospitality in Time of Crisis Earns Texans Special Awards," *Houston Chronicle*, April 14, 2006, B4; John Biemer, "DuPage Seeks More Crisis Helpers," *Chicago Tribune*, January 13, 2005, 7; Shamus Toomey, "Bush Campaign Whistle-Stops through Suburbs," *Chicago Tribune*, July, 23, 2004, 3.

57. See, for example, Sheryl Stolberg, "Grand Vision Fizzled, Boosters Concede," *Houston Chronicle*, January 27, 2008, A28; Sheryl Stolberg, "Bush's 2002 State of the Union Volunteerism Initiative Is Seen as Sputtering," *New York Times*, January 27, 2008, A19; Alan Gathright, Jim Herron, "Catastrophe on a Shoestring," *San Francisco Chronicle*, August 16, 2004, A1; Dan Barry, "A Nation at War: At War at Home," *New York Times*, April 9, 2003, B13; Mimi Hall, "Bush's Volunteer Plan Takes a Hit," *USA Today*, January 27, 2003, 8A.

58. Peggy O'Hare, Salatheia Bryant, and Bill Murphy, "Katrina: The Aftermath — Evacuees Turned Away at the Astrodome Gates," *Houston Chronicle*, September 1, 2005, A19.

59. See, for example, Andy Newman, "Look Out; Citizen Snoops Wanted," *New York Times*, July 21, 2003, B13; Clarence Page, "Snooping Around Could Turn Tricky," *Chicago Tribune*, July 28, 2002, 9; Debra Picket, "Cable Guys Aren't Meant to be U.S. Spies," *Chicago Sun-Times*, July 19, 2002, 2. Operation TIPS has since been scuttled by Congress. See Homeland Security Act of 2002, U.S. Code Title 6, sec. 460 (Supp. 5 2006).

60. *National Strategy*, 12.

61. U.S. National Office of Citizen Corps, "Harris County, Texas Citizen Corps' Response to Hurricane Katrina," *citizencorps.gov*, accessed September 21, 2008, http://www.citizencorps.gov/councils/goodstories.shtm.

62. U.S. National Office of Citizen Corps, "Boca Raton CERT's Breakfast with Firefighters Program," *citizencorps.gov*, accessed September 21, 2008, http://www.citizencorps.gov/councils/ goodstories.shtm.

63. Ike Seamans, "National Security: A Serious Matter," *Miami Herald*, February 28, 2003, 7B.

64. U.S. Federal Emergency Management Agency, *Are You Ready? An In-Depth Guide to Citizen Preparedness*, no. IS-22 (Washington: Federal Emergency Management Agency, 2004), http://www.fema.gov/pdf/areyouready/areyouready_ full.pdf (accessed September 21, 2008).

65. U.S. Federal Emergency Management Agency, *Disaster Preparedness Coloring Book*, no. 243E (Washington: Federal Emergency Management Agency, 1993), accessed September 21, 2008, http://www.fema.gov/library/viewRecord.do?id=Record.do?id=1640.

66. U.S. Citizen Corps National Office, "CERT Frequently Asked Questions," *citizencorps.gov*, accessed September 21, 2008, http://www.citizencorps.gov/cert/faq.shtm.

67. Peter (Ken Foree) in *Dawn*.

68. *28 Days Later*, directed by Danny Boyle (DNA Films, 2002).

69. Max Brooks, *The Zombie Survival Guide: Complete Protection from the Living Dead* (New York: Three Rivers Press, 2003).

70. Ibid., 62–63.

71. Kyle Ladd, e-mail message to author, March 13, 2005.

72. Kyle Ladd, telephone interview by author, July 3, 2008.

73. Ibid.

74. Ibid.

75. Zombie Squad, Inc., "What Is ZS?" *zombiehunters.org*, accessed September 21, 2008, http://zombiehunters. org/who.php.

76. Zombie Squad, Inc., "Welcome to the Official Zombie Squad Website," *zombiehunters.org*, accessed September 21, 2008, http://zombihunters.org/index/php.

77. Zombie Squad, Inc., "What is Zombie Squad?" *zombiehunters.org*, accessed September 21, 2008, http://zombiehunters.org/faq.php.

78. Ladd, e-mail.

79. Ibid.

80. "What is Zombie Squad?"

81. Ladd, e-mail. When asked about Citizen Corps, CERT, et al., during a telephone interview with the author in 2008, Ladd noted that ZS is well aware of these organizations but has no official relationship with them, although CERT members, he said, have attended ZS training events. Ladd was reluctant to go on record

with his estimation of these groups' efficacy but noted they are "getting better." He also considers mainstream aid organizations such as the Red Cross and Citizen Corps partners rather than competitors. Zombie Squad's primary focus, Ladd states, is not on collecting donations or responding to disasters but on motivating individuals to get involved in their communities and to prepare and train *before* disaster strikes.

82. Ladd, e-mail.

83. Ibid.

84. Zombie Squad, Inc., "Zombie Squad Forum," *zombiehunters.org*, accessed September 21, 2008, http://zombiehunters.org/forum/.

85. Zombie Squad, Inc., "Zombie Squad Forum Rules," *zombiehunters.org*, accessed September 21, 2008, http://zombiehunters.org/forum/viewtopic.php?f=44&t=19895.

86. Ladd, July 3, 2008.

87. See "Zombie Squad Forum."

88. Zombie Squad, Inc., "Zombie Squad Chapters." *zombiehunters.org*, accessed September 21, 2008, http://zombiehunters.org/chapters/index.php.

89. Zombie Squad, Inc., "Where We Are," *zombiehunters.org*, accessed September 21, 2008, http://zombie hunters.org/map.php.

90. Zombie Squad, Inc., "News & Upcoming Events." *zombiehunters.org*, accessed September 21, 2008, http://zombiehunters.org.

91. Zombie Squad, Inc., "Zombie Con," *zombiehunters.org*, accessed September 21, 2008, http://zombie hunters.org/zomcon.php.

92. Ibid. One can only imagine that Romero would approve.

93. Kyle Ladd, e-mail message to author, June 22, 2008.

94. Ibid.

95. Ladd, e-mail.

96. Ladd, telephone.

97. Ibid.

98. Ibid.

99. Ladd, e-mail.

100. Peter Dendle, *Zombie Movie Encyclopedia* (Jefferson, NC: McFarland, 2001), 12.

101. Dr. Millard Rausch (Richard France) in *Dawn*.

102. "Zombie Squad Forum Rules."

103. Ibid.

104. See, for example, Gagne, 38; Stephen Harper, "'Night of the Living Dead': Reappraising an Undead Classic," *Bright Lights Film Journal*, no. 50 (November 2005), accessed September 21, 2008, http://www.brightlightsfilm.com/50/night.htm; Christopher Sharret, "Genocidal Spectacles and the Ideology of Death," in *Bad: Infamy, Darkness, Evil, and Slime on Screen*, ed. by Murray Pomerance (Albany: State University of New York Press, 2004), 65, 72–74; Sumiko Higashi, "'Night of the Living Dead': A Horror Film About the Horrors of the Vietnam Era," in *From Hanoi to Hollywood: The Vietnam War in American Film*, ed. Linda Dittmar and Gene Michaud (New Brunswick, NJ: Rutgers University Press, 1990), 175–178; Williams, 26–27, 32.

105. See, for example, Gagne, 5, 87–88; "Zombies, Malls, and the Consumerism Debate: George Romero's 'Dawn of the Dead,'" *Americana: Journal of American Popular Culture (1900 to Present)* 1, no. 2 (Fall 2002), accessed September 21, 2008, http://www.americanpopular culture.com/journal/articles/fall_2002/harper.htm; A. Loudermilk, "Eating 'Dawn' in the Dark: Zombie Desire and Commodified Identity in George A. Romero's 'Dawn of the Dead,'" *Journal of Consumer Culture* 3, no. 1 (March 2003): 83–108; Wood, 105–106.

106. See, for example, Walter Chaw, "'Day of the Dead,'" *filmfreakcentral.net*, accessed September 21, 2008, http://filmfreak central.net/dvdreviews/dayofthedead.htm; Barry Keith Grant, "Taking Back the 'Night of the Living Dead': George Romero, Feminism, and the Horror Film," in *The Dread of Difference: Gender and the Horror Film*, ed. Barry Keith Grant (Austin: University of Texas Press, 1996), 200; Kim Paffenroth, *Gospel of the Living Dead: George Romero's Visions of Hell on Earth* (Waco: TX: Baylor University Press, 2006), 79, 82, 85; Williams, 132.

107. See, for example, Kyle Ladd, "What Do We Mean When We Say Zombies?" *zombiehunters.org*, accessed September 21, 2008, http://zombiehunters.org/forum/viewtopic.php?f=44&t=19895. Writes Ladd: "It is VERY important that everyone realizes that when we discuss the walking dead we are not talking about other groups of living people. Zombie is a metaphor for disaster. If you have to think of zombies as ... analog[ies] then treat [them] as ... hurricanes, earthquakes, floods, etc." A similar parallel, as R.H.W. Dillard points out, is explicitly drawn in *Night*: "They [the zombies] have no identities and are really no different from any other natural disaster; Tom specifically compares them to a flood, and he is right." R.H.W. Dillard, "'Night of the Living Dead': It's Not Like Just a Wind That's Passing Through," in *American Horrors: Essays on the Modern American Horror Film* (Urbana: University of Illinois Press, 1987), 14, 21.

This insistent depoliticizing, however, brooks little sympathy for the wretched state of the undead. *Land* was widely criticized by ZS members for overemphasizing residual zombie humanity and group identity. See discussion following Fred_Fury's post, "Just Saw Land of the Dead," *zombiehunters.org*, June 25, 2005, accessed

September 21, 2008, http://zombiehunters. org/forum/viewtopic.php?f=13&t=4537&st=0&sk=t&sd=a&start =48.

108. See the "Introductions" section of the "Zombie Squad Forum," accessed September 21, 2008, http://zombiehunters.org/ forum/viewforum.php?f=10.

109. *National Strategy*, 12.

110. Ibid., iii.

111. Ibid., viii, 12.

# About the Contributors

**Aalya Ahmad** teaches "The Monstrous Feminist: Gender and the Horrific in Popular Culture" at the Pauline Jewett Institute of Women's and Gender Studies at Carleton University, Ottawa, Canada. Her doctoral dissertation was a comparative literary study of contemporary horror fiction. She is currently collaborating on a collection of essays about the pedagogy of horror.

**Andrea Austin** is associate professor of English and film studies at Wilfrid Laurier University, Ontario, Canada. She has published on cybercultures, cyberpunk fiction, the history of science and technology, and aesthetics and simulation theory. Her most recent article (in *2012*, Joseph Gelfer, ed., McFarland, 2010) considers the competing narratives of evolution and miracle in Roland Emmerich's *2012*. Her current book project explores the controversial subject of human cloning and the moral problems it raises in film, in scientific practice, and in legal precedent.

**Stephanie Boluk** is a postdoctoral fellow in the Media Studies program at Vassar College. She has published in *Electronic Book Review*, *Leonardo Electronic Almanac*, *Postmodern Culture*, and *Journal for Early Modern Cultural Studies*.

**Brian Greenspan** is an associate professor in the Department of English and the doctoral program in cultural mediations at Carleton University. He is the founding director of the Hypertext and Hypermedia Lab and co-designer of the StoryTrek locative narrative system. His research interests include utopian narratives, digital cultures, and the intersections between them.

**Terry Harpold** is associate professor of English, film, and media studies at the University of Florida. His essays on science fiction and science fiction film have appeared in several edited collections and in journals such as *Bulletin de la Société Jules Verne* and *Science Fiction Studies*.

**Randy Laist** is currently assistant professor of English at Goodwin College in East Hartford, Connecticut. He is the author of *Technology and Postmodern Subjectivity in Don DeLillo's Novels* and the editor of a McFarland volume on the television show *Lost*. He has published numerous articles on Herman Melville, Nathaniel Hawthorne, and Norman Mailer, and also publishes on media studies, ecocriticism, and pedagogical theory.

**Nicole LaRose** is assistant professor of English at the University of Houston-Downtown. Her teaching and research focuses on 20th and 21st century British literature and culture, particularly representations of London. She has previously published on William Wordsworth's and Martin Amis's conception of the city in *Interdisciplinary Literary Studies* and *Critique*, respectively. She is currently working on a monograph on apocalyptic London, the mapping of a city in crisis, and the unlikely characters who navigate the metropolis.

**Sarah Juliet Lauro** is currently finishing a dissertation titled "The Modern Zombie: The Revolution of Resurrection in the Empirical Age" from UC Davis. She has published on the zombie's importance to critical theory (with Karen Embry, "A Zombie Manifesto," *boundary 2*, Spring 2008), and co-edited a collection of essays on the zombie in film, art, literature and culture called *Better Off Dead: The Evolution of the Zombie as Post-human* (with Deborah Christie, Fordham University Press, Spring 2011). Her next project concerns corpses in art and literature.

**Wylie Lenz** is a Ph.D. candidate in the English Department at the University of Florida, where he is writing his dissertation on the figure of the railroad tramp in American literature and popular culture. His has previously published on the zombie in *Journal for Early Modern Cultural Studies*.

**Tyson E. Lewis** is an assistant professor of educational philosophy at Montclair State University. He has published widely in journals such as *Rethinking Marxism, Cultural Critique, Culture, Theory and Critique,* and *Theory and Event.* He is also author of two books, including *Education Out of Bounds: Reimagining Cultural Studies for a Posthuman Age* (2010) and *The Aesthetics of Education* (forthcoming).

**Phillip Mahoney** is a Ph.D. candidate at Temple University, where he is studying representations of collectives in American literature. An example of his work on crowd psychology can be found in the online journal *Kritikos.* His essay "*Tropic of Cancer* and Sexual Discourse: A Critical Hole" appears in the 2008 issue of the *International Henry Miller Journal.*

**Shaka McGlotten** is an assistant professor of media, society, and the arts at Purchase College, where he teaches courses on media, ethnography, and digital culture. His research and writing focuses on the mutual intensification between digital media culture and the creativity of queer sociality.

**Sean Moreland** earned his Ph.D. in English literature from the University of Ottawa, where he currently teaches part time. His research interests include modern American fiction and horror fiction and film. His recent articles include "Tortured into Aught of the Sublime: Poe's Fall of the House of Burke, Ussher and Kant" in *Deciphering Poe* (forthcoming 2011) and "Becoming-Death: The Lollywood Gothic of Khwaja Sarfraz's Zinda Laash," co-authored with Summer Pervez in *Draculas, Vampires and Other Undead Forms: Essays on Gender, Race and Culture* (2009).

**Kim Paffenroth** is professor of religious studies at Iona College. After writing several books on the Bible and theology, he turned his analysis towards horror films and literature, writing *Gospel of the Living Dead: George Romero's Visions of Hell on Earth* (2006), which won the 2006 Bram Stoker Award. He has since written several zombie novels: *Dying to Live: A Novel of Life Among the Undead, Dying to Live: Life Sentence,* and *Valley of the Dead,* all from Permuted Press.

**Gyllian Phillips** is associate professor of English at Nipissing University in North Bay, Ontario, Canada. She has published and presented on musical settings of Edith Sitwell and Gertrude Stein. Her current work focuses on the associations between primitivism, modernism and horror. Most recently, she has published "Imaginary Africa and London's urban wasteland in Edith Sitwell's 'Gold Coast Customs'" in *Twentieth Century Literature* (2010).

**Karen Randell** is principal lecturer in film and programme leader of film & television at Southampton Solent University, UK. She is co-editor of *Screen Methods: Comparative Readings in Film Studies* (2005), *The War Body on Screen* (2008) and *Reframing 9/11: Film, Popular Culture and the "War on Terror"* (2010).

**Scott Reed** is an assistant professor of English at Georgia Gwinnett College, where he is actively developing ways to dovetail gaming with writing pedagogy. His current research focus is on the convergences between game studies and rhetoric & composition studies, with particular attention to theories of invention and rhetorical agency. He has contributed to the online journal *Kairos* and to the forthcoming collection *Rhetoric/Composition/Play: How Electronic Games Mediate Composition Theory (and Vice Versa).*

**Brendan Riley** is an associate professor of English at Columbia College Chicago, where he has been teaching, among other things, a January-session course called "Zombies in Popular Media" since 2007. He has published essays on detectives, comics, writing, and monster movies.

**Chris Vials** is an assistant professor at the University of Connecticut-Storrs and the author of *Realism for the Masses: Aesthetics, Popular Front Pluralism, and U.S. Culture, 1935–1947* (2009). His work has also appeared in *Criticism* and *The Journal of Asian American Studies*. Vials' current project looks at the legacy of 1930s left-liberal antifascism in postwar U.S. culture, and what insights it offers for reading the American political right.

**Christopher Zealand** is an attorney with the National Rifle Association in Fairfax, Virginia, and a graduate of the University of Michigan Law School and Frostburg State University. His essay "Guns to the Left of Me: Firearms Ownership as a Neglected Civil Right" was the winning entry in the 2006 NRA Civil Rights Defense Fund Law Student Scholarship Writing Contest.

# Index